Liberalism's Last Man

∴

Liberalism's Last Man

∴

HAYEK IN THE AGE OF
POLITICAL CAPITALISM

Vikash Yadav

THE UNIVERSITY OF CHICAGO PRESS
CHICAGO AND LONDON

The University of Chicago Press, Chicago 60637
The University of Chicago Press, Ltd., London
© 2023 by The University of Chicago
Published 2023
Printed in the United States of America

32 31 30 29 28 27 26 25 24   2 3 4 5

ISBN-13: 978-0-226-82147-4 (cloth)
ISBN-13: 978-0-226-82736-0 (e-book)
DOI: https://doi.org/10.7208/chicago/9780226827360.001.0001

Library of Congress Cataloging-in-Publication Data

Names: Yadav, Vikash, author.
Title: Liberalism's last man : Hayek in the age of political capitalism /
Vikash Yadav.
Description: Chicago : The University of Chicago Press, 2023. |
Includes bibliographical references and index.
Identifiers: LCCN 2022053981 | ISBN 9780226821474 (cloth) |
ISBN 9780226827360 (ebook)
Subjects: LCSH: Hayek, Friedrich A. von (Friedrich August),
1899-1992—Political and social views. | Liberalism. |
Economic history—21st century.
Classification: LCC HB101.H39 Y34 2023 | DDC 330.092—dc23/eng/20230104
LC record available at https://lccn.loc.gov/2022053981

Contents

Preface

While Friedrich A. Hayek's economic ideas and debates have been carefully examined, applied, formalized, extended,[1] contextualized,[2] and frequently dismissed or vilified,[3] his political philosophy has been comparatively neglected outside the purview of a dedicated circle of Hayek scholars, many of whom are economists by training.[4] Even though Hayek's fame as a public intellectual was built upon an embarrassingly popular political pamphlet, his political ideas have languished in plain sight. Conservatives use Hayek as a prop to lend intellectual gravitas to their policy ideas, but his work is not read carefully—perhaps indicating that it is more complex than one might assume. Even his rejection of the label "conservative" is casually disregarded.[5] And although Hayek lived long enough to see the triumph of the free market over state planning and to receive the Nobel Memorial Prize in Economic Sciences, his ideas are not widely taught in the academy. Generations of academics in the social sciences and humanities have at least a passing familiarity with the nineteenth-century ideas of Karl Marx and Friedrich Engels, but they have scarcely any knowledge of the man whom even his contemporary critics acknowledge as the most successful intellectual of the twentieth century.[6]

Regardless of the conspicuous neglect, Hayek continues to haunt our intellectual debates. On subjects from Bitcoin to bailouts, Hayek's name is readily evoked to provide a pedigree or totem to a set of ideas and policies. Political economists use Hayek as a milestone to mark their supposedly superior theoretical advancements.[7] Radical leftists view Hayek as a foil in the guise of a reactionary neoliberal, although he was anything but reactionary. Conservatives view Hayek as a midwife to the revolution set in motion by Margaret Thatcher and Ronald Reagan, although the economist's actual influence on specific policy matters is doubtful. These cursory engagements and polarized interpretations rehash the intellectual battles of the twentieth century but ignore the prospect that the challenge to liberalism in the twenty-first century will come not from socialism and centralized state planning, but from a divergent strain of capitalism that has evolved in East Asia.

This book is an attempt to take the core of Hayek's *political* thought seriously, although blurring the disciplinary boundary between technical economics and political institutions was integral to Hayek's broader project.[8] This book embraces Hayek's *Road to Serfdom* as a political text worthy of close reading,[9] even if it is at times much more than a political pamphlet.[10]

As Bruce Caldwell has noted, *The Road to Serfdom* was part of Hayek's much larger "Abuse of Reason" project. Hayek hoped to write an intellectual history that excavated the fundamental principles of social development from the father of socialism, Henri de Saint-Simon, to the rise of national socialism.[11] However, by the end of 1940 Hayek chose to publish only a small portion of the project as a political pamphlet that would become *The Road to Serfdom*.[12] Of course, Hayek would elaborate his political thought in more detail in subsequent decades, most notably in *The Constitution of Liberty* (1960), *Law, Legislation, and Liberty* (vols. 1–3, 1973, 1976, 1979), and *The Fatal Conceit* (1988). However, *The Road to Serfdom* remains his most widely read text by the general public and as such marks the starting point for understanding Hayek's political thought.

The aim of my book is to provide a critical companion to the unadorned text; it is a restatement or explication of Hayek's ideas for the twenty-first century. This book is primarily a close reading of *The Road to Serfdom*; it is not an attempt to provide a holistic interpretation of Hayek over the long arc of his career. The effort to present Hayek retrospectively as embodying a consistent intellectual position in a career that spanned decades will not withstand scrutiny. This book is generally organized to follow the structure of Hayek's text. My objective is to write neither a biography nor an intellectual history that traces the origins and situates the context of Hayek's journey; excellent narratives that trace and contextualize the arc of Hayek's fall from grace and redemption already exist.[13] The project does not seek to canonize Hayek; while his thought is complex, subtle, and erudite, it has flaws and weaknesses that must be noted. Thus, this book is a reading or exegesis of Hayek's political thought that assesses what is relevant for the century that is unfolding. The target of the text is young minds seeking to understand the merits of liberalism in an age when the leading liberal power is experiencing hegemonic decline, rising income inequality, growing corruption, and increased populism. My project reflects Hayek's own revivalist project: "If old truths are to retain their hold on men's minds, they must be restated in the language and concepts of successive generations."[14]

Chapter Outline

The introduction makes the case for a revival of liberalism in the twenty-first century. The rise of a form of political economy that the economist Branko Milanovic has labeled "political capitalism" in parts of East Asia, particularly China, Vietnam, and Singapore, as well as growing issues of inequality and cronyism in liberal polities, lends urgency to the need to reexamine the ideals on which "liberal meritocratic capitalist" societies are based. At the same time, the emergence of global and regional value chains linking firms across rival economic systems, massive debt-fueled international consumption patterns, and the decline of the American world order (AWO) limit the strategies available to strengthen liberal capitalism. In fact, there are increasing protectionist pressures as liberal economies witness relative decline. Revisiting Hayek's political text helps us to understand why liberalism was first abandoned in the early twentieth century and how to strengthen this ideology in preparation for the next major battle of ideas. The chapter advocates pruning the branches of Hayek's argument that are no longer productive (e.g., Hayek's Eurocentrism) in order to open new lines of thought, while guarding against dismissive simplifications (e.g., the slippery-slope critique) of Hayek's ideas or attempts to muddle passages from Hayek's political theory with snippets of his personal biography in order to paint a sinister caricature.

The substantive chapters are all arranged in a format that mirrors that of Hayek's book. Broadly, each chapter begins with a discussion of Hayek's epigraph for his chapter. The reason I have chosen to linger on the epigraphs is that they help situate Hayek as a remarkably astute scholar of liberalism and an intellectual historian, rather than merely a polemical pamphleteer. The epigraphs are a trail of breadcrumbs left by Hayek inviting the reader to a deeper conversation about liberalism and its enemies. After discussing the epigraph, each chapter seeks to summarize, critique, and (where appropriate) extend the chapter's argument to engage the rival form of capitalism that is unfolding in Asia.

Chapter 1 explains Hayek's argument that laissez-faire liberalism was abandoned even before World War I owing to a counterrevolution of illiberal ideas refined in German intellectual circles. The chapter maps Hayek's political space in order to lay out his argument of the commonalities between the illiberal ideologies of socialism and national socialism. The emergence of political capitalism in the twenty-first century, rather than simply replaying the defining conflicts of the twentieth century, implies that the challenge to liberalism will come from a new vertex. Unlike socialism and national socialism, the new rivalry exists within variants of a hegemonic capitalism. Nevertheless, the battle of ideas must be engaged, particularly as even high-income countries are increasingly tempted to adopt a range of illiberal policies on the flow of goods and bodies and to elect populist leaders who promise to use coercive means to implement those policies.[15]

In chapter 2, Hayek locates the ideological origins of socialism in efforts to squelch the French Revolution. Hayek argues that socialism disguised its authoritarian pedigree by appropriating and bifurcating the liberal concept of freedom. Socialism's prioritization of "economic freedom" over "political freedom" continues to resonate in political capitalism's derogation of human and civil rights to the right to subsistence or the right to development. Hayek will offer a response to socialism's insistence on the antecedent nature of economic freedom by advocating for a minimum income. The rationale for Hayek's policy solution requires careful unpacking to distinguish it from the extravagant promises of socialist prophecy. It will be argued that innovative policy solutions will only grow in popularity in the twenty-first century as liberal, meritocratic, capitalist societies struggle to create a "people's capitalism" that manages growing income inequality and thereby restores preeminence to its variant of capitalism.

Chapter 3 discusses Hayek's classification of socialism and national socialism as a species of the genus "collectivism," united in their reliance on centralized planning. The chapter defends Hayek's taxon by examining commonalities and critiquing a reading of Walter Benjamin's "artwork essay," which seems to frame fascism and socialism/communism as polar opposites. Next, the characteristics of liberalism in contrast to those of collectivism are laid out. Hayek's fierce attack on centralized planning across the political spectrum is moderated by his acceptance of the legitimacy of state regulation, including environmental regulations. The discussion distinguishes Hayek's moderate liberalism from dogmatic variants of libertarianism. Finally, Hayek's understanding of planning for competition also complicates the distinction between liberal states and the industrial policies and corporatist arrangements of developmental states.

The fourth chapter explains Hayek's critique of centralized planning in the context of increasing societal complexity and emerging technological possibilities. The chapter critiques both technophiles, who believe that advances in artificial intelligence and machine learning justify a revival of centralized planning, and those who seek to use the state to force technology adoption by limiting market competition. The chapter emphasizes the ways in which Hayek's embrace of radical uncertainty and spontaneous orders might be even more relevant for the contemporary phase of globalization and technological development.

The fifth chapter exposes a flaw in Hayek's argument about the inherent tension between centralized economic planning and parliamentary democracy. Hayek argues that collectivism requires the establishment of a comprehensive and hierarchical ethical code. Hayek conditions his support for democratic regimes because of the extent to which democratic procedures can be used by proponents of centralized planning to engineer greater agreement than actually exists and to delegate authority to an opaque bureaucracy. He even argues that authoritarian regimes may preserve greater cultural and spiritual freedom than some democracies. Unfortunately, Hayek's conditional support of democracy renders his argument vulnerable to proponents of political capitalism, who would agree that the virtues of authoritarian regimes may exceed those of their democratic rivals. Hayek will not propose an institutional solution to buttress democracy until near the end of his book.

Chapter 6 concerns the rule of law as a mechanism to restrain centralized planning. As political capitalism deliberately sets aside the rule *of* law in favor of "rule *by* law," Hayek's defense of the rule of law in a free-enterprise system requires careful analysis. Hayek's assumption that the rule of law prevents arbitrary governance (i.e., centralized planning) occludes his ability to contemplate a scenario in which deliberately creating an unstable legal environment and endemic corruption is functional for enhancing state autonomy and rapid economic growth.

In the seventh chapter, Hayek argues (through a somewhat misleading epigraph from Hilaire Belloc's book *The Servile State*) that because the economy interconnects with every sphere of the lifeworld, economic decisions are antecedent to all other freedoms. Of course, within a liberal order there are a number of gray areas to be negotiated between the autonomous individual and the subjugating state. Socialism traditionally sought to overcome these complex trade-offs by promising an era of "potential plenty" generated by centralizing production that would liberate the individual. In recent decades the socialist discourse has shifted, in an effort to bridge the red-green divide, from promises of plenty to promises of sustainability. The transparently eco-authoritarian demand to create a "Climate Lenin" is contrasted with Hayek's flexible, humble, and open approach to address the challenge of climate change.

Chapter 8 grapples with Hayek's tolerance of economic, religious, and racial inequality. While Hayek presents a refreshingly frank discussion of inequalities in a commercial society, his tolerance for inequality as opposed to advocacy for greater formal equality is a missed opportunity in the argument. Hayek is correct to warn that efforts to promote social justice in a collectivist society through the redistribution of income may ultimately cross an unmarked threshold beyond which the extension of political and economic control becomes comprehensive. While centralized planning has fallen in popularity, Hayek's conception of inequality may still be fruitfully contrasted with Amartya Sen's "capability-enhancement" approach to illustrate the enduring value of Hayek's logical, political, and moral argument for equality rather than equity.

Chapter 9 presents Hayek's argument in support of a minimum income and social insurance for citizens of a given polity in order to limit coercion in the marketplace. Hayek is careful to circumscribe these provisions in such a way that the competitive market order is maintained. He contrasts the market with the barracks to explicate the relationship between choice and risk. Hayek's primary concern is to foster a moral society that values liberty more highly than security. In essence, Hayek's preference ordering is diametrically opposed to the values that sustain political capitalism.

In the tenth chapter, Hayek argues that the repellent features of totalitarian regimes are due not to historical accident, but to ethical and social incentive structures. In other words, the embrace of totalitarian political regimes (e.g., fascism or communism) cannot be reformed through a more careful and routinized selection of upstanding leaders. Regardless of the moral character of political leaders, successful totalitarian rule requires the disregard of conventional morality and the coercive imposition of a hierarchy of values in a collectivist framework. The unscrupulous and uninhibited are thus more likely to acquire power in this context and overwhelm those collectivists (e.g., democratic socialists) who feel restrained by democratic institutions and norms. Moreover, the ethics of a collectivist system are likely to be radically different from the high-minded moral principles or objectives that brought it into being. Thus, Hayek's critique of "strongman" rule as reflecting an impatience with the pace of political and economic development under liberal democracy and grounded on a naive understanding of the relationship between morality and political incentives provides useful counterarguments to the growing preference globally for rapid economic growth under political capitalism. However, it is worth noting that unlike totalitarian regimes, political-capitalist regimes strategically fuse collectivist and individualist ethics.

The eleventh chapter links the necessity of propaganda and dogmatic indoctrination in planned societies to the impossibility of reaching full agreement on a hierarchically ranked list of values. Unsurprisingly, then, the myths on which public policy in collectivist societies ultimately rest are often the product merely of instinctive prejudice. Hayek argues that, as the totalitarian state develops, not only is truth sacrificed, but absurdities multiply, and an intense dislike of abstract thought emerges. Hayek's conception of propaganda is too narrow and oversimplified. Historically, totalitarian regimes have continued to fund basic science and advanced technology research. Political-capitalist regimes, which often have inherited propaganda bureaucracies and techniques from their totalitarian predecessors, increasingly use sophisticated information operations to manage public opinion in their core areas but apply cruder and more coercive techniques on their periphery.

Chapter 12 traces the trajectory of leading socialist intellectuals who converted to fascism in order to crush liberalism. The puzzling thing is how the views of a reactionary minority came to be held by the great majority in different societies. Hayek's argument concerns the socialization of the state and the nationalization of social democracy. The mechanisms through which illiberal ideas become mainstream is worth outlining as political capitalism congeals into a putatively superior alternative to liberal meritocratic capitalism. Notably, liberalism is still targeted for two of its defining features: its internationalism and its link to democratic government. Political capitalism is increasingly marked by nationalism and elements of corporatism, but the end result is far from national socialism.

Chapter 13 represents a fierce critique of the theory of realism in international relations, scientists and engineers who served the Nazi regime, monopolistic owners of capital, and collusive union leaders. For Hayek, these individuals are an example of the totalitarians living among us. The argument belies the popular notion that only ignorant and gullible masses manipulated by a demagogue support authoritarianism. The chapter is useful in understanding elites' attraction for authoritarian capitalism. Hayek is right to warn elites that a totalitarian state will seek to subordinate autonomous bases of power and criticism; however, the use of anticorruption campaigns and rule-by-law tactics of contemporary political-capitalist regimes implies that authoritarian capitalist states can retain autonomy without capturing all bases of private power.

Chapter 14 builds Hayek's case for nonrational submission to impersonal market forces against the perennial belief that high-income economies have entered a "postmaterialist" age and transcended the material considerations of capitalism. Hayek argues that the market is a nonrational order that lies between instinct and reason. The order is built upon moral and cultural foundations, including the irrationality of religion. Despite its nonrational character, submission enables the growth of civilization. Hayek's critique of the refusal to submit to nonrational forces echoes the argument of Adam Smith against the "man of system." Failure to submit to market forces and accept the reality of trade-offs opens the door to pseudotheories of "potential plenty" and utopian schemes to improve general prosperity. For Hayek, utopian schemes and shortcuts undertaken to transcend market forces and relieve individuals of the responsibility to make trade-offs endanger individual freedom and morality. While postmaterialist discourse rings increasingly hollow in affluent societies (even with rising awareness of human-induced climate change), political-capitalist regimes are under no illusion that a postmaterialist age is dawning.

In chapter 15 Hayek argues against the realists, particularly E. H. Carr, in favor of a postnationalist, interstate federalism that champions individual workers and entrepreneurs regardless of location or race. Hayek argues against the realists' neocolonial strategy of using intergovernmental institutions to regulate the affairs of colonized peoples after the war. He does not completely rule out the role of intergovernmental organizations (e.g., regional (con)federations), as such organizations can play a critical role in limiting the power of the state to coerce individuals. Thus, Hayek displaces the centrality of the nation-state without naturalizing the domination of great powers. Notably, political-capitalist regimes have also shown a remarkable ability to use (asymmetric) federalism domestically and development assistance internationally to enhance state power, improve performance, and reduce interstate friction. Finally, the use of surgically targeted tariffs by political-capitalist regimes to weaken adversarial federations in trade wars makes the return to liberalism in international trade more urgent.

The conclusion argues that liberal meritocratic capitalism will not be able to compete with political capitalism in terms of economic performance, and that liberal states are losing the ability to shape a world order supportive of liberalism; therefore, liberal meritocratic societies will need to reform themselves and prioritize the moral foundations of individual freedom.

Introduction

The generally flaccid response of liberal and libertarian scholars to nearly four decades of expansive leftist critique of the concept of "neoliberalism" has left a lacuna in academia even as capitalism in its various guises has spread globally. For the first time in human history, almost all of the planet is economically organized under the flag of capitalism.[1] And while liberal governance is increasingly in retreat globally,[2] it remains an admired ideal. In this context, a mechanical form of economic policy-making (i.e., a revived laissez-faire) has come to legitimate itself solely on the promise of economic growth—a benchmark that may have limited connection to the expansion of individual freedom—while masking increasingly rigid income inequality and a crony-capitalist actuality. It is time to update and reinvigorate the cause of economic and political liberalism, to cast off the cronyism and state protection that bleeds the economy of its vigor and face the intellectual challenges emanating from all parties on the horizon.

Friedrich A. Hayek's *Road to Serfdom* (1944) is the seminal twentieth-century text in defense of economic liberalism. Hence, any recovery and restatement of economic liberalism for the twenty-first century should begin by sifting the arguments laid out there. Published near the end of World War II, the book sought to steel Britain against the intellectual battle with centralized planning that lay ahead of victory by once again restating the liberal values on which Britain's freedom and prosperity were built.[3] Hayek argues that liberalism faced a challenge from the import of German ideas (e.g., Hegel's statism, Marx's socialism, List's economic nationalism, Schmoller's historicism).[4] Defeating those ideas by defending the rationale of liberal political economy, Hayek thought, would clear the terrain for a revival and restatement of liberalism.

To some, the need for an intellectual revival of liberalism may seem less pressing today, given the near universality of capitalism and the lingering prestige of liberal democracy, but clouds of dissent from the liberal order have been amassing for some time. Liberalism once more faces threats from revived and intellectually reconstructed communists and fascists as well as less systematic new challenges from environmentalists and (in some regions) religious textualists. And while socialism, understood as control of the commanding heights of the economy, centralized planning, and one-party domination, has been marginalized in high-income countries, it remains popular as an ideology in middle- and low-income countries, particularly in South America.[5] Moreover, "democratic socialism" has demonstrated significant popular appeal in high-income countries in recent years. However, the twenty-first century is unlikely to be characterized by a simple ideological reenactment of the Cold War, in large part because the failed and discredited ideologies of fascism and communism lack broad popular appeal today.

Political Capitalism

The most pressing new challenge to liberalism in the twenty-first century stems not from a nostalgic revival of communism or fascism—although paroxysms are to be expected—but from the emergence of what Milanovic has labeled "political capitalism" in countries such as China, Vietnam, and Singapore.[6] Political capitalism is an alternative form of capitalism associated with efficient technocratic bureaucracy, the absence of the rule of law, and the autonomy of the state in matters of private capital and civil society.[7] Political capitalism, as an ideal-type model, is usually the product either of a communist revolution or of a revolutionary one-party state that successfully leveled precolonial cultural impediments in order to achieve economic transformation and political sovereignty.[8] These states are technocratic and oriented toward legitimacy based on economic performance and political competence under the banner of a ruthless one-party state that rules by selectively using the law as a weapon against dissidents and opponents. Political-capitalist states are highly autonomous from the owners of capital when they need to be and capable of formulating a nationalist (i.e., mercantilist) policy agenda.[9] The selective use of anticorruption purges is one mechanism for maintaining state autonomy (although a highly disciplined party apparatus could achieve the same effect without tolerating high levels of corruption). These societies are highly inequitable, owing at least in part to the discretionary authority of the law-administering bureaucracy and decision makers' public policy preferences for economic performance over social equity.[10] The state keeps corruption and dissent in check because of its need to deliver tangible economic performance and to demonstrate competence in crisis management. Despite the authoritarian nature of political capitalism, these are capitalist economies characterized by (1) a majority of production in the private sphere, (2) a majority of workers operating as wage laborers, and (3) a majority of production decision-making that is market determined (i.e., not centrally planned).[11] In essence, the competition on the global stage is no longer between alternate systems of economic organization, but between alternate variants of capitalism.

Since the birth of industrial capitalism, there have always been varieties of capitalism and even illiberal forms of capitalism, but there has arguably not been a great power rivalry between liberal and illiberal capitalism since at least the mid-twentieth century.

Is Milanovic's political-capitalist category, as exemplified by China, accurate? Panthea Pourmalek writes, "Milanovic's characterization of political capitalism is especially well-founded and concise."[12] She adds, "The conceptions of political and liberal meritocratic capitalism prove to be both novel and compelling." While Pourmalek agrees that the model is attractive to many countries, it is fair to be slightly skeptical that the model would generate similar levels of success elsewhere:

> In terms of replication beyond China, the success of implementing political capitalism is contingent upon the presence of a decentralized authoritarian structure. Decentralization encourages non-localized elites to implement successful policies with the incentive of moving up within the political system, while an authoritarian centre acts as a backbone that is able to both reward such policies and maintain a united regime. This unique set of conditions grants political capitalism some potential for export, but do not necessarily guarantee economic success elsewhere, especially to the extent of China's.[13]

Pourmalek's tepid skepticism is warranted, but it is unlikely to deter leaders attracted to China's approach.

In a broad critique, Robert Kuttner begins by arguing that China's political capitalism is only one variant of capitalism, even in East Asia. Milanovic might agree, but his argument is a Weberian discussion of polarized ideal types that serve as a heuristic device for discovering a wider range of categories. Kuttner adds that many Chinese firms are willing to operate at a loss in order to gain global market share and hence are not quite capitalist:

> In many Chinese industries, contrary to Milanovic's contention, the paramount goal is to gain worldwide market share even if that requires

operating at a loss for a long time, not to pursue "production for profit." Free enterprises cannot withstand operating at a loss year after year, as many Chinese companies do. They can do it because the state provides extensive subsidies both to state-owned enterprises and to nominally private companies in targeted industries.[14]

However, this criticism is not valid. It is worth noting that in the United States the bastion of market capitalism, Amazon, did not record its first profit until 2003, almost a decade after its founding.[15] Similar stories can be told about FedEx, Tesla, ESPN, and Turner Broadcasting.[16] Extensive state subsidies are also used by private firms. Tesla (formerly Tesla Motors) received $2.44 billion in subsidies from eighty-two federal grants and twenty-seven state and local awards.[17] More generally, the state provision of welfare benefits for the poor may be viewed as a de facto subsidy to low-wage employers.

Kuttner even disputes Milanovic's notion that China uses free labor, stating, though without providing any evidence, that "much of the Chinese labor force is close to slave labor."[18] There are scattered instances of labor exploitation in China, including in the electronics and construction sectors,[19] and arguably in the Xinjiang Uyghur Autonomous Region, but it is unfair to argue that the majority of the labor force is close to an enslaved one. Kuttner goes on to argue that free unions are not permitted, but this line of argument is not relevant to the assertion that the majority of Chinese firms hire legally free laborers who are paid a wage as compensation for their work.

Kuttner also disagrees that China is characterized by "decentralized cooperation"; he asserts that, with the exception of some spontaneous enterprises, China's entire economic system is based on state planning.[20] This is a common but oversimplified and outdated conception of the Chinese economy. As Anthony Go Yeh, Fiona F. Yang, and Jiejing Wang note, the Chinese economy is increasingly characterized by market competition:

In 1978, the commodities allocated by the state were under 256 categories. This number was dramatically reduced to 24 in 1987 and 17 in 1989. By the end of 1991, less than 30% of the prices of commodities and goods were decided by the state. The prices of economic resources can fluctuate according to the changing relationship between supply and demand. The withdrawal of state intervention and the rise of non-state sectors have also broken the "iron rice bowl" and "fraternal cooperation" of the state enterprises. The state enterprises were granted great flexibility for their production, but they also lost the shelter provided by the state and were confronted with intense market competition. By allowing the market economy to "grow out of the plan," the Chinese state has essentially externalised the market mechanism.[21]

This is not to argue that contemporary China is a pure free market: the state/party continues to play the role of ultimate decision maker, regulator, and competitor, particularly through a significant—if diminishing—number of state-owned enterprises (SOEs).[22] Nevertheless, Milanovic's portrait of decentralized cooperation is more accurate than Kuttner's outdated image of China's party-state governance. It is true that the Chinese state reintroduced an element of centralized planning after abandoning it in the 1990s. However, with the exception of compulsory environmental and poverty-alleviation targets, most contemporary state planning at the national level in China reflects the hopes and objectives of policy makers—that is, these are "vision statements" or (at best) "indicative planning" documents.[23] National planning is meant to convey to decentralized actors that they need to take environmental issues seriously (which the evidence does not indicate they do). Barry Naughton argues that Chinese "planning" is not much different from state-level planning in the United States: "But described in this way, China's planning process is not terribly different from how it is done in, for example, the state of California, where binding targets are established through legislation and regulation. In China, the target is enforced through administrative action, but decentralized actors are left free to choose specific steps."[24] The national plans or vision statements do lead to a dense proliferation of sectoral and local plans that convey state priorities and guide the allocation of state resources in the targeted sectors and regions. Whether localized planning is effective or coherent as a plan or industrial policy is rather doubtful, however, as there are complex layers of overlapping and contradictory plans in any given priority issue area. Argues Naughton, "This complexity means it is quite difficult to determine the net incidence of planning, much less its effectiveness. Resources pour into the highest priority sectors, which brings in more investors and creates unpredictable competition down the road. With so many plans and industrial policies, it is in some ways difficult to say whether China has any plan or a coherent industrial policy."[25] Thus, while China has robustly returned to using planning documents in the twenty-first century, there is not much evidence that centralized planning documents at the national, regional, sectoral, or local level effectively or efficiently shape development—particularly as China seeks to move beyond the solitary pursuit of high rates of economic growth.

An alternative, but equally misguided, approach has been simply to dismiss political capitalism, as Daron Acemoglu and James A. Robinson have done with regard to China, because such states are apparently predestined for stagnation owing to their reliance on "extractive political institutions" (although apparently they have made halting steps toward certain "inclusive economic institutions," which, according to the authors, explains the expansive period of growth).[26] Such reasoning in defense of liberal democratic capitalism is wishful thinking that ignores over four decades of sustained economic growth under an authoritarian one-party state. The absence of the rule of law (i.e., the reliance on rule *by* law, or laws that apply to all except the governing authority and ruling elite), including the insecurity of property rights, is fundamental to political capitalism; without it, the rule of the party and its autonomy vis-à-vis private capital would be forfeit. The Chinese state is prosperous precisely because it is not an example of Acemoglu and Robinson's "shackled leviathan."[27] In other words, political capitalism is deliberately exclusive and property rights are intentionally kept insecure, but growth is neither necessarily "extractive" (with a few limited inclusive economic institutions tacked on to explain growth) nor "unsustainable" over a long period.[28]

By "extractive growth," Acemoglu and Robinson refer to situations in which elites allocate resources to high-productivity activities that they themselves control or to situations in which a measure of inclusive economic institutions is permitted by elites who do not believe those institutions will threaten their political dominance.[29] However, state allocation of resources has been declining as market competition has increased. Milanovic points out that China's industrial output generated by SOEs has dropped from 100 percent in 1978 to just over 20 percent in 2015. In the agricultural sector, almost all output is now privately produced by self-employed farmers. Overall, the private sector now accounts for more than half of fixed investment. The share of SOE workers in total urban employment has plunged from nearly 80 percent in 1978 to less than 16 percent since 2015.[30] Moreover, as Barry Naughton notes, "State-owned enterprises pay profit taxes and a changing—but relatively small—proportion of after-tax profits to their governmental owners (these are included in budgetary revenues). The majority of profits remain in the firm, where it is subject to government influence but not direct government allocation."[31] Of course, the financial sector is dominated by state-owned banks, and patterns of lending are subject to governmental influence. However, the after-tax profits of state-owned financial and nonfinancial enterprises, as well as land revenues, which are wholly owned by the state, have cooled since a peak of 13.2 percent of the gross domestic product (GDP) in 2010 to 9.2 percent of GDP in 2015. Overall, when one looks at budgetary revenues, social insurance premiums, land revenues, and net income from SOEs, China's government had direct or indirect control of 38 percent of GDP in 2015.[32] In other words, the data does not quite demonstrate an extractive growth model in contemporary China based on either state control of capital allocation or strictly limited use of inclusive economic institutions. On the contrary, China is primarily a capitalist economy, albeit one characterized by a large and well-resourced state that has the potential to be intrusive. But despite its interventionist potential and growing wealth, the Chinese state has released control over many productive assets, particularly in agriculture and (non-capital-intensive and non-human-capital-intensive) industry, giving way to competition.

Nevertheless, Acemoglu and Robinson would reply that *sustainable* growth requires harnessing the power of "creative destruction," or innovation through socially inclusive economic institutions. States that are "catching up" to established high-income economies may coast on existing technology. However, eventually these states will need to innovate. The problem with this facet of Acemoglu and Robinson's argument is that it mistakes invention for innovation. Moreover, while they concede that ". . . Chinese entrepreneurs are showing a lot of ingenuity," they do not believe that Chinese firms are generally innovative.[33] However, this is a rather restrictive understanding of innovation. Chinese firms are innovative in their ability to translate inventions into commercially viable products at reasonable cost.[34] In fact, the ability of Chinese firms to extract profits from old inventions through new product development, new process development, or new product architecture indicates that the Chinese are perhaps even more commercially innovative than their inventive counterparts.[35]

Acemoglu and Robinson famously predicted in 2012 that China's growth ". . . is also likely to come to an end, particularly once China reaches the standards of living level of a middle-income country."[36] Since 2016, China's gross national income (GNI) per capita has been well above the mean of "upper middle income countries," according to the World Bank.[37] And Chinese GDP growth rates, although moderating from a peak of 15 percent in 1984, remained above 6 percent from 2012 to 2019.[38] Notably, this high growth has been sustained despite clear signs of an increasing centralization of power under President Xi Jinping—a move *away* from more inclusive political institutions. In 2019 Acemoglu and Robinson dramatically revised their prediction: "Chinese growth is not likely to peter out in the next few years. But as with other episodes of despotic growth, its existential challenge lies in unleashing large-scale experimentation and innovation. Like all previous instances of despotic growth it is unlikely to succeed in this."[39] However, the pressing challenge of political capitalism, which has significant appeal in many parts of the world, cannot be dismissed with a revised prophecy.

To be clear, the fear of political capitalism expressed in this book is neither that it will create prosperity in Asia—after all, a better standard of living for millions is a welcome development for all of humanity, and in a globally interconnected world the fruits of prosperity and innovation will eventually be shared widely—nor that a resurgent China will displace American hegemony, for hegemonic decline is inevitable; rather, it is that political capitalism represents a prosperous future with limited scope for individual autonomy and freedom. It would be wise to treat political capitalism as a viable alternative and a worthy adversary to liberalism.

THE VALUE OF LIBERTY

At this point, a supporter of political capitalism might justifiably inquire: if political capitalism generates sustained prosperity and order for its citizens and allows a measure of autonomy in the private sphere, what is the problem? Various political freedoms are certainly restricted, but why is that problematic, given that this regime type has lifted millions out of extreme poverty? Why should we as political capitalists revisit the work of a liberal thinker such as Hayek? After all, even Hayek, whose primary concern was the utilization of knowledge by individuals and the social utilization of knowledge through the market, would have to concede that, despite the inefficiencies generated by discretionary decision-making and arbitrary coercion, a political-capitalist system does generate prosperity.

Hayek would likely reply that individual liberty is "the source and condition of most moral values." Moreover, citing Henry Bayard Philips, Hayek notes that restrictions on liberty reduce the rate of civilizational progress, as it reduces "the number of things tried." Philips adds that the freedom of action granted to the individual to "go his own way" will on average "serve the rest of us better than under any orders we know how to give." The value of liberty is for Hayek a function of our imperfect foresight regarding how to attain our goals in the future. Liberty, by creating a diversity of ways of being, helps us to adjust to the unpredictable and provides opportunities to advance civilization in the face of new challenges. One might add that political freedom also generates varied political institutions among and within liberal states, which in turn creates new mechanisms to preserve and advance civilization.[40]

Of course, the points above defend liberty only for its instrumental value. As John Gray notes, Hayek famously refuses to accord to liberty a distinct political value or virtue, arguing that liberty cannot be defined in isolation from concepts such as justice and security. Even Hayek's (negative) definition of liberty appears to be procedural (i.e., abstract, universal rules are not coercive), consensual (i.e., I am not coerced if I or at least a majority consent to general and abstract laws that might be applied to me), and contingent on foresight for avoidability (i.e., we are not coerced if we know in advance and avoid a situation in which we might be coerced).[41] Nevertheless, a careful study of Hayek's work can articulate the instrumental value of liberty.[42] Roland Kley argues that the reason Hayek defends liberalism primarily on its technical ability to use information acquired by individuals efficiently, rather than on the normative value of individual liberty, is that liberalism and socialism generally share many values.[43] The main value divergence between liberalism and socialism is the issue of distributive justice. Kley's argument helps to highlight the fact that the challenge posed by political capitalism is quite distinct from that presented by socialism. Political capitalism shares a common means with liberal capitalism, but a distinctly different order of values.

At the root of Hayek's failure to articulate a satisfactory theory of the intrinsic value of liberty, at least from Gray's perspective, is the reliance on Kantian universalizability, which is neither necessary nor sufficient to ensure a liberal order; a common-law tradition or even a tyranny may be better at securing individual liberty.[44] Gray's critique of Hayek's understanding of liberty may even be seen in the contemporary context as opening a space for a return to a normative defense of the intrinsic value of liberty, perhaps as more of a moral and political practice than a concept deduced from abstract principles.[45] While such a philosophical endeavor is outside the scope of this book, it will become necessary as the performance of political-capitalist regimes continues apace. The point of this book, however, is to map the challenge that political capitalism will pose for liberalism and to see what intellectual weaponry from the battle with socialism can be repurposed.

Liberal Meritocratic Capitalism

Meanwhile in the West, liberal meritocratic capitalism, which prides itself on being a system of natural liberty that is open to talent and poses no formal legal or religious barriers to achievement (i.e., "meritocratic equality"), along with free education and restrictions on intergenerational transfers of advantages to promote fluid social mobility (i.e., "liberal equality"), is becoming rigid.[46] The United States, which has served as a beacon for the liberal meritocratic version of capitalism since the 1980s and its Keynesian predecessor after World War II, is witnessing a decline in social mobility owing to an erosion of the quality of the free education system and the rollback of restrictions on intergenerational transfer of wealth.[47] The US political system is increasingly being captured by and steered toward the interests of those who derive the majority of their income from the ownership of capital.

A liberal capitalism that cannot tackle its own increasingly ossifying income inequality and the fusion of political and economic corruption will inevitably slouch toward a plutocratic form that culminates in political or authoritarian capitalism.[48] If political capitalism, as opposed to socialism or national socialism, is the major challenge to liberal (meritocratic) capitalism, then it is necessary to rethink aspects of Hayek's argument to prepare for the century ahead. The challenge therefore comes not from elements of centralized planning, much less "hot socialism," but from the effort to build a capitalist market economy that can deliver sustained economic growth and political stability despite rampant corruption and systematic violations of the rule of law and even stable private-property rights.

A second major new challenge for liberalism unfolding in the twenty-first century is the linkage between select countries through extensive global value chains (GVCs) or regional value chains. Richard Baldwin argues that as a direct consequence of the information and communication technology (ICT) revolution, globalization since the 1990s has promoted a "Great Convergence" in manufacturing between the G7 (i.e., the United States, Germany, Japan, France, Britain, Canada, and Italy) high-wage/high-income countries and six formerly low-wage/low-income countries (i.e., China, Korea, India, Poland, Indonesia, and Thailand).[49] New technologies have enabled corporations to spatially "unbundle" their management and production functions without losing control of corporate know-how. With the exception of India, which has carved out its own unique path, the countries able to participate in the Great Convergence all exist near a major G7 industrial center. The Great Convergence has touched a wider circle of states by pushing up demand for commodities from primary product–exporting countries.[50] At the same time, dramatic leaps in ICT, particularly in the area of artificial intelligence, have accelerated the mechanization of production tasks.

The latest phase of globalization and mechanization has been occurring not merely in certain sectors of the economy, but at the level of production stages and occupations across the entire economy. This means that occupations and processes within firms may be enhanced or harmed through the process of globalization/regionalization and mechanization. The end result is the denationalization of comparative advantage.[51] The implication of the newest phase of globalization is that rival economic variants of capitalism are deeply intertwined. Whereas the communist countries during the Cold War were autarchic and nationalist even vis-à-vis one another,[52] the new globalization is intensively interdependent, even beyond the issue of debt-financed trade.[53] Strategies for coping with the new globalization by degrading the competitiveness of rival states or cutting trade linkages altogether are shortsighted and unlikely to succeed.

A third major challenge in this century is the significant decline in the ability of the United States to engage in liberal ordering of the global architecture for international trade and cooperation. American hegemony has been unraveling at least since the start of the new millennium through challenges by revisionist or discontented great powers, new patronage opportunities for weaker client states, and new transnational networks for antiliberal activists.[54] It is highly unlikely that the United States will be able to course-correct at this stage, and there is no realistic prospect that Germany or Japan can step up to the task in the foreseeable future.[55]

Of course, the "American world order" was never as American in design, as comprehensive in scope, or as consistently benign and consensual as American scholars have at times claimed.[56] Its norms were never firmly internalized outside of Europe and North America,[57] so it is unlikely that the new great powers will simply pick up the liberal mantle from the United States, as it had done from the United Kingdom. In fact, because the American world order was subsumed under the Cold War order, the United States often acted in ways that were highly illiberal in terms of human rights and democracy among client states.[58]

Nevertheless, an even further diminished capacity to shape the world order to support liberal political and economic approaches will generate a challenging environment for liberalism. At the very least, Western policy makers will have to reevaluate their ideas about the promotion of democracy and free-market policies. Unlike the "unipolar moment" following the end of the Cold War, the United States and European Union now have fewer instruments with which to pressure weaker states to engage in political reform and economic structural adjustment. For example, imposing conditionality on multilateral loans has little effect when weak states can apply for loans from the "no-strings-attached" lending institutions set up by the revisionist and rising powers. At the same time, mercantilist states will be able to continue to exploit the existing liberal international free-trade architecture with minimal consequences, and consequently political pressure will build within liberal states to impose increasingly protectionist and illiberal measures to protect domestic industries. Even liberal norms related to fundamental human rights that were embedded in a series of international regimes, as well as the general norms of "good governance" touted by teams of consultants during the heyday of the Pax Americana, are eroding at a remarkable pace. Today, very few states feel obligated to listen to the United States pontificate about the sanctity of human rights or the value of free and fair elections. Of course, the United States will maintain its military primacy for decades, but the deployment of that instrument is already understood as largely ineffective, even against the weakest of states. Thus, the power of example as opposed to the example of power will have to be the primary approach to building an environment supportive of liberalism.[59]

The First Liberal Revival

Arguably, the classical liberalism of Adam Smith and John Stuart Mill had already been restated in the late nineteenth century. Critics will argue that the repeated failure of liberalism renders another revival a dubious project. For example, Keith Tribe claims that Hayek simply failed to acknowledge the historical and philosophical reasons that the first revival of liberalism failed. Liberalism—or, in his argument, the Liberal Party in Great Britain—came to be associated with a series of progressive political demands that would eventually lead to demands for a larger state. Furthermore, the enfranchisement of the working class gave rise to the Labour Party, which then marginalized the Liberal Party.[60]

Tribe argues that centralization of state power at the national level was the inevitable consequence of liberal social reforms, which demanded uniform provision of services and the generation of revenue adequate for the state to fund these demands.[61] As we will see, Hayek would disagree that a state that promotes equality under the rule of law requires centralization of provision and concentration of power as opposed to a minimum income, voluntary provision, and a reliance on the market mechanism to coordinate individual wants and needs. The Liberal Party's demand for centralized provision and state expansion is not the liberalism that Hayek was seeking to revive; nor is it inevitable that the expansion of democracy requires the creation of a welfare state, as the democratic countries of East Asia demonstrate.

Additionally, Tribe argues that the English liberal state was limited in the nineteenth century only because of the financial impact of fighting the Napoleonic Wars, and that the state was not "limited" in its colonies, such as India and Australia. In this line of argument, Tribe somewhat overstates the penetration of the colonial state in places such as India, which, despite the colonizers' pretentiousness and brutality, was actually quite limited in both size and scope, given the magnitude and complexity of the Indian subcontinent and the general mercantile focus of the colonial state. Tribe mistakes the assemblage of the Raj for its actual institutional presence and power.[62] In any case, Tribe's argument that the British state was so heavily indebted after the Napoleonic era that it could not expand seems odd. Tribe admits that "revenue was overwhelmingly indirect, so that the costs of navy and army together (£79.1m) [in the financial year 1913–14] were almost matched by revenues from taxes on the sale of alcohol, tobacco, tea, and sugar alone (£71.5m)."[63] Certainly, a state that had yet to rely more heavily on direct forms of taxation had room to expand and even a justification for doing so. The puzzle, which Tribe cannot explain, is why the British state did not expand prior to World War I if more direct means of repaying its debts were available and the new liberalism as an ideology had already died off by the end of the nineteenth century.

Philosophically, Tribe argues that Hayek's project did not overcome Carl Schmitt's devastating critique of parliamentary democracy.[64] Tribe sees Hayek as appealing nostalgically to "a golden age of the English liberal state" in response to Schmitt's critique, rather than explaining how order and liberty could be defended in an age of an unconstrained democratic state. Tribe is too dismissive of the power of embedded cultural norms and a constitutional order in shaping and constraining state behavior even in instances where the sovereign authority appears outside the law.[65] In any case, Hayek's concept of sovereignty, as laid out in the three volumes of *Law, Legislation, and Liberty*, would need to be more carefully unpacked to assess whether Hayek countered Schmitt's critique. Regardless, it is ironic to accuse Hayek of falsely blaming the demise of liberalism on the import of foreign ideas while also condemning him for failing to overcome the critique of the philosopher of the Third Reich.

In summary, for Tribe the demise of the liberal state was due to internal factors brought on by liberalism itself (i.e., democracy and progressive social policies) and exogenous factors (i.e., military spending and war debt), rather than to the import of foreign ideas from Germany. Hence, it is useless to revive liberalism for a second (or third) time as politics on the ground have surpassed its utility. However, Tribe's argument is not compelling, because the kinds of progressive reforms demanded by the Liberal Party were not a reflection of the type of classical liberalism that Hayek hoped to revive. In any case, Hayek anticipated this critique, and he begins the first chapter of *The Road to Serfdom* with a response.

A more potent critique against a liberal revival, although not specifically directed at Hayek, comes from Milanovic. He writes that although Marxism cannot explain the turn away from socialism and back to capitalism at the end of the Cold War, liberalism cannot explain why Europeans turned away from capitalism to support fascism and communism in the early twentieth century.[66] If fascism and communism were simply mistaken overcorrections of capitalism's mistakes, why were those mistakes committed in the first place? Milanovic writes:

> Why did fascism and communism become powerful if humanity—and certainly the advanced liberal capitalist countries—was on the right path in 1914? We encounter here a fundamental problem that the liberal capitalist view of history faces: explaining the outbreak of the most destructive war in history (up to that point) within a system that, from a liberal point of view, was fully consonant with the highest, most developed and peaceful way of organizing human society. How to explain that a liberal international order where all the key players were capitalist and globalist, and moreover, were actual, partial, or aspiring democracies (as was certainly the case for the Western Allies but also for Germany, Austria-Hungary, and Russia, which were all moving in that direction) could end up in a state of general carnage.[67]

Hayek anticipated this line of critique in his first chapter by arguing that the road to liberalism had been abandoned in favor of historicist, statist, socialist, and economically nationalist ideas imported from the Continent well before World War I.[68] In fact, Hayek argued that liberalism reached the summit of its eastward expansion from England around 1870 and then began to retreat in the face of opposition by a set of ideas from the East (of Europe). England became a net importer of ideas, and from the mid-1880s onward Germany became the center ". . . from which the ideas destined to govern the world in the twentieth century spread east and west."[69] Ideas, institutions, and policies that reflected a contempt of liberal ideals were imported and adapted, and the old ways were abandoned as outmoded.[70]

Preparing for the Next Liberal Revival

Regardless of these historical critiques, to the contemporary scholar encountering Hayek's *Road to Serfdom*, the text appears dated and flawed. A revival of liberalism appears ill-fated if we do not at least acknowledge these critiques and slough off the unnecessary aspects of Hayek's thought.

First, Hayek anchors his apology for individual freedom on an outmoded teleological narrative and failed political project that aimed to solder seamlessly and exclusively the civilizations of ancient Greece and

Rome to the contemporary West—as if the fecund and complex civilization of Ionia could be so easily captured and marshaled into the service of a system of power. This is not to deny that the study of ancient Greek and Roman civilizations is undoubtedly fundamental to understanding aspects of the self-identity of Western societies even today. The appropriation of Hellenic and Roman civilizations on behalf of the West to anchor notions of individual freedom is no longer particularly useful, and in any case it is easily discarded without damage to Hayek's core ideas.

Second, and flowing from the first, the effort to excommunicate fascism and socialism from the Western tradition, when both emerged originally in the West, while scarcely mentioning the exploitative brutality of colonial conquest, slavery, and racism in Western societies seems misleading and is unlikely to resonate with many contemporary students or scholars. A contemporary defense of liberalism has little use for dubious claims of pure lineage and nobility; this pristine narrative should also be discarded.

Third, and related to the first point, Hayek's general unfamiliarity with non-Western philosophical developments that also endorsed nascent conceptions of reason, human freedom, limits on state power, and individual rights renders his work parochial and provincial outside of the West.[71] One could argue that it succumbs to a variant of the historicism that Hayek detested. Given the broad global appeal of liberalism from East Asia to Latin America, a less parochial framework would be wise. Hayek himself was cosmopolitan by temperament, and he was keenly aware of his international influence. There is no reason to limit liberalism to its Western strain.

Fourth, the methodological individualism in Hayek's early work appears at first glance to be not only in tension with his later turn toward cultural evolution but also naive in the wake of post-structural theories of the panoptic-disciplinary grounding of liberal societies.[72] A synthesis between Hayek's methodological individualism and Foucault's structuralism/post-structuralism is imaginable, and a way can be seen through the work of Alexis de Tocqueville and Friedrich Nietzsche, although it would require extensive theoretical compromises—and is beyond the scope of this book. A knowing subject who is aware of the disciplinary structures that summon, bind, and animate the individualized body would entail a more restricted notion of autonomy than liberalism currently postulates. Nevertheless, a more nuanced conceptualization of the individual and their agency is warranted, and an interpretation of Hayek's work is that he developed well beyond any "dogmatic," "reductive," or "atomistic" individualism.[73] For those who remain unconvinced by methodological individualism, Hayek's individualism must be posited as an a priori assumption, first principle, or unquestionable theoretical "hard core" from which liberalism's (Lakatosian) research program generates testable hypotheses about the nature of social and economic organization.[74]

Fifth, Hayek has often been misread as arguing that social democracy, or the welfare state more broadly, would inevitably result in totalitarianism. The durability and performance of social-democratic countries is then used to simplistically refute Hayek. *The Road to Serfdom* was even maligned as a slippery-slope argument by Hayek's friend and intellectual rival John Maynard Keynes.[75] As Hayek made clear in his later work, Keynes clearly misunderstood Hayek's intellectual framing, and this oversimplification was dismissive and unthoughtful. Noted Hayek in his preface to the 1956 edition of *The Road to Serfdom*:

> Of course, six years of socialist government in England have not produced anything resembling a totalitarian state. But those who argue that that this has disproved the thesis of *The Road to Serfdom* have really missed one of its main points: that the most important change which extensive government control produces is a psychological change, an alteration in the character of the people. This is necessarily a slow affair, a process which extends not over a few years but perhaps over one or two generations. The important point is that the political ideals of a people and its attitude toward authority are as much the effect as the cause of the political institutions under which it lives. This means, among other things, that even a strong tradition of political liberty is no safeguard if the danger is precisely that new institutions and policies will gradually undermine and destroy that spirit. The consequences can of course be averted if that spirit reasserts itself in time and the people not only throw out the party which has been leading them further and further in the dangerous direction but also recognize the nature of the danger and resolutely change their course. There is not much ground to believe that the latter has happened in England.[76]

This prefatory note establishes that Hayek was not arguing a slippery-slope position, nor did he view the turn toward socialist totalitarianism in Great Britain as predestined. Nevertheless, Hayek's concerns about the impact of extensive government control were not wholly unfounded, as events in Great Britain after the publication of *The Road to Serfdom* illustrated. In particular, the Attlee Labour government's (1945–51) reintroduction of Defence Regulation 58A and the Control of Engagement Order (1947) in peacetime to direct laborers to take "essential" work or face fines and/ or up to three months' imprisonment was a troubling development, even if the regulations were seldom enforced.[77] While Hayek did believe that some members of the British Labour Party were less inhibited about using coercion than Germany's Social Democrats during the Weimar Republic (1918–33), he regarded the Attlee administration as more incompetent than totalitarian.[78]

Even if the Attlee government took Britain farther down the road to serfdom, it was clear that Hayek did not argue from a determinist's standpoint. In the introduction to the original book, Hayek writes:

> The danger is not immediate, it is true, and conditions in England and the United States are still so remote from those witnessed in recent years in Germany as to make it difficult to believe that we are moving in the same direction. Yet, though the road be long, it is one on which it becomes more difficult to turn back as one advances. If in the long run we are the makers of our own fate, in the short run we are the captives of the ideas we have created. Only if we recognize the danger in time can we hope to avert it.[79]

There is scope for agency, although it requires intellectual struggle. Hayek repeats the point after a paragraph:

> The supreme tragedy is still not seen that in Germany it was largely people of good will, men who were admired and held up as models in the democratic countries, who prepared the way for, if they did not actually create, the forces which now stand for everything they detest. Yet our chance of averting a similar fate depends on our facing the danger and on our being prepared to revise even our most cherished hopes and ambitions if they should prove to be the source of the danger.[80]

Hayek reiterates the point a third time in the next paragraph: "All parallels between developments in different countries are, of course, deceptive; but I am not basing my argument mainly on such parallels. Nor am I arguing that these developments are inevitable. If they were, there would be no point in writing this."[81] Given these repeated caveats at the outset of the argument, only a shallow or willful misreading of Hayek's argument can explain the use of the slippery-slope label to dismiss Hayek's thesis. Hayek's book is neither a slippery-slope argument nor a prophecy; it is an admonition to turn back from the long road. Moreover, as we see from the dedication of his book to "the socialists of all parties," Hayek is particularly interested in persuading his intellectual opponents, rather than merely reaffirming the prior convictions of liberals. In fact, as Chris Matthew Sciabarra reminds us, Hayek often agreed with progressive socialists on many issues:

> Hayek believed he had much more in common with progressive social-ists on specific social issues than with conservatives. He agreed with socialists on most questions of value. Yet he opposed central planning because it was both counterproductive and subversive of its own stated ultimate ends. In a unique synthesis, Hayek integrated a classical liberal commitment to the free market, a classical conservative commitment to evolutionism, and elements of a profoundly radical, dialectical method of social inquiry.[82]

This passage from Sciabarra indicates that Hayek's argument should not be regarded as reactionary or alarmist. Hayek disagreed with socialists mainly about means, not ultimate values. The core of Hayek's argument in *The Road to Serfdom* is not a debate about "planning or no planning" but, as Peter J. Boettke and Scott M. King reiterate, ". . . who is going to plan and for whom is the planning intended."[83]

Hayek's warnings about the impact of state paternalism on the spirit of political liberty echoes Tocqueville's concerns about despotism in Amer-ica. Hayek quotes Tocqueville's *Democracy in America* directly:

> The will of man is not shattered but softened, bent and guided; men are seldom forced by it to act, but they are constantly restrained from act-ing. Such a power does not destroy, but it prevents existence; it does not tyrannize, but it compresses, enervates, extinguishes, and stupefies a people, till each nation is reduced to be nothing better than a flock of timid and industrial animals, of which government is the shepherd.[84]

A restatement of liberalism must emphasize the impact of government policy on the political character of a people without implying a slippery slope or predestined outcome once a society moves away from liberalism.

Finally, Hayek's public apologetics on behalf of and silence toward the human-rights abuses of the brutal authoritarian capitalist regime of Gen-eral Augusto Pinochet (1915–2006; President, 1974–90), despite the com-plex context in which it occurred,[85] severely undermined Hayek's philo-sophical defense of liberalism and individual liberty. Although Hayek's abhorrence of illiberal democracy was long standing and drew inspiration from Tocqueville, his support for a brutal military dictatorship did tarnish his reputation.[86] Hayek's defense of Pinochet as a "liberal dictator" and his belief that the dictatorship was merely a transitional regime on the path to a stable, limited, and liberal democracy was a severe and unforgivable mistake. Similarly, his belief in the 1960s that the Portuguese dictator Oliveira Salazar could be guided toward the creation of a limited democracy was naive.[87] These errors set back the cause of liberalism globally. Hayek's actions did not match his own philosophy, articulated in his earlier writings, and thus a revival of liberalism must divorce the two elements, retaining only an emphasis on Hayek's philosophy.

Despite these major drawbacks and misreadings, Hayek's ideas contain nuggets of enduring truth and insight that merit our attention if we seek to preserve and enhance the (limited) autonomy of individuals against a repackaged collectivism and the seductive appeal of authoritarian capitalism. Rather than attempting to excuse or exonerate the shortcomings of Hayek's project and his political missteps, by focusing on Hayek's text and ideas this book seeks to recover the enduring insights that will permit a robust defense and restatement of liberalism in the contemporary era.

The method employed here is a close reading of Hayek's text. The goal is to illuminate hidden meaning, open up lines of thought, and draw connections that contemporary students approaching the text may not readily note or grasp. This book is conceptualized as a meditation upon, a companion alongside, and a supplement to Hayek's *Road to Serfdom*; it is not meant as a substitute for the original.

CHAPTER ONE

The Abandoned Road

A program whose basic thesis is, not that the system of free enterprise for profit has failed in this generation, but that it has not yet been tried.

Franklin Delano Roosevelt (1938)

Hayek enigmatically opens *The Road to Serfdom*'s first chapter, "The Abandoned Road," by invoking a speech by US President Franklin Delano Roosevelt.[1] Although Roosevelt is commonly seen as a market interventionist and the architect of the New Deal, his fundamental beliefs were aligned with liberalism. In response to William Trufant Foster and Waddill Catchings's pre-Keynesian economic text *The Road to Plenty* (1928), Roosevelt had written in the margin of his copy, "Too good to be true—You can't get something for nothing."[2] Roosevelt was deeply conflicted about the state expansion over which he presided. In fact, in 1933 Roosevelt had initially blamed the previous administration's "loose fiscal policy" for creating a drag on the government. His first acts were budget cuts targeting veterans and government employees.[3] He was reflexively a fiscal conservative. Even in 1937, after a peak federal deficit, Roosevelt claimed (rather disingenuously) to have cut spending and balanced the budget, "exclusive of the extraordinary relief expenditures which began with the new Administration."[4] Thus, Roosevelt's 1938 call for a return of the faithful to a competitive market order in the Second New Deal of 1935 was, perhaps, sincere. In particular, Roosevelt sought to combat the "economic royalists" or business elites who abhorred competition in practice despite their rhetoric to the contrary.[5] Hayek understood that the ideals of the United States and United Kingdom had undergone such a transformation since the Great Depression that Roosevelt's words would seem puzzling. And yet the words echoed the faith of the revivalist; economic liberalism had failed not because it did not work, but because it had not been tried in earnest. Thus, the title of the chapter is a reference to the abandonment of the road to liberalism before the destination was reached. The chapter, and the book more broadly, comprise an exhortation to turn back from the road to servitude and return to the high road, though, to quote Milton, "long is the way and hard."[6]

It is also worth mentioning that Keynes, Hayek's friend and intellectual rival, attacked Roosevelt's "stimulus" (the National Recovery Act of 1933). Keynes had argued for $4.8 billion a year in stimulus (which was equivalent to 11 percent of US national income at the time), but actual US spending never approached that level. In 1937–38 the US economy fell back into recession owing, from Keynes's perspective, to Roosevelt's reluctance to increase spending. For Keynesians, the United States would not climb out of its rut until it began spending on armaments prior to World War II.[7]

Ironically, Hayek would gain the support of the faction of the American business community that was deeply hostile to both New Deal liberalism and Keynesianism after the publication of *The Road to Serfdom*.[8] Jasper Elliot Crane, a retired vice president of the DuPont Company and a major conservative activist and donor, met with Hayek in May 1946. Shortly thereafter William H. Luhnow, of the Volker Fund, inquired whether Hayek would write a "Road to Serfdom" about trends in the United States. Loren Miller, who had first introduced Crane to Hayek, thought that Crane might be interested in Luhnow's proposed project.[9] Although Hayek tried to cultivate Crane as a fundraiser for his Mont Pelerin Society, Crane privately expressed anti-Semitic concerns about Hayek's heritage and ideological misgivings about Hayek's tolerance of intellectual diversity.[10] Ultimately, the financial support of anti–New Deal American businessmen did not seem to be impaired by the opening epigraph of Hayek's book or by Hayek's mild distrust of the propensity of capitalists to form monopolies.[11]

Alternatively, of course, one might read Hayek's epigraph as seizing on a kernel of truth from the words of a political opponent—a practice that becomes a pattern throughout *The Road to Serfdom*, as we will see.

∴

In a seeming allusion to the opening of Karl Marx and Friedrich Engels's *Communist Manifesto*, which in turn was an allusion to the opening of William Shakespeare's *Hamlet*,[12] Hayek commences his political text with a discussion of the malevolent spirit that is haunting the West: "When the course of civilization takes an unexpected turn—when, instead of the continuous progress which we have come to expect, we find ourselves threatened by evils associated by us with past ages of barbarism—we naturally blame anything but ourselves."[13] He asks rhetorically who is to blame for the derailment of the Spencerian expectation of continuous progress instilled in Westerners since the Industrial Revolution. Despite the best of intentions to generate freedom and prosperity, only bondage and misery have resulted:

Have we not all striven according to our best lights, and have not many of our finest minds incessantly worked to make this a better world? Have not all our efforts and hopes been directed toward greater freedom, justice, and prosperity? If the outcome is so different from our aims—if, instead of freedom and prosperity, bondage and misery stare us in the face—is it not clear that sinister forces must have foiled our intentions, that we are the victims of some evil power which must be conquered before we can resume the road to better things?[14]

Writing in the midst of a global war, the misery is plain to his audience, as is the desire to see the war as an aberration from the path to progress begun with the birth of the commercial society. But Hayek is not content with such a simple explanation; moreover, he seeks to lay the groundwork for an inversion of Smith's "invisible hand." In Hayek's variant of Smith's memorable metaphor,[15] it is the noble intentions of the collective civilization that set the stage for an epic tragedy:

However much we may differ when we name the culprit—whether it is the wicked capitalist or the vicious spirit of a particular nation, the stupidity of our elders, or a social system not yet, although we have struggled against it for half a century, fully overthrown—we all are, or at least were until recently, certain of one thing: that the leading ideas which during the last generation have become common to most people of good will and have determined the major changes in our social life cannot have been wrong.[16]

Hayek is critical of a mindset that seeks to either externalize ("the vicious spirit of a particular nation") or find scapegoats for ("the wicked capitalist," "the stupidity of our elders," "a social system not yet . . . fully overthrown") the civilizational turmoil in which the West finds itself toward the end of World War II. Instead, Hayek proposes that it is the pursuit of "our most cherished ideals" that has produced its unintended opposite.[17] In essence, the battle to institute progressive state control over the market and overthrow the remnants of laissez-faire, were regarded as uniformly appropriate by the intellectual elite on *all* sides of the war. As Hayek noted in his introduction,

The problem is not why the Germans as such are vicious, which congenitally they are probably no more than other peoples, but to determine the circumstances which during the last seventy years have made possible the progressive growth and the ultimate victory of a particular set of ideas, and why in the end this victory has brought the most vicious elements among them to the top.[18]

The task is to move beyond stereotyping and scapegoating to understand how a century and a half of a battle of ideas between liberalism and socialism eventually fostered an environment in which the most ruthless individuals on all sides acquired political power.

Hayek believes that even before the two world wars, the liberal values for which the Western Allies were fighting as he wrote were endangered at home. Thus, even a victory on the battlefield abroad would need to be complemented with an ideological victory at home. Without a confrontation of the basic problems of social order in the West, Hayek feared his adopted homeland would eventually succumb to the totalitarian impulses of Germany, Italy, or the Union of Soviet Socialist Republics (USSR).

Hayek realized that his audience would have difficulty envisioning that the radical ideologies that arose on the European subcontinent had already arisen, or even originated,[19] in "the Anglo-Saxon nations."[20] He reminds his audience, however, that Germany, Italy, and Russia were all part of a common European civilization, and their rapid and malevolent ideological evolution prior to the war stemmed from a common cultural base. Thus, Hayek's book was constructed as a warning that these radical ideologies had already taken root in familiar soil, whatever the war's outcome. And that the transformation that had happened so subtly and rapidly as to seem almost inevitable and irresistible over there could happen at home.

To demonstrate that liberalism was under assault before World War I, Hayek asserts that the notion that the world prior to World War II was governed by the principle of laissez-faire was itself an illusion. He argues that the state regulation of day-to-day affairs of society in liberal countries had already commenced well before the Great Depression.[21] In essence, the transformation of society away from rugged individualism and limited government had already begun.

Western Civilization

Unfortunately, at this critical juncture, instead of expanding on the erosion of individualism and liberalism, Hayek digresses to argue that his compatriots were ". . . moving away from the basic ideas on which Western civilization has been built."[22] Although this line of argument is unsurprising for its

time, the argument seems rather unnecessary and overstated, since rational capitalism and liberal political philosophy were themselves relatively
recent developments in the long arc of European intellectual and economic
history. Moreover, a transhistorical notion of "the West" is arguably too
vague and internally contradictory to withstand critical interrogation.
However, to the extent that Hayek detects in the turn toward socialism a
break with specific British intellectuals of the seventeenth, eighteenth, and
nineteenth centuries, he was on solid ground. In *The Counter Revolution of
Science* (1941) Hayek had traced the source of rationalism that he associ-
ates with the hubris of socialist state planning to René Descartes (1596–
1650) and subsequently to Saint-Simon (1760–1825) and Auguste Comte
(1798–1857).[23] To detect a divergence within European thought in the
early modern period that eventually leads to a preference for state planning and socialism in one strand and for individual freedom in the other is
unobjectionable.

To stretch liberalism back to its foundations in Christian, Roman, and
Greek notions of the individual, however, is a rather selective appropriation of intellectual history.[24] It is as convincing a parlor trick as tracing the
origins of socialism back to Christian, Roman, and Greek notions of the
community. In any case, scientific socialism and national socialism emerged
first in the West. If there were a coherent concept of Western civilization, it
would also need to acknowledge its paternity of these ideologies as well as
liberalism. Hayek's logic is more persuasive where he notes that socialism
and national socialism represent a sharp deviation from liberalism.

Tactically, this framing of his argument is also an error, because it firmly
aligns economic liberalism with the West alone. The pairing of liberalism
and the West thereby strengthens authoritarianism outside the West. Argues the Nobel Laureate economist Amartya Sen:

> Authoritarian lines of reasoning in Asia—and more generally in non-
> Western societies—often receive indirect backing from modes of thought
> in the West itself. There is clearly a tendency in America and Europe to
> assume, if only implicitly, the primacy of political freedom and democ-
> racy as a fundamental and ancient feature of Western culture—one not
> to be easily found in Asia. It is, as it were, a contrast between the authori-
> tarianism allegedly implicit in, say, Confucianism vis-à-vis the respect
> for individual liberty and autonomy allegedly deeply rooted in Western
> liberal culture. Western promoters of personal and political liberty in the
> non-Western world often see this as bringing Occidental values to Asia
> and Africa. The world is invited to join the club of "Western democracy"
> and to admire and endorse traditional "Western values."[25]

Liberalism rightly aspires to be a universally valid set of ideas; notions of individualism, tolerance, and limited government are found in many cultures across history, albeit unsystematically. This unsystematic development of the values of freedom and democracy outside of Western societies is actually no different from what one finds in the classical Western authors themselves. Sen states:

> Values that European Enlightenment and other relatively recent developments have made common and widespread cannot really be seen as part of the long-run Western heritage—experienced in the West over millennia. What we do find in the writings by particular Western classical authors (for example, Aristotle) is support for selected *components* of the comprehensive notion that makes up the contemporary idea of political liberty. But support for such components can be found in many writings in Asian traditions as well.[26]

Sen argues that since "non-freedom perspectives" are present in thinkers from Plato to Confucius, the heart of the matter is whether "freedom-oriented perspectives" (i.e., individual freedom, tolerance, and egalitarianism) are *absent* from Asian traditions. Sen cites Buddhism as a clear example characterized by the value of freedom. Buddhism emphasizes volition and free choice; nobility of conduct must be achieved in the context of freedom.[27] The Emperor Ashoka (c. 304–232 BCE), who converted to Buddhism around 260 BCE, emphasized uniform and universal tolerance across his empire.[28] Similarly, the Mughal emperor Akbar (1542–1605) emphasized religious and social tolerance across the Indian subcontinent.[29]

Gurcharan Das traces the roots of liberty on the subcontinent to the concept of *raj dharma*, or the dharma of the king:

> Dharma can mean many things—duty, virtue, righteousness—but it is chiefly concerned with doing the right thing. Dharma also means law, and it preceded the state and placed limits on the king's power in premodern India. The king did not give the law as in China. Dharma was above the state, and the king was expected to uphold it for the benefit of the people. The king also did not interpret the law, unlike in China; it was the Brahmin who interpreted the law. Hence, a liberal division of power was created early on, which contributed to a weak Indian state at birth. But it also prevented oppression by the state. . . .[30]

In any case, while state strength varied across the premodern subcontinent, kings in Indian history were generally distant figures who did not

touch the lives of ordinary persons. The individual was constrained not
so much by the state as by the village, the caste or sect, and the family.
The role of the state was to uphold the "ordered heterogeneity" of Indian
society.[31]

Even Confucianism, known for its emphasis on order and discipline
and (supposedly) lacking in lexical equivalents to key liberal concepts,[32]
does not emphasize blind obedience to the state; truth is prioritized over
power.[33] Moreover, one's family has greater value than one's state.[34] Confucius (fifth century BCE) believed that individuals had the freedom to
choose between different ends. In the Confucian philosophy of Mengzi
(fourth century BCE), individuals possess the capacity to weigh competing options and choose from them; and in the work of Xunzi (third century
BCE) one sees a concept of the mind's autonomy as well as a vision of moral
responsibility by a free agent.[35] While modern neo-Confucianism tends to
emphasize positive freedom and personal ethics, it does not condone totalitarianism. In fact, the philosophy of Mou Tsung-san (1909–1995) argues
for the "blossoming" of democracy by means of self-negation (i.e., the recognition of equality).[36] In any case, Chinese liberals in the early twentieth
century, such as Chang Fo-ch'üan (1908–1994), affirmed a conception of
"negative freedom" and a confirmation of human dignity. As Roy Tseng
argues, "Chang's liberalism without a doubt entails the universalistic belief
that there are common human values, namely human rights, transcending
various traditions and cultural barriers."[37] Hayek, who had once hoped to
study under Max Weber,[38] would have been wiser to take seriously Weber's
parenthetical remark at the outset of *The Protestant Ethic and the Spirit of
Capitalism*:

> A product of modern European civilization, studying any problem of
> universal history, is bound to ask himself to what combination of cir-
> cumstances the fact should be attributed that in Western civilization, and
> in Western civilization only, cultural phenomena have appeared that (as
> we like to think) lie in a line of development having universal significance
> and value.[39]

Similarly, Weber's invocation of Goethe in *The Protestant Ethic* indicates
the need for a greater humility: "Specialists without spirit, sensualists without heart; this nullity imagines that it has attained a level of civilization
never before achieved."[40] Despite his apparent Eurocentrism, however,
Hayek's theories transcend provincialism. The political theorist Chandran
Kukathas once posed the question "Does Hayek Speak to Asia?" in a short
speech to the Mont Pelerin Society. Kukathas's answer frames an interest-

ing tension between Hayek's respect for local knowledge production and an understanding of civilization as a society that makes possible change for the sake of change. In Kukathas's account, Hayek simultaneously clears space for Asian societies, which will find their own path, while destroying the conservative refuge of "Asian values" authoritarianism. Hayek's statement to Asia is not to be too easily seduced by the West. In this respect, Kukathas presents a Hayek who rises above the provincial concerns of Western civilization to champion an internationalist outlook.[41]

Individualism

What *is* useful in Hayek's historical digression is his explanation of the essential features of individualism associated with liberalism: ". . . the respect for the individual man *qua* man, that is, the recognition of his own views and tastes as supreme in his own sphere, however narrowly that may be circumscribed, and the belief that it is desirable that men should develop their own individual gifts and bents."[42] Hayek's individualism represents a rejection of individualism understood as mere selfishness. Liberalism views the individual as occupying a space of autonomy, at least when it comes to matters of opinion, belief, thought, and taste (notably, the preservation of individual autonomy does not apply to issues of fact or science). The historical mission of liberalism is to expand this kernel of autonomy so that ". . . men could at least attempt to shape their own life, where man gained the opportunity of knowing and choosing between different forms of life. . . ."[43] Hayek argues that "tolerance" is the word that best conveys the essence of the notion of freedom and liberty in a liberal society.[44]

Hayek dates the birth of "individualist civilization" and "modern man" to the European Renaissance, although he gestures to Christian, Greek, and Roman foundations. He contends that the late seventeenth century and the eighteenth century witnessed a revival and expansion of this form of individualism not seen since the Renaissance. In this light, it is perhaps worth noting that the notion of the abstract individual is not absent from all non-Western cultures. In the Hindu *Bhagavad Gītā* (first century CE), for example, although social roles shape outward behavior and moral frameworks, the individual is severed from their family and community to "cultivate a soteriological psychology."[45] There are parallels with the soteriological psychology cultivated in the first part of John Bunyan's allegory *The Pilgrim's Progress* (1678) that (tentatively) helped to lay the basis for the modern (i.e., Protestant) conception of individualism.[46] Although Hinduism has not fostered the emergence of liberal individualism in the same way as secularized Protestantism, the building blocks for a liberal ideology are present.

Hayek lists wars, political oppression, and the subjugation of the bourgeoisie as forces that submerged the Renaissance in continental Europe, but he neglects to mention the ways in which settler colonialism and imperialism often confined the spread and development of these noble ideas in political practice to a narrow elite well into the twentieth century. His conception of individualism is significantly different from the emphasis on narrow self-interest in contemporary neoclassical microeconomics. Notably, Adam Smith also did not embrace selfishness as the basis for the commercial society; he emphasized mutual ocular surveillance as the bedrock that would underpin the moral order and an appeal to the interests of others as the basis for market exchange.[47] While mechanical notions of individualism have permitted the development of sophisticated microeconomic models, they have made the vision of humanity unidimensional, abstract, and brittle. Importantly, however, Hayek does not postulate a heroic form of individual agency. Rather, he notes that individuals should at least be permitted to attempt to shape their own lives and to have the opportunity to know and choose between different forms of life. Chance, structural forces, and mutual competition implicitly limit human agency in Hayek's framework. Nevertheless, Hayek argues that the scope of individual agency should be maximized (where appropriate) in a liberal order, despite the existence of constraints.

It should also be noted that Hayek's understanding of individualism is silent on the prospect for efficacious collective action through practical and tacit knowledge sharing such as emerged during the Occupy Wall Street protests in 2011–12.[48] However, one might assume that Mancur Olson's "logic of collective action" and Robert Michels's "iron law of oligarchy" might limit the efficaciousness or authenticity of "acephalous" social movements.[49]

The theoretical importance of the spread of individualism, for Hayek, is that freeing individuals from the shackles of custom in ordinary life permits the emergence of an unintended and spontaneous economic order: "The conscious realization that the spontaneous and uncontrolled efforts of individuals were capable of producing a complex order of economic activities could come only after this development had made some progress."[50] Political freedom or autonomy is therefore antecedent to the "free growth of economic activity," and the latter is an unintended by-product of the former. This historic sequencing is important to keep in mind for those who would seek to create a spontaneous economic order without political liberalization.

Political freedom also enables the growth of science and technology. Hayek notes that mechanical inventions had emerged in earlier ages but were promptly suppressed when linked to an extended industrial use.[51] Without the liberalization of the political sphere, industrial freedom could not open new pathways. It is the Industrial Revolution that both raises the standard of living of all classes and exposes intolerable "dark spots in society" that need to be addressed.[52]

Idealism

It is important to appreciate that Hayek's political philosophy is idealist, in the sense that he asserts the primacy of ideas: "That a change of ideas and the force of human will have made the world what it is now, though men did not foresee the results, and that no spontaneous change in the facts obliged us thus to adapt our thought is perhaps particularly difficult for Anglo-Saxon nations to see."[53] Although Hayek may have retained elements of a dialectical method,[54] he rejects the historical-materialist component of Marx's thought.[55] Ideas have primacy in shaping the world, even if those ideas are dimly understood by the agents of history. However, a society's cherished ideals may not reflect the actual ideas at work. For example, according to Hayek, by 1931 the United Kingdom and the United States had both strayed far from the liberal path they were on before World War I, but many British and American citizens were unaware of the one onto which they had strayed, and the divergence from liberalism would only increase after the onset of the Great Depression.[56] In other words, discovering the principles on which a society actually operates requires intellectual excavation.

While Hayek certainly rejects Marxist historical materialism, it should be noted that Hayek embodies a form of Leninism in his systematic efforts to create the intellectual vanguard of twentieth-century liberalism through the Mont Pelerin Society (MPS).[57] The MPS served as a "Neoliberal thought collective" during the high tide of Keynesianism.[58] Hayek also admired the courage of Marxists to dream of a utopia, although he attacked socialists for their utopian schemes.[59] In essence, Hayek supported utopian thinking when it aligned with the proper means and ends of society. As Hayek would spell out later in *Law, Legislation, and Liberty*:

> It is not to be denied that to some extent the guiding model of the overall order will always be an utopia, something to which the existing situation will be only a distant approximation and which many people will regard

as wholly impractical. Yet it is only by constantly holding up the guiding conception of an internally consistent model which could be realized by the consistent application of the same principles, that anything like an effective framework for a functioning spontaneous order will be achieved. Adam Smith thought that "to expect, indeed, that freedom of trade should ever be entirely restored in Great Britain is as absurd as to expect an Oceana or Utopia should ever be established in it." Yet seventy years later, largely as a result of his work, it was achieved.[60]

However, unlike his colleague Karl Popper, whose aim was to apply critical rationality to social problems to prevent utopian thinking, Hayek's chief fear was well-meaning incrementalism in public policy.[61] Moreover, Hayek eschewed narrow empiricism combined with incrementalism in guiding public policy:

> The myopic view of science that concentrates on the study of particular facts because they alone are empirically observable, and whose advocates even pride themselves on not being guided by such a conception of the overall order as can be obtained only by what they call "abstract speculation," by no means increases our power of shaping a desirable order, but in fact deprives us of all effective guidance for successful action. The spurious "realism" which deceives itself in believing that it can dispense with any guiding conception of the nature of the overall order, and confines itself to an examination of particular "techniques" for achieving particular results, is in reality highly unrealistic. Especially when this attitude leads, as it frequently does, to a judgment of the advisability of particular measures by consideration of the "practicability" in the given political climate of opinion, it often tends merely to drive us further into an impasse. Such must be the ultimate results of successive measures which all tend to destroy the overall order that their advocates at the same time tacitly assume to exist.[62]

Freedom and Commerce

Hayek historically links the expansion of individual autonomy and the historic development of commerce in Europe's urban centers.[63] It is worth emphasizing that political freedom from serfdom and customary life preceded the elaboration of economic freedom in Europe.[64] The spread of commerce and the accumulation of capital in turn create support for a particular form of social and political life that emphasizes tolerance and individual autonomy. Although the sociological assertion seems rather mono-causal,[65] it is not incorrect to assert a correlation between the development of European commercial centers and the expansion of individual freedoms in the late seventeenth and eighteenth centuries. To this extent, Hayek reiterates Adam Smith's stadial theory of European history.[66]

Hayek also notes that it was the pairing of venture capital with scientific and industrial inventions that dramatically advanced the pace of scientific discovery, transformed the standard of living, and opened new political possibilities for Europeans and to a lesser extent their settler colonies during this period. In other words, the expansion of wealth in Europe is also linked to the harnessing of new ideas to venture capital.

A more critical perspective requires us to acknowledge the link between these commercial centers, monopolistic colonial enterprises, and the slave trade, which stifled freedom in other parts of the world. However, the fact that the blossoming of individual freedom was coeval with the emergence of monopolistic corporations and chattel slavery is not an indictment of liberty or liberal economics. State conferred monopolies and human slavery are the hallmarks of illiberalism; in a liberal framework, the roots of human freedom in one part of the planet need not necessarily rely on the enslavement and exploitation of another. As Adam Smith noted, the East India Company distorted the natural economic development of the Indian subcontinent.[67] The exploitation of the colonies was deeply misguided and economically shortsighted.

The Pace of Progress

Hayek properly frames the timeline and metric for measuring the effects of capital accumulation: "To appreciate what it meant to those who took part in it, we must measure it by the hopes and wishes men held when it began: and there can be no doubt that its success surpassed man's wildest dreams. . . ."[68] Often the timeframe for contemporary, critical assessments of capitalism is merely a few business cycles or a few decades at most. To comprehend the cumulatively ameliorative effects of capitalism, one needs to expand the time horizon. The metric for Hayek is not merely the improved material standard of living, but ". . . the new sense of power over their own fate, the belief in the unbounded possibilities of improving their own lot, which the success already achieved created among men."[69] Defenders of capitalism often make the mistake of legitimating capitalism and liberal economic policies solely on the basis of economic gain, but as authoritarian or political capitalism is clearly capable of making dramatic gains in economic output, the proper metric for those who value individual autonomy is more qualitative, political, and metaphysical.

An Evolving Creed

Hayek insists that liberalism is not a stationary creed. Rather, it is based on a generalizable principle that political society ought to be organized in a way that "makes as much use as possible of the spontaneous forces of society, and resort[s] as little as possible to coercion."[70] The articulation of an adaptive principle for liberalism sublates Hayek's earlier effort to anchor liberalism in a specific Eurocentric philosophical tradition and reveals a cosmopolitan potential. In essence, one need not attempt to revive the failed project to link the West to the emergence of liberty in order to appreciate Hayek's underlying argument.

The Prestige of Ideas

Hayek argues that the prestige of ideas and economic development are somewhat intertwined. He locates the reversal of liberal ideas and the spread of antiliberal doctrines in Germany from the late nineteenth century forward.[71] Germany not only attained great material progress during this period but also had developed a rigorous intellectual infrastructure over the preceding century: although socialist ideas did not originate in Germany, they were perfected there. Hayek argues that the contempt shown by German scholars for liberalism induced even the people of the West "to believe that their own former convictions had merely been rationalizations of selfish interests, that free trade was a doctrine invented to further British interests, and that the political ideals of England and America were hopelessly outmoded and a thing to be ashamed of."[72] The underlying argument is that the prestige of ideas can deceive a people into turning against their own heritage, even when that heritage has generated immense prosperity. The argument seems anti-intellectual, but it might also be read as a warning to those who would neglect the need for engaging with foreign intellectual ideas. In other words, in each age the battle of ideas must be enjoined.

If Hayek is correct that the prestige of ideas is intertwined with economic development, then liberals ought to be paying careful attention to the development of political capitalism in East Asia. Today Singapore is nearly tied with the United States in terms of GDP per capita, and China is the second-largest economy in terms of GDP (nominal) and the largest in PPP (purchasing power parity).

Mapping Illiberalism

Most importantly for the subsequent chapters, Hayek posits a deep affinity between the two most prominent forms of illiberalism, national socialism and socialism/communism.[73] In contrast to the conventional conceptualization of a polarized left-right political spectrum or plane, Hayek offers a curved political spectrum in which the radical left mirrors the radical right.[74] National socialism is thus the culmination of socialist trends in Europe (and Germany in particular since the later part of the Bismarckian era[75]) rather than its antithesis. Liberalism stands uniformly opposed to both socialism and national socialism. Hayek's insight forces a meditation on the commonalities of communist and fascist regimes: centralized planning, attenuated rights, physical coercion of individuals, and militarism. Hayek provides anecdotal empirical support for this controversial conceptualization later in the text when he quotes a set of firsthand accounts of life in the Soviet Union by Max Eastman, W. H. Chamberlin, and F. A. Voigt.[76] Those who experienced life in the early Soviet Union frequently saw the parallels between socialism and fascism unprompted.

Today, even ardent radical leftist intellectuals concede certain parallels at least between Stalinism and Hitlerism, even if they continue to insist that communism is philosophically an outgrowth of the Enlightenment and oriented toward liberation, while fascism was a "radical evil." For example, Slavoj Žižek, while rejecting the liberal project of rationally comparing variants of totalitarianism, goes so far as to write:

> We should have the honesty to acknowledge that the Stalinist purges were in a way more "irrational" than the Fascist violence: its excess is an unmistakable sign that, in contrast to Fascism, Stalinism was a case of an authentic revolution perverted. Under Fascism, even in Nazi Germany, it was possible to survive, to maintain the appearance of a "normal" everyday life, if one did not involve oneself in any oppositional political activity (and, of course, if one were not Jewish). Under Stalin in the late 1930s, on the other hand, nobody was safe: anyone could be unexpectedly denounced, arrested and shot as a traitor. The irrationality of Nazism was "condensed" in anti-semitism—in its belief in the Jewish plot—while the irrationality of Stalinism pervaded the entire social body. For that

reason, Nazi police investigators looked for proofs and traces of active opposition to the regime, whereas Stalin's investigators were happy to fabricate evidence, invent plots etc.[77]

Of course, the excesses of Stalinism relative to those of fascism are taken by Žižek as signs that a pure communist revolution was "perverted," while fascism's disciplined totalitarianism is a sign that it had no such enlightened heritage and was mainly a conservative revolution in response to apparently inherent class antagonisms in capitalism. Nonetheless, regardless of the debatable philosophical differences, it is clear that communism regularly devolved into forms of totalitarianism that were comparable to fascist totalitarianism.

Hayek's political spectrum also entails a rejection of nineteenth-century laissez-faire liberalism. He excoriates liberals who employ a "wooden insistence" on rough rules of thumb, that is, the principles of laissez-faire.[78] Economic liberalism must not become a mechanical framework or unyielding prejudice against the state; a market solution does not apply automatically to all policy questions. It is the austere and mechanical character of "neoliberalism," "market fundamentalism," or "dis-embedded markets" that has been most assailed by leftist critics from Karl Polanyi onward.[79] A careful reading of Hayek demonstrates that there is neither fundamentalism nor mechanistic logic in Hayek's restatement of liberalism. It is also for this reason that Hayek should not be confused with an American libertarian. While Hayek's work may be useful to libertarians, it cannot be reduced to slogans and simplistic formulas. At the same time, Hayek hoped that the new liberalism (i.e., neoliberalism) would dare to dream of a utopia. Figure 1.1 is a provisional attempt to elaborate Hayek's understanding of the political/ideological space in which he operated.

As a point of reference, figure 1.1 also includes Keynesianism. Keynesian thought, although an attempt by a liberal humanist to save liberal capitalism from the threat of socialism after World War II, would have appeared to Hayek as moving too far on the path to collectivism.[80] Of course, Milton Friedman's version of neoliberalism (monetarism) was built on the Keynesian system of aggregate economics, so the gulf between Keynesianism and neoliberalism ought not be overemphasized.[81]

It is also worth noting that Hayek does not use the term "totalitarian" as a synonym for "authoritarian." A totalitarian regime is the polar opposite of a liberal regime, whereas an authoritarian regime is the opposite of a democratic regime. A totalitarian regime is one that seeks to organize the whole of society toward the pursuit of a specific goal and refuses to recognize an autonomous sphere wherein the individual's pursuit of their own ends is

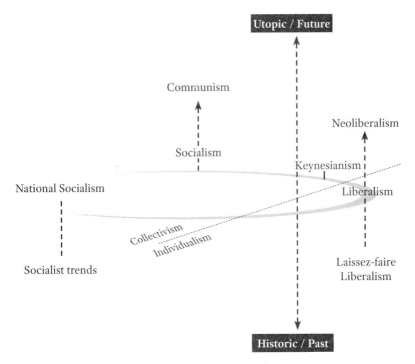

FIGURE 1.1. Hayek's curved political spectrum.

supreme. An authoritarian regime is one in which legitimate authority is concentrated in an individual or a small group and not subject to popular oversight. In Hayek's framework, particularly in his postwar writing, it is conceivable that an authoritarian regime could be "liberal" if it accepted and adhered to self-imposed limits on its power. Similarly, a democratic regime could be illiberal and totalitarian if it succumbed to Tocqueville's "tyranny of the majority" and failed to protect the rights of minorities. Liberalism and democracy are often compatible, but for Hayek these are not equivalent concepts.

Although fascism and communism have been reconstituted and reenergized through transnational networks as liberalism wanes in the twenty-first century, the most pressing challenge to liberalism is political capitalism, particularly as embodied in the political economies of China, Vietnam, and Singapore. Fascism and communism remain mired in nostalgia and, like conservativism, lack an understanding of economic forces.[82] Political capitalism as a variant of the capitalist mode of production seeks to master economic forces but is not reliant on centralized planning or militarism as essential features, although rights are attenuated and the use of physical coercion against dissidents who cannot be subdued by the law is not uncommon. (Of course, to be fair, the liberal meritocratic capitalist state, although it tends to treat private property as sacrosanct for citizens, is not immune from using physical coercion against dissidents.) What political capitalism and the strains of socialism have in common is (1) an impatience with the slow pace of liberal policy and (2) an acceptance of authoritarian political control. However, unlike socialism and national socialism, political capitalism seeks to supplement (as opposed to supplant) the spontaneous forces of a free society with a macroenvironment oriented toward advancing nationalist goals.[83] Political capitalism sits uneasily in this mapping of political space at the vertex of the axis between individualism and collectivism and the axis of historic and utopic ideologies.

Conclusion

The system of thought that Hayek introduces is substantially at odds with much of contemporary neoclassical economic thought. Hayek's ontology is characterized by chance and uncertainty; his epistemological metrics are qualitative and philosophical, and his scope is a patient appreciation for the long view. Similarly, Hayek's idealism stands in sharp contrast to the historical materialism of Marx and Engels. Hayek seeks to ground his idealism in its cultural milieu, but he offers hints that liberalism is a flexible and adaptive doctrine that can and should be tailored to the needs of contemporary society. In other words, Hayek's liberal ideas are not necessarily confined to the West. Hayek's framework is therefore useful in preparing liberalism for the challenge posed by the rise of illiberal or political capitalism, particularly in East Asia.

The Garden Analogy

In replacing the wooden disposition of laissez-faire liberals, Hayek offers the analogy of the gardener to guide the liberal's attitude toward society.[1] Like the gardener who seeks to understand the conditions that are most favorable to the growth of a plant, the liberal must carefully study the structures and functions of society's many branches. The aim is to assist, and where necessary supplement, the growth of each organism. The analogy clarifies that the attitude taken toward social amelioration must be thoughtful and patient, with only occasional interventions. Mechanical rules of thumb cannot substitute for patiently acquired knowledge and wisdom and may even lead to failure when misapplied.

The gardener analogy is also meant to counteract the impression that economic liberalism is a negative creed that stands only to prevent weedlike policies that threaten the efficient operation of the marketplace and offers to the layperson only a share in the common progress of society (which the layperson takes for granted anyway). The gardener needs not only to weed her garden but also to facilitate optimal growth.

Through the gardening analogy, the demand for socialism is thus understood as a kind of impatience with gradual rates of improvement in the standard of living.[2] Moreover, socialism seeks to frame the material distribution of wealth, as opposed to the philosophical expansion of individual freedom, as the metric of a just economic policy. Hence, it is not surprising that collectivists exhibit irritation at the "antisocial privileges" defended by liberals.

Hayek warns, however, that the effort to accelerate economic growth and achieve a more equitable distribution of wealth threatens to endanger the very system that created dramatic improvements in prosperity over the last few centuries. If the expansion of human freedom sustained economic expansion and the scientific revolution, then, logically speaking, seeking to constrain individual freedom would impair the ability of a society to accelerate growth.

Hayek premises his analogy on understanding society in terms of an organic metaphor. The deeper message is to adhere to a precautionary principle in the management of complexity. The message, while not logically opposed to radical economic solutions (e.g., "shock therapy") in societies transitioning away from authoritarianism, would imply caution even in such situations.

CHAPTER TWO

The Great Utopia

What has always made the state a hell on earth has been precisely that man has tried to make it his heaven.

Friedrich Hölderlin (1797)

The chapter's epigraph is a quote from the German Romantic poet Johann Christian Friedrich Hölderlin's (1770–1843) only novel, *Hyperion* (2 vols., 1797 and 1799). Howard Gaskill translates the passage from which Hayek's quote is taken thus:

> "Say what you will, you grant too much power to the state. It may not demand what it cannot enforce. Yet what love gives the spirit cannot be enforced. Let it leave that untouched, or we should take its precious law and nail it to the pillory! By heaven! he little knows how much he sins who would turn the state into a school of morals. It's this that's always made the state into a hell, that man has tried to make it his heaven.
>
> "The state is the coarse husk round life's kernel and nothing more. It's the wall around the garden of human fruits and flowers.
>
> "But what help is the wall around the garden when the soil lies parched? Then all that helps is rainfall from heaven.
>
> "O rainfall from heaven! O inspiration! You will bring again to us the springtime of the peoples. The state cannot command you hither. But let it not hinder you, then you will come, come you will, with your almighty joys, wreathe us in golden clouds and lift us high above mortality, and we shall marvel and wonder whether we're still who we were, we, the needy who'd ask the stars if a blossoming spring awaited us there—do you ask me when this shall come to pass? . . ."[1]

The passage demonstrates a classically liberal consciousness with a radical bent (as exhibited by the oblique reference to the "springtime of the peoples," a European antimonarchical uprising in 1848) that believes in redemptive beauty and communion with nature.

This affirmative reference to a German Romantic poet in the midst of

World War II is perhaps meant to reinforce for the reader Hayek's complex attitude toward German culture. A sweeping denigration of German culture was never the objective of Hayek's polemical text, and he takes pains to show that the true origins of socialism are French and English rather than German. At the same time, *Hyperion* was not written to praise the German people. The protagonist and namesake of Hölderlin's novel indicates that the German people are politically and spiritually fragmented, egotistical, and slavish—the very antithesis of the ancient Greeks.[2] While Hölderlin wrote for an elite German audience, his censure of the German people in the novel is severe, even if it was intended to edify and unite.

A small irony of citing Hölderlin in defense of economic liberalism is that the poet was also deeply influential in shaping the national-socialist ideology of the philosopher Martin Heidegger.[3] Hölderlin served as the centerpiece of Heidegger's aesthetics. Of course, as even the brief passage above makes evident, Heidegger distorted and evacuated the poet from his intellectual context. At the same time, Hölderlin would undoubtedly have looked askance at Hayek's plunder of his epistolary novel for a didactic epigraph.[4]

The logic of the actual passage quoted by Hayek is an inversion of Adam Smith's famous "invisible hand" metaphor, which is a central trope in *The Road to Serfdom*. Instead of narrowly circumscribed efforts of individuals to secure their return on investment producing the unintended effect of a wealthy society, Hölderlin describes an infernal state brought about by noble intentions. Hayek's aim throughout the book, and particularly this chapter, is to argue against well-intentioned, pragmatic, and incremental changes to public policy, particularly through the mechanism of centralized planning. In this chapter, the "great utopia" is a reference to the well-intentioned goals of democratic socialism.

∵

Hayek's second chapter is a critique of the history, philosophy, and rhetorical tactics of socialism and, by extension, communism. Before proceeding, a brief note of terminology may be useful.

Terminology

Communism refers to the utopian stage of socioeconomic organization that supposedly follows upon the achievement of socialism's objective of creating a classless society and paving the way for the withering away of the state. When Hayek refers to socialism, he means, ". . . unambiguously, the nationalization of the means of production and the type of centralized economic planning which this made possible and necessary."[5]

Socialism does not include the welfare state or "social democracy." A welfare state continues to rely on prices as a guide to policy-making; it is not a centrally planned socialist economy with a central planning bureau.[6] Hayek does not consider the Nordic countries, for example, with their market economies, heavy taxation, and redistributive welfare states, to be socialistically organized. Thus, "social democracy"—the effort to use reformist public policy to compensate individuals for perceived market failures—is not the target of his argument.

Hayek is deeply skeptical, however, of the sincerity of "democratic socialists"—those who would seek to use parliamentary means to achieve a mode of economic organization in which the means of production is wholly or predominantly socially owned. Although he recognizes the noble intentions of democratic socialists, including several of his colleagues at the London School of Economics, Hayek sees logical contradictions in formulating an ideologically unified economic plan through democratic means when a sizable minority disagrees with either the means or ends.[7] Using democratic means to effect a socialist revolution is as logical to Hayek as executing each step in a military campaign through democratic means. He doubts the political feasibility of the entire democratic socialist project and believes that the actual political consequences of attempting such a transformation are occluded by utopian thinking: "That democratic socialism, the great utopia of the last few generations, is not only unachievable, but that to strive for it produces something so utterly different that few of those who now wish it would be prepared to accept the consequences, many will not believe until the connection has been laid bare in all its aspects."[8] In essence, the struggle to attain democratic socialism opens the gateway to brutal socialism and totalitarianism. Of course, Hayek is not a deterministic thinker, and it is an error to read him as arguing that any regulation of the market leads inevitably to more regulation, ending finally in tyranny and totalitarianism.[9] In fact, as will be argued, Hayek was not hostile to market regulations that were applied uniformly, and he supported a form of minimum income for all citizens. What Hayek is warning is that "totalitarianism is not a historical accident that emerges solely because of a poor choice of leaders under a socialist regime. Totalitarianism, Hayek shows, is the *logical* outcome of the institutional order of socialist planning."[10]

In any case, Hayek is not the first to issue a warning. The threat of socialism to liberalism and individual freedom was recognized almost a century before Hayek was writing. He cites Tocqueville's 1848 speech on the floor of France's Constituent Assembly against "the right to work" (i.e., government-guaranteed employment at a set wage rate) and socialism.[11]

Socialism's Genealogy and Popularity

The central puzzle of the chapter is to explain why socialism has gained in popularity within liberal societies, given the early warnings of liberal thinkers. Hayek goes so far as to state that socialism has displaced liberalism among contemporary progressives.[12] This unsupported claim appears to be a matter of personal perception, although it was probably a fair assessment, given the intellectual climate of London and Cambridge, where Hayek circulated at the time. His thesis is that the triumph of socialist thought among progressives occurred only through socialism's appropriating to itself the conceptual tools of liberalism.

Hayek posits that the origins of socialism are reactionary and authoritarian. Historically, Hayek asserts that socialist ideology was a response to the liberalism of the French Revolution. Socialists sought to impose order.[13] The first socialists clearly did not value human freedom or freedom of thought, nor did they seek to mask their contempt for such values. Socialism sought "a strong dictatorial government" to "terminate the revolution," even if it meant treating those who did not obey "as cattle."[14]

Hayek argues that socialism allied itself to freedom and democracy only after the antimonarchical wave known as the Springtime of Nations or Springtime of the Peoples that swept Europe in 1848. However, democratic socialism remained suspicious of individualism and dissent. Hayek deploys Tocqueville to argue that democracy expands individual liberty, while socialism uses democracy to "seek equality in restraint and servitude."[15] Obviously, democracy as a technical instrument for selecting political leaders and holding them accountable can be used for different ends. Tocqueville's point, however, is that liberalism and socialism approach the concept of equality from orthogonal angles; liberalism seeks equality in liberty, while socialism seeks equality in outcomes.[16]

Hayek argues that socialism masks its emphasis on "equality in restraint and servitude" by creating the notion of "economic freedom" to supplant the liberal notion of "political freedom." The socialist argument is that without a certain level of income, political freedom becomes meaningless. Hence, economic freedom must be prioritized. With socialist rhetoric, "freedom" changes from the absence of arbitrary coercive power to the release from economic compulsion or necessity. The socialist conception of freedom is synonymous with power or wealth.[17] Socialism promises greater economic growth, but it seeks to redistribute wealth primarily through fiat.[18] Wealth redistribution is necessitated by the fact that socialism has no economic solution for increasing innovation or efficiency.

Socialist Promises and Reality

Hayek warns that not only are socialism's promises of greater wealth undeliverable, but are also likely to lead to servitude.[19] However, Hayek's argument does not hinge on a slippery slope. Hayek is asserting that liberalism and socialism are inherently contradictory ideologies, even though socialism claims to be the heir of the liberal tradition. Hayek's aim is to highlight the contradictions between the two philosophies so that it becomes apparent why socialism is not oriented toward political freedom.

Today, there are ample sources that demonstrate the massive human bonfire created by Communist Party dictatorships a century after the October Revolution, which birthed the Soviet Union and its protectorates, as well as a host of notorious communist dictatorships, including those of Cambodia, China, Cuba, Ethiopia, North Korea, Laos, Somalia, and Vietnam. However, Hayek was writing well before such information had been widely and systematically documented; therefore, his prescient analysis relies on anecdotes. Hayek cites, for example, the radical socialist Max Forrester Eastman's direct observation of Stalin's Great Purge. Eastman noted the similarities between the tyrannies of communism and fascism and argued that "Stalinism" was actually a form of superfascism. Moreover, Eastman asserted that Stalinism *is* socialism in the sense that it was the ". . . inevitable although unforeseen political accompaniment of the nationalization and collectivization which [Stalin] had relied upon as part of his plan for erecting a classless society."[20] It would be an error to reduce communism to Stalinism, but Eastman's observations would apply to a range of communist dictatorships (e.g., North Korea and Cambodia).

Hayek's discussion of communism is still important today. Decades after the collapse of the Soviet Union and the transition of most communist regimes to authoritarian or political capitalism, there is a propensity for contemporary radical theorists to downplay the dismal historical economic performance of the vast majority of actually existing communist states as merely a failed experiment,[21] or, derisively, as an exercise in "state monopoly capitalism" or "state capitalism."[22] Of course, to fail to recognize that tyranny was the probable outcome of socialism is to misunderstand the level of coercion needed to move from private ownership of capital and toward the semblance of a "classless" society on a large scale. To accept or even desire the "necessary violence" of the "dictatorship of the proletariat," as some contemporary radical theorists do, is obviously sadistic. Such sadistic fantasies only make Hayek's thesis of the linkage between totalitarian communism and fascism self-evident.[23]

However, given the social inequities, ecological spectacles, and political challenges that contemporary capitalism regularly generates, or at least is blamed for generating, and regardless of the ways in which these difficulties stem from a distortion of capitalism's liberal political and economic heritage, the battle of ideas with alternatives to capitalism is far from over. The banner of utopian, revolutionary, dogmatic alternatives to liberal democracy and free markets will always carry a certain seductive appeal among the intelligentsia, particularly to those who have little training in political economy or economics and thus little interest in discussing how economic structures relate to the values of a market-based society.

To conclude the chapter, Hayek returns to his conception of the curved political spectrum and argues that for the communist, as well as the fascist, the main enemy is the liberal, because the latter believes in individual freedom. The socialist, however, remains a potential recruit for both the communist and the fascist. The logic is that the socialist has already moved away from support for individual freedom. Ironically, the general population tends still to believe that socialism and (political) freedom can be combined.[24] While Hayek's reasoning is plausible, the notion of a curved political spectrum is likely to generate a measure of resistance; hence, some further thoughts might be useful.

The notion of a political spectrum understood as a plane with political positions arrayed from left/progressive to right/conservative probably dates back to the French Revolution. The notion of fascism, which arose to prominence only in the 1920s, as antithetical to socialism is even more recent. Nevertheless, the understanding of fascism as antipodal to socialism is entrenched in both the social sciences and the humanities.

Among social scientists and historians, the purportedly oppugnant relationship between fascism and socialism is often traced to the alliance among fascists, industrialists, and large landowners, as contrasted with the alliance among socialists, the intelligentsia, and the peasantry/proletariat. However, Hayek argued in 1933 that capitalists who allied with fascists were either misled about the true nature of fascism or that these capitalists were already under the sway of socialist ideas. Hayek noted that the Nazis primarily opposed the "internationalism" (i.e., the supposed Jewishness) of the socialists, not the socialists' economic policies per se.[25] He argued that fascists shared with socialists a deep hatred of all aspects of capitalism, that is, "individualistic profit seeking, large scale enterprise, banks, joint-stock companies, department stores, 'international finance and loan capital,' [and] the system of 'interest slavery' in general. . . ."[26] Moreover, socialists and fascists shared an antirational disposition, which Hayek traced to Marx's teaching on the class-conditioned (as opposed to universal) nature of thinking. Hayek argued that the fascists merely extended Marx's anti-Enlightenment notion to other social groups, for example, other nations or races.[27] Fascism is distinct from socialism: the former is a middle-class or petit-bourgeois socialism, while the latter is proletarian. Additionally, fascism permits a greater measure of de jure property rights, although these are attenuated. Similarly, fascism permits market competition but prefers the organization of guilds or syndicates to regulate the activities of artisans. Finally, state control over key industries, limits on income earning, restrictions on the international flow of people and goods, and of course a centralized dictatorship mark fascism and socialism as consanguine.[28]

To link and summarize these last two main points together, the liberal defends individual freedom and makes modest promises of economic growth; socialists of all stripes make extravagant and unrealistic promises and systematically destroy individual liberty.

A Liberal Response

MINIMUM INCOME

Hayek's advocacy for a minimum income, later in *The Road to Serfdom*,[29] is an implicit acknowledgment of the socialist complaint that without a certain level of income, participation in the marketplace becomes compulsory and therefore in contradiction to liberal principles. Thus, Hayek writes:

> There is no reason why in a society which has reached the general level of wealth which ours has attained the first kind of security should not be guaranteed to all without endangering general freedom. There are difficult questions about the precise standard which should thus be assured; there is particularly the important question whether those who thus rely on the community should indefinitely enjoy all the same liberties as the rest. An incautious handling of these questions might well cause serious and perhaps even dangerous political problems; but there can be no doubt that some minimum of food, shelter, and clothing, sufficient to preserve health and the capacity to work, can be assured to everybody. Indeed for a considerable part of the population of England this sort of security has long been achieved.[30]

A central distinction between Hayekian liberals and socialists rests on the distinction between arbitrary and universal redistributions of income. Hayek believes that socialism facilitates an arbitrary (i.e., politicized) redistribution of wealth; therefore, he (initially) supports a "universal" or uniform redistribution to eliminate overt forms of coercion in the marketplace.

It may be objected at this point that Hayek is interested in the provision of basic security and not the prevention of coercion. However, as Norman P. Barry notes with regard to Hayek's tightly circumscribed conceptualization of "coercion" in *The Constitution of Liberty*, individuals who lack basic security cannot avoid placing themselves in situations where they have forewarning of potential coercion by the state (e.g., loitering and vagrancy laws).[31] To this extent, the provision of security and the prevention of coercion are two sides of the same coin.

Hayek also endorses the provision of comprehensive social insurance against specific risks to prevent market coercion and ensure security:

> Nor is there any reason why the state should not assist the individuals in providing for those common hazards of life against which, because of their uncertainty, few individuals can make adequate provision. Where, as in the case of sickness and accident, neither the desire to avoid such calamities nor the efforts to overcome their consequences are as a rule weakened by the provision of assistance—where, in short, we deal with genuinely insurable risks—the case for the state's helping to organize a comprehensive system of social insurance is very strong.[32]

Juan Ramón Rallo argues, correctly, that Hayek never explicitly goes so far as to endorse an unconditional, universally applicable, and perpetual policy such as a universal basic income (UBI). However, Rallo is mistaken in his claim that Hayek's desire to provide a minimum income is linked to the provision of comprehensive social insurance organized by the state. In fact, these are two separate policy ideas endorsed by Hayek in *The Road to Serfdom*. The use of the word "nor" in the paragraph after discussing a minimum income and before Hayek introduces the topic of social insurance indicates these are separate proposals. Nevertheless, Rallo is correct that later in *The Road to Serfdom* Hayek suggests that some form of means testing (e.g., voluntary military service) might be preferable to universal access to a minimum income.[33] By the time Hayek wrote *The Constitution of Liberty*, he explicitly endorsed a means test for access to a minimum income.[34] Finally, in *Hayek on Hayek*, he did argue that unemployment insurance schemes were very similar to his vision of minimum income.[35]

While a means test or conditional work requirement (e.g., military service) is morally reasonable when an individual is requesting assistance from society, and still distinct from the arbitrary criteria of social-justice advocates, Hayek weakened his argument by stepping away from a universal approach, since the state is thus empowered to adjudicate legitimate need and the problem of dispersed and incomplete knowledge reappears (even if means testing based on income does not pose a severe challenge in gathering information for a capable state).

A minimum income also distinguishes Hayek's liberal approach from socialist redistribution. Hayek argues that socialists make "irresponsible" and undeliverable promises of a great increase in material wealth, but the heart of their ideology is merely an egalitarian redistributive impulse, not a strategy to overcome problems of scarcity in nature. Hence, while liberalism offers a minimum income, socialism promises a robust income. Hayek sees in socialism a demand to redistribute wealth primarily in order to eliminate "the great existing disparities in the range of choice of different people."[36] Hayek's insight is that disparities in income generate disparities in available choices. The equal redistribution of income would therefore require a restriction on the range of choices available to those who currently earn above the mean and thus a restriction on the range of choices overall. Of course, funding a minimum income would most likely entail an increase in taxes on higher incomes unless all elements of the inefficient tax and transfer system were disassembled to render the policy fiscally neutral.[37]

By supporting a minimum income, Hayek hopes to neutralize the socialist demand for economic freedom in order to reemphasize the contours of political freedom or liberty in the liberal sense. However, as noted, Hayek is aware of the confusion that has resulted from socialism's appropriation of the liberal concept of "freedom." Moreover, grandiose promises of increased wealth have succeeded in luring progressives away from liberalism's more modest position.

THATCHER'S "PEOPLE'S CAPITALISM"

In the face of the extravagant promises of socialism and the actual economic performance of political capitalism, liberal meritocratic capitalism will need to go beyond the provision of minimum income if it is to retain adherents. One policy proposal is to mitigate growing income inequality by creating a greater balance in the sources of income for workers. This concept, known as "People's Capitalism," was first put forth by the British prime minister Margaret Thatcher in 1977 to encourage employee stock ownership plans (ESOPs) of formerly state-owned companies.[38] Milanovic concurs that providing greater access for workers to own capital would help to reduce "capital concentration," along with reforms in tax policy to incentivize greater equity ownership by small to medium shareholders and taxation on intergenerational income.[39] Because the wealthy draw a disproportionate (relative to the poor) amount of their income from ownership of capital and the economic system provides greater benefits for income derived from capital ownership, equalizing endowments across the population would generate greater equality without large redistributions of income.[40] This is particularly true because twentieth-century mechanisms for taming inequality (i.e., trade unionism, mass education, high taxes, and government transfers) are of limited utility in the current phase of globalization, which is characterized by high levels of capital and labor mobility and a maximization of the marginal returns on mass education in high-income countries.[41] Taiwan provides a real-world example of a state that has significantly reduced income inequality by creating a balance between labor and capital income without engaging in massive redistribution or building a large welfare state.[42]

Political Capitalism and Economic Freedom

In the twenty-first century, political-capitalist states, which have adopted the conceptual tools of socialism, often argue (either directly or indirectly) that they must prioritize economic freedom before political freedom. In orthodox socialism, this preference ordering is commonly known as the "hierarchy of rights" doctrine, in which economic, social, and cultural rights are perpetually antecedent to human, civil, and political rights.[43] Thus, China, which is a signatory to the Universal Declaration of Human Rights and various other international human-rights treaties, used to argue that the right to development should take precedence over civil and political rights.[44] Political rights without the ability to achieve basic economic self-sufficiency were deemed irrelevant. (Of course, regardless of the state's public rhetoric, the governance principle of party leadership, as expressed in the 1982 constitution, permanently subordinated individual rights to the authority of the party/state.[45]) In actuality, growth-oriented economic policies were fundamental to maintaining political repression and enabling the perpetual deferral of human rights.[46] In fact, Chinese intellectuals under the shadow of Xi Jinping are increasingly unrestrained in rationalizing political repression as fundamental to economic prosperity. Qin Hui, at Tsinghua

University, for example, argues that China is globally competitive because of its "low-human-rights advantage."[47] In a similar vein, Wang Yiwei, at Renmin University, argues that strengthening its dictatorship maximizes China's comparative advantage relative to the electorally volatile Western democracies.[48] In other words, the argument is shifting from prioritizing economic development before political freedom to arguing that political repression confers a comparative advantage that promotes economic development. While other scholars, such as Han Dayuan at Renmin University and Yu Chongsheng and Liu Yuanliang at Wuhan University, critiqued the increasing concentration of power in the hands of the president (before the Nineteenth Party Congress in 2017, which removed the two-term limit), their arguments concerned the danger of recreating a cult of personality and the advantages of institutionalized collective governance rather than championing human rights and political freedom.[49] In any case, since 2017 critics of increasing authoritarianism in mainland China have either gone silent or declared their full-throated support for Xi.[50]

The Vietnamese case with regard to the relationship between economic and political freedom was briefly complicated by the fact that Ho Chi Minh cited the American Declaration of Independence (1776) and the Declaration of the Rights of Man and Citizen (1789) in his 1945 Declaration of Independence for Vietnam. The references to the Western natural-law tradition, which essentially makes human rights sacrosanct, contradicted a historical-materialist Marxist view of the legal regime as merely a part of the "super-structure" and thus ultimately the product of economic relations as dominated by the owners of the means of production.[51] Of course, the concept of natural rights was eventually sidelined (along with the right to private property) in favor of "citizens' rights" as a product of positive law. With economic liberalization in 1986, partial protection of private property,[52] freedom to trade, and freedom of movement were formally reintroduced in the 1992 constitution. However, the state continued to conflate human rights with the rights of citizens, to view rights as a product of positive law (as opposed to natural law), and to fail to provide an obligation to protect or at least prevent the derogation of human rights.[53] In essence, even after liberalization, the state viewed political rights through the lens of socialism and therefore positive law. Political rights remained subordinate to the state's economic development policies. Thus, the changes to the constitutional order seemed primarily motivated by a desire to help the state reintegrate with the international community and meet the explicit terms of international donor agencies (e.g., the United Nations Development Programme).[54] After listening to comments from citizens and legal experts, the Communist Party of Vietnam (CPV) attempted, with significant reservations, to fix the contradictions with a new constitution in 2013. While this new constitution did address the conflation of human and citizen rights, the state remained "cautious over expanding the scope of political and civil rights," particularly those rights that could threaten the CPV's monopoly on power.[55] In any case, the written constitution remains quite distinct from political practice in Vietnam.

The "constitutional authoritarian" or "soft-authoritarian" character of Singapore also deviates slightly from the bifurcation and subordination of political to economic freedom. Singaporean elites have consistently argued that individual political freedoms must be restricted, not to promote economic development per se, but to prevent individuals from becoming "divided, alienated and apathetic." To paraphrase Lee Kuan Yew, Singapore's first prime minister, a "well ordered society" is necessary to preserve the state.[56] Of course, the ruling People's Action Party (PAP) realizes that economic growth flows from social stability, and that continual economic growth confers legitimacy on the ruling party and the state.[57] The Singaporean state also directly protects the legitimacy of the ruling party and state by eliminating (potential) opposition groups suspected of espousing radical ideologies. After one "anticommunist" action, Operation Coldstore in 1963, in which more than a hundred left-wing activists were detained, including members of a leftist offshoot of the PAP, the Barisan Socialis (Socialist Front), a major emerging opposition party was effectively crippled.[58] Similarly, in 1987 Operation Spectrum led to the detention of twenty-two individuals under the Internal Security Act on the allegation of a "Marxist conspiracy" to overthrow the state. Kenneth Paul Tan argues that the group was "deemed a threat to Singapore's security and the maintenance of public order."[59] Opposition politicians from registered parties still face an intimidating gauntlet of regulations and libel laws that have resulted in the jailing or bankruptcy of dissidents. Furthermore, the PAP's use of gerrymandering and the withholding of funds from opposition wards disincentivizes protest voting. The weakness of opposition parties in Singapore also happens to strengthen the PAP's argument that were opposition parties to come to power, it would damage the economy.[60] In essence, Singapore justifies its ongoing limits on political freedom by arguing that economic freedom and prosperity would be endangered by political liberalization. Moreover, very high levels of income inequality, a significant disparity between the income of "foreign talent" and local Singaporeans, a forced savings system that limits private consumption, and the high cost of living have created the phenomenon of "poor people in a rich country," further adding to political quiescence and economic vulnerability on the island.[61]

Conclusion

Thus, the challenge of political capitalism, particularly in China, Vietnam, and Singapore, is that these regimes have delivered and sustained rapid economic growth without substantively expanding political freedom for their citizens. Liberalism is unable to compete with the levels of sustained, long-term economic growth one finds in political-capitalist regimes. Even if one is skeptical of the reliability of data from China or critical of the aggregated data (i.e., GDP vs. GNP [gross national product]) from Singapore,[62] it is undeniable that these countries have dramatically changed their economies in the last several decades. The remaining attraction of liberalism, then, is mainly that it protects individual freedom (metaphysically and psychologically as well as qualitatively and politically) while generating modest economic growth over time. Hayek would likely acknowledge the difficulty of the challenge posed by political capitalism and point toward a minimum income as a mechanism to relieve the anxiety of those desperate for a modicum of economic security.

CHAPTER THREE

Individualism and Collectivism

The socialists believe in two things which are absolutely different and perhaps even contradictory: freedom and organization.

Élie Halévy (1938)

The epigraph, from the French philosopher and liberal republican *dreyfusard* Élie Halévy (1870–1937), pits individual freedom against collective organization as discrete and potentially antithetical concepts.[1] Ironically, the young Halévy, who was sympathetic to socialism, had argued in 1906 that there was no real "antithesis between liberty and socialism."[2] While Halévy was never a socialist, he did not embrace economic liberalism. He associated economic liberalism, particularly in the work of Adam Smith, Frédéric Bastiat, and Carl Menger, with a form of "providentialism" (i.e., a belief that events are the products of divine intervention), which he deemed no better than the position of anti-*dreyfusard* Catholics fighting against a separation of church and state in France.[3]

Economic liberalism's providentialism is exhibited by the faith that the proper understanding of interests and limitations on intervention by man-made institutions would naturally create human happiness and prosperity. In contrast to this providentialism, Halévy argued, through a study of Bentham's utilitarian philosophy and political economy, that there were two modes of identifying interests: natural (independent of human institutions) and artificial (the product of deliberate design). Where natural interests were not spontaneously harmonious, the lawmaker would need to either impose pain to balance the pleasure of certain actions or use institutions to artificially identify collective interests. Halévy argued that the classical economists Adam Smith and David Ricardo understood that inequality was necessary under conditions of natural-resource scarcity and differential rent from land. Interests could not be spontaneously harmonized in this context. Thus, the Classical school relied on the state to support the interests of the rich against the poor in the interest of society as whole. Bentham's utilitarians sought to use state intervention to educate the masses to accept the "rules" of political economy. The authoritarian character of the Utilitarian school came be moderated as its proponents discovered ways to use state institutions to approximate the natural identi-fication of interests through marketlike mechanisms (e.g., democratic vot-ing procedures).[4] Hayek would later reject Halévy's dichotomous theory of interest identification and argue that harmonious interest can develop through spontaneously arising institutions that endure through a process of social selection as those institutions confer prosperity on a society.[5]

Despite the differences between their liberalisms, there was a common ground. Halévy was the main source for Hayek's genealogy of socialism, which traced its origins to Saint-Simon and his followers (e.g., Comte, Thomas Hodgskin, and Louis Blanc, among others), as described in the previous chapter.[6] Halévy's work helped Hayek to hone his critique of so-cialism to its reliance on the cult of organization. H. Stuart Jones argues that it was the influence of Halévy, along with Hayek's encounter with Walther Rathenau's ideas on economic planning during World War I—rather than the British alliance with the USSR at the time he was writing—that led Hayek to de-emphasize Marxism and Soviet socialism in *The Road to Serf-dom.*[7] It is in regard to Saint-Simon's emphasis on the reorganization of soci-ety for a common purpose that Halévy and Hayek find their mutual enemy.

Halévy, as a Platonist philosopher, identifies in early Franco-English so-cialism a dialectical tension between the desire to liberate workers from the slavery of industrial capitalism and the need to strengthen the state to pro-tect the weak segments of society. While the former goal appears poised to fulfill the promise of political liberalism and individualism, the latter must subordinate the individual to the state, since a natural harmonization of interests is not feasible. Halévy traces the demise of the emancipatory or "democratic" branch of socialism (including Marxism) and the rise of its "aristocratic" branch (characterized by Hegel), which triumphed with the coming of wartime planning in 1914. To this extent, Halévy foreshadows Hayek's broader argument in this chapter of *The Road to Serfdom.*[8]

Are Halévy's insights still relevant? In the twentieth century, if Halévy were correct, the principal internal contradiction in socialism was that socialists sought to achieve liberation of the individual (i.e., freedom) through organization (i.e., centralized planning). For both Halévy and Hayek, the means violate the ends. In the twenty-first century, the central internal contradiction of political capitalism is the desire to strengthen the postcolonial state (i.e., to encourage national development) by combining economic decentralization (the market) with the political subordination of the individual. The emancipatory project of socialism has been abandoned or deferred indefinitely, but the means of harmonizing interests remain internally contradictory.

∴

Collectivism: Planning without Freedom

In the third chapter, Hayek implicitly builds on Halévy's insights by broadening and delineating the contours of collectivism relative to liberalism. He begins by elaborating the confusing polyvalence inherent in the term "socialism." The ideology is simultaneously synonymous with a set of ideals or ends (i.e., social justice, starting-point equity, endpoint equality, and economic security) and a set of methods for achieving those ideals (i.e., the abolition of both private enterprise and the private ownership of the means of production, and the imposition of bureaucratic centralized planning).[9] While social democrats and democratic socialists may reject the deployment of coercive means, there is little dispute that their shared goals or ideals are similar to those of revolutionary socialists.

Hayek explores the additional complication that a method associated with achieving socialism, namely centralized planning, may also serve other ideologies (e.g., fascism). After all, whether one believes in an egalitarian redistribution of income or a hierarchical/racial redistribution of income, the ends require centralized planning as the means. Thus, Hayek proposes that socialism is a species of collectivism. He posits that national socialism, socialism, and democratic socialism are separate species of this genus. The label "collectivism" may seem facile and partisan when one considers only the ends of each ideology. However, much like Weber in his definition of the modern state,[10] Hayek emphasizes the commonality of means rather than the open-ended pursuit of ends. The means establishes the lowest common denominator between political ideologies. Thus, what unites various forms of collectivism is the common means for achieving their stated ends, that is, centralized planning (see fig. 2.1).

The objective of collectivist planning is any given distributive ideal. The ideal may be egalitarian, but it might equally be hierarchical, patriarchal, racial, or any number of other systems. Hayek readily concedes that even the creation of a market economy may require rational planning (e.g., the establishment of laws, a judiciary, and an enforcement mechanism). However, collectivist planners would not view the establishment of a market as a form of planning. Collectivist planning seeks ". . . the central direction

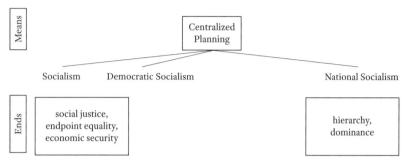

FIGURE 2.1. "Collectivism."

of economic activity according to a single plan, laying down how the resources of society should be 'consciously directed' to serve particular ends
in a definite way."[11]

Hayek's critique of centralized planning and the selection of a particular ideologically determined end goal requires further unpacking. Hayek
rejects the entire conception of redistributive justice on the basis of insufficient knowledge acquisition capability in humans.[12] His logic is that
centralized planners, despite pretensions to pastoral care, do not have the
ability to ascertain efficiently the individual needs of any large polity, particularly as those needs change dynamically from moment to moment. At
the core of Hayek's theory is a belief in the limits of human knowledge.
Only a market economy, buttressed by the rule of law, has the ability to
ascertain constantly changing individual needs. Moreover, and unlike the
situation with the free market, the effort of centralized state planners to
provide an ideologically determined end goal has the result of suppressing
freedom of at least some (if not the majority of) individuals.[13]

FASCISM AND PLANNING

At this point, those who view fascism as a "bourgeois reaction" to
socialism—owing in large part to a misreading of Antonio Gramsci's *Prison
Notebooks*[14]—will object that centralized planning was not a feature of fascism. Simply put, this is factually incorrect. As Traute Rafalski wrote in her
study of Italian fascism:

> "Planning" was the universal cry. It was extolled in concepts and
> speeches, some of whose authors had come from the ranks of the nation-
> alist movement and futurism, and now, within the fascist regime, saw
> some potential room for political action as strategists in crisis resolution.
> "Planability," especially long-term, was also the call of those Italian eco-

nomic interests most up to international standards, again with Agnelli/ Fiat setting the pace. By 1926 Agnelli had already formulated what he meant by planability. The calculability of intrafirm relations, absolutely indispensable from the standpoint of management, which had indeed been restored with the defeat and assimilation of the working class (from 1922 onwards, with the installation of the fascist regime) was not enough. Rather, it had to be extended beyond the factory to the whole of society, for only an organization of the society as a whole in accordance with the (new) demands of production could ensure long-term planability of production, especially in years of drastic changes in the world economy.[15]

In Nazi Germany, multiyear planning was characterized most prominently by a specialized economic bureaucracy, under Hermann Göring, that oversaw price controls and economic coercion in a manner similar to that seen in the Soviet Union. As Peter Temin emphasizes, ". . . the Nazi economy shared many characteristics with the dominant socialist economy of the time. The National Socialists were socialist in practice as well as in name."[16] The Nazi state generally preferred to purchase industrial goods from private firms at fixed prices. Private property was therefore nominally maintained for non-Jewish, urban citizens,[17] but its use was considered conditional. Failure to meet the terms of contract would lead to state appropriation of the firm (albeit with compensation); the pursuit of private gain outside of the Four-Year Plan could be met with terrorism, the concentration camp, or execution.[18] The state did manage one SOE, Hermann Göring Works, which employed over half a million people. The main purpose of the Hermann Göring Works was to increase competitive pressure on private firms and further Germany's autarchic goals.[19] The state firmly controlled capital and financial markets, with government financing dominating investment.[20]

AESTHETIC POLITICS AND POLITICAL AESTHETICS

Even those who will concede that fascism championed centralized planning often resist linking fascism and socialism. Obviously, as discussed earlier, the conceptualization of political ideology on a spectrum from left to right creates the illusion that fascism and communism are polar opposites, but there are other reinforcing conceptualizations. Among humanists, for example, Walter Benjamin's 1935 essay, "The Work of Art in the Age of Mechanical Reproduction," framed fascism once and for all as the aestheticization of politics, and communism as the politicization of aesthetics or art. Examples of aesthetic politics often cited include the Nazi

Party's emphasis on iconic imagery (e.g., the swastika), the ritualized use of art, monumental architecture, and the public spectacle—not to mention racial purity theories and praxis. Such a formulation cast communism as antithetical to fascism, with dramatic effects on the ways in which the political spectrum is understood and taught. Recent scholarship, however, has challenged this simplistic, binary interpretation of Benjamin's writing (although not the broader notion that communism is fundamentally antithetical to fascism). As Jon Simons argues, Benjamin only opposed the aestheticization of politics *by fascism*. Benjamin did not imply that other ideologies (including communism) do not partake in an aestheticization of politics or that the aestheticization of politics is inherently fascist.[21] Moreover, it is apparent that fascism also relies on the politicization of art, so that a simplistic reading is untenable. The aestheticization of politics to which Benjamin referred was a response to the technological reproduction of art and a broader crisis of modernity in the twentieth century. Benjamin would certainly agree that communism held greater potential for combining technology and art to create a new aura, or at least collective engagement. However, as Simons argues, both fascism and communism rely on the masses. The latter views the masses as a collective with the will for self-reproduction, while the former regards the masses as "an impenetrable, compact entity" to be summoned in rallies, sporting events, and war.[22] Nevertheless, the inherent prejudice against tracing the commonalities between fascists and communists is unwarranted. In other words, while there are differences between fascism and communism, it is naive to claim that these ideologies are polar opposites.

Liberalism: Competition and Freedom

By way of contrast to collectivism and centralized planning, liberalism utilizes decentralization and planning at the individual/firm level, which is coordinated through the market operating under a system of limited government, a generalized and abstract rule of law, and an enforceable protection of private-property rights. However, Hayek emphasizes that he is not advocating merely a return to laissez-faire. The forces of competition among individuals and firms need to be harnessed and organized by the state within a strong legal framework. The legal framework itself may need modification in order to facilitate competition. Of course, Hayek is not dogmatic; where competition is not likely to be effective or beneficial, competition need not be promoted by the state.[23]

The advantage of competition (i.e., individualized or firm-level planning) over centralized planning is that the former permits social coordination and mutual adjustment without submission to the authority of the planner or bureaucrat. Allegiance to abstract and uniform rules of competition set by the government preserves individual liberty while facilitating an epistemological process that reveals optimal outcomes in dynamic contexts. Competition permits social coordination and adjustment with a minimum of coercion.[24] Conversely, the regimentation of economic life that accompanies centralized planning places states in a position that is oppressive and tyrannical.[25]

The presence of competition should not be interpreted to indicate the absence of regulation. As discussed below, Hayek indicates that the state has a positive role in regulating methods of production, including in such areas as protecting the environment.

REGULATION AND THE ENVIRONMENT

Since environmentalists and anticapitalists regularly malign capitalism for its environmental impact and seek to portray environmental harm as endemic to capitalism, it is worth emphasizing Hayek's conception of government regulation and competition in a liberal society. He states clearly:

> Though all such controls on the methods of production impose extra costs (i.e., make it necessary to use more resources to produce a given output), they may be well worth while. To prohibit the use of certain poisonous substances or to require special precautions in their use, to limit working hours or to require certain sanitary arrangements, is fully compatible with the preservation of competition. The only question here is whether in the particular instance the advantages gained are greater than the social costs which they impose. Nor is the preservation of competition incompatible with an extensive system of social services—so long as the organization of these services is not designed in such a way as to make competition ineffective over wide fields.[26]

In other words, environmental (or health and safety) regulations applied equally to all manufacturers are consistent with the promotion of competition, unless they are actually designed to render competition ineffective. When anticapitalists and environmentalists argue that liberalism and capitalism are inherently harmful to the environment and society, the actual target of their ire should be redirected from liberalism as an ideology to collusive corporations and captured politicians.

Moreover, Hayek argues that the legal code of a competitive market system needs to be robust and dynamic, not minimalist and static. It is a gross caricature to argue that liberalism seeks to "roll back" the state. Hayek would certainly agree that in particular instances, what is needed is certainly not fewer laws and regulations but more laws and updated regulations in order to facilitate competition.[27]

In those cases where the private benefits cannot be captured (and hence goods are not supplied adequately in the marketplace) or social harms contained by organized competition, Hayek sees a need to substitute competition with direct regulation by authority.[28] Hayek quotes Adam Smith again to emphasize that where competition is ineffective or the costs are too great to be supplied by individuals or a small group, there is a "wide and unquestioned field for state activity." Furthermore, Hayek adds, "In no system that could be rationally defined would the state just do nothing."[29]

Political Capitalism: Competition without Freedom

In the twenty-first century, the challenge to Hayek's framework is that political capitalism may seek to foster or permit competition among domestic firms to shape production and resource allocation, but the use of competition in an illiberal context does not imply the need to protect individual liberty. In other words, market competition may just be encouraged by political-capitalist states to force quality improvements and technology upgrading while individuals, including owners of firms, continue to be subject to arbitrary repression.

SOEs AND SWFs

It will be objected that political-capitalist states such as China are often characterized by SOEs, so market competition is chimerical and therefore not part of a discovery process. However, the Chinese state's share of industrial output has consistently declined from above 50 percent at the turn of the century to just above 20 percent today. In any case, the proportion of rural and urban dwellers employed by state- and collectively owned enterprises amounts to no more than 9 percent.[30] This is not to deny that China uses its antimonopoly law to discriminate against multinational corporations (MNCs) and favor SOEs in its domestic market. However, nationalist discrimination aside, the Chinese state has clearly adopted a policy of reducing the number of SOEs and confining them to strategic industries (e.g., oil and gas exploration, banking, transportation, telecommunications, and electricity supply);[31] the remaining sectors of the economy are open to competition. Of course, it is true that while contemporary China permits a much greater degree of competition than before, it has not abandoned its commitment to SOEs in principle. As part of an industrial policy to create "national champions," the Chinese state has encouraged a few SOEs to expand abroad. By concentrating its resources, China hopes to create a few SOEs that are ". . . large and powerful enough to compete with the most competitive MNCs in the world."[32] In 2020 three SOEs (Sinopec, State Grid, and China National Petroleum) were ranked in the top ten of *Fortune*'s Global 500, based on annual revenue.[33]

Needless to say, despite increased domestic competition between firms, China has become markedly more authoritarian since around 2010, with acute repression in certain areas (e.g., Xinjiang, Tibet, and Hong Kong), and nationwide "campaign-style law enforcement," such as the "Sweep Away Black and Eliminate Evil" campaign of 2018–20. In fact, the "Sweep Away Black and Eliminate Evil" campaign, although mainly intended to curb racketeering and usury networks, also targets monopolies in ". . . construction, transport, mining, manufacturing, warehousing and logistics, production and operation sites and other industries and fields, including the supply of sand and other building materials . . ." as a threat to economic competitiveness.[34] The campaign permits local officials to seize the property and assets of criminals to fund local government initiatives. Unsurprisingly, the campaign has been associated with extrajudicial police actions and forced confessions to help officers meet their quotas. The campaign also encompasses Internet surveillance against those who spread rumors or increase dissent. Li Wenliang, the Wuhan doctor who first warned his friends about a suspected new SARS virus in 2019, was arrested under this campaign and forced to sign a confession for spreading rumors.[35] Thus, the desire for more competitive, efficient markets may be seen as fueling more intensive authoritarianism.

The situation is similar in Vietnam, where the share of employees in all forms of SOEs dropped from over 60 percent in 2000 to less than 20 percent by 2012. The share of SOEs in the economy also dropped from over 14 percent to less than 2 percent by 2012.[36] The state has encouraged competition between public and private enterprises and has restructured SOEs such that in terms of incentives they are more like private firms. Specifically, even prior to liberalization the state permitted nonplanned production, a share in realized profits, a dual-price policy, and market trading for inputs. After liberalization, the state permitted SOEs to retain all after-tax profits, began to cut state subsidies, and began to allow autonomy in production decisions, flexibility in labor management and wages, and even partnerships with foreign firms.[37] All of these economic reforms failed to translate into greater protections for individual liberty. If anything, repression has mutated and intensified with new tactics:

> These tactics are: targeting lawyers who represent political prisoners; using criminal charges to deflect criticism that those sentenced are political prisoners; tolerating physical attacks by non-uniform[ed] police and thugs against dissidents; recruiting an army of Internet polemicists to monitor and detect online anti-government activists, bloggers and Facebook users; and adopting coercive powers on websites that are trying to make the critical jump from individual blogs to multi-authored and edited news portals, a critical transition for the development of an independent media. More recently, the regime has used a tactic that can be termed as "political deportation"; that is, to "expel" and let its citizen-dissidents live in exile overseas.[38]

Singapore's SOEs are professionally managed and must be profitable to remain in business. These firms are organized under a single holding company, Temasek Holdings, which is one of the state's two sovereign wealth funds (SWFs). SWFs invest in local enterprises in the hope of globalizing their products. Singaporean SOEs are found in foreign capital investment partnerships, the defense industry, and spin-offs from natural monopolies and utilities. The SOEs and SWFs employ a considerable portion of the population, who constitute what Chua Beng Huat terms the "state capitalist sector."[39] Since the 1980s the state has increasingly shifted away from an interventionist role and toward a partnership with the business sector. The state has announced policies of extensive privatization, deregulation, and liberalization. However, the state continues to play a key role in the provision of public services and steering markets.[40] While the state encourages competition, entrepreneurship, and innovation among firms, it concentrates on improving the quality of public services. The state is still committed to the prestige of its hyperefficient and meritocratic bureaucracy, but it views itself as a catalyst encouraging private businesses to deliver services.[41] Despite the state's lighter touch with respect to business, repression has increased. Mark Thompson writes,

> . . . Singapore's state-centric governance and an increasingly out-of-touch PAP leadership has struggled to handle issues of immigration and rising income/inequalities. [Along with] growing repression after the 2015 election. This is a reminder that at the end of the day PAP power rests on coercion, however strong its governance performance (once) was, suggesting liberalism has not so much been disavowed as disallowed.[42]

The main point is that while illiberal states no longer rely as heavily as before on centralized planning through SOEs or interventionist policies aimed at private firms, competition under political capitalism does not require extending substantive protections to individual liberties and may even function under systemic coercion. Unsurprisingly, Vietnam and China rank 121st and 129th overall out of 162 countries in the 2020 Human Freedom Index. Singapore, buoyed by its 2nd place rank in "economic freedom," did better, with a 28th place rank overall.[43] In terms of "personal freedom," however, the Human Freedom Index put Singapore 53rd, Vietnam 110th, and China 125th.[44]

QUESTIONING INDUSTRIAL POLICY

The continuing role for the developmental state, despite shifts in emphasis, in shaping industrial policy and "picking winners" or concentrating on the quality of public services should not be taken as an indication that the state's guiding hand explains economic growth accelerations. Even within China there is debate about whether industrial policy actually works to promote innovation and development. As Li Daokui, a professor of economics at Tsinghua University, observes, the best companies in China rarely start with state backing.[45] Professor Zhang Weiying, a self-proclaimed Hayekian at Peking University, notes that in the 1990s the Chinese government invested heavily in building a television industry, only to have cathode ray tubes become outdated.[46] It may be that China will succeed economically, in large part, in spite of industrial policy and massive investment in fixed capital by the state.[47]

In Singapore, the state's desire to create formidable "national champions" also led to increased mergers and acquisitions with government-linked corporations and changes in government tax and incentive measures in a bid to shift from a regional to a global strategy in the wake of the Asian financial crisis in 1997–98.[48] However, a study of the regionalization scheme using a sample of forty-one firms found that the incentives offered were little used, and therefore state intervention had little impact, particularly in projects where private firms partnered with the government.[49] The state had greater success (at least from the perspective of local firms) in areas where it merely acted to provide information and to assist local businesses to make contacts in foreign markets.[50]

Indeed, academic proponents of the "developmental state," whose detailed research once illuminated the industrial policies of Japan, Korea, and Taiwan, have come to downplay a mechanical vision of industrial policy and state piloted development. Stephan Haggard writes: "The phrase 'picking winners' has become a particularly unhelpful trope for understanding how industrial policy worked in East Asia. The idea that East Asia was blessed by an omniscient, far-seeing, and welfare-enhancing state has given rise to the injunction that such states are rare and that prudence justifies an abstemious approach to government intervention."[51] Haggard prefers to think of industrial policy as a process, one that ". . . did not involve insulated bureaucrats 'picking winners,' but rather political institutions that facilitated coordination among states and private actors engaged in an iterative process of learning."[52]

Thus, it is not clear that political capitalism's use of bureaucratic guidance and state-structured competition was the actual catalyst for a sustained acceleration in growth. There may be other factors that better explain why an economy is increasing its productive output. All of this implies that the trade-off between economic growth and individual freedom may be overstated. The Japanese developmental state, although it emerged during a period of one-party rule, most likely belies the notion that individual rights must be sacrificed for rapid economic growth. Haggard also notes that despite the caricature of developmental states as authoritarian, ". . . developmental states also rested on complementary investments in human capital that proved a critical input to the growth process."[53]

In any case, to the extent that East Asian developmental states enhanced export capability by organizing competitions for export licenses, these practices could be considered liberal in Hayek's framework.[54]

CORPORATIST STATES

An alternate explanation for East Asia's growth acceleration frames the leading states as "corporatist."[55] A corporatist state is one in which a limited number of interest groups (or "syndicates") is organized or recognized by the state to facilitate economic planning and social stability. To the extent that East Asian developmental states are also corporatist states, competition is suppressed and planning is "left in the hands of the independent monopolies of the separate industries."[56] With regard to corporatist or syndicalist arrangements, Hayek writes:

> By destroying competition in industry after industry, this policy puts the consumer at the mercy of the joint monopolist action of capitalists and workers in the best organized industries. . . . Such independent planning by industrial monopolies would, in fact, produce effects opposite to those at which the argument for planning aims. Once this stage is reached, the only alternative to a return to competition is the control of

the monopolies by the state—a control which if it is to be made effective, must become progressively more complete and detailed."[57]

Hayek prophesied that "grave defects" of the corporatist approach would become increasingly obvious over time. Nevertheless, while causality is difficult to demonstrate, it is clear that several East Asian developmental states had corporatist structures and that corporatism did not dampen export-led growth strategies or lead to the immiseration of domestic consumers—in large part because wages increased as developmental states increased productivity and moved toward more sophisticated manufacturing in their GVCs. In other words, this line of argument was a misstep for Hayek, who had previously placed the weight of his argument in *The Road to Serfdom* on the moral and sociocultural impact of suppressed competition rather than its economic impact. (Hayek will return to the relationship between corporatism and political capitalism in chapter 12.)

Conclusion

As Halévy first noted, socialism's preference for centralized planning (or "organization," to use his word) as a means for artificially harmonizing interests and strengthening a progressive state comes directly at the expense of emancipating the individual from economic exploitation and drudgery. Hayek builds upon and expands Halévy's observation by arguing that "collectivism," a category that encompasses both socialism and fascism, uses a common means (i.e., centralized planning) to pursue divergent ends. By way of contrast, liberalism generally seeks to harmonize interests through decentralization and market competition without subordinating the individual. Of course, Hayek reminds us that liberalism is flexible, pragmatic, and dynamic. Thus, it is not surprising that state intervention is necessary to establish, regulate, and harness competitive forces; the free market must be planned and regulated.

Political capitalism inherits the collectivist project of strengthening the (postcolonial) state but discards the reliance on centralized planning (for the most part) as well as the dream of emancipating the individual. Despite the lingering presence of SOEs, political capitalism is increasingly characterized by market competition—even if that competition is organized, manipulated, and managed by the state. Nevertheless, the myth of an omniscient, elite bureaucracy that "picks winners" and guides "national champions" through carefully crafted industrial policy has been shelved, even by the developmental state theorists who first proposed it as an explanation for the original East Asian economic miracle. In any case, state-organized market competition is not an inherently illiberal practice.

Hayek would take issue, however, with corporatist institutions and strategies as supplementary explanations for economic growth among developmental states. Corporatist strategies enforce labor discipline and manage wage increases in order to facilitate sustainable growth in the face of international competition. Hayek disputes the long-term economic potential of corporatism due to rent extraction from consumers by monopolistic firms and unions inherent in the model. From a contemporary perspective, Hayek's prophecy about corporatism is not compelling. While workers in fascist Italy were immiserated by corporatist arrangements (as discussed in the next chapter), workers/consumers in export-oriented East Asian states with corporatist institutions have witnessed dramatic improvements in their standard of living.

Hayek's argument would have been stronger if he had returned to the philosophical critique of Halévy with which he begins the chapter. Hayek should have argued that the artificial harmonization of contending interests through state repression and manipulation via corporatist institutions ultimately comes at the cost of individual liberation, which may impact happiness, societal trust, innovation, and regime legitimacy.

CHAPTER FOUR

The "Inevitability" of Planning

> We were the first to assert that the more complicated the forms assumed by civilization, the more restricted the freedom of the individual must become.
>
> Benito Mussolini (1929)

This epigraph, although poorly understood, briefly took on a life of its own in American politics. In February 2019, Texas Senator John Cornyn enigmatically repeated this quotation on the social media platform Twitter. Quoting an Italian fascist without any context earned the senator a few sharp rebukes, including one from the democratic socialist Representative Alexandria Ocasio-Cortez (D-NY, 14th district), who disputed the notion that a "living wage" was tantamount to "socialism."[1] Nonetheless, Cornyn insisted that democratic socialists need to be reminded that their ideology is incompatible with freedom. In other words, Cornyn sought to frame fascism as the natural outgrowth of Mussolini's youth as a socialist. This framing was fuliginous to those unfamiliar with Hayek's arguments but not inaccurate, as the policy demands of Mussolini's party, Fasci Italiani di Combattimento, were clearly socialist: universal suffrage, economic restructuring with technocratic administration and workers' representation, a minimum wage, an eight-hour workday, state insurance against injury, state pensions, infrastructure improvements, and nationalization of the armaments industry.[2] The senator later clarified that he took the quote directly from the fourth chapter of Hayek's *The Road to Serfdom*. Of course, Senator Cornyn either failed to mention or was unaware that Hayek also supported a minimum income.

In its day, the quote, from the Italian dictator Benito Mussolini (1883–1945), was likely meant to be taken by Hayek's readers as preposterous. Italy under Mussolini's fascism in 1929 was hardly a leading civilization or one more challenged by "complexity" than any other European economy. Hayek's readers would have known this; Hayek simply hoped to illustrate that the use of (purported) technological or social progress to justify collectivism should be regarded with deep skepticism. Moreover, the notion that market competition and individual freedom need to be restricted because of growing complexity gets the relationship exactly backward. Hayek will argue that social complexity and technological advances mandate greater competition and individual freedom. Nevertheless, it is worth discussing the political economy of Italian fascism to correct the popular myth that economic development mandates a curtailment of economic freedom.

Mussolini's reference to restrictions on individual freedom is understated. The Italian fascist regime unleashed ruthless violence against labor union leaders, socialists, and other dissidents, hobbling these groups by 1923, only a year after coming to power. Resistance was completely crushed by 1926, when the full dictatorship was established and all guarantees of personal rights from the liberal Piedmont constitution were subverted.[3] In addition to withdrawing rights, the state actively sought to organize the social life of citizens outside of the workplace.[4]

In terms of economic management, after an initial liberal phase the fascist government revalued the lira by returning to the gold standard in 1927 and increased import duties in order to favor new, inward-oriented industries (e.g., chemical manufacturing and mechanical engineering) over older, export-oriented staples (e.g., textiles and food). The dictatorship also discouraged domestic competition and fostered the domination of the economy by a few large firms in order to increase their profitability. Not only the wages but also the rights of workers were curtailed as the regime struggled to solve its economic malaise. At the time of Mussolini's statement in 1929, real wages in Italy had fallen considerably. From June 1927 to December 1928 wages fell about 20 percent; there was a further reduction of 10 percent in 1929. By 1934 wages of industrial workers had fallen by an estimated 30 to 40 percent from 1926 levels. Agricultural wages similarly dropped precipitously in the same period.[5] The fascist regime even permitted employers to prolong the workday without paying overtime.[6] Eventually, a forty-hour workweek was instituted as a kind of work-sharing program to try to solve the growing unemployment problem. While laborers were organized under syndicates, these organizations were state organs and not organizations of the working class.[7] Moreover, the syndicates strongly favored the owners of industry and sought to increase their profitability without completely alienating the working class.[8] The interventionist economic policies of the fascist regime caused a slowdown in productivity growth, and efforts to shift the economy structurally from agriculture toward industry had a negligible impact on productivity.[9] The pursuit of autarchy resulted in Italy becoming more and more of a command economy.[10] The main driver of growth was capital accumulation rather than productivity enhancement. In other words, the regime's restrictions on individual freedoms and intervention in the market did not correlate with better management of the industrial economy.

Despite Mussolini's manifest incompetence at economic management, his reputation as the archetypal strongman endures as a potent symbol of decisive and competent leadership, particularly in the economic sphere. His name is practically synonymous with the myth that the fascists, regardless of their brutal tactics, "made the trains run on time." In fact, in 1932 Republican Senator David A. Reed of Pennsylvania said in an address to Congress and President Herbert Hoover:

> Mr. President, I do not often envy other countries their governments, but I say that if this country ever needed a Mussolini, it needs one now. I am not proposing that we make Mr. Hoover our Mussolini, I am not proposing that we should abdicate the authority that is in us, but if we are to get economies made they have to be made by someone who has the power to make the order and stand by it. Leave it to the Congress and we will fiddle around all summer trying to satisfy every lobbyist, and we will get nowhere. The country does not want that. The country wants stern action, and action taken quickly.[11]

Reed believed that Mussolini, who at that time was celebrating his tenth year in power, was a man of authority and action, and that management of a troubled economy mainly requires decisive leadership. Reed, who was otherwise averse to the immigration of southern Italians and Eastern Europeans, had been seduced by the soft power of fascist propaganda newsreels and adulatory American press coverage of the "Modern Caesar."[12] Nevertheless, in times of economic crisis and distress there is always a temptation to seek out a charismatic leader, because the economy is popularly understood as malleable to a masculine will, in the manner of a wild beast;[13] or, alternatively, the strongman is desired as a counterforce to unruly workers who are seen to be disrupting the "immortal laws of economics" through collective agitation.[14]

In sum, there is clearly popular confusion about the relationship between fascism and its economic policies. First, while it is correct that Italian fascism endorsed a range of socialist policies, not all redistributive policies are antithetical to liberalism and capitalism. In fact, some economic redistribution may be necessary for a free market and an open society to function with minimal coercion. Second, while fascists endorsed a range of socialist policies when seeking power, in practice workers were brutally subordinated in a vain attempt to revive the economy during the interwar period. Third, the belief among admirers of authoritarianism that a complex economy requires decisive leadership and centralized planning to "make the trains run on time" is based on accreted myths rather than historical analysis. The actual record of macroeconomic management under Italian fascism was dismal. As noted, Hayek argues that the solution to managing ever greater economic complexity and technological sophistication is neither decisive leadership nor centralized planning, but increased competition and individual freedom.

∵

Collectivism and Technology

Collectivists attempt to justify centralized planning not on its desirability, but because of the pace of technological change and the subsequent emergence of monopolies in major industries. Hayek argues that while there was a growth in monopolies in the first half of the twentieth century, the extent of monopolies dominating sectors of the market was exaggerated.

Today, the trend toward economies of scale, large firms, and the "concentration of industry" that seemed inevitable in the mid-twentieth century has clearly abated. In fact, one could argue that the pace of technological change has helped to minimize the number of monopolies and shorten their durability where they do emerge. The ICT revolution and advances in mechanization, robotics, and artificial intelligence, coupled with the emergence of GVCs has spurred dramatic changes in manufacturing. Manufacturing processes can now be separated over vast spaces without losses in coordination, efficiency, or timeliness.[15] Moreover, the shift from flows of finished products to flows of components, along with the strategic positioning of assembly points, has displaced the intrafactory division of labor that characterized the twentieth-century industrial process.[16] Hayek's assertion against the superior efficiency of large-scale manufacturing in the mid-twentieth century is therefore confirmed by trends in the twenty-first century, although some monopolies persist.[17]

Hayek asserts that some reasons for the emergence and persistence of monopolies are collusive agreement, protectionist tariffs, and other public policies.[18] Moreover, the emergence of monopolies is a feature of "comparatively young industrial countries," and their experiences should not be used as a general model of "advanced" or "late-stage" capitalism.[19] Hayek, following in the footsteps of Adam Smith, does not defend monopolies or oligopolies. Moreover, Hayek is correct to be skeptical of linear projection

THE "INEVITABILITY" OF PLANNING › 69

models that haunt socialist and communist thinking (e.g., Sombart's theory of monopoly capitalism, or Lenin's theory of imperialism). If capitalism has demonstrated anything since Adam Smith, it is that this mode of social organization is flexible, dynamic, adaptable, resilient, nonlinear, and unpredictable.

Hayek adds that complexity does not necessitate centralization. The growth of complexity implies the "increasing difficulty of obtaining a coherent picture of the complete economic process." Hayek argues that competition is actually best suited to mutual coordination in complex and dynamic contexts. In fact, competition is the only method by which coordination can be achieved in such contexts.[20] Competition enables the price system to function, thereby permitting individuals to adjust their behavior in response to new information.[21]

AI AND COMPUTERIZED PLANNING

In 2016 and 2017 Jack Ma, the billionaire entrepreneur who founded China's e-commerce giant the Alibaba Group and the financial services technology firm Ant Group, stated that with big data, networks, and modern computing, real-time planning of the Chinese economy was now possible:

> The planned economy I am talking about is not the same as the one used by the Soviet Union or at the beginning of the founding of the People's Republic of China. The biggest difference between the market economy and planned economy is that the former has the invisible hand of market forces. In the era of big data, the abilities of human beings in obtaining and processing data are greater than you can imagine.
>
> With the help of artificial intelligence or multiple intelligence, our perception of the world will be elevated to a new level. As such, big data will make the market smarter and make it possible to plan and predict market forces so as to allow us to finally achieve a planned economy.[22]

The dream of computerized economic planning can be traced back to the 1960s. L. V. Kantorovich understood the problem of centralized economic planning as one that basically entailed combining a given vector of resources with a finite number of techniques to maximize the fulfillment of a plan's target. Kantorovich assumed that a linear programming algorithm could devise the most efficient use of resources for each technique. Unfortunately for Kantorovich, computing power in the 1960s was simply too limited to demonstrate his hypothesis on an economy-wide basis.[23]

In 1970 the Salvador Allende regime in Chile invited the British "management cybernetics" consultant Stafford Beer to create Project Cybersyn (or Synco in Spanish). Allende's government hoped to organize a socialist economy and use computer feedback for indicative planning to direct production, with the hope of eventually achieving complete automation.[24] A network of five hundred Telex machines was used to gather real-time data from factories on output, energy use, labor levels, and so on.[25] In some cases, information traveled from factories to the Telex operators by donkey. In any case, the data was transmitted to two mainframe computers in Santiago and ultimately to a *Star Trek*–inspired control room where planners could make decisions. The project ended abruptly in September 1973 with the coup d'état that would bring General Pinochet to power. As a side note, while Hayek had condemned the Allende regime as South America's only totalitarian experiment, it is unlikely that he knew about Project Cybersyn.[26] If he had, he would certainly have seen it as a step toward comprehensive economic planning and hence as confirmation of his characterization of Allende's regime.

The dream today is that data on sales of consumer goods (by companies such as Alibaba or Amazon) will help AI overcome information problems. One difficulty, however, is that simple input-output (IO)-model economies rapidly increase in complexity as the number of industries increases. It would take a computer (with one 64-bit ARM core running at 1.6Ghz) approximately 33 years to compute a one-year plan for an economy with 50,000 industries using a linear programming solver, and 2,417 years to generate a five-year plan for the same economy.[27] Moreover, while this plan would specify the output available for consumption, it does not address output of raw materials and replacement of capital goods, which would be necessary in any comprehensive plan of total output.[28] These models also do not assess output quality, worker wages, monetary issues, political stability, and a host of other variables that shape production.

A simpler, iterative algorithm based on insights from marginal utility theory and neural networks combined with parallel operating supercomputers could significantly reduce the time required to make the necessary calculations technically feasible under certain assumptions about fixed capital.[29] However, even an algorithm that mimics the "low complexity coordination algorithms" of ordinary consumers cannot accommodate innovation or exogenous shocks.

Limitations on structured data as well as changes in the utility of existing data over time can also impact the prospects for machine learning. Jesús Fernández-Villaverde, a professor of economics at the University of Pennsylvania, writes:

Monetary policy is a relatively straightforward topic with fewer moving parts than other kinds of economic policy. Could machine learning ever replace the Federal Market Open Committee (FOMC, the main policy instrument of the Federal Reserve System)? I am skeptical. For one thing, the FOMC usually has a limited amount of data. In the United States, we only have reliable data for output, consumption, and investment after World War II and, even then, only at a quarterly level. If we count them, from 1947:Q1 (the first "good" observation in terms of the accuracy of our measurement) until 2021:Q2 (the last observation as I write this), we have 298 data points. This is far fewer than acceptable for machine learning techniques.

Furthermore, the US economy has radically changed, which limits the relevance of older data. We have moved from an economy dominated by manufacturing into an economy driven by services, and financial innovations have transformed the relationship between financial and real variables. The evolving structure of the economy shifts the relationships between the data points, making it harder for machine learning to find clear patterns. These structural changes mean that econometricians often do not use observations before the early 1980s when they estimate the effects of monetary policy on output. In fact, such estimates change sharply depending on whether we include early observations. Moreover, the economy is bound to continue to change, meaning we will continue to have to deal with newer and newer data.[30]

Finally, even if all these data problems could be technically overcome, Hayek would argue there is a more fundamental limitation. Fernández-Villaverde continues:

> The fundamental problem with relying on machine learning to recognize economic trends and determine economic policy coincides with the reasons that Friedrich Hayek gave against conventional, socialist central planning. . . . The objections to central planning are that the information planners need is dispersed and, in the absence of a market system, agents will never have the right incentives to reveal it or to create new information through entrepreneurial and innovative activity.[31]

Adds Zhang Weiying:

> Although knowledge and data are useful for entrepreneurs, the real entrepreneurial spirit goes beyond that. Decision-making based only on data is scientific but not entrepreneurial.

Entrepreneurs need to see what is behind the knowledge and data, and different entrepreneurs may see different things.

Such uncertainty means that we cannot predict the future based on the past, and that's why we need entrepreneurs. If we could simply use data to predict the future, then we would only need managers or robots instead of entrepreneurs.[32]

As a postscript, it is noteworthy that Jack Ma, only a few years after his prophecy about computerized state planning, began to argue that government regulators should use a lighter touch with tech companies because the market should decide how new industries and artificial intelligence develop.[33] Eventually Ma fell afoul of the Chinese government for harshly criticizing the state's financial regulators in public.[34] He disappeared from public view for several months, and the government blocked an initial public offering by his financial services company and launched an antitrust investigation into the Alibaba Group, wiping billions from his companies' market capitalization. Ma has since been seen only in sporadic press reports.[35] The fundamental problem of freedom in a centrally planned economy will not be resolved through AI.

ELECTRIC VEHICLES, SOLAR PANELS, AND MONOPOLY

An alternative to the belief that complexity mandates planning or that artificial intelligence can facilitate planning in a complex reality is the belief that scientific progress and social concerns require placing limits on competition, or even granting a monopoly. In other words, proponents argue that a new technology will either fail to develop or fail to become affordable to the majority of consumers if it is forced to compete with existing industries. Hayek is not wholly unsympathetic to certain instances of this line of argument, even though it is easily muddled by its proponents:

> This type of argument is not necessarily fraudulent, as the critical reader will perhaps suspect: the obvious answer—that if a new technique for satisfying our wants really is better, it ought to be able to stand up against all competition—does not dispose of all instances to which this argument refers. No doubt in many cases it is used merely as a form of special pleading by interested parties. Even more often it is probably based on a confusion between technical excellence from a narrow engineering point of view and desirability from the point of view of society as a whole.[36]

Although the argument wears many guises today (e.g., legislation to force a technology switch, tax incentives, taxpayer-funded rebates, etc.), there is a familiar impulse. The argument begins with the logic: if everyone *opted* to use technology x, prices for the use of that technology would drop to affordable levels. The argument then changes from the voluntary adoption of a new technology to the use of financial incentives, financial penalties, and finally legal coercion on the manufacturer or consumer. Although arguing from a pre-environmental framework, Hayek concedes that such arguments are at least logically valid: "It is, for example, at least conceivable that the British automobile industry might be able to supply a car cheaper and better than cars used to be in the United States if everyone in England were made to use the same kind of car or that the use of electricity for all purposes could be made cheaper than coal or gas if everybody could be made to use only electricity."[37] Compulsory standardization, such as the requirement that all future passenger vehicles use rechargeable electric batteries rather than internal combustion engines, might create conditions that lower prices for those products or generate sufficient positive externalities to compensate the consumer for their loss of choice. However, Hayek states that one cannot argue that technical progress *requires* compulsory standardization. Compulsory standardization brings products to the market faster than if consumers were provided with freedom of choice, but if consumers prefer not to take advantage of the benefits of a new technology, or if they prefer to wait until market forces bring the technology to fruition at an acceptable cost, there is no need for compulsion. The only cases in which compulsory standardization should be contemplated are those technologies that are undeniably necessary for the consumer's health and safety, particular those technologies whose mass adoption is highly time sensitive.

In general, however, Hayek would advocate forgoing the immediate gains that would accrue from compulsory standardization of a technology to preserve freedom of choice. His position is informed by his philosophy of knowledge, which assumes the role of radical uncertainty. Hayek argues that channeling future decisions on the basis of present knowledge is dangerous, given the fundamental unpredictability of knowledge:

> Though in the short run the price we have to pay for variety and freedom of choice may sometimes be high, in the long run even material progress will depend on this very variety, because we can never predict from which of the many forms in which a good or service can be provided something better may develop. It cannot, of course, be asserted that the

preservation of freedom at the expense of some addition to our present material comfort will be thus rewarded in all instances. But the argument for freedom is precisely that we ought to leave room for the unforeseeable free growth.[38]

Hayek supports a precautionary principle even in cases where, on the basis of current knowledge, the adoption of a new technology brings only advantages and may actually do no harm. Hayek is correct to imply that knowledge based on laboratory and static conditions may change in a dynamic context.

Scientists and Coercion

Hayek notes that scientists often advocate using the power of the state to make adoption of their favored technological solution compulsory. The obvious reason is simply that ". . . almost every one of the technical ideals of our experts could be realized within a comparatively short time if to achieve them were made the sole aim of humanity."[39] Unfortunately, he notes that there are an almost infinite number of desirable and beneficial outcomes, but only a limited number that can actually be achieved in a lifetime by directing the entire energy of a population.

Hayek does not deny that there are instances in which state planning produces technical excellence (e.g., Germany's interstate highways) for a specified problem, and he would agree that marshaling massive state resources may generate scientific discoveries (e.g., the public-private partnership that led to the COVID-19 vaccine) and justifiably help to manage a threat to public health,[40] but he rejects the notion that excellence or a scientific breakthrough in one area builds the case for centralized state planning and state coercion in general. Even in cases where planning produces an excellent solution, for example, it is to be wondered whether such allocation of resources was economically efficient or even necessary. For example, a capacious modern highway, while no doubt aesthetically pleasing and convenient for its users, may actually indicate a failure of efficient resource allocation from other priorities:[41] "Anyone who has driven along the famous German motor roads and found the amount of traffic on them less than on many a secondary road in England can have little doubt that, so far as peace purposes are concerned, there was little justification for them."[42] In fact, the aesthetic preference for massive physical infrastructure systems (e.g., superhighways and bullet trains), which has become a preoccupation of middle-income countries in Asia desperately and perpetually in search of acquiring the symbols of modernity, is a perfect example of the use of state resources to circumvent rational persuasion and to impose a particular order of values on a society, often with limited regard for questions of efficient resource allocation. Ironically, the desire to build superhighways in middle-income countries is coming at the exact moment that high-income countries are increasingly dismantling their ring roads in order to restore the value of communities and create more livable cities.

By conceding that there are some technical ideals that could be advanced through state coercion, Hayek's argument is actually quite generous to scientists. Hayek should have distinguished more clearly between technical solutions to specific problems and the pursuit of technical ideals in this final portion of the chapter. While specified technical problems can be resolved, there are no technical ideals to which humanity or even all the members of a small society could be uniformly compelled to implement. The state may marshal immense collective resources for specified technical problems, but that is altogether different from altering the behavior and value ordering of a collection of individuals. Hayek would have to concur that the exercise of power incites resistance and subversion. As Michel Foucault observes, while resistance may lead to a dramatic rupture, most often it is mobile and transitory. But points of resistance, even when they are defeated, generate cleavages in the social body that fracture unities and effect regroupings.[43]

Beyond limitations inherent in the exercise of power, a complex adaptive system is subject to Hayek's "knowledge problem." While physical and social scientists may understand general principles of complex systems and the patterns that result, they may not be able to predict specific responses to specific events or even the range of likely responses. In particular, social systems are composed of creative actors who perpetually drive processes of social change. While some day-to-day regularities are predictable, longer-term forecasting requires "knowledge of factors in advance of their emergence."[44]

Conclusion

For Hayek, deploying advanced technology to manage social complexity is unnecessary. The technophile's long-standing dream of coordinating individuals in society through the use of computer-processed data is both misguided and redundant. The dream is misguided because it is premised on a flawed ontology and epistemology. Despite dramatic advances in computing power and the emergence of artificial intelligence, the persistence of radical uncertainty in social affairs and interpretive ambiguity in coding places constraints on the utility of aggregated social data over the long term. In any case, the project is unnecessary because there is already a mechanism to coordinate individuals in society efficiently with a minimum of coercion: the free market. As a discovery process, competition in the marketplace is often the most efficient mechanism to reveal capabilities, quality, and desires in a dynamic context.

By the same token, centralized planning and the power of the state should not generally be used to accelerate the adoption of new technologies, except in areas critical to consumer health and safety. Logically, state incentives, prohibitions, and coercion to compel the mass adoption of a technology will certainly result in lower prices per unit. However, the forced adoption of a technology fails to respect the individual's rank ordering of values, to appreciate the dynamic nature of individual needs from moment to moment, and to predict unforeseeable changes from factors that have yet to emerge.

Compared to authoritarian approaches, liberalism is more efficient in managing complexity and provides better safeguards in integrating new technologies.

CHAPTER FIVE

Planning and Democracy

> The statesman who should attempt to direct private people in what manner
> they ought to employ their capitals, would not only load himself with a most
> unnecessary attention, but assume an authority which could safely be trusted
> to no council and senate whatever; and which would nowhere be so danger-
> ous as in the hands of a man who had folly and presumption enough to fancy
> himself fit to exercise it.
>
> Adam Smith (1776)

The passage by Smith from which Hayek takes his epigraph should not be
taken out of context lest it appear as a dogmatic statement. Smith's admonition pertained to the establishment of protected (i.e., monopolistic) domestic markets for the produce of domestic industry.[1] Smith did not intend
a blanket rejection of all efforts by the statesman to shape the ways in which
private people might employ their capital. For instance, Smith endorsed a
politically privileged position for the Bank of England over other private
commercial banks, at a time before the Bank of England had established
itself as the central bank and the sole issuer of currency.[2] Smith also supported the protection of domestic industries related to the defense of the
state and in cases where discrimination against the exports of one's own
country dictated a demand for retaliation.[3]

Nevertheless, the passage is an opening salvo for Hayek's rejection of the
imposition of values by the stateman on the individual.

∵

Fabricating the Common Good

In contrast to the liberal creed, what unifies the varieties of collectivism is
an intolerance for the seeming anarchy of individuals pursuing their own
aims autonomously from either the state or the collective. The desire of
collectivists of all stripes to organize the whole of society and its resources
is reliant on the establishment of a thin notion of the "common good" or

"general welfare."[4] Hayek counters that establishing a notion of the common good requires ". . . a complete ethical code in which all the different human values are allotted their due place." Nevertheless, a scale of values or complete code prescribing how to choose among competing values and needs cannot be set for any complex society—at least not without the use of repression or callous indifference. Any set of common goals must be organized hierarchically, and this goes against the general trend in civilization of the development of morality, which has given progressively greater freedom to the autonomous individual. Writes Hayek, "The fact that we are constantly choosing between different values without a social code prescribing how we ought to choose does not surprise us and does not suggest to us that our moral code is incomplete."[5] In contemporary society, Hayek argues, morals are not guides but outer limits ". . . circumscribing the sphere within which the individual could behave as he liked."[6] Even choosing a "unitary economic plan" would seek to invert the trend of expanding autonomy.

Hayek's argument is not fully compelling, for it assumes that disciplinary and surveillance technologies do not always already shape, constrain, and animate individual choice in a commercial society. While these technologies (or "discourses") may not be directed from a central point, the notion that the sphere of individual autonomy has been continuously expanded is contested.[7]

Although Hayek agrees that a common (albeit limited) purpose might exist in periods of war,[8] or in more mundane situations where individual views coincide in the pursuit of social ends,[9] there is nothing barring individuals from combining to realize common goals. But Hayek cautions: "The limits of this sphere are determined by the extent to which the individuals agree on particular ends; and the probability that they will agree on a particular course of action necessarily decreases as the scope of such action extends."[10] Moreover, while Hayek does not argue the point here, he believes that there are different forms of morality appropriate to both small groups and the extended society. A very small group may have a common scale of values, but such morality is not possible for a complex society. Not only does an extended society lack a uniform scale of values, but a dictator or centralized bureaucracy cannot address the infinite variety of different needs and wants of an extensive population.[11] By contrast, a competitive market is a decentralized and spontaneous information collection and transmission device. Hayek is arguing that market competition is a discovery process that reveals the complex and constantly changing values of individuals in a complex society. Of course, it is logically possible that individual goals may coincide and create incentives for collective action, but where there is no agreement, the market can sort out different values and the level of effort individuals expend in seeking to attain specific goals.

Democracy and Planning

Hayek understands democracy as the product of an antecedent liberal economic order. When a state moves away from liberal values and toward economic planning, Hayek believes that the political system will need to assert greater agreement than that which actually exists. Moreover, even where agreement exists on the need for a planned economy, the goals of planning may not be agreed upon.

The problem of setting goals in a planned economy, and even of administering rules, is usually moved out of the political sphere and into the field of a technocratic elite who are buffered from accountability. The turn toward technocrats reduces democratic institutions to "talk shops," where grievances are merely aired, not addressed. Hayek argues that socialism cannot allow itself to be constrained by democratic governance. The reason that he paints socialism as necessarily antidemocratic is that a truly planned economy would be derailed if democratic processes were to permit the rise of an administration hostile to economic planning. In such a case, economic planning could only be set for the medium term at best.[12]

Hayek understands a planned economy as a project that fails in multiple stages. With each failure of planning to achieve its promised objectives, there is a demand for greater centralization of planning, culminating in the demand for an economic dictatorship.[13] Thus, for Hayek, a collectivist path inevitably destroys democracy.

Democracy and Freedom

What is Hayek's understanding of a democracy? Hayek argues that only within a capitalist system in which individuals have the right to possess and dispose of private property is democracy possible.[14] Thus, the purpose of a democratic state is to protect individual freedom through the rule of law (i.e., the limitation of arbitrary power). But a democracy can easily degenerate into a tyranny of the majority, and hence Hayek does not fetishize it. By the same token, Hayek does not believe that all dictatorships eliminate freedom. In fact, he notes that some authoritarian regimes have preserved greater cultural and spiritual freedom than some democracies. However, he believes that a planned economy leads to a demand for a dictatorial planner because this is the most effective mechanism for implementing the ideals of a planned economy.

While Hayek is certainly correct to echo Tocqueville's warning that democracy can decay into a tyranny, Hayek's qualified attachment to democracy opens the door to the endorsement of authoritarian or political capitalism. Although Hayek is careful to argue that authoritarian regimes sustain merely "cultural and spiritual freedom," his argument appears rather weak when one considers that authoritarian states have no particular attachment to individual freedom, and that there are no restrictions on the arbitrary use of coercive power.

Democratic Accountability

Hayek argues that liberal democratic institutions are unable to provide meaningful input or accountability in a centrally planned economy. The implicit logic here is that the limits to democratic input in the planning process stem in large part from the inherent value of pluralism in society. Regardless, after successive failures to achieve planned targets, the sovereign state will inevitably seek decisive authority to assert control over an economy; otherwise it would have to turn away from planning altogether. Centralized economic planning inherently confers power to one group over all others, since most planners believe that ". . . a directed economy must be run along dictatorial lines."[15] Hayek argues that it is a contradiction to assert that democracy can sustain itself in a planned economy so long as the democratic authority is excluded from economic policy-making.[16] A meaningful exercise of democratic accountability must be able to overturn the dictates of a centralized economic planning bureau after an election brings a different administration to power.

Centralized economic planning sets the stage for totalitarianism by transferring power to a "staff of experts" and vesting final authority in a "commander-in-chief." It is not just the unaccountable structure of decision-making, but also the intensively intrusive scope of economic planning, that poses a threat to liberty. The ability to shape consumption through the regulation of production and prices, the ability to shape an individual's choice of occupation, and the ability to determine the value of values generate a form of unlimited tyranny heretofore unknown.

Economic control, whether exerted by the state or a private monopolistic firm, is a form of coercion. The coercion is all the more dangerous when exerted by a state, since it also claims a monopoly on the legitimate use of violence over a given territory.[17] By contrast, submission to competitive market forces permits social coordination and adjustment by prices that are "not determined by the conscious will of anybody."[18] In a market economy, when individuals face economic losses, they are not necessarily coerced, because individuals retain the right to dispose of their possessions based on what is least important or useful. Of course, the ability to exercise one's freedom of choice carries with it risks and responsibilities.[19]

Conclusion

Hayek consistently views democratic institutional arrangements as a means of protecting individual liberty. Where democratic mechanisms are insufficient to protect liberty, or where democracy gives way to the tyranny of the majority, alternative institutional arrangements are required. Hayek is not denigrating the role of institutions; he firmly believed that the error of laissez-faire liberalism was its general perception as a negative creed that did not emphasize the importance of institutional bulwarks supporting and enabling the free individual.

Nevertheless, he weakens his argument for reviving liberalism by entertaining the prospect that an authoritarian regime might better protect individual freedom than an illiberal democracy. Hayek will turn to interstate federalism toward the end of the book as a liberal solution to limit state coercion of individuals and thus strengthen liberal democracy. Building institutional safeguards for individual freedom is the way forward for a revived liberalism.

CHAPTER SIX

Planning and the Rule of Law

> Recent studies in the sociology of law once more confirm that the fundamental principle of formal law by which every case must be judged according to general rational precepts, which have as few exceptions as possible and are based on logical subsumptions, obtains only for the liberal competitive phase of capitalism [and not, as Max Weber once believed, for capitalism in general].
>
> Karl Mannheim (1940)

The epigraph, by the émigré sociologist of wide-scale planning at the London School of Economics Karl Mannheim (1893–1947), seems to have been intended as a backhanded compliment to liberal capitalism.[1] Mannheim, a scholar of conservative German reactions to the French Revolution, had become a critic of capitalism. He believed that capitalism systematically inhibited the kinds of "moral relationships" between individuals that were needed in a modern mass society. As detailed below, Mannheim would call on the British state to intervene in society to promote necessary mores and values among the youth. Unsurprisingly, Mannheim's non-Marxist critique of capitalism would soon draw the ire of his academic colleagues (including Max Horkheimer, and eventually also Herbert Marcuse and Theodor Adorno) at the Frankfurt School of critical theory located down the hall in the Institut für Sozialforschung (Institute for Social Research) at Goethe University in Frankfurt am Main.[2]

Despite his battles with the Marxists of the Frankfurt School, Hayek was also deeply critical of Mannheim's work. Mannheim's vision of anomic capitalism creating atomized individuals clashed with Hayek's Smithian belief that the market rendered individuals cooperatively interdependent without reliance on state or personal coercion. Moreover, Mannheim's advocacy of centralized planning, which extended into the social sphere, was in Hayek's view a virulent threat to individual freedom. Mannheim would have countered that parliamentary control could ensure against the erosion of individual freedom and the rise of bureaucratic absolutism in a planned society, at least until the individual could adjust to the new social order:

... the planned retention of ancient liberties is a guarantee against exaggerated dogmatism in planning. We have learnt to realize that even when society has passed to a new stage in many spheres of its existence, some of the old forms of adjustment could still continue. Wherever it is possible and the plan is not endangered every effort must be made to maintain the primary form of freedom—freedom for individual adjustment. . . .

Of course once society has reached the stage of planning[,] separatism and local autonomy cannot be allowed to have the last word as at the stage of invention.[3]

However, as Hayek already argued in the previous chapter, parliaments cannot delegate tasks to a bureaucracy where there is no agreement on end goals. And because agreement on ends in a complex society is difficult, a parliament would be ineffective in preventing bureaucratic absolutism. At best, the parliament would be reduced to tinkering at the margins of plans that emanate from the bureaucracy itself.

Hayek's attack on Mannheim would be aided by Karl Popper. Much like Hayek, Popper used Mannheim as his foil in *The Poverty of Historicism* (1957) and *The Open Society* (1945). Jefferson Pooley describes Hayek and Popper as "vituperative" critics of their colleague's sociology.[4] Michael Polanyi would also join in the assault on Mannheim with the publication of *Science, Faith, and Society* (1946).

In fact, the attacks were so pointed that Mannheim felt that *The Road to Serfdom* was a personal attack directed at him.[5] While Mannheim's understanding of his place in Hayek's work is somewhat conceited, in the first chapter of *The Road to Serfdom* Hayek did include Mannheim alongside G. W. F. Hegel, Karl Marx, Friedrich List, Gustav von Schmoller, and Werner Sombart in a list of Germanic intellectuals who helped to rout the forces of English liberalism on the Continent.[6] Though Hayek viewed Mannheim as the least powerful of this pantheon, Mannheim's work on planning did need to be countered. Of course, despite the intellectual animus between Hayek and Mannheim, it is worth noting that Hayek's mentor and friend Ludwig von Mises, along with several other leading intellectuals, worked tirelessly to secure employment for Mannheim and many other academics who were dismissed and persecuted by the Nazi regime in the interwar period.[7]

In terms of the "sociology of law" discussed in the epigraph, Mannheim believed that the "monopoly stage" of "late capitalism" produced juridical irrationalities, as contracting parties were no longer equal in political and economic power. Judicial decisions move from formal law to an individual judge's discretion. In Mannheim's sociology, the law becomes prejudiced against the powerless and operates in favor of those with political and economic power. This results in what he labels as "fascism," despite the persistence of democratic rule, in the sense that there is inequality before the law.[8]

Hayek must have viewed Mannheim's assertion that it is only in the "liberal competitive phase of capitalism" that the rule of law is operative with a mixture of both bemusement and disdain: bemusement at Mannheim's admission (following in the footsteps of Max Weber) of the central role of the rule of law in capitalism, and disdain for Mannheim's assumption that capitalism had morphed out of its competitive phase. The assumption that law functions differently at different stages of social development is problematic for Hayek.[9] In a memorandum on "Nazi-Socialism," Hayek argues that antiliberalism is manifest in arguments that destroy the belief in the universality and unity of human reason. The "sociology of knowledge," a phrase directly associated with Mannheim, was a form of intellectual relativism that ". . . denied the existence of truths which could be recognized independently of race, nation, or class. . . ."[10] The consequence of this mode of thinking is to delegitimize liberal institutions (e.g., the concept of the rule of law) and to place sentiment above rational thinking and positionality above universality.

The assumption that "monopoly capitalism" or "late capitalism" would soon be transcended led Mannheim to see a need to initiate comprehensive planning. Mannheim had argued in 1930 that laissez-faire had not only produced structural maladjustment (e.g., mass unemployment) but also chaos in every other sphere of social life. Mannheim contended that comprehensive planning was therefore necessary to go beyond economics to touch the "life of society" itself and restore an organic community of the sort present in smaller towns. He stated that it would be very desirable if "everything beyond economics were arranged by the spontaneous self-regulating powers of group life." But since this spontaneous self-regulation was not forthcoming, Mannheim modestly posited, "interference in the life of the spirit" was inevitable.[11] At other times, however, Mannheim was more bombastic. He saw humanity as sitting on the cusp of a new age of comprehensive planning; he argued that mankind was ". . . tending more and more to regulate the whole of its social life. . . ." Indeed, Mannheim argues that social science is (out of necessity) far more advanced than the natural sciences and able to treat the ills of society at this particular historical stage as if it were a discrete subsystem:

> When we have gone so far as to regulate the movements of clouds and . . .
> when we have controlled climate in the same way as it is becoming nec-

essary for us to control social factors, and when we try to draw into the framework of our regulation all the laws of biology in their concrete interactions, then we will be faced with the same problem in the world of nature as now confronts us in the world of society: namely the treatment of a particular historical and local stage in the total system of nature as a relatively self-contained whole, working according to certain principles which are peculiar to it.[12]

In essence, Mannheim's position was the polar opposite of Hayek's faith in the spontaneous order.

Mannheim's ideas acquired particular influence among conservative British politicians during the interwar period after Prime Minister Winston Churchill appointed R. A. Butler president of the Board of Education, a cabinet position, in 1941. As Butler pondered the postwar reconstruction of education, he summoned Mannheim, whose book *Man and Society in an Age of Reconstruction* had appeared in translation that year. Mannheim was also associated with the Moot, an ecumenical Christian group that included the noted poet and playwright T. S. Eliot, even though Mannheim was not a Christian. Mannheim's ideas about state-directed moral reform generally accorded with Butler's vision, although Butler was not quite comfortable with Mannheim's role for the state in coordinating the "life of the spirit." In fairness, Mannheim was not calling for a totalitarian state, but he did believe that the state had a role to play in strategically stimulating social solidarity where it was weak, in an analog to the Keynesian state in the economic sphere.[13] Mannheim's stated aim was to instill a minimal sense of decency and moral obligation. However, his policy instrument, a committee composed of academics and legislators who would meet weekly to advise policy makers, journalists, and opinion makers in society, certainly raised eyebrows, even within the Moot group. Tim Rogan argues that Mannheim's policy idea mirrored Hayek's plan to create the Mont Pelerin Society (MPS) as an influential group of thought leaders.[14] On the surface there is a parallel, but the MPS decided at the first meeting of its board of directors in 1948 not to seek political influence, issue manifestos, or set up political agendas; it remained primarily an academic debating club.[15]

In any case, Butler's 1942 report on the aims of education would recommend, alongside several uncontroversial measures to limit class privilege and increase technical education, that the state should actively promote religious education, and that compulsorily registered youth should be required to engage in service to the community, regulated by the state. The aim was to foster a "new morality" and values that he saw as missing in mass society. Critics, including Hayek, seized on these elements of the report to decry the report's authoritarian undertones.[16] The work of the committee was sidelined, and the reform ideas were abandoned. After 1942 Butler would pursue the promotion of religious education through an alliance with the archbishop of Canterbury.

∴

Taming the State

For Hayek, democracy is laudable to the extent that it is able to restrain arbitrary power and thus prevent the destruction of individual freedom. While democracy is clearly incompatible with socialism in Hayek's theory, democracy does not automatically enhance individual freedom.[17]

The restraint of arbitrary power and thus the enhancement of freedom are subsumed under the concept of the rule of law. The rule-of-law concept (as it evolved from the *Rechtsstaat* concept in Germany) implies that the tyranny of the majority, or unfettered democracy utilizing the coercive apparatus of the state, needs to be constitutionally constrained.[18] The concept is in force when the state's coercive power is bound by fixed, principled, generalized, nondiscriminatory rules that are announced beforehand.[19] The rule of law renders the law stable and impartial; it provides the enduring rules of the game.

Thus, Hayek's endorsement of the rule of law is based upon its ability to

1. constrain the discretionary authority of legislators and administrators, thereby preventing *ad hoc* measures to limit individual freedom;[20] and
2. create a predictable environment that permits individual planning with a fair degree of certainty about how and under what circumstances the state's coercive apparatus will be used.[21]

In essence, the rule of law is a "meta-legal principle" necessary to tame the behavior of a democratic state and to create a predictable terrain for the consequences of individual actions.

Predictability for the individual under the rule of law coincides with creating uncertainty and unknowability for the state:

> Formal rules are thus merely instrumental in the sense that they are expected to be useful to yet unknown people, for purposes for which these people will decide to use them, and in circumstances which cannot be foreseen in detail. In fact, that we do *not* know their concrete effect, that

we do *not* know what particular ends these rules will further, or which particular people they will assist, that they are merely given the form most likely to benefit all the people affected by them, is the most important criterion of formal rules. . . . They do not involve a choice between particular ends or particular people, because we just cannot know beforehand by whom and in what way they will be used.[22]

The state accepts being blindfolded in order to free the individual. The rule of law is therefore a precondition for individual freedom in a societal context.[23] Of course, the enactment of any formal laws necessarily encroaches on individual freedom, but the rule of law limits executive discretion in order to sustain individual freedom in a society. Despite these encroachments, for liberal thinkers, there is no liberty without law.[24]

The rule of law (again, in the *Rechtsstaat* tradition) also requires that the state obey "principled, generalized, nondiscriminatory rules," which implies that

3. the law cannot discriminate in favor of or against persons or groups; the law applies equally to all.[25] This means the liberal democratic state can neither engage in rectifying historical injustices nor redistributing resources to assist a favored group. The state sets the conditions for the use of available resources but individuals must determine the ends.[26]

The rule of law aims to create a politically neutral state; a state guided by the rule of law is an umpire, not a coach.

Moreover, one could argue that the *principle of self-limitation* (points 1 and 2 above) from arbitrary action creates a necessary, albeit fluid, boundary between the public and private spheres. While the private sphere is not sacrosanct, it is protected from arbitrary encroachment by the state. The *principle of equality* or nondiscrimination before the law (point 3 above) also limits the state. It implies that the state and its agents are subject to the law. The state thus acknowledges the limits on its own knowledge, capacities, and powers. The equality principle acts against the use of the state's resources for personal gain or particularistic/partisan interests. The equality principle creates a boundary between the state and particularistic interests or partisan bias. In other words, the principle of equality creates state autonomy from segments of society.[27]

Hayek's outlook on the law should be contrasted with legal positivism, which asserts that legal validity stems from its procedural origins in government rather than its adherence to abstract principles or moral criteria. For Hayek, procedural validity is unrelated to the rule of law, and an absence of the rule of law does not indicate lawlessness or even the violation of for-mally legal statutes.[28] The absence of the rule of law does not preclude rule *by* law. Hayek blamed legal positivism for eclipsing the tradition of lim-ited government and opening the door to dictatorship in Europe. Having earned his first PhD in law (with the legal positivist Hans Kelsen as one of his professors and examiners at the University of Vienna), Hayek would develop his own evolutionary theory of law and a critique of legal positiv-ism in later works, particularly *The Constitution of Liberty* (1960) and *Law, Legislation, and Liberty* (vols. 1–3, 1973, 1976, and 1979).[29]

Planning as Arbitrary

Hayek argues that the absence of the rule of law is functional for central-ized planning or "arbitrary" government. His argument is counterintuitive, since one generally assumes that long-term planning requires or prefers a stable and predictable policy environment. However, Hayek views the rule of law as a constraint on the state's flexibility and a mechanism to "de-politicize" the law. Thus, the absence of the rule of law permits a govern-ment to direct the means of production dynamically toward particular ends or beneficiaries.[30] A state that seeks to make rapid, dynamic, relative gains in the international system or to redress perceived historical injustices will be deeply hostile to the adoption of the rule of law, as it leaves resource production and allocation to be based on individual desires as opposed to elite ambition acting in the name of the collective.[31]

Planning is thus not fixed but flexible, not principled but tactical, not general but selective, not disinterested but discriminatory. Therefore, planning cannot operate on abstract principles, particularly if it aims to achieve rapid catch-up or social justice. Of course, plans will be articulated as based on abstract government regulations while providing a measure of reasonable discretion for the program administrator. The reliance on im-plicit standards of fairness or reasonableness by state officials only masks the arbitrary and ad hoc nature of discretionary decisions. Moreover, the state is invariably drawn into microdecisions about resource allocation. Ul-timately, the planning state must comprehensively rank interests—who is worthier of assistance—arbitrarily in order to implement its policies.

Another complication that develops with planning policy outcomes is that a state's knowledge of the beneficiaries of a planned policy not only eliminates the impartiality of the state, it transforms the state into a "moral" institution that imposes the state's preferences on moral questions.[32] Hayek's aim here is to warn that the pursuit of social justice through affirmative action/positive discrimination or state-led industrialization is a tactic common to socialists as well as national socialists. These policies have the unintended consequence of eliminating the notion of universally applicable rules and formal equality before the law.[33] Notably, Hayek cites Carl Schmitt, the most prominent legal theorist of national socialism, who opposed the liberal rule of law with a notion of the "just state," which relied upon a legal interpretive doctrine grounded on instinct rather than rule following.[34]

In elaborating his argument, Hayek seeks to dispel the image of a passive and reactive, laissez-faire state juxtaposed with an active and anticipatory planner state. He notes that ". . . every state must act and every action of the state interferes with something or other." Liberalism is not opposed to regulation, so long as rules are intended as permanent and not specifically designed to favor or harm particular persons.[35]

Political Capitalism and the Rule of Law

As noted earlier, Hayek's dichotomous, "ideal-type" framework consisting of liberal and centrally planned societies masks hybrid possibilities, particularly Milanovic's "political capitalism."[36] A political-capitalist regime combines a state that deliberately relies upon a limited application of the rule of law to enhance state autonomy with a market-based production of resources.

At the surface level, the laws of a political-capitalist state may resemble and even derive from the laws of a liberal state and international norms. It is in practice where the divergence from the rule of law is felt. For example, Wendy Ng writes with regard to the origins of China's law regulating competition:

> China has adopted and accepted many international competition law norms into its formal competition law and practice. The AML [Anti-Monopoly Law] itself is broadly consistent with international norms, though there are departures from those norms in some areas as the law has been tailored to reflect China's specific circumstances. The Chinese authorities also frame their decisions to be within the bounds of the formal language, concepts, tools and analytical approaches reflected in international competition law norms, even in cases where it seems that industrial policy or other non-competition factors may have been rel-

evant in the decision-making. Hence, in both the law and in its decisional practice, China has demonstrated formal conformance with what is considered to be international best practice.[37]

In essence, through intellectual gymnastics, formal conformance with international norms is used disingenuously to mask the underlying factors that actually shape decision-making.

In Vietnam, as noted earlier, the CPV revised its constitution twice (1992 and 2013) after initiating liberalization in the late 1980s to better accord with the international human-rights norms supported by donor agencies, trade partners, and intergovernmental organizations; and to create a more predictable legal environment for commercial activity. Vietnam has participated in the Universal Periodic Review of the UN Human Rights Council and it is a signatory to the ASEAN Charter, which codifies adherence to the rule of law and protection of human rights.[38] Officially, of course, Vietnam has merely sought to promote a "socialist" rule-of-law concept for the "socialist law-based state" to support its "socialist-oriented" market economy.[39] Historically, however, the state has shown little regard for law-based governance, even disbanding its Ministry of Justice from 1959 to 1980. The CPV has preferred to rule on the basis of neo-Confucian "revolutionary moral principles" and emulation of the personal virtue of Ho Chi Minh.[40] Ultimately, as in China, socialist legality is predicated upon the supremacy of the Communist Party, a positivist conception of law, and the prioritization of collective interests over individual rights. The CPV itself has recognized that the "laws and discipline of the state" are consistently violated, inconsistently enforced owing to corruption, or simply not implemented by the party/state.[41] Thus, in practice, the rule of law is neutered by the party's resistance to the notion of an independent judiciary and even the devolution of power to state units that might become autonomous from the ruling party.

In Singapore, the constitution derives ultimately, via the 1957 Constitution of the Federation of Malaya, from the 1950 Indian Constitution. The Constitution of Singapore has a bill of rights (with restrictions), and the judiciary is constituted as an independent branch of government. The constitution is officially the supreme law of the land, and the judiciary may nullify any law that violates it.[42] In practice, however, nullification of laws has been remarkably rare. The court has even been accused by critics of a "thin positivist" conception of the law, while defenders argue that ". . . the courts have never shirked from exercising judicial review. . . ."[43] Nevertheless, through a constitutional amendment, the legislature has curtailed judicial review in cases related to the Internal Security Act.[44] "Ouster clauses," which prevent acts or decisions from being challenged in court, permit the state to stand above the law on the grounds of "necessity" in cases of preventive detention and licensing laws for public assemblies. A compliant judiciary also (allegedly) facilitates ". . . the suppression of political dissent through speech-restrictive defamation and contempt of court laws."[45]

Thus, despite constitutional lineages and conformance to international norms, in political-capitalist states the restraint of governmental power, a core attribute of the rule of law, is limited. The political-capitalist state is not organized to act as merely an administrative authority operating under public law:[46] the state, and by extension the ruling party, are effectively above the law in such regimes.

The preceding is not meant to deny that a political-capitalist state could have broad areas in which the rule of law appears to outsiders to be robust. Even in China, there are segments of the market (e.g., the international investment regime) characterized by the "bare elements" of the rule of law, such as "universality, predictability, non-retrospectivity, and the principle of legality."[47] However, these pockets of the rule of law exist primarily to reassure foreign investors that their investments will not be nationalized without compensation and that they will have the ability to repatriate investments or seek legal redress. Nevertheless, the fine print of investment agreements illustrates that the Chinese state, for example, is not forbidden from appropriation of investments to protect the public welfare (e.g., public health, safety, and environment), and the state is permitted to discriminate against foreign firms provided that the nonextension of national treatment is set out in laws and regulations.[48]

In Vietnam, despite dramatic liberalization and efforts to strengthen the rule of law, including enacting an Investment Law in 2005 to reassure investors against fears of nationalization or confiscation, consultants argue that major investment risks remain: "Key risks include weak adherence to the rule of law and inadequate mechanism to enforce intellectual property rights protection, compounded by the prevalence of corruption that weighs down the market's potential."[49] Moreover, the dominance of SOEs in particular economic sectors is correlated with a slow pace of liberalization to foreign investment in those areas. In any case, foreign firms still face challenges when applying for investment licenses in these areas. While Vietnam permits foreign investment in all but six sectors and regulates 267 sectors, there are over 6,400 conditions related to these sectors.[50] Thus, Vietnam does not project a convincing image of a state guided by the rule of law, and its actual practices, when not directly hampered by rampant corruption, reveal discriminatory and burdensome practices toward foreign investors.

Singapore is exceptional in this regard; it does not seek to retain the right to discriminate against foreign firms. The primary reason is that the city-state has been unsuccessful, for the most part, in its efforts to nurture and expand local small and medium-sized enterprises.[51] In fact, although the Singaporean government has worked assiduously to mitigate risks, transportation costs, and labor unrest for multinational corporations,[52] it has not spurred the growth of a domestic entrepreneurial class, relying instead on forced savings from citizens that are funneled into sovereign wealth funds to increase capital accumulation.

In terms of economic management, the merely nominal status or curtailed scope of the rule of law does not result in a substantive reliance on comprehensive, centralized planning under political capitalism. Sectoral "master plans" may persist to guide foreign investment in targeted industries, but these plans are often vague aspirational statements that mainly create confusion by overlapping different ministries and layers of government.[53] Instead of actually relying on comprehensive planning, political-capitalist states often seek to create an environment that is conducive for a broad strategy of mercantilism (e.g., through currency manipulation, tariff barriers, discrimination against foreign firms, etc.) or national economic development (e.g., attracting foreign direct investment from firms with the potential to create spillover effects). In other words, the state relies on the market to allocate most resources but is willing to intervene whenever it deems it necessary for a course correction. Even Singapore, a remarkably open entrepôt economy, at times relies robustly on "economic realism and/or mercantilism," owing to the city-state's vulnerable geostrategic location and reliance on foreign trade.[54] Some of the evidence for this lies in Singapore's accumulation of foreign exchange reserves, which at one time were the highest in the world in per capita terms, to improve export competitiveness through a managed floating exchange rate.[55]

The political-capitalist state is involved in actively managing the market. As Wendy Ng explains, "The Chinese Communist Party has stated that the market plays a decisive (though not complete) role in allocating resources and that the government's role is to, inter alia, oversee the market, maintain market order and intervene and remedy market failures. The relationship between the state and the market in the economy is one that is close and entwined. . . ."[56]

However, political capitalism is not merely a synonym for a kind of "regulatory capitalism." Eleanor Fox adds that market intervention is not limited just to cases of "market failure":

China's enhanced state involvement implies that the state is free to control markets, even very well-functioning markets—for example, the state may step in when markets are tipping towards foreign suppliers or are undercutting state-owned enterprises (SOEs) or Chinese brands or simply when the opportunity arises to condition a deal on a promise of a flow to China of natural resources or foreign technology. China may override the market to get outcomes that are more favourable to China than competition would produce.[57]

Ng would concur that market interventions in China may also be politically motivated:

> . . . due to the lack of transparency surrounding decision-making and governance in China, this state-centered approach to competition law might not lead to stable, predictable or transparent outcomes across and within industries, actors and categories of prohibited conduct, as the interests and roles of the state—which may or may not be consistent with competitive outcomes—can change depending on a number of known and unknown factors. In this context, it is understandable why commentators criticize that some AML outcomes are motivated by non-competition and political concerns and depart from (at least the spirit of) international competition law norms.[58]

Of course, the existence of competition law (as well as bureaucratic entities designed to enforce the Anti-Monopoly Law) in China indicates that there is a tension between state guidance of markets and the state's defense of the markets.[59]

The use of rule-of-law rhetoric helps to entrench illiberal regimes. In this regard, it is worth noting that the Chinese word for "rule of law" (*fazhi*) was added to the Chinese Constitution in 1999. Since joining the World Trade Organization in 2001, Chinese officials have made efforts to promote a rule-of-law system in order to attract foreign investors. President Xi Jinping has emphasized the policy of "governing the nation under law."[60] While the use of the term would not correspond to Hayek's understanding, since the law and judicial institutions are subordinate to the Chinese Communist Party, it is clear that China is seeking, at least nominally, to create the impression of greater equality before the law and the notion of accountability for corrupt state officials. The appearance of a law-governed society may help to legitimate an authoritarian regime, particularly in the context of a failed economic ideology.[61]

Similarly, in Vietnam debates about fostering the rule of law shortly after liberalization centered around an analogous Vietnamese concept (*nha nuoc phap quyen*), which is better translated as "rule *by* law." Vietnamese policy makers were attracted to these concepts precisely because they en-hance existing centralized economic and legal mechanisms.[62] The idea of a "socialist law-based state" is meant to balance the rule of law sought by foreign investors with the rule of the party.[63] The top-down reform process and the discourse of law is understood as a mechanism to strengthen the party/state, not weaken it.

In Singapore, the state's creation of a highly disciplined, safe, and law-abiding society has been a major selling point for foreign firms and workers. As H. H. Khondker observes, "The more foreign FDI [*sic*] flows in to Singa-pore, the higher the legitimacy of the state."[64] Moreover, the discourse has the added benefit of legitimating restrictions on individual liberty:

> Paramount to [the] Singapore state's criminology discourse is the need for an orderly, safe and well-controlled environment that is conducive for urban living but also for global corporate businesses to thrive. As a fledg-ing globalizing city, the need to make Singapore a safe haven for foreign investors has often been strongly emphasized by state actors. Through regular government campaigns and public education programmes that reinforce the message of creating a safe and orderly nation-state with law abiding citizens to boot, a huge premium has been placed on having a well-ordered society, even if this means at the expense of individual liberty.[65]

Through the Internal Security Act, the state retains the right to arrest and preventively detain individuals without trial for up to two years.[66] As noted earlier, the act is not subject to judicial review. Paradoxically, by constrain-ing the rule of law, the authoritarian state is able to project the image of a lawful society and legitimize its rule.

Although limiting the rule of law permits the political-capitalist state to be autonomous from interest groups in society, the state is not distant from the business, entrepreneurial, and industrial elite.[67] The developmen-tal state theorist Peter Evans once labeled this phenomenon, that is, when a state seeks linkages to business groups without becoming captured by those interests, "embedded autonomy."[68]

In contemporary China, the party *nomenklatura* actively cultivates strong links with private business,[69] but the state is not captured by those interests. Members of the party become entrepreneurs, and entrepreneurs are encouraged to join the party. Patronage is vital for entrepreneurs' ac-cess to loans from state-owned banks and to contracts from the state.[70] The effect is strong group cohesion and a reliance on political connections and loyalty as opposed to merit. A symbiotic relationship develops in which businesses are permitted and encouraged to prosper so long as entrepreneurs do not seek to challenge or criticize the party leadership.[71] If the state is challenged, however, an amensalistic relationship emerges, as the weaker partner is destroyed without consequence to the stronger partner. As noted earlier, anticorruption campaigns are a useful mechanism for purging troublesome entrepreneurs as well as party officials.

In Vietnam, the top-down image of the controlled and technocratic reform process often conceals ". . . not only a complex process of elite consensus building which seeks to be politically inclusive, but also a high level of sensitivity to local demands and protests."[72] A significant portion of the private sector in Vietnam actually originated from within the state itself or at the fringes of the state as "bureaucratic entrepreneurs" explored opportunities created by market liberalization.[73] Highly factionalized "state-business blocs" also emerged as SOEs were given greater autonomy on a commercial basis and opportunities for profiteering "off the books" emerged. Business associations have also emerged to create new deliberative spaces and networking opportunities that inform policy makers.[74] Thus, there are strong links between state, parastatal, and societal interest groups. Informal relations are often used by state actors to engage in rent seeking and for private actors to seek lax enforcement of regulations. The state has attempted to manage the ensuing corruption by further restructuring SOEs, raising the salaries of public officials, and implementing a slew of anticorruption laws, including the execution of corrupt executives.[75] Nevertheless, large-scale corruption is endemic, and the Vietnamese state is less capable of disciplining its power elite than either China or Singapore.

In Singapore, which is often portrayed as the alienated administrative state par excellence, the state remains "highly enmeshed through familial ties and friendship networks where the distinction between private and public remains blurred."[76] At the sociological level, individual career paths, interests, and roles frequently intertwine the public and the private. Nevertheless, the state has demonstrated over and over that it can withdraw assistance from targeted industries and that it can completely discipline the labor force, nongovernmental organizations, and the media.[77]

Conclusion

In sum, compared to the highly inefficient, centrally planned economies of the twentieth century, an advantage of contemporary political capitalism, from the perspective of authoritarian leaders, is that it can harness market efficiencies in the allocation of resources and continuously increase output within an illiberal political framework. The model demonstrates that neither the principle of self-limitation of the state (and its attendant security of property rights) nor the principle of equality of all citizens before the law is necessary to ensure economic growth and state autonomy. And unlike the illiberal rentier states of the Persian Gulf, which have achieved economic prosperity primarily by capturing rents from natural resources, political capitalism appeals to a wide range of low- and middle-income states that, like China and Singapore, are food- and energy-insecure and zealously seek to protect their hard-won sovereignty.[78] Moreover, China has indicated that it is interested in exporting its development model to countries seeking a "new alternative" to accelerate development while retaining their sovereignty. Even if China did not actively seek to spread its model, given China's role in the global economy, lawyers and strategists working for multinational firms seeking to do business in China will need to study China's legal system, particularly its business law and approach to competition policy.[79] Even if China were uninterested in reshaping the world in its own image, its status in the global economy confers upon it a tutelary role. Similarly, while Singapore may not be interested in exporting the "Singapore Consensus," it is a model for other countries, particularly in Asia.[80]

The rule of law is easily mimicked and subverted under political capitalism with little consequence. Liberalism will make little headway arguing for the rule of law's centrality in generating prosperity.

CHAPTER SEVEN

Economic Control and Totalitarianism

The control of the production of wealth is the control of human life itself.

Hilaire Belloc (1946)

The epigraph is a quote from the French-British writer and activist Hilaire Belloc's book *The Servile State* (1912).[1] Belloc's work is often seen as a precursor to Hayek's *Road to Serfdom*, because the earlier work is usually read as an antisocialist tract. However, Edward McPhail argues that Belloc's work is not a critique of collectivism, state socialism, or totalitarianism, but rather an argument against unbridled capitalism. The "servile state" is Belloc's description of an incrementally expansive state in which the proletariat trade their freedom for security and sufficiency in response to the instability generated by a capitalist economy. The effect of this trade-off is the entrenchment of the capital- and property-owning classes, along with a highly skewed distribution of wealth.[2]

Belloc traced the rise of capitalism to the dissolution of the monasteries in sixteenth-century England and the subsequent expropriation of their wealth, and thus to a movement away from the widespread ownership of private property under medieval institutions and Christian norms. The servile state develops as a necessary compensatory mechanism for the propertyless masses as a consequence of the rise of rapacious owners of property and capital in the subsequent period. The servile state is not a socialist state, for it primarily changes the legal status of propertyless workers rather than taking control of the means of production.[3]

Hayek clearly understood that Belloc's servile state was categorically separate from both socialism and capitalism.[4] However, Hayek, like George Orwell, believed that Belloc presciently explained how the advance of socialist doctrine in a capitalist society could lay the groundwork for the rise of Nazism in Germany. McPhail objects that if Nazi Germany is characterized as a servile state, Belloc would argue that its root cause was capitalism, not the spread of socialist ideas.[5] For Belloc, the "control of the production of wealth" was problematic because it was in the hands of the capitalist firm—not the state—which rendered the worker relatively powerless.[6]

Thus, it would appear that Hayek misread Belloc. Hayek mistook Belloc's contempt for socialism, particularly piecemeal Fabian socialism, as an endorsement of capitalism. In reality, Belloc was aiming to carve out a position that rejected both capitalism and socialism. For Belloc, the piecemeal efforts to ameliorate the insecurity and precarious subsistence of the proletariat results in a servile state, which entrenches a rapacious capitalist class, while for Hayek, the cumulative and ever-expansive centralized planning by the state opens the gates to totalitarianism.

∵

The Centrality of Economic Decision-Making

Modernity, in Max Weber's conceptualization, entails the separation of the spheres of the lifeworld. Overlapping areas of endeavor (e.g., art, religion, science, and politics) in a traditional society come to be distinct and autonomous areas. For example, art is pursued for its own sake rather than for the glory of religion, science comes to be divorced from religion, and so on, Similarly, areas of study become discrete and disciplinary despite obvious interconnections. Thus, the economy comes to be imagined as a distinct and discrete sphere of human activity separate from politics, art, and religion, for example, and economics is nominally divorced from the study of politics, moral philosophy, aesthetics, and the like.

Building on the epigraph from Belloc, Hayek rejects the notion of the economy as a separate sphere of the lifeworld in order to counter the notion that centralized planning "only" impacts economic matters. Regardless of the epistemological and disciplinary boundaries of neoclassical economics, Hayek asserts that the economy as a field is necessarily interconnected with every other sphere of the lifeworld, particularly politics. To this extent, Hayek's argument represents an effort to take economics back to its origins in political economy and moral philosophy. In fact, Hayek aims to demonstrate that the freedom to make economic decisions is antecedent to all other freedoms. There is no Maslovian "hierarchy of needs" that would relegate base material (i.e., economic) matters to a lower order of concern. Control of the economy through centralized state planning is therefore tantamount to the effective control of life itself, since the economy cannot be examined in isolation. The economy reflects the weight of relative values in society, the range of choices, and the horizon for self-actualization of every individual. Thus, Hayek argues, "To be controlled in our economic pursuits means to be always controlled unless we declare our specific purpose. Or, since when we declare our specific purpose we shall also have to get it approved, we should really be controlled in everything."[7]

Marginal Man

In the absence of centralized planning, when individuals possess the ability to freely dispose of their property, economic loss will only deprive individuals of those items that they consider to be the least important. In Hayek's framework, economic loss and gain occur only at the margins. Of course, he implicitly assumes (1) the operation of a free market, (2) the existence of nearly universal secondary markets for the disposal of assets, and (3) the existence of a basic social safety net—otherwise dramatic economic adjustments would not be at the margins. Individuals in a free-market economy constantly adjust their assets to match their expected income with their preferred order of values. It is because individuals in a market society engage in this process constantly and because there are certain values that seemingly transcend material valuation (or "filthy lucre," as Hayek puts it) that individuals come to undervalue quotidian economic adjustments. Centralized planning seeks to subsume the individual's role by aggregating and collectively declaring the social order of values, including the status of what constitutes the marginal. By surrendering intimate economic decision-making to the state, Hayek warns us that the planner comes to decide what it is we should value and what we should be willing to discard.

The fundamental political question for Hayek is therefore not *cui bono* (who benefits), but *qui iudicat* (who decides). The essence of freedom in Hayek's framework emerges from individuals (or at most a household) making intimate decisions about their own preferences on a perpetual basis. (Hayek does not mention the possibility that free individuals might collectively choose to reassign a small proportion of economic power; here he only deals with the polar ends of the spectrum.)[8] A wholesale collective reassignment of economic power would obviously be an inherent loss of freedom for at least some individuals. An example of complete subordination to the power of the state is provided in Hayek's brief discussion of foreign exchange controls. Hayek notes that prohibiting citizens from acquiring foreign currency limits an individual's ultimate exit option and even the individual's exposure to a wide range of opinion through imported books and journals.[9]

There is, of course, a considerable gray area between complete autonomy from the state and complete submission to state tyranny. In this realm, the question is: how much autonomy do individuals need to retain to remain free? In almost all societies a measure of economic power is transferred to the state and redistributed by its agents. Given Hayek's support for a minimum income and his recognition of complex interdependence as a permanent feature of the market, he would not object to a portion of economic power being redistributed. Thus, Hayek is not making a demand for complete autonomy of decision-making—that would be naive and illusory in any case—but a general preference for placing greater decision-making on the individual level as opposed to the collective.

Controlling Production

Hayek understands that centralized planning does not need to control consumption directly in order to constrict individual freedom. So long as the state can control production, the individual loses their freedom even while retaining the illusion of free choice in consumption.[10] Hayek's concern is not so much about state predation through monopoly power, but restrictions on the type, range, and quantity of goods available for consumption, as well as the ability of the state to discriminate between individuals in their pursuit of particular ends (e.g., to charge different prices for a good on the basis of ascriptive or social categories). Restrictions and discrimination limit freedom when the citizen does not have the ability to take their business elsewhere.

State control of production may also impact the individual's freedom to choose their occupation, which naturally influences individual happiness, given the role of work in shaping the lives of adults. The notion that a state could dictate one's choice of occupation appears ridiculous today, yet Hayek's fear would materialize in the welfare state of postwar Great Britain. As noted in the introduction, the Labour Government (1945–51) did reintroduce Defence Regulation 58A and the Control of Engagement Order (1947) in peacetime to direct laborers to take "essential" work or face fines and/or up to three months' imprisonment.[11] Even though the acts were not widely implemented, they demonstrated that a planned economy might seek to direct employment and thereby restrict individual freedom of choice in very fundamental areas of life.

It is notable that Hayek is not arguing in defense of the status quo. The mere possibility of alternative employment, although clearly better than the absence of that possibility, is cold comfort for those working in intolerable conditions with little real prospect of attaining better employment. Hayek readily concedes that the state could and should do more to spread knowledge and assist in social mobility:

This is not to say that in this respect all is for the best in our present world, or has been so in the most liberal past, and that there is not much that could be done to improve the opportunities of choice open to the people. Here as elsewhere the state can do a great deal to help the spreading of knowledge and information and to assist mobility. But the point is that the kind of state action which really would increase opportunity is almost precisely the opposite of the "planning" which is now generally advocated and practiced.[12]

In other words, the state need not be confined to a passive role with regard to inequality and social rigidity. In fact, as Raymond Plant notes, not only does the (neo)liberal state need to demonstrate concern about coercion by individuals and the enforcement of rule of law to ensure mutual noncoercion, but the liberal state must also ensure negative equality of opportunity, that is, the removal of obstacles placed in the way of individuals by the intentional actions of others. Of course, a line is drawn between a state removing obstacles to equal opportunity (*Rechtsstaat*) and one positively seeking to equalize the ability to take advantage of opportunities (*Wohlfahrtsstaat*), as the latter is a violation of the rule of law.[13] While centralized planning is predicated on controlling the flow in and out of employment channels and grand promises of rapid and comprehensive social transformation, the dissemination of knowledge and information by the liberal state to help encourage social mobility and reduce inequality is certainly possible within the framework of a decentralized market economy and the rule of law.[14]

It may be objected that Hayek's later work is fairly indifferent to concerns about economic inequality. In fact, one could argue that later in his career, Hayek more forthrightly asks the state to accept economic inequality as the amoral by-product of a spontaneous (i.e., unintended) and competitive market order. However, such a reading of Hayek's later work needs to be slightly moderated to avoid generating a caricature. For example, Hayek argued that economic growth is the best mechanism for improving the absolute *and* relative position of those in the lowest-income groups. In other words, Hayek is not a neo-Malthusian; rather, he wishes to generate a higher standard of living for the poor through economic growth:

> But on the whole it would seem that the fact which, contrary to a widely held belief, has contributed most during the last two hundred years to increase not only the absolute but also the relative position of those in the lowest income groups has been the general growth of wealth which has tended to raise the income of the lowest groups more than the relatively higher ones. This, of course, is a consequence of the circumstance that,

once the Malthusian devil has been exorcized, the growth of aggregate wealth tends to make labour more scarce than capital.[15]

Note here that the increase in "relative" position is comparing the lowest-income groups to the "relatively higher ones." This indicates at least a general concern to demonstrate a reduction in inequality even in his later writings.

In any case, from a post-Hayekian perspective, reducing social rigidity and inequality through state action that is noncoercive, oriented toward experimental learning, and does not generate severe knowledge and information problems may also be necessary if liberalism is to be revived.[16]

Trade-offs and Utopian Thought

Next, Hayek argues that the desire to be relieved of making tough economic trade-offs is what fuels utopian thinking, which promises to make trade-offs vanish. In reality, however, the preservation of core values (e.g., life and health, beauty and virtue, honor and peace of mind) are obtained at significant material cost and regularly requires the sacrifice of lesser needs. This condition is perpetual and inescapable since "all our ends compete for the same means; and we could not strive for anything but these absolute values if they were on no account to be endangered."[17] Hayek's convoluted prose adds unnecessary opacity to his argument. His points in this subsection seem to be that:

1. in a competitive, market-oriented society, most things can be had directly or indirectly in exchange for money;
2. regardless of one's ultimate goals, the means to attain those goals is usually through the acquisition of money, often through activity which risks life and health;
3. because we have multiple goals and only finite resources, we must make trade-offs;
4. because others seek similar goals, there is competition for attaining what we contemptuously call "material comforts" but are in reality our higher goals; and
5. we would not strive for our ultimate goals if those goals were immune from scarcity.

The idea that a society could eliminate the risk to life and health incurred in earning income if only it were willing to bear the cost is fanciful. Hayek uses the example of highway fatalities and argues that we could reduce automobile accidents to zero if we abolished all automobiles. While the scenario is logically valid, the full cost is not bearable, since the reason that these risks arise is a desire to achieve our end goals. Hayek is not arguing against mitigating risks or regulating workplace safety, but he is chastising those who seek to portray scenarios without trade-offs or competition.

Socialist propaganda about ushering in an era of "potential plenty" is the target of Hayek's concern. The claim that overthrowing capitalism, with its business cycles and occasional productive overcapacity, would lead to an era of plenty relies on either dishonest or wishful thinking. Socialism lacks an academically compelling explanation for how production could be efficiently increased in the absence of market competition.[18] Hayek agrees that planning predicated on creating a more just and equitable distribution of resources is on more solid ground than planning that argues from a technical economic perspective. However, Hayek believes that universal agreement on an ordering of value is not possible, and that imposing such a standard would create more oppression and discontent than the "much-abused free play of economic forces."[19]

From Eco-Marxism to Climate Leninism

In the twenty-first century, socialism no longer claims to offer a path toward "plenty"; rather, it has come to embrace environmental "sustainability," in the face of growing popular concern about human-induced climate change. Through a rereading of Marx and Engels, a path to bridging the divide between "Red" and "Green" factions of the Left has been underway for several decades. The claim by environmentalists that Marx and Engels were infatuated with "productivism" (or "Prometheanism") and had an uncritical attitude toward the "development of productive forces" is rejected by contemporary communists and socialists. In fairness, there are select passages from Marx (and even Engels) that show a critical perspective on productive forces, although these lines of thought are undeveloped.[20] However, Paul Burkett (*Marx and Nature*, 1999) and John Bellamy Foster (*Marx's Ecology*, 2000) argue there is neither a preference in Marx's writing for material wealth over nature nor praise for the bourgeoisie's subjugation of nature. Even eco-Marxists such as Andreas Malm find such revisionist claims a bit ridiculous: "There seems to be some wishful reading going on here. Foster and Burkett take the Marx they like best and claim that no other Karl can be found. But if there is not a trace of Prometheanism in his writings, the fact that it was undisputed orthodoxy among the generations of classical Marxism simply becomes inexplicable."[21] In addition to the familiar efforts at writing a hagiography of Marx, the solutions for climate change proposed by eco-Marxists and climate Leninists are pretty predictable: "In order to stabilize the rise of global temperatures at 1.5°C, emissions will have to be reduced by 8 percent a year until you meet net zero. This sort of change is totally impossible to do simply by tinkering with market mechanisms or introducing some carbon taxes; rather, it will require a massive expansion of state ownership and comprehensive economic planning."[22] The demand for eco-authoritarianism, a green leviathan, or a climate Lenin is being fueled by climate panic as the effects of climate change are becoming more palpable.[23] Thus, while the ends have changed, the means remain unreflectively statist and coercive in this strand of the radical Left.

Eco-Hayek

Although Hayek does not address sustainability or broader environmental issues in detail in *The Road to Serfdom*, one can extract his perspective on conservation and preservation of the environment from the general principles he articulates in *The Road to Serfdom* and from his more direct discussion in *The Constitution of Liberty*.

For example, climate change as a complex phenomenon (i.e., one characterized by nonlinear trends and a huge number of interacting elements) generally enhances the case for individual freedom in the allocation of resources. Hayek would contend that a complex phenomenon is subject to the knowledge problem, whereby a centralized intelligence cannot grasp the totality and therefore is not optimally managed through a directive intelligence.[24] But Hayek's outlook on environmental issues is flexible and open to direct state regulation where necessary. In *The Constitution of Liberty*, he writes that while most environmental problems arise out of an incomplete specification of property rights,[25] special legal provisions and state action may be necessary in certain cases to ensure an efficient use.[26] Hayek does not believe that a competitive market is the sole mechanism for solving complex coordination problems. In regard to environmental issues, Hayek says in *The Road to Serfdom*:

> There are, finally, undoubted fields where no legal arrangements can create the main condition on which the usefulness of the system of competition and private property depends: namely, the owner benefits from all the useful services rendered by his property and suffers for all the damages caused to others by its use. Where for example, it is impracticable

to make the enjoyment of certain services dependent on the payment of a price, competition will not produce the services; and the price system becomes similarly ineffective when the damage caused to others by certain uses of property cannot be effectively charged to the owner of that property. In all these instances there is a divergence between the items which enter into private calculation and those which affect social welfare; and, whenever this divergence becomes important, some method other than competition may have to be found to supply the services in question. Thus neither the provision of signposts on the road nor, in most circumstances, that of the roads themselves can be paid for by every individual user. Nor can certain harmful effects of deforestation, of some methods of farming, or of the smoke and noise of factories be confined to the owner of the property in question or to those who are willing to submit to the damage for an agreed compensation. In such instances we must find some substitute for the regulation by the price mechanism. But the fact that we have to resort to the substitution of direct regulation by authority where the conditions for the proper working of competition cannot be created does not prove that we should suppress competition where it can be made to function.[27]

In *The Constitution of Liberty*, Hayek argues that there may even be instances in which the state may know more facts concerning "probable future developments" than individual owners of natural resources. Nevertheless, Hayek adds, "there will always exist . . . an even greater store of knowledge of special circumstances that ought to be taken into account in decisions about specific resources which only individual owners will possess and which can never be concentrated within a single authority."[28] Thus, even if the government knows facts that the individual is not in a position to know (e.g., the probable macroeconomic effects of carbon dioxide [CO_2] emissions), the government will be ignorant of how specific individuals can optimize resource use in their own local contexts. Thus, institutions should be designed to disperse downward the generic knowledge available to the government. The failure to permit decentralized agents (e.g., individuals, firms, voluntary organizations) from experimenting with solutions generally limits efficient learning and adjustment in complex adaptive systems. Alternatively stated, decentralized decision-making limits the probability of selecting a mistaken policy choice. The aim of environmental policy should be to promote institutional experimentation and feedback.[29]

Arguing from a more conservative Austrian perspective, Graham Dawson reminds us that the state's preference for environmental regulation on the basis of aesthetic, historical, or scientific criteria is actually based on an ethical rank ordering rather than superior technical knowledge.[30] Although lacking a compelling argument, Dawson's contention is that Hayek favors "collective effort" to preserve the environment only where income maximization has been disqualified as a legitimate use for the resource in question. For Dawson, the prioritization of scientific or aesthetic criteria for the sake of a "public good" logically assumes that there is a "public at large," a claim that he believes is invalid.[31] This rather cantankerous argument ignores that Hayek does supply a clear explanation for when an aesthetic or scientific preference should be paramount:

> . . . the situation is different where the aim is the provision of amenities of or opportunities for recreation, or the preservation of natural beauty or of historical sites or places of scientific interest, etc. The kinds of services that such amenities render to the public at large, which often enable the individual beneficiary to derive advantages for which he cannot be charged a price, and the size of the tracts of land usually required make this an appropriate field for collective effort.
>
> The case for natural parks, nature reservations, etc., is exactly of the same sort for similar amenities which municipalities provide on a smaller scale. There is much to be said for their being provided as far as possible by voluntary organizations, such as the National Trust in Great Britain, rather than through the compulsory powers of government. But there can be no objection to the government's providing such amenities where it happens to be the owner of the land in question or, indeed, where it has to acquire it out of funds raised by taxation or perhaps even by compulsory purchase, so long as the community approves this, in full awareness of the cost, and realizes that this is one aim competing with others and not a unique objective overriding all other needs. If the taxpayer knows the full extent of the bill he will have to foot and has the last word in the decision, there is nothing further to be said about these problems in general terms.[32]

In other words, the "public at large" is the democratic electorate of a sovereign state, which votes to pay for the use of government revenues to pursue aesthetic, historic, or scientific preservation of the environment.

Andries Nentjes argues that Hayek's position is perfectly compatible with state creation and regulation of tradable emissions permits:

> The government is the appropriate organization to carry out and finance environmental research on quantity of emissions, their expected growth, their diffusion and the ultimate impacts of the pollutants. The govern-

ment is also the organization to weight the environmental benefits of lower pollution loads against the estimated costs of emission control. It is, then, the government that must decide how much of the public good pollution control should be provided.... Deciding upon and announcing a time path of annual emission caps is, then, the first step in "dispersing downward all the generic knowledge available to the government."[33]

Dawson would object that markets for tradable emissions permits require "precise and reliable information about the costs and benefits of climate change mitigation if they are to operate effectively and efficiently."[34] He is skeptical of the very existence of precise information on the impact of CO_2 emissions on atmospheric concentrations of CO_2, the impact of concentrations on mean global temperature, and the impact of rising temperature on physical phenomena such as rising sea levels. Of course, Hayek only argued that the state may have greater knowledge of "probable future developments"; there is no requirement that the state be omniscient. Hayek accepts that government addresses issues that involve negative externalities and tentative judgments about scientific research.[35] The government, firms, and individuals can all discover more precise relationships once property in the "right of use" has been established and scarcity in the emissions space has been created by freely distributing or auctioning permits.[36]

Conclusion

Control over economic decision-making is a fundamental and intimate aspect of human freedom; economic decision-making cannot be relegated to a subordinate concern in pursuit of "higher values." Nevertheless, the state has a legitimate role in these intimate areas of economic decision-making, where it may have greater knowledge of probable future developments, where property rights cannot be adequately specified, where markets are insufficient to ensure efficient use, and/or to preserve democratically agreed-upon (aesthetic, scientific, historical) and publicly funded priorities. However, a durable policy solution to a collective problem (e.g., climate change) still needs to address the knowledge problem and preserve the ability of individuals to rank-order their own values by adjusting their assets at the margin. A moderate liberalism is thus suited to the implementation of durable policy solutions simultaneously with the preservation of individual liberty.

[CHAPTER EIGHT]

Who, Whom?

The finest opportunity ever given to the world was thrown away because the passion for equality made vain the hope for freedom.

Lord Acton (1895–99)

The epigraph, taken from Lord (John Emerich Edward Dalberg-) Acton's *Lectures on the French Revolution* (1895–99), signals that the pursuit of equality comes at the expense of freedom.[1] To this extent the passage echoes Tocqueville's statement to Nassau Senior: "The great misfortune of France is the preference of *égalité* to liberty."[2] Nonetheless, the quotation is rather stark and easily misconstrued, given the nuance in Hayek's position on income inequality in a competitive market system.

Thus, it is important to understand Acton's quote in context. Acton, who was influenced by Edmund Burke, believed that liberty had to be limited to be possessed.[3] Moreover, Acton associated freedom with civilization and the state; freedom did not exist in a state of nature.[4] In other words, liberty is the fruit of a state in which there are institutional checks on power.

The quote Hayek uses for this chapter refers specifically to the French Revolution, a liberal revolution against an absolute monarch and a feudal order that Acton on the whole supported. Acton's critiques of the French Revolution relate partially to its assault on the Catholic Church, which stripped that institution of its privileges after August 1789; and primarily to the rise of a dictatorial regime under the Girondins and Jacobins/ Montagnards from July 1792 to July 1794. Although Acton was a devout Catholic, he detested the Gallican Church, which he viewed as compromised by its association with absolutism.[5] His objection to the legal and financial neutering of the Church was only that it removed an institutional check on political power. Similarly, although Acton approved the violent overthrow of the absolutist monarchy in France, he could not condone the use of violence once the ancien régime had been removed from power.[6] It was the failure of the French to understand the American Revolution's movement from violence and military conflict to constructive constitutionalism and limitations on democratic power that irked Acton. He also noted the hypocrisy of a revolutionary regime that declared the Rights of Man one day and then suspended those rights for the inhabitants of its colonies the next day.[7]

Acton was not a proponent of laissez-faire liberalism. As Christopher Lazarski notes, "Acton was shocked by the attitude of some liberals that 'the best thing for the poor is not to be born, and the next best, to die in childhood' and viewed it as fundamentally illiberal."[8] Acton's liberalism proceeded not from an abstract theory, but from the citizens, who decide what is good or bad for their community.[9] While Acton would have felt that free trade was an essential component of any liberal regime, he would also have included poverty relief, basic health care for the disadvantaged, freedom of association for labor, and education.[10] For Acton, protecting the weak and destitute was an ingredient in the advancement of civilization and therefore liberty. In other words, Acton's preference for liberty was not inimical to the pursuit of greater equality; it was only opposed to the pursuit of equality as an abstract and absolute end in itself. While Acton did not comment much on socialism, he shared socialists' concern for the poor and believed that labor ought to represent itself and defend its interests against property owners. Beyond these shared concerns, however, he viewed socialism as not just delusional but actually dangerous to freedom and civilization.[11]

Acton's prudent and sympathetic humanism (imperfectly) informs Hayek's views on the relationship between liberty and equality.

∴

Hayek argues that the virtue of market competition is precisely that one cannot know in advance who will succeed and who will fail. Hayek readily concedes that success is not a product of merit but entails a significant component of luck and unforeseeable circumstances. In a competitive market, the individual must rely on their own ability, hustle, and luck. The stark alternative, from Hayek's perspective, is a system in which an unaccountable state official decides the allocation of resources.

Hayek readily admits that in a market system chances of success are not equal. A system of private property that permits intergenerational transmission of wealth ensures that some have a highly weighted and undeserved advantage. He argues for prudent reduction in this form of inequality of opportunity through public policy: "There is, indeed, a strong case for reducing this inequality of opportunity as far as congenital differences permit and as it is possible to do so without destroying the impersonal character of the process by which everybody has to take his chance and no person's view about what is right and desirable overrules that of others."[12] Nevertheless, even with the imperfections in the competitive market, Hayek believes that freedom is greater for the poor in a competitive society than a collectivist one. Moreover, while the odds are stacked against the poor when it comes to achieving great financial success, it is at least possible in a competitive society: "Although under competition the probability that a man who starts poor will reach great wealth is much smaller than is true of the man who has inherited property, it is not only possible for the former, but the competitive system is the only one where it depends solely on him and not on the favors of the mighty, and where nobody can prevent a man from attempting to achieve this result."[13] Hayek seems to idealize the competitive system when he argues, ". . . there are no absolute impediments, no dangers to bodily security and freedom, that confine him by brute force to the task and the environment to which a superior has assigned him."[14] Such a portrait clearly ignores the history of physical persecution of racial, ethnic, and religious minorities in the competitive market societies of North America and Western Europe even in his time. Of course, Hayek would not endorse a society with such illiberal arrangements, but he is negligent in ignoring the long history of the oppression of minorities.

To attack and discredit the virtues of a collectivist society, Hayek cites evidence from Leon Trotsky that levels of inequality in Soviet Russia (in 1939) were not substantially less than in a capitalist society.[15] In other words, the collectivist society promises equality but actually delivers results similar to those of a competitive society.

In the twenty-first century, the challenge for post-Hayekian liberalism and liberal meritocratic capitalism is to reduce inequality to maintain this competitive system. Liberal systems that permit intergenerational transmission of wealth with minimal obstruction, limit funding to public education, and allow the fusion of economic and political power are destined to transition to a plutocratic system. Hayek's suggestion that inequality ought to be mitigated through public policy is a rational response.

Race and Justice

In the context of a broader discussion on planning, Hayek inserts a brief sentence on racial and religious minorities: "Who can seriously doubt that a member of a small racial or religious minority will be freer with no property so long as fellow-members of his community have property and are therefore able to employ him, than he would be if private property were

abolished and he became owner of a nominal share in the communal property."[16] In essence, through the phrase "his community," Hayek seems to
accommodate discriminatory and segregationist practices (e.g., Jim Crow
laws and Jewish ghettos) on the grounds that it is better than a return to
slavery or serfdom. This frankly reflects a disappointing passivity toward
racial and religious discrimination, even for the era in which Hayek was
writing, and it is at odds with his fundamental belief in human freedom
and liberalism. Where there were racial or religious (or other prejudicial)
barriers to entry in a competitive market, Hayek should have championed
nondiscrimination through a strict insistence on the universality of the law
and the removal of intentional barriers to equal opportunity, rather than
offering the cold comfort that having a meager share of private property in
a segregated system is better than having no private property. When a political majority is hostile toward a minority, it may seem that there is little
to be done; however, liberalism prides itself on having worked to free the
individual from religious dogma, feudal hierarchy, rigid patriarchy, serfdom, and chattel slavery in the face of intense hostility.

In any case, the dichotomous framing between a meager freedom and
dictatorial communism is not rhetorically compelling today, for these are
not the alternative options on offer. A competitive society that actively
combats unlawful discrimination based on race, gender, religion, and sexual orientation is far preferable to a passive system that only points to absolute intergenerational gains.

One can speculate on how Hayek might respond by examining his general discussion of structural forces of the market:

> There will always be inequalities which appear unjust to those who suffer
> from them, disappointments which will appear unmerited, and strokes
> of misfortune which those hit have not deserved. But when these things
> occur in a society which is consciously directed, the way in which people
> will react will be very different from what it is when they are nobody's
> conscious choice.
>
> Inequality is undoubtedly more readily borne, and affects the dignity
> of the person much less, if it is determined by impersonal forces than
> when it is due to design. In a competitive society it is no slight to a per-
> son, no offense to his dignity, to be told by any particular firm that it has
> no need for his services or that it cannot offer him a better job.[17]

While Hayek's frankness about injustice is refreshing, it is not compelling except in situations where one faces a stark alternative between

a minimally competitive and a comprehensively collective society. More-over, as Brian Lee Crowley's penetrating critique notes, despite Hayek's aversion to state coercion, the theory sanctions restrictive social insti-tutions (e.g., the market) and places them beyond rational criticism. Hayek's approach leads to skepticism about the ability of citizens to or-ganize and manage the res publica collectively or even to engage in criti-cal moral reasoning; he enshrines the market in the place of individual or collective reason.[18]

As a student of Tocqueville, whose "Three Races" chapter in *Democracy in America* arguably prefigures contemporary critical race theory, Hayek should have understood that the defense of liberty can easily be a mask for defending privilege.[19] Furthermore, as Tocqueville noted, to the extent that the state succumbs to the prejudices of the privileged, the state loses its status under liberalism as a neutral arbiter of conflict.[20] While deference to the structural forces of the market may be borne lightly, discrimination may also take on structural characteristics. Thus, a de jure segregated sys-tem in which market competition is segmented by impersonal forces of prejudice and inequality is unlikely to be readily borne or to deflect from the dignity of the individual. It is unlikely that a segmented market will be characterized by comparable occupations—in fact, American history reveals a tendency to reserve the "roughest work" for those most discrimi-nated against.[21] A segmented market (e.g., a segregated labor market) cre-ates not only real privileges and deprivations but also inefficiencies. At the very least, a liberal should encourage the market integration of fragmented communities (to the extent that individuals in those communities desire integration and assimilation) through *doux commerce* rather than a ratio-nalization of segmentation as superior to collectivism.

In fact, Lord Acton had argued that where "political and national bound-aries coincide, society ceases to advance, and nations relapse into a condi-tion corresponding to that of men who renounce intercourse with their fellow men."[22] The preservation of diversity was fundamental for liberty; where unity became the primary objective of the state, the possibility of absolutism opened up. In his aphoristic style, Lord Acton stated in *Essays on Freedom and Power* that liberty "provokes diversity, and diversity pre-serves liberty."[23] The very vitality of a liberal state and civilization is indexed by the extent to which it integrates its various national groups. Of course, as a Victorian intellectual, Acton believed that "inferior races" would benefit by living in a political union with "superior races," but his prejudice was mainly cultural in that Victorian culture was a yardstick rather than a So-cial Darwinian notion.[24] Acton favored race mixing or "miscegenation" on moral and biological grounds, since the "mixture of races" was at the heart of Christianity.[25]

Production and Distribution

As Hayek delves deeper into the mechanics of centralized planning, he argues that a collectivist society cannot avoid shaping the distribution of income. While most state planners would prefer to concentrate on the organization of industry and leave the distribution of income mainly to impersonal market forces (operating within certain bounds), the exercise of control over industrial organization necessarily impacts the distribution of income. For Hayek, because of the deep interdependence between economic phenomena, meddling in the market "beyond a certain degree" necessitates that planners extend their controls until the controls become comprehensive.[26] What is unknowable, however, is where the line is that begins the process resulting in a desire for comprehensive control. The argument is not a slippery slope, but for Hayek there is a threshold beyond which it becomes impossible to operate a planned economy without perpetually deepening the level of control.

The main takeaway for Hayek is that the market order, even in a competitive society, is about submission, but the psychological burden of submitting to impersonal market forces is much lighter than that imposed by submission to a particular individual. Of course, Hayek implicitly assumes that individuals lack the ability (individually or collectively) to exert influence over patrons or decision makers, as is common in traditional patron-client societies. In essence, the political relationship between the planner/director and the planned/directed is apparently a diode. Regardless, on a societal scale, such countervailing pressures would likely have limited significance in a feudal or collectivist system.

Despite Hayek's general acceptance of unmerited inequality in a healthy liberal society and competitive market, one detects a revulsion toward the reintroduction of submission to powerful individuals (i.e., serfdom). The submission of the individual to the authority of a powerful individual backed by coercive capabilities literally undoes the most important accomplishment of the commercial society that brought an end to the Middle Ages. As conveyed in Adam Smith's historical narrative of the silent demise of the great allodial lords in Western Europe, the power of the great lords was attacked first through the introduction of feudal laws and institutions to strengthen the hand of the king and moderate the authority of the lords.

While the feudal laws and institutions had minimal success, the market forces of the commercial society led the lords unwittingly to exchange their source of power for luxuries and extravagances:

> But what all the violence of the feudal institutions could never have effected, the silent and insensible operation of foreign commerce and manufactures gradually brought about. These gradually furnished the great proprietors with something for which they could exchange the whole surplus produce of their lands, and which they could consume themselves without sharing it either with tenants or retainers. All for ourselves, and nothing for other people, seems, in every age of the world, to have been the vile maxim of the masters of mankind. As soon, therefore, as they could find a method of consuming the whole value of their rents themselves, they had no disposition to share them with any other persons. For a pair of diamond buckles perhaps, or for something as frivolous and useless, they exchanged the maintenance, or what is the same thing, the price of the maintenance of a thousand men for a year, and with it the whole weight and authority which it could give them. The buckles, however, were to be all their own, and no other human creature was to have any share of them; whereas in the more ancient method of expence they must have shared with at least a thousand people. With the judges that were to determine the preference, this difference was perfectly decisive; and thus, for the gratification of the most childish, the meanest and the most sordid of all vanities, they gradually bartered their whole power and authority.[27]

Equality and Capability Enhancement

Hayek argues that those who would still opt for a planned society despite the psychological burden of submission should not mislead themselves into thinking that the political problem of equitable distribution can be evaded. The central questions in a planned society remain: Who plans for whom? Or, who gets what when, and how?[28]

Although Hayek's argument is less relevant in a postsocialist era, his arguments on equitable redistribution are still pertinent for those who embrace Amartya Sen's "capability-enhancement" approach to economic development and social justice as an alternative to "neoliberalism." Sen's argument is that certain individuals need additional assistance to achieve similar levels of functioning. Although Sen's outlook is oriented toward enabling participation in the marketplace (rather than outcomes), he does not provide clear criteria on who would allocate resources and judge whose life is adequately compensated to facilitate a life the recipient of resources would have reason to value. Sen frequently looks to the state to provide public goods to create equity, but he also indicates that he does not see basic social institutions as an "inalienable right."[29] In essence, the provision of public goods is meant only as a supplement to the amount that can be supplied by the individual. Social institutions are instrumental, not intrinsically valuable; if individuals can supply services for themselves, there is no intrinsic need for public provision. Thus, public benefits should be based on an assessment of a person's "actual functioning" and supplemented with additional information. Notably, however, Sen does not address the surveillance mechanisms needed for a state bureaucracy to overcome its informational deficit.

Because Hayek critiques slogans of "greater equality" as an inadequate guiding principle for planners, he would be leery of the demand for "equity"—even from a careful thinker and fellow Smithian liberal such as Sen. In particular, while Sen increases the complexity of thinking about issues of equality and freedom, he does not address how observing actual functioning (supplemented with additional information) would prevent arbitrary and subjective bureaucratic decision-making in actuality. In other words, Sen's approach does not adequately consider the danger of building a state that is partial and discriminatory. Hayek will seek to ensure a floor of social provision to all citizens without prejudicing the state in the next chapter.

Where Sen and Hayek might wholeheartedly agree, however, is that attempts to eliminate inequality completely may be much more harmful than intended. As Sen writes, "And yet attempts to eradicate inequality can, in many circumstances, lead to loss for most—sometimes even for all."[30] It is also worth remembering that Sen's capability-enhancement approach is not necessarily an endorsement of the welfare state as a mechanism for tackling inequality. In fact, Sen sees merit in the parsimonious American approach relative to the West European welfare state. For Sen, there is dignity in work, and thus European smugness in terms of progress on income inequality masks a deeper problem of higher unemployment.[31]

Conclusion

The chapter grappled with notions of equality and submission to impersonal forces against an older order consisting of hierarchy and submission to embodied (i.e., personal, patriarchal, racial, and social) authority. Echoing Smith, Hayek correctly argues that submission to anonymous market forces promotes freedom, since it liberates the individual from submission to embodied authority. While the individual is not liberated from structural forces or chance, the burden of submitting to the anonymous forces of the market is less burdensome for most. Nevertheless, Hayek missteps by encouraging discriminated-against minorities to take (a fatalistic) solace in their limited freedom rather than championing a strict insistence on the universality of the law and the removal of barriers to equal opportunity to help root out discrimination. Liberalism, which once drew vigor from its role in guiding the abolitionist movement, will need to return to a more strident posture toward discrimination if it is to be revived. If liberty must be limited through institutional checks to be actualized, as Burke and Acton argue, the liberal state cannot go far beyond ensuring equality without ensnaring itself in questions of who will decide, and for whom. Although the degree to which a liberal state can pursue equity (or "capability enhancement") is highly debatable, at the very least formal equality before the law and equality of opportunity (in the negative sense) must be vigorously ensured.

[CHAPTER NINE]

Security and Freedom

The whole of society will have become a single office and a single factory with equality of work and equality of pay.

Nikolai [Vladimir] Lenin (1917)

In a country where the sole employer is the State, opposition means death by slow starvation. The old principle: who does not work shall not eat, has been replaced by a new one: who does not obey shall not eat.

Leon Trotsky (1937)

Hayek's ninth chapter opens with a stunning passage from Lenin's essay "The Economic Basis of the Withering Away of the State," in *The State and Revolution* (1917).[1] The passage requires contextualization. The quote, set only two decades before Trotsky's denunciation of Stalinism and the Soviet Union, dreams of a world in which society would be unified on the model of an office or factory, and substantive equality would overcome the income inequality generated by the market.

Lenin's chapter focused on harmonizing and elaborating the views of Marx and Engels on the prophesied status of the state after a future communist revolution. Lenin contends that, despite arguments that Marx actually envisioned a strong role for the state under communism in distinction to Engels, both men assumed the state would "wither away" after a transition from capitalism to communism. The passage quoted by Hayek occurs in the context of a future armed dictatorship of the vanguard of the proletariat, a period in which the communists would crush the resistance of the capitalists to the revolution, thereby paving the way for the state to wither away gradually and spontaneously. Lenin envisioned, parallel to wresting violent control of the state apparatus, a socialist reorganization of the state in which *all* citizens would take part in public administration. Lenin acknowledges that universal literacy and "training and discipline" of the masses would be prerequisites to the collective administration of the state, but he believes these characteristics had already emerged in the advanced capitalist societies. In essence, Lenin seeks to show how the state

117

would continue to function for a period of time after the overthrow of the capitalists and their bureaucrats.[2]

Although Lenin is brutally Machiavellian in his understanding of how to secure a revolution, his argument indicates a deeply naive and static understanding of a complex and dynamic economy. He believes that the smooth operation of an economy is merely a matter of control over production and distribution and a simple accounting of labor and products. Lenin does admit the need for a separate scientifically trained class of engineers, agronomists, and so on, but he assumes this class will be efficiently and productively subordinated to the will of the armed proletariat—presumably owing to ideological persuasion or the threat of violence, since the Revolution would abolish any skill premium.[3] He believes that all literate and numerate persons will be able to independently supervise, record, and issue receipts to exercise control over the remaining capitalists and "intellectual gentry" who would be converted to employees of the state alongside all other citizens. The system envisioned is one of universalized, general, and constant mutual surveillance by a society composed of citizen-bureaucrats. Notably, Lenin envisioned this generalization of "factory discipline" to society as a whole as merely a transitory stage on the path to a communist utopia.

To be clear, Lenin was not describing a communist "state," but a transitional stage between capitalism and communism. The quoted passage from Lenin is a description of an intentionally designed albeit (apparently) ephemeral totalitarian society. The quote by Trotsky about the state as the sole employer, juxtaposed with Lenin's discussion of society under the dictatorship of the proletariat serves to link the totalitarian society with the socialist state.[4] Undoubtedly, Hayek would argue that the link between a totalitarian society and a socialist state was inevitable over time.

However, Trotsky's quote was meant primarily as a critique of a socialist revolution in an economically backward society; it was not a critique of socialism or communism per se. Trotsky understood that "When there is little goods [sic], the purchasers are compelled to stand in line. When the lines are very long, it is necessary to appoint a policeman to keep order."[5] For Trotsky, the authoritarian pathologies of the Bolshevik Revolution were tied to its economic backwardness and its consequent need to expand the bureaucratic and police apparatus to decide who gets goods and who has to wait. The Soviet state would not wither away, because the bureaucracy had risen above society and given birth to a privileged minority.[6] Trotsky would not have accepted the notion that the Soviet Union was either capitalist or socialist. The Soviet state was a novel regime in which the means of production and the state itself belonged to the bureaucracy.[7]

For Trotsky, a (Marxian) socialist state/society needed genuine democracy and global scope to be acceptable; a centralized economy dominated by SOEs was insufficient to seize the mantle of socialism.[8] The Soviet Union was a weak transitional regime that could either return to capitalism, if the workers were defeated, or progress toward socialism, if the workers succeeded in overthrowing the bureaucratic caste.[9] Stalin's use of increasingly brutal methods to terrorize, purge, and exterminate segments of the population ultimately demonstrated how far the Soviet state was from its promised utopia—and even raised the question of whether the utopia could be realized.

Hayek's insight about the totalitarian tendency of socialism is essentially that the centralization and displacement of market dynamics by the state opens the door for a brutal totalitarian regime. Trotsky would have agreed with Hayek on this point and would additionally emphasize the crucial role of the price mechanism:

> The obedient professors managed to create an entire theory according to which Soviet price, in contrast to market price, has an exclusively planning or directive character. That is, it is not an economic but an administrative category, and thus serves the better for the redistribution of the people's income in the interests of socialism. The professors forgot to explain how you can "guide" a price without knowing the real costs, and how you can estimate real costs if all prices express the will of a bureaucracy and not the amount of socially necessary labor expended.[10]

To this extent, Trotsky offers a direct critique of Lenin's "citizen-bureaucrats" who surveil and keep account: "A rationalization of the economy is unthinkable without accurate accounts. Accounts are irreconcilable with the caprices of a bureaucracy."[11] He understood all too well that prices were markers not merely in the unequal distribution of purchasing power, but also of political power. Prices undergird social relations between segments of society. A change in prices can threaten the stability of the regime if the social relations formed at a particular price point become unglued as prices shift. Market-determined prices and profits also tend to reveal the errors of bureaucratic guidance of the economy. While holding fast to the necessity of a measure of planning (i.e., coordination of the basic sectors of the state economy) in socialism, Trotsky was prescient in understanding that market-determined prices constrain the power of the bureaucrat "from below." For Trotsky, the purpose of planning was to adapt the state economy to the peasant market.[12]

In an odd parallel with Trotsky's critique of Lenin and the Soviet Union, Hayek seeks to lay out the costs and benefits of purchasing economic security from the bureaucrat.

∵

Liberty and Security

Hayek argues that above a certain threshold there is a trade-off between security and freedom. Of course, a degree of limited economic security is vital to ensure that each individual develops a proper mental disposition toward freedom. The provision of absolute security, however, may endanger the liberty it is meant to foster by impairing the market mechanism. Thus, a measure of limited security for all is legitimate; the provision of absolute security is warranted only in exceptional cases where absolute independence of thought is paramount (e.g., judges): "There is no reason why in a society which has reached a general level of wealth which ours has attained the first kind of security should not be guaranteed to all without endangering general freedom."[13] In other words, Hayek advocates for a minimum income and social insurance (e.g., national health insurance) for all citizens of a given polity.[14] Such income and insurance is at the very least necessary to "preserve health and the capacity to work."[15] Moreover, the state ought also to assist individuals whose property is devastated by natural disasters. Hayek reasons that few individuals can make adequate provision against the "common hazards of life," such as sickness or accident, and the state's assistance does not generate moral hazard—rational individuals will still seek to avoid calamities and illness.[16]

Hayek even argues for government measures to combat "recurrent waves of large-scale unemployment."[17] While he indicates that an approach to combating unemployment via regulation of the monetary supply is consistent with liberalism, he is not intrinsically opposed to a Keynesian approach reliant on the use of public-works programs on a large scale.

Hayek's humane argument is often surprising to those who hold a caricatured view of economic liberalism and is often either criticized or casually forgotten by American libertarians of a fundamentalist disposition. While the notion of a welfare state is currently associated with the political Left, its historical origins actually lie on the right of the political spectrum, in Bismarck's Germany. The "Iron Chancellor" believed that the state should "cultivate the view also among the propertyless classes of the population, those who are the most numerous and the least educated, that the state is not only an institution of necessity, but also one of welfare. By recognizable and distinct advantages they must be led to look upon the state not as an agency devised solely for the protection of the better situation classes of society, but also one of welfare."[18] Undoubtedly, the kaiser and his chancellor were motivated more by a fear of political upheaval as industrial capitalism developed in Germany than by any humanitarian instinct. Moreover, it is clear that the provision of welfare reinforced hierarchy and merely displaced the feudal concept of noblesse oblige from the aristocracy to the state. The point, though, is that although the welfare state is treated with hostility and suspicion by conservatives and libertarians in the United States, the provision of welfare by the state is not inherently a creature of the Left. As Eugene Goodheart has argued, "European conservatives distinguish, as American conservatives and libertarians do not, between, on the one hand, establishing a safety net to protect the economically vulnerable and, on the other, egalitarianism."[19] While Hayek was not a European conservative, he too could distinguish between social protection and egalitarianism.

Hayek does not address how the state will pay for a minimum income, although he does suggest at one point that military service might be a plausible exchange for it.[20] The author indicates that a range of policy proposals to provide a minimum income and social insurance is possible, and that different policies might rely to differing degrees on competition or the limitation thereof.

While the provision of social and unemployment insurance requires planning and state bureaucracy, it need not require a level of planning that seeks to supplant the market.[21] Hayek is cautious, however, and warns against governmental policies whose volume and direction might increase the individual's dependency on the state.

Liberty versus Security

To move beyond a minimal level of social insurance and minimum income and prevent diminutions in income, however, introduces "insidious" effects on liberty.[22] Many societies, including the United States, have enacted agreements to create "embedded liberal" markets and generate social stability by limiting competition, particularly in sunset industries.[23] For Hayek, protection against diminutions in income in a competitive economy cannot be offered to all without eliminating the freedom to choose one's employment, since aggregate changes in employment will generate losses of output in various sectors and imbalance the economy. If pecuniary incentives and penalties are taken away, then only ideology—or coercion—will remain to motivate workers and adjust output. Moreover, if remuneration is a mechanism through which the market communicates the value of an individual's contribution to the collective, attempting to distort the market signals will corrupt the signaling mechanism and increase inefficiencies in the market. Protecting only a subset of jobs that are uncompetitive will create perverse incentives and provide security to some (e.g., union workers) at the expense of all others (e.g., day laborers or seasonal farmworkers).[24]

Hayek's point is to emphasize the ways in which the extended order of the market operates through anonymous incentives and penalties. And while the penalties, such as a reduction in real wages or unemployment, can be devastating, he is arguing that the anonymous order is much less coercive than its alternative. Even in a planned economy (or a corporation, for that matter, although Hayek does not make that point here), where a worker is not responsible for the risk or a recipient for the gain of their actions, the worker can only be responsible for following established rules and pleasing superiors. In essence, economic security in a planned economy (or even a private corporation to an extent) is purchased through servility.

The essential point for Hayek is that in a commercial society, the choice and risk rest with the individual. For Hayek, the alternative ideal type is the military society, in which the individual is relieved of both choice and risk.[25] Hayek is not criticizing the military life; he believes the security of the barracks is tolerable so long as individuals have the option to return to a competitive market if life in the military becomes too irksome.[26]

Hayek's fear is that the provision of security for certain sectors of the job market creates the incentive for a free people to value security more highly than their liberty. Any regulation of competition through barriers to market entry or limits on output substitutes the regular variability in wages, prices, and income for rather violent fluctuations in employment and production.[27] The only way to sustain such a volatile order, then, is to disparage risk-taking and elevate the status of secure, salaried employment through the use of state-sponsored propaganda.

Conclusion

To return to the chapter's epigraph and fuse Hayek and Trotsky temporarily, what is lost in the purchase of absolute security from the state is the power of the market to constrain the bureaucrat "from below." The distortion of the price signals through guaranteed employment and security facilitates the arbitrary discretion of the bureaucratic planner. Moreover, the provision of absolute economic security may foster a culture of servility among a formerly free people, which is Hayek's underlying fear for postwar Great Britain in *The Road to Serfdom*.

Lenin ingeniously aimed to displace the power of the state bureaucracy in transitioning to communism by transforming every citizen into a bureaucrat. Of course, his solution would only have opened the door wider to a totalitarian state of mutual surveillance and coercion. A decade after Lenin's theorizing, Trotsky was able to decipher that the bureaucracy had completely engulfed the Soviet state. However, Trotsky surmised that this was mainly a product of Russia's economic backwardness and clung to the hope that a socialist revolution in an advanced society would avoid a similar fate. Of course, a socialist revolution did not occur in any advanced industrial economy, and even in Eastern Europe the economic performance of socialist countries at any (initial) income level was worse than that of the capitalist countries of Western Europe from 1950 to 1989.[28] Thus, Trotsky's hope for building a genuinely democratic socialist state in the context of economic plenty was rendered futile.

Hayek argues for a moderate position in balancing liberty and security. While a basic minimum of security ought to be provided by a humane and civilized state, there is no alternative but for the individual to accept the marginal risks and insecurity that come from functioning with freedom in the marketplace. Thus, Hayek seeks to cultivate stoicism and resilience with respect to the anonymous forces of the marketplace in the liberal individual. Liberals ought to emphasize these core values as they build a more humane society.

CHAPTER TEN

Why the Worst Get on Top

Power tends to corrupt, and absolute power corrupts absolutely.

Lord Acton (1887)

In his letter to Mandell Creighton (April 5, 1887), written after he had penned his famous maxim quoted in the epigraph, Acton added: "Great men are almost always bad men; even when they exercise influence and not authority: still more when you superadd the tendency or the certainty of corruption by authority. There is no worse heresy than that the office sanctifies the holder of it."[1] Hayek's epigraph invites us to consider the relationship between one's structural position and one's morality. This chapter concerns the question of why certain types of individuals come to dominate in totalitarian societies.

Acton's complex critique of absolutism, whether monarchical, aristocratic, or democratic, resonated with Hayek. Specifically, Acton's discussion of the acquisition of absolute power under the first Roman emperor, Caesar Augustus (27 BCE–14 CE), the adopted son of Julius Caesar, provides a useful lens through which to critique the emergences of absolutist-populist regimes across the political spectrum.

Augustus assumed the office of (plebeian) tribune, ordinarily a sacrosanct, annually elected position, that was empowered to check and even veto the power of the Roman Senate on behalf of the common people. As Lazarski notes, "The emperor as a tribune enjoyed inviolability and embodied the sovereignty of the Roman people."[2] According to Acton, it was the Roman people who transferred their sovereignty and absolute power to the emperor in order to end bloodshed and secure prosperity:

> Thrice the senate proposed to Augustus the supreme power of making laws. He declared that the power of the tribunes already supplied him with all that was required. It enabled him to preserve the forms of a simulated republic. The most popular of all the magistracies of Rome furnished the marrow of Imperialism. For the Empire was created, not by usurpation, but by the legal act of a jubilant people eager to close the

era of bloodshed and to secure the largess of grain and coin. . . . The people transferred to the Emperor the plenitude of their own sovereignty. To limit his delegated power was to challenge their omnipotence, to renew the issue between the many and the few which had been decided at Pharsalus and Philippi. The Romans upheld the absolutism of the Empire because it was their own.[3]

The transfer of absolute power nullified any protection of minorities: "The elementary antagonism between liberty and democracy, between the welfare of minorities and the supremacy of masses, became manifest. The friend of one was a traitor to the other."[4] Acton adds, "The dogma that absolute power may, by the hypothesis of a popular origins, be as legitimate as constitutional freedom, began, by the combined support of the people and the throne, to darken the air."[5] For Hayek, it is this final delusion, the attempt to mask and absolve absolute power by hypothesizing its popular origins and destination, that marks the collectivist enterprise: ". . . the desire to organize social life according to a unitary plan itself springs largely from a desire for power."[6] Whereas power, particularly concentrated power, is the enemy of liberal philosophy, the appropriation, centralization, and refinement of power is a necessity for collectivists. Hayek states that ". . . in order to achieve their end, collectivists must create power—power over men wielded by other men—of a magnitude never before known, and that their success will depend on the extent to which they achieve such power."[7] Collectivists delude themselves into believing that transferring power from private individuals to society, rather than a Hobbesian Leviathan, for instance, somehow extinguishes the exercise of power: ". . . many liberal socialists are guided in their endeavors by the tragic illusion that by depriving private individuals of the power they possess in an individualist system, and by transferring this power to society, they can thereby extinguish power." For Hayek, the problem is that concentrating power for use in a single plan results in "infinitely heightened" power. Hyperbole aside, what Hayek means here is that the concentration of power in the hands of a planning board creates a degree or intensity of power that is far greater than the sum of its parts.[8] Hayek rejects as a false equivalence the notion that the power of a socialist planning board is merely the equivalent of the sum of the power of all the private boards of directors of corporations. In a competitive economy, boards of directors cannot logically collude and combine powers, for if they do it is not a competitive system. In any case, Hayek argues that economic power is distinct from political power. The former is always limited in a competitive system, even though it may be used coercively; the latter may create a degree of dependence that is indistinguishable from slavery. For liberals, maintaining a separation between economic and political power is fundamental to the preservation of freedom; for collectivists, substituting political for economic power is viewed as central to the provision of social justice and fusing political and economic power is necessary for social planning.

In essence, then, centralized planning confers absolute power on the planners.

∵

Hayek seeks to dispel the notion that a benign form of totalitarianism is possible. His argument is structural and institutional. In other words, the totalitarian regimes in Germany and Russia did not arise from the moral depravity of individual Nazis or Stalinists per se; rather, the rise of unscrupulous individuals to leadership positions in a totalitarian party is an inevitable consequence of the party's system of incentives and punishments. While culture, individual morality, and personal ideals might retard the immediate transition to totalitarianism in some countries that undergo fascist or communist transitions, in the long run the default outcome is, sooner or later, inevitable. In other words, actors have agency, but the structural incentives and constraints ultimately shape outcomes. The reason for this fate is that totalitarian parties do not seek to create a new social contract on which all can agree, but rather coercively impose the views of a plurality or minority on the rest of society.[9] In such a context, populism and demagoguery will triumph over ordinary morality, refined tastes, and intellectual prowess if the totalitarian party is strong enough to coerce the majority of society. Even if the aspiring dictator has benign intentions, ". . . the totalitarian dictator would soon have to choose between disregard of ordinary morals and failure."[10] The totalitarian party's internal incentive structure rewards those who are less scrupulous about disregarding ordinary morals.

The moral-relativist response to Hayek's assertions is to argue that immoral and unscrupulous politicians are common in all regime types. However, Hayek states that the ". . . whole moral atmosphere under collectivism" is utterly different from "individualist Western civilization."[11] To a detached reader, the argument appears reasonably plausible, as it is difficult to think of counterexamples to match the level of moral depravity and mechanical slaughter of citizens one commonly finds in totalitarian regimes. However, one need not confine Hayek's alternative to "individualist Western Civilization."

Hayek's brilliant maneuver here is switching from discussions of the "moral necessity" for a collectivist solution (i.e., the "moral framework" that individuals would need to possess to make a collectivist regime succeed) toward an examination of the moral results of collectivist regimes.[12] In one fell swoop, Hayek dethrones the pretentious moral superiority of collectivism and shifts the debate. Hayek's logic is, unsurprisingly, reliant on an inversion of Adam Smith's invisible hand: high-minded moral aspirations generate a system that rewards the least moral.

The Incentive Structure

The incentive structure in a totalitarian party (and regime) ultimately stems from impatience at the pace of political and economic change. Writes Hayek, ". . . the general demand for quick and determined government action is the dominating element in the situation, dissatisfaction with the slow and cumbersome course of democratic procedure that makes action for action's sake the goal."[13] The demand for decisive action generates a two-pronged response: (1) the emergence of a "strongman" who takes decisive action for its own sake, and (2) the emergence of a new type of party, "organized on military lines."

The militarily organized political party seeks first to dominate the private life of its members. The party transforms and mediates even intimate private relations. For example, the term "friend" is dropped in favor of "comrade"; basic greetings and salutations are inflected with political gestures and overtones. The effort to infect civil society with overtly politicized discourse and symbols runs parallel to the voluntary subordination of the party faithful to the whims of the strongman. (And although Hayek does not say it, the strongman will necessarily make irrational demands upon the party faithful, since his objective is to test their loyalty.) The voluntary subordination of the party faithful precedes the forceful imposition of a totalitarian will on the rest of society.

Hayek argues that the old socialists were reluctant to use force to impose their will on the masses because of their democratic ideals, a trait that the national socialists and revolutionary communists were more than willing to discard. The failure of the old-guard socialists was primarily a function of their inability to understand that, aside from the free market, coordination of contending interests in a mass society is difficult to achieve on a voluntary basis. Moral suasion is insufficient to persuade the majority to act against their self-interest; ethical and principled socialists are doomed to fail. In any case, the unwillingness of the old socialists to meet the structural imperatives consigned them to impotence and irrelevance in the political system.

Hayek specifies that the worst personalities rise to the top of totalitarian parties and regimes for three reasons: (1) a plurality, characterized by low moral and intellectual standards, willing to accept the imposition of a uniform hierarchy of values; (2) the gullibility and excitability of the masses, which rewards demagogues, who can direct their passions; and (3) the ease with which negative and destructive political agendas can unite the masses compared to positive and constructive programs, which incentivizes those who foment hatred and destruction over those who seek harmony and constructive policy solutions to problems.

First, Hayek assumes that higher levels of education and intelligence correspond to a wider differentiation and refinement of tastes and values, and therefore a greater resistance to the imposition of a hierarchy of values. Conversely, those with lower education and intelligence will have greater ability to agree on a hierarchy of values. Hayek says that the largest groups in society that share a common view are those with "lower moral and intellectual standards" and in those areas where "primitive and 'common' instincts and tastes prevail." This plurality forms the base of the totalitarian party. He is not necessarily arguing that the ordinary folk are immoral or "deplorable"; rather, he is saying the groups with lower moral and intellectual standards will be numerically larger than groups with higher standards.[14] This part of Hayek's argument is not persuasive, and despite Hayek's qualifications, it still reads as elitist because the dichotomous metaphorical language (e.g., "high" and "low" standards) he uses is so loaded. There is no logical reason, for example, that a plurality could not subscribe to a simple worldview characterized by decency and a regard for individual autonomy. Similarly, a plurality could also have relatively high moral standards, regardless of the mean level of education or intelligence of the group, depending perhaps on the role of religion, culture, political and economic stability in a society. The imposition of a hierarchy of values on a plurality with high moral standards (e.g., by a church) but modest intelligence need not be linked to totalitarianism per se. In any case, Hayek fails to explain why the low standards of the masses incentivize the "worst" to rise to leadership positions within the party. He may have simply assumed that those with low moral and intellectual standards seek a leader whose personal values is no higher than their own. Or, as Max Weber stated in his lecture "Politics as a Vocation" (1918), "When American workers were asked why they allowed themselves to be governed by politicians whom they admitted they despised, the answer was: 'We prefer having people in office whom we can spit upon, rather than a caste of officials who spit upon us.'"[15]

Second, Hayek argues that because a large segment of the population is "docile and gullible," a demagogue would easily be able to gain the support of those who have no strong convictions but are prepared to accept a "ready-made system of values." This group will expand the ranks of the totalitarian party. The idea that a demagogue with sufficient media access could arouse the passions of otherwise politically neutral individuals to swell the ranks of a totalitarian party is certainly plausible. If Hayek's assessment about the general characteristics of the masses is correct, then this fact would clearly incentivize demagogic leaders to rise to positions of prominence.

Third, Hayek argues that it is easier for individuals to agree on a negative or destructive political program (e.g., hatred, envy) than on a positive or constructive political program. The fundamental political distinction between "us" and "them" is thus useful for ruthless leaders who are willing to bind a group together with unreserved allegiance at the expense of internal scapegoats and external enemies. Here Hayek draws a parallel between the anti-Semitism of Nazi Germany and the anti-kulak sentiment of the Soviet Union. The argument is persuasive for the two examples given, but it could be noted that Italian fascism did not originally have a strong anti-Semitic component.

Each of these three permissive conditions would be more persuasive if Hayek had simply argued that they expand when a society is subjected to an economic or political shock.

From Universal to Particular

Hayek makes a keen insight by noting the ways in which collectivism, even socialism, reinforces national borders, racialism, and classism.[16] Hayek argues that collectivism requires particularism, because as the group expands in membership, the particularistic trait (whether race, class, or nationality) is vital to retaining a common identity.

Hayek notes that collectivism on a world scale is generally unimaginable. Using the example of British India, Hayek argues that socialism, which imagines distributional equality, would falter if that equality were applied beyond national borders:

> If the English proletariat, for instance, is entitled to an equal share of the income now derived from his country's capital resources, and of the control of their use, because they are the result of exploitation, so on the same principle all the Indians would be entitled not only to the income from but also to the use of a proportional share of the British capital.

But what socialists seriously contemplate the equal division of existing capital resources among the people of the world? They all regard the capital as belonging not to humanity but to the nation—though even within the nation few would dare to advocate that the richer regions should be deprived of some of "their" capital equipment in order to help the poorer regions. What socialists proclaim as a duty toward the fellow-members of the existing states they are not prepared to grant to the foreigner.[17]

Those in the United States, the European Union, and Japan who support the demand for a more equitable distribution of wealth in their own society do not seem to realize that the same demand on a global scale would imply a dramatic reduction in their own income and standard of living, given the fact that almost all Europeans, Americans, and Japanese, including much of the lower class in these areas, occupy the upper decile of global income distribution. It is much easier to direct the anger of the masses at the top 1 percent of income earners in their own society than to demand that the masses themselves surrender a significant share of their own income to assist the global poor.

Twisting the knife further, Hayek adds that ". . . socialism so long as it remains theoretical is internationalist, while as soon as it is put into practice, whether in Russia or in Germany, it becomes violently nationalist. . . ."[18] The important point here is that the false distinction that socialists assert between their pristine theoretical vision and the actual socialist states that have mutated into totalitarian monstrosities is not an aberration. Hayek believes that the humanistic morals on which socialism is based are practicable only in small groups. It is not surprising that socialism immediately retreats from broad humanitarianism to the "narrow particularism of totalitarianism" (nation, race, or class).

In the footnotes, Hayek quotes a passage from Friedrich Nietzsche's *Thus Spake Zarathustra* as illustrative of the collectivist mentality. In "On the Thousand and One Goals," Zarathustra says, "A thousand goals have existed hitherto, for a thousand people existed. But the fetter for the thousand necks is still lacking, the one goal is still lacking. Humanity has no goal yet. But tell me, I pray, my brethren: if the goal be lacking to humanity, is not humanity itself lacking?"[19] The point is, of course, that the collectivist sees the failure to yoke humanity to one goal not as a failure of the task, but as a shortcoming of humanity, in that it has not prepared itself for enslavement. Thus, it is not surprising that collectivists often argue that the failure of actual socialism to correspond to the broad humanitarianism of theoretical socialism is the fault of the leadership or the society on which the experiment was conducted, not the inherent contradiction between the vision and practical implementation.

Another factor pushing collectivism toward particularism is individual psychology. Relying on the work of the American theologian Reinhold Niebuhr, Hayek argues that individuals join groups only if doing so confers a sense of superiority over others. The collective permits individuals to indulge violent instincts that they would ordinarily seek to curb. Groups become the repository of vices that the morally restrained individual would ordinarily find repugnant. In reality, it is through the act of delegating vice to larger and larger collectives that individuals come to see themselves as moral.

Finally, Hayek argues that collectivist planning is antagonistic toward internationalism—that is, the free flow of goods, capital, and ideas across borders—because these flows efface the ability to plan. Not only is socialism linked to nationalism in practice, but Hayek cites Halévy's observation that even Fabian socialists such as Sidney Webb, Beatrice Webb, and George Bernard Shaw (three of the four cofounders of the London School of Economics) were "ostentatiously imperialist." Hayek notes that even Marx and Engels held smaller nations, such as Poland, in contempt.[20]

Collectivist Ethics

Hayek argues that collectivist ethics flow from (1) the necessity for common goals and (2) the desire to confer maximal power on the group (i.e., the party) to implement those goals. By contrast, individualist ethics flow from (1) the desire to leave the individual's conscience as free as possible to apply their own rules and (2) a set of general rules that the individual is required or permitted to observe in all circumstances.[21] Individualism prescribes or prohibits certain actions regardless of context. Collectivism prioritizes the group's goals regardless of the means. Although Hayek is juxtaposing two Weberian "ideal types" to accentuate fundamental differences that are unlikely to correspond to the messiness of reality, it is clear that collectivist and individualist ethics develop from radically different starting points.

Hayek sees collectivist ethics as a residual artifact of the morality of hunter-gatherer bands brought into the contemporary era.[22] This is not to argue that a collectivist ethics is to be uniformly despised. For example, Hayek notes the generalizations commonly associated with Prussians, the epitome of a collectivist society: industriousness, self-discipline, conscientiousness, orderliness, fidelity to duty, obedience, and courage in the face of physical danger. Hayek concedes that these are "useful" characteristics. At the same time, a collectivist society is deficient in those qualities that allow a free society to function.[23] Hayek's counterintuitive point is to argue that individualist ethics are social virtues.

An individualistic ethic "makes control from above less necessary and at the same time more difficult." In other words, an individualist ethic promotes the kind of personality that permits the development of strong bonds between free individuals and a healthy distrust of centralized authority. While Adam Smith's commercial society is ultimately based on mutual ocular surveillance, which serves as an incubator for the emergence of a conscience, Hayek's commercial society is based upon and reinforces the traits of kindliness, humor, modesty, tolerance, respect for privacy, and a belief in the good intentions of one's neighbor.[24] These virtues flourish where an individualist or commercial society prevails; and an individualist or commercial society flourishes where these virtues prevail.

By contrast, a collectivist ethic is ultimately destructive of the social fabric. Hayek argues that when the ends justify the means, there are no moral restraints on individual behavior. The totalitarian party/state has no use for individuals whose morality is anchored beyond the confines of the party. The worst get on top in totalitarian regimes because there is nothing in such regimes to satisfy the idealistic desires of principled individuals. As Hayek states, "The only tastes which are satisfied are the taste for power as such and the pleasure of being obeyed and of being part of a well-functioning and immensely powerful machine to which everything else must give way."[25] All of the incentives are for those who are morally unconstrained.

The Ethics of Political Capitalism

How does one apply Hayek's contrast between collectivism and individualism in contemporary societies that are simultaneously collectivist and capitalist? Perhaps a clue to how Hayek would answer this question rests in his understanding of Prusso-German culture. Although Hayek, writing in the midst of World War II, lists the collectivist qualities or stereotypes commonly associated with "typical Prussians," he also presents a more complex portrait of German culture: "Until recently, at least, in those parts of Germany which have been longest exposed to the civilizing forces of commerce, the old commercial towns of the south and west and the Hanse towns, the general moral concepts were probably much more akin to those of the Western people than to those which have now become dominant all over Germany."[26] One must assume, therefore, that political-capitalist societies ought to be internally differentiated regardless of the overarching presence of an authoritarian state that propounds a collectivist ethos.

In contemporary China, for example, anecdotal evidence and empirical research confirm that there is internal differentiation—or, at the very least, that there is a wide gulf between the culture of the financial capital, Shanghai, and that of the political capital, Beijing.[27] Weigang Gong, Meng Zhu, Burak Gürel, and Tian Xie find that there are also significant regional and county-level variations in the distribution of individualism/collectivism indicators, conceptualized as a continuum. They attribute these variations to the strength of lineage organizations in various provinces and (to a much lesser extent) rice theory, which posits that the cooperative needs of rice farming cultivate a collectivist ethos in areas where that crop is predominant.[28] Consequently, these legacies shape the willingness to accommodate or resist the emergence of a more individualist ethos since China's liberalization.

Steele and Lynch would add that the strategic movement from Maoist collectivism to the increasing accommodation of individualism since liberalization has also precipitated a shift in the ruling party's ideology. The Chinese Communist Party has recast itself from the vanguard of socialism to the defender of national pride since at least the Tiananmen Square Massacre.[29] While nationalism remains a collectivist ideology, the shift permits greater scope for a commercial society. Steele and Lynch's analysis of the World Values Survey, conducted in China since 1990, indicates that individualist factors have become more important over time in predicting conceptions of subjective well-being relative to collectivist factors, which have become less important over time.[30] Long, Parnell, and Dent note differentiation even at the level of the firm. Managers of SOEs, which are more dependent than other businesses on access to government financing, retain a traditional emphasis on collectivist traits and Marxist philosophy, while managers at private firms pursue a hybrid approach emphasizing both collective and individualist virtues.[31] Qiu Cheng and Kinglun Ngok, while noting provincial level and rural/urban-floating/urban–level variations, also find differentiation at the level of individual Chinese citizens, with consequent impacts on attitudes toward the state's antipoverty policies. Those who are motivated by economic individualism tend to be more satisfied with the efficiency of state antipoverty policies.[32]

In Vietnam, researchers still find a strong collectivist and Confucian culture, particularly among women. However, values associated with globalization (e.g., individualism and personal freedom) have begun to influence Vietnamese attitudes and behaviors.[33] This is most observable at the family level, with increasing nuclearization (with an average family size of 3.4)

134 ‹ CHAPTER TEN

and individualization in mate selection, although in the (less commercial) northern provinces there is still a particularly strong preference for male children. Divorce rates have also increased nationwide since economic liberalization, particularly in urban areas.[34]

As a pluralist society composed of three major ethnic groups (Chinese, Malay, and Indian) who mainly migrated to the city-state, Singaporean diversity is foundational for the state's management of social relations.[35] Although the state seeks to naturalize a collectivist cultural ethos under the banner of "Asian values," the state is also vested in reifying cultural distinctions that legitimate state management of relations between communities. Moreover, the ruling party's efforts to promote "Asian values" and "communitarianism" as counters to a seemingly decadent, Western, liberal individualism are internally contradicted by the ruling party's simultaneous emphasis on individualistic self-reliance and meritocracy as explanations for economic inequality.[36] Unlike totalitarian regimes, which seek to sever any morality that lies beyond the control of the party, the Singaporean state pivots between collectivism and individualism as needed, and despite seeming contradictions.

Conclusion

In sum, Hayek's differentiation between individualist and collectivist ethics as a basis for understanding alternative values that either support or resist a commercial society and a liberal state is still valid. Under a political-capitalist regime, however, there can be significant variation in the presence of individualist ethics. Individualist ethics are essential in cultivating stoicism and resilience toward market forces. At the same time, however, with greater access to foreign cultures, political-capitalist regimes are less able to shape the ethics of their societies. Political-capitalist regimes must constantly pivot between collectivism and individualism to legitimate the regime despite expanding internal contradictions. A revived liberalism will increase these contradictions by restoring the prestige attached to individualism as an essential component of a great civilization.

[CHAPTER ELEVEN]

The End of Truth

It is significant that the nationalization of thought has proceeded everywhere
pari passu with the nationalization of industry.

E. H. Carr (1939)

Edward Hallett Carr argued that along with military and economic power,
propaganda is a necessary instrument of the modern state and a natural
corollary of the expansion of the franchise.[1] By "propaganda" Carr meant
both the organization of domestic opinion and the targeted effort to influence public opinion in foreign countries. Citing Hitler's *Mein Kampf*, Carr
also distinguished between the intelligentsia's "scientific exposition" and
propaganda that targets the masses.[2] He argued that with larger numbers
of individuals whose opinions matter politically, the modern state must use
propaganda to reinforce the regime's legitimacy, rationalize foreign policy,
and generally direct the thought of its citizens. As an instrument of foreign
policy, propaganda could be used to demoralize enemy forces and delegitimize foreign regime types, or merely to promote an understanding of the
initiating regime's outlook. He states that the concentration of economic
power in the nineteenth century revealed the illusory liberal conception of
political freedom. His argument is that the prejudice against a state's use of
propaganda to organize domestic opinion is as anachronistic as the prejudice against the state control of industry and trade.[3] As an illiberal, a collectivist, and a realist, Carr has no tolerance for the notion that individuals
should be free to express their opinions. Carr argues that opinion is merely
the product of subjection to innumerable forms of propaganda. Even in
democracies, Carr believes, centralized control of opinion by the state is
inevitable, because large corporations have little choice but to cooperate
with the state.[4] Moreover, as democratic states compete with totalitarian regimes, the failure to control and organize opinion places states at a
disadvantage.[5]

Carr is thus exemplary of a cynical worldview that viewed the state's
centralized deployment of propaganda to direct opinion domestically
and abroad as necessary and morally unproblematic in modern societies.[6]

While Hayek agrees that centrally planned societies require the dissemination of propaganda, he views this development as highly problematic from
a moral perspective.

∴

Hayek's Theory of Propaganda

Hayek outlines the ways in which propaganda and dogmatic indoctrination are necessary elements of a comprehensively planned society, since
full agreement on values in a large social order is not possible.

The use of propaganda not only reduces the necessity of physical coercion but brings the goals of the citizen into complete conformance with
those of the state. The effect, when the state holds a monopoly on the
means of communication, is less awareness by the subjects of a totalitarian
regime of their own oppression. Obviously, the use of propaganda is not
confined to totalitarian regimes, but in a liberal polity the instruments of
propaganda are unmonopolized and uncoordinated by the state. Thus, the
magnitude and intensity of propaganda in a totalitarian country is much
greater than elsewhere, since individuals in a totalitarian state are isolated
from alternative sources of information.

Hayek's main concern with the use of propaganda in a totalitarian society is its destruction of the "sense of truth" and the consequent impact on
all morals in that society. The erosion of truth occurs because propaganda
cannot confine itself to discussing ultimate values; it must extend to questions of "facts," since the state needs to justify the relationship between
public policies and outcomes that support particular ultimate values. In
order to link means and ends, the totalitarian state must create agreement
about the facts on which particular policies are based. Moreover, the planner needs to rationalize the often arbitrary decisions made by bureaucrats
implementing public policies in a manner that appeals to the masses. Rationalization proceeds by constructing theories, that is, "assertions about
the connection between facts."[7]

The pseudoscientific theories (or what Hayek also calls "myths") on
which public policy in collectivist societies rest are often merely the product of instinctive prejudice. For example, Hayek cites Oswald Spengler's
pseudoscientific theory of "blood and soil," which argued that a proper
state consists of a people of a uniform race occupying their own land. This
spurious theory, which derived from an irrational prejudice against Jews,

served to undergird the Nazi regime's hereditary farm laws, which permitted the state to seize land from "non-Germans."[8] The totalitarian state develops these myths into a series of beliefs about cause and effect and ideals expressing ultimate values. In this case, it was assumed that a homogeneous peasantry would supply the "racially pure" bloodlines for the German *Volk*. Facts that challenge or fail to support either the theories or the ultimate values must be discarded.

Hayek argues that popular acceptance of new ultimate values proceeds by using the same terminology as the old values to which the masses adhered loyally but modifying the meaning of the words. Thus, for example, collectivists insist that their ideas will also deliver "liberty" and "freedom," but their approach will ensure "collective freedom." Hayek offers a backhanded compliment to his colleague and rival Karl Mannheim for at least being honest enough to state that the old liberal conception of freedom is an obstacle to the collectivist.[9] Hayek correctly identifies the danger that stems from the despoliation of language.[10] Communication and hence political life become impossible when words come to mean their opposites.

Ultimately and unsurprisingly, intimidation and coercion are used against those who remain skeptical of either the means or the ends of the state. The government fears the spread of doubt about the state's ultimate ends. The result is that a whole apparatus must be erected to spread knowledge and filter out information that might cause doubt. The criteria for including or excluding information is its probable impact on morale rather than truth or falsehood. Eventually, even the pretense of searching for truth is abandoned. Not only is truth sacrificed, but absurdities multiply, and an intense dislike of abstract thought and art emerges because these are not easily classifiable. Thus, one learns from the totalitarian regimes that Einstein's theory of relativity was simultaneously labeled a Semitic assault on Nazi science in Germany and in conflict with Marxist dogma in the Soviet Union.[11] All activity must ultimately be subsumed by and for the state apparatus; activities and thought may not proceed for their own sake. The object of fear is spontaneity. Any new and original thought potentially threatens the planner and the ultimate values of the state and the community.

Hayek acknowledges that the tendency toward the subversion of truth is present in pockets of liberal society, particularly in communities with a "collectivist faith" threatened by the advance of science. Paradoxically, the imposition of values and the suppression of truth are often cynically justified by the claim that there is no real freedom of thought in society anymore in any case. Thought is allegedly already manipulated by the ruling class, for example. Thus, the effort to control the direction in which thought travels is conceptualized as merely redirecting thinking in a more desirable direction.

Propaganda and Totalitarianism

Hayek's theory of propaganda is oversimplified; one is left with the impression that totalitarian regimes subvert and reject science altogether in favor of political dogma and pseudoscientific theories or myths. While elements of his theory are correct, the historical record of totalitarian regimes paints a more complex picture. The semblance of scientific debate was utilized by totalitarian regimes, even under Stalin's reign of terror, to enhance the ruler's personal legitimacy. Under Hitler's regime, basic science research continued, and technological research advanced the lethality of the state's war fighting capabilities as well as the militarized state's autarchic ambitions. Moreover, the frontiers of scientific, technological, and medical research all expanded as basic ethical and humanitarian standards were reformulated.[12]

STALINIST SCIENCE

In the Soviet Union, only a year into the Great Purge (1936–38), in which nearly a million individuals were executed, Joseph Stalin instigated a debate on the political economy of socialism that would be active from 1941 until his death in 1952. The dictator insisted on an open, pluralist, and non-dogmatic debate, in part to elevate his own status to that of a true Marxist intellectual on a par with Marx, Engels, and Lenin and in part to distract from his (arbitrary and tyrannical) economic policies. Notably, Stalin appealed to the "scientific laws" of socialism in orchestrating the debate, which was initially confined to eleven participants but eventually included almost all of the Soviet intelligentsia.[13] Of course, the ritualized debate was carried out in a climate of generalized terror. Participants would have been aware of the terrible fates of Nikolai Bukharin and Leon Trotsky when they dared to oppose Stalin's policies,[14] as well as earlier purges of the "old intelligentsia" in 1928–30.[15] Those who adopted critical positions in Stalin's political-economy debate were strategically excluded. For example, Nikolai Voznesensky, the director of the state planning committee, was tried for treason in a secret trial and executed in 1949; the economist L. D. Yaroshenko was imprisoned in Siberia for several months in 1952 but released after Stalin's death.

While no intellectual credibility accrued to participants in the debate, it was evident that the totalitarian state could use economic debate to legitimize the head of state. Given the general atmosphere of terror in the USSR, most participants hesitated to develop their initial positions in the debate or even attempt to apply party doctrine to their discipline without clear, personally delivered signals from the dictator. The inevitable stalemate gave Stalin the opportunity to "settle" the intellectual battle at the Party Congress, as if he were the most accomplished academic. Stalin's appeal to reject Marxist-Leninist dogma was also productive in creating space for economists to attempt to rationalize his arbitrary economic policies.[16] Far from rejecting science, Stalin's "scientificity" about the laws of economics was useful for excusing the current failure of economic policies and pointing toward a prosperous and harmonious future.[17] (As a side note, Hayek would likely have been aware of the contents of these "debates," as the *American Economic Review* published a translation of the first debate in 1944 and a shorter version even appeared in the *New York Times*.[18])

Of course, the Soviet regime's use of academics was not restricted to economists.[19] Naturally, the regime favored "middle of the road" scientists who would simply carry out the tasks assigned to them.[20] At the same time, however, scientists and academics were not merely the passive victims of an exploitative totalitarian state. For example, Soviet geographers saw the announcement of the Stalin Plan (1948–53), an ambitious plan to increase and stabilize harvests in the forest-steppe region of the USSR that neighbored Europe, as an opportunity to enhance the prestige and usefulness of their science alongside that of agronomists, foresters, botanists, geologists, soil scientists, meteorologists, hydrological engineers, and so on.[21] The Soviet state, despite its penchant for politicide and cult of personality, did fund scientific research, particularly after World War II. In the fourth Five-Year Plan, for example, funding for research institutes increased by almost a third.[22] Moreover, much like the Nazi regime's activities in the concentration camps, the Stalinist state conducted medical research on prisoners in laboratories throughout the five hundred labor camps and colonies of the Gulag system. Unlike the Nazi doctors, however, many of the Soviet medical researchers and scientists were themselves prisoners.[23]

Nevertheless, even with funding increases after the war, the late-Stalinist period was marked by repeated waves of purges, including those of academics and scientists, as well as ideological attacks on core ideas in mathematics, physics, chemistry, biology, physiology, and medicine. New archival research has revealed, however, that many of these purges and ideological battles were triggered by professional jealousies, institutional rivalries, and academic politics among the academics themselves.[24] In other words, the totalitarian state intervened in academic debates at the request of academic factions rather than merely repressing intellectuals to curry favor with the masses.

NAZI SCIENCE

In Nazi Germany, research institutes smoothly transitioned their work, processes, and personnel from the preceding Weimar Republic. Scientists apparently exhibited "moral indifference" to cooperation with Nazi policies and military agencies as well as a lack of solidarity with dismissed Jewish colleagues.[25] Of course, in some cases the scientists might have been unaware of the ways in which the military violated ethical standards to test new products (e.g., the use of 170 concentration-camp prisoners to test the durability of synthetic leather shoes).[26] In other cases, the immoral complicity of scientists is undeniable (e.g., the Dachau hypothermia experiments).[27] Regardless, German society did not simply succumb to the subversion of scientific truth by the regime; science and knowledge production did not come to a halt under the totalitarian state. Even in the humanities, intellectuals contributed to the rationalization of Nazi policies and laid the groundwork for genocide.[28] It is not the case that only a few scientists and scholars collaborated or were tricked into working with the regime; the Nazi regime promoted the humanities, social sciences, and physical sciences.

The regime sought to portray to the German public that its policies were grounded in evidentiary science and not merely pseudoscientific theories or myths. For example, the state's pursuit of scientifically informed public policies against smoking (i.e., lung cancer epidemiology), occupational carcinogens (e.g., asbestos), nutrition, and environmental protection was years ahead of other countries.[29] Antismoking research, which was personally funded by Hitler, was an extension of Nazi ideals of bodily purity and racial hygiene.[30] Thus, far from being repressive of science, the Nazi regime saw itself as a "hygienic state" or a manifestation of "applied biology": the state promised to remove a range of "pollutants" from the Aryan body and the body politic.[31]

The once-dominant postwar image of Nazi "organizational incompetence" in terms of science research and policies is belied by the number of innovations across many fields that resulted and the vigorous recruitment of German scientists by the Allied powers after the war.[32] Aside from the increasingly integral role of cruelty, a fact common to several countries—including the United States—during and after the war, the role of science and the quest for scientific truth were not particularly subverted under the Nazi regime.[33]

Hayek was clearly aware that scientists and scholars collaborated with the Nazi regime. In fact, he excoriates servile scientists and engineers in chapter 13. Of course, because Hayek was writing during the war, he would not have had a complete picture of how science was operating under the regime. Thus, while Hayek cannot be faulted for what he could not have known, what is needed today is a more complex picture of when propaganda is selectively deployed and the historical relationship between science (or academia more broadly) and propaganda under totalitarianism.

A useful beginning to creating a more sophisticated theory is Robert Proctor's argument that the dichotomizing of individualism and collectivism misses the crucial point about who was included in the collective:

> . . . what went wrong in the Nazi period is not best understood as a subordination of the good of the individual to the good of the whole. Rather, one has to understand who was included within "the whole" and who was banished. It was not, after all, "the individual" in the abstract who suffered but particular kinds of individuals. Public health protections were extended to the "healthy" majority, while so-called "enemies of the people" were first excluded and then exterminated. Medicine was complicit in both ends of this moral scale: in public health reforms that brought the majority of Germans cleaner air and water, and in "health reforms" that involved sterilization and eventually wholesale murder.[34]

Moreover, the argument that the centralized deployment of propaganda undermines the sense of truth, and hence all ethics and morality in society, is too broad. As Proctor notes, ethics were taught to medical students under the Nazi regime. The ethics were racist and sexist, to be sure, but there was a clear set of ethical standards and laws. For example, physicians could be sued for failing to inform patients of the severity of their illness, and there were laws against cruelty to animals in scientific experiments.[35]

Nonetheless, Hayek's observation about the imposition of ultimate values does help to unpack the horrors unleashed by Nazi science. As Proctor continues: "Most Nazi doctors did not lie, or cheat, or misrepresent their credentials. They did not falsify or fabricate data to an unusual degree, and there is little evidence of plagiarism. The evil must be sought elsewhere. The primary failing of Nazi medicine, I would argue, was the failure of physicians to challenge the rotten, substantive core of Nazi values."[36] The Nazi imposition of a hierarchy of ultimate values through state propaganda did not eliminate the existence of ethical codes or even the sense of morality among academics, scientists, and medical practitioners; but the substantive core of Nazi values did circumscribe the scope of ethical responsibility and moral behavior to the German *Volk*. "Healthy" German citizens were never experimented upon; nonetheless, the presumption of valuable life did not extend much beyond that category.[37]

Propaganda and Political Capitalism

In contemporary political-capitalist regimes, the increasing expansion of the market economy and the erosion of the state's monopoly on information production and dissemination generates new social networks and political pressures. To survive, a regime must continue to prevent alternative political solidarities and reinforce regime legitimacy. A political-capitalist state that neglects the use of propaganda risks political instability owing to rising income inequality, rampant corruption, and the absence of the rule of law.

PROPAGANDA IN CHINA

The Chinese Communist Party originally developed its propaganda system through a careful study of Soviet, Nazi, and other totalitarian states,[38] and while ideological content continues to be infused into the educational system as well as the traditional media and cultural life, the state has perceived the need for more intensive indoctrination of its citizens, principally to combat exposure to counternarratives online that might challenge the hierarchy of values set by the party/state or the role of the current party/state as guardians of those values. The ultimate aim is, as Hayek theorized, to protect the sanctity of the party's hierarchy of values. As Rogier Creemers argues, "At a broader level, the reassertion of online control has accompanied systemic efforts to impose top-down, predefined notions of civility and public morality, such as the Socialist core value system and the untranslatable (and ungraspable) concept of *suzhi*[.] In contrast, counternarratives are marginalized."[39] In contrast to Hayek's theory of propaganda under totalitarianism, however, Chinese state propaganda under political capitalism does not appear to have the effect of undermining all notions of morality. Instead, the state projects itself as the guardian of public morality and societal stability, although a certain level of cynicism toward state propaganda is noticeable.

Another purpose of propaganda in a political-capitalist regime such as

China, for example, is to "contain the spontaneity of the Chinese citizenry and create a predictable environment."[40] After the 1976 Tiananmen Incident, the 1979 Democracy Wall protests, and the 1989 Tiananmen Square Massacre, the Chinese state particularly fears spontaneous and unforeseen events that may flow from unfettered public interactions, which generate alternative solidarities across social and spatial barriers. Thus, while a political-capitalist regime seeks to encourage spontaneity in a large and unified marketplace, it attempts to prevent spontaneity in the public square. This task is achieved strategically by fragmenting the communications infrastructure for the national public audience and limiting the spillover of political ideas across social status and locality.[41] Instrumentally, the political-capitalist state (unlike its totalitarian predecessor) is willing to use both public agencies and private (social media) companies to achieve these goals. Alternatively stated, the political-capitalist state uses the spontaneity of the marketplace to contain spontaneity in the public square.

In 2013 Xi's government announced its intention to "occupy the [online] public opinion battlefield" by combining propaganda work and opinion management with advanced data-gathering and -processing techniques. The militarized metaphor has set the tone for the state's activities. Hence, for the general population, the state seeks not only to preventively filter keywords, images, and information considered politically sensitive, but also to proactively promote patriotism, guide public opinion, and advance the party's current policy agenda, as well as to aggressively discover and punish dissenters.[42] Private corporations have been enlisted for their ability to technologically enhance the surveillance capacities of the state. For example, Alibaba, an e-commerce website, and Baidu, a search engine and artificial intelligence technology company, provide technology data for the state's Social Credit System. Alipay and WeChat have collaborated with the state to provide contact tracing in the wake of the COVID-19 pandemic.[43]

As a Leninist organization, the state prioritizes the ideological discipline of its party cadres. While the party traditionally relied on historically established indoctrination techniques, rampant corruption and growing exposure to alternative ideas began to erode the party's confidence, while new technological developments seemed to expand the frontiers for indoctrination. Consequently, the Chinese Communist Party's Propaganda (or "Publicity") Department launched the Xuexi Qiangguo (Study the Powerful Nation, or XQ) digital platform application in January 2019. The aim of XQ is "political learning," specifically the political thought of President Xi Jinping, who (like Stalin in this regard) has sought to cultivate a cult of personality and to elevate himself as an intellectual on par with Marx and Lenin, as well as Mao Zedong and Deng Xiaoping. The basic format of the

XQ digital platform is an extension of traditional propaganda techniques from the Maoist era:

> Mao was a master propagandist in his own right, and he and his re-gime used a variety of "thought control" techniques throughout their rule. These included mass mobilization campaigns; the construction of "models" to be emulated; the creation of study groups and ideological monitors throughout society; incarceration for the purpose of "brain-washing"; the promulgation of a steady stream of documents to be mem-orized; control of the subject matter to be taught throughout the educa-tional system; control of the content of newspaper articles and editorials; development of a nationwide system of loudspeakers that reached into every neighborhood and village; domination of the broadcast media; the use of propaganda teams (*xuanchuan dui*) to indoctrinate specific seg-ments of the population; and other methods.[44]

But communications technology now allows the party to more quickly de-tect and reward or punish individuals in real time. Party members are all ob-ligated to use the XQ platform and join "study groups" with other members in their communities. Non–party members may also join the platform, but all users must provide their real names and phone numbers. Some employ-ers and universities require employees and students to use XQ and to ob-tain a certain minimum score each day. By June 2020, a year and a half after its launch, the platform had 180 million users. Users earn points by watch-ing propaganda videos, reading articles, and taking quizzes. User scores are ranked nationally, and party officials have access to data on individual users and their scores.[45] The XQ program aims to use data mining and real-time analytics to "match, track, and steer" users toward political objectives (as opposed to the monetization of online activity pursued by commer-cial services) and to monitor those with low scores offline.[46] The platform restricts user personalization and prioritizes news about President Xi in order to deliver a consistent ideological message from aggregated official news sources. Beyond passive exposure, XQ seeks to spur "active learning" through daily, weekly, special, and challenge quizzes.

The use of digital technology theoretically enhances the penetration of state propaganda into society. However, it is unclear whether usage of the XQ app, for example, actually increases user attachment to the party, or whether high quiz scores translate to increased political knowledge. Liang, Chen, and Zhao argue that many users are extrinsically motivated by the app's "gamification" features and offline rewards such as commodities in exchange for points, as well as access to events, a special XQ theme park, and even dedicated subway train cars for "good" citizens.[47] Other users re-sist political content and use the app mainly to watch entertainment pro-grams. There are also paid services that will help users to falsely earn forty to fifty points per day.[48] Beyond XQ, the exposure of Chinese netizens to online rumors may work to undermine official news reports. Kang and Zhu state that better-informed Chinese citizens tend to consider government propaganda "crude, heavy-handed, and preposterous."[49]

It would be difficult to argue that the Chinese state's extensive use of propaganda has undermined the notion of truth and hence the morals of the society in core areas of the state. While there is clear evidence of skep-ticism and cynicism in society to state propaganda, notions of truth and the role of science in society have not been wholly subordinated (except where scientific facts challenge the regime's crisis management legitimacy, as in the early stages of the COVID-19 pandemic). Moreover, the state has a strong interest in cultivating a particular notion of social morality. How-ever, as a settler colonial state engaged in a "civilizing" mission,[50] China does not readily extend the benefits of ethics to non-Han peoples residing along the internal periphery, such as Xinjiang province.

Xinjiang

Chinese government propaganda intended to win support for official poli-cies has had very limited success in its northwestern Xinjiang Uyghur Au-tonomous Region (XUAR) since the foundation of the Chinese state in 1949 and the establishment of the XUAR in 1955. Today, nearly half of the approximately twenty-five million inhabitants of the region are Uyghurs, a Turkic Muslim ethnic group; another 10 percent of the population belong to other Turkic Muslim minority groups; and the remaining 40 percent of the population are Han Chinese. Unable to win over the non-Han peoples, the party/state has shifted to regulating the Uyghur group's "values, be-liefs, and loyalties."[51] In particular, the government aims to promote "eth-nic unity" or harmony and "de-extremization" or antiradicalization (in a manner that oddly resonates with the efforts of the Singaporean case, dis-cussed below).[52] The party/state has sought to use religious organizations and the clergy of the Uyghur community to "unite and educate believers in areas of patriotism, territorial integrity, ethnic unity, and social stability."[53] Preaching against these ideas has been deemed illegal and extremist. Anti-extremization efforts, in addition to prohibiting actions and speech acts that promote a radical religious ideology, have also resulted in regulations banning ". . . attempts to obstruct the fusion of nationalities, disseminating the *halal* concept [e.g., ritually lawful meat], wearing or compelling of others to wear veils, growing beards, selecting religious names for children, practicing religious weddings and divorces, obstructing state education, or spreading extremist information."[54] The state has adopted Chinese as the language of instruction and banned the use of the Uyghur language in school activities. Since 2014 the party has required over 200,000 of its members to live in Uyghur villages, where they hold talks, gather intelligence, and distribute propaganda materials.[55] The party also uses GPS technology, facial recognition algorithms, and machine learning to monitor, categorize, and discipline the population.[56]

Of course, efforts to dominate the population extend well beyond the use of propaganda and surveillance to physical coercion. After economic liberalization,[57] the Chinese state had adopted a policy of "relatively" limited interference in the family and religious affairs of the country's non-Han peoples.[58] However, at the turn of the century the state shifted toward more intensive regulation and militarized policing of Uyghur and other Turkic Muslim minority population groups in response to the state's perception of increased threats from regional extremist groups.[59]

The first crackdown on minorities after economic liberalization came in 1996–97. Crackdowns accelerated after September 11, 2001, under the banner of the US-led Global War on Terrorism, since China believed the United States had greenlighted using the specter of terrorism to advance state objectives. In 2009 two hundred were killed in mass violence between Uyghur and Han Chinese citizens in Urumqi.[60] In 2013 there were multiple violent incidents, including a suicide car attack in Tiananmen Square. In 2014 a terrorist attack at Urumqi's south railway station killed three; and a knife attack left thirty-one civilians at the Kunming railway station dead, instigating the latest and most severe crackdown.[61] Since that time, over one million Uyghurs and other members of non-Han ethnic groups have allegedly been sent to one of many "reeducation camps" or "counterextremism camps" and subjected to "arbitrary detention, forced birth control and sterilization, religious restrictions, sexual abuse, torture, family separation, and forced labor. . . ."[62]

The Chinese state continues to view Uyghurs who identify as Muslim or Turkic as effectively aligned with either Islamic terrorists or Western human-rights organizations that threaten to block the rise of China.[63] Uyghurs are thus seen as Chinese so long as they do not identify with their own religion or language—characteristics that form the essence of their ethnic identity. The Uyghurs and other Turkic minorities are a source of insecurity because of their *lack* of Chinese national identity.[64] Barring complete assimilation and pacification or successful secession, the political situation along China's periphery in Xinjiang (as well as Tibet and Inner Mongolia) is at a stalemate.

The main effect of the Chinese surveillance state in the XUAR is not so much the end of truth but the erosion of trust. As James Leibold writes, "In societies where social and political monitoring is normalized, there is a commensurate deterioration of social cohesion and rise in public suspicion."[65] The Chinese surveillance state in the XUAR has been compared to the German Democratic Republic's Stasi, which assembled detailed dossiers on six million East Germans. Although there is more room to maneuver in the XUAR, owing mainly to the incompetence of state officials, the complexity of the bureaucracy, and interbureaucratic rivalries, the surveillance society creates paranoia even within families and between community members. The erosion of trust, particularly between the Han and Uyghur communities, then has measurable impacts on economic growth.[66] For liberals, the fate of the Turkic minorities of the XUAR is a reminder of the dark underbelly of political capitalism's derogation of civil and human rights in the pursuit of rapid economic development—a pursuit that is undermined in the process of building a surveillance state.

PROPAGANDA IN VIETNAM

Vietnamese propaganda efforts, symbolized by the still-present neighborhood loudspeaker system established during the "American War," has been supplemented with state-run media and a complex censorship regime, as well as more sophisticated social media information management efforts and SMS messaging.[67] Although the authoritarian government had initially been reluctant to even permit the Internet in 1997, the party/state has accepted the trade-off of commercial gains from a networked society for the costs of mitigating risks to regime legitimacy. The party/state employs approximately 80,000 propagandists to monitor and direct online discussions of political topics. This figure undoubtedly includes almost 10,000 soldiers from "Force 47" of the Vietnam People's Army recruited specifically for cyberwarfare against "toxic" information.[68] Individual CPV members also employ propagandists to defend themselves from criticism by rival propagandists working for other CPV members.[69] In the Vietnamese digital ecosystem, truth may be a liability. As Mai Duong writes,

> The facts, figures and photos published on anonymous blogs generate a lot of political discourse among the online community, but the sources of this information are seldom revealed. This reality challenges the qual-

ity of blog-based arguments resulting in readers having to face the risk of being driven into a matrix of information where propaganda, truth, truthiness and lies are all mixed up together.[70]

However, the population is not passive or naive in its reception of state propaganda; messages are often contested through viral posts and rumors that the state is only intermittently able to block or stop. Moreover, the arrival of fiberoptic cable and mobile broadband technology in 2009 have helped in the emergence of a "semi-autonomous" civil society as social media usage has skyrocketed.[71] The authoritarian regime has responded to these developments by promulgating or amending a slew of regulations to limit speech acts that are subversive toward the party/state.[72] The party/state has also relied on periodic crackdowns on protestors and the prosecution of dissidents, as well as blocking oppositional websites and platforms and bombarding social media with "positive" messages about the regime.[73]

What do these propaganda tactics and coercive measures indicate about political capitalism? As will be recalled, political capitalism is associated with postcommunist societies (e.g., China and Vietnam) or one-party states (e.g., Singapore) in the formerly colonized world. For the former group, the legacy of the totalitarian era, in which the state had a monopoly on information dissemination, and the absence of substantive liberal protections of individual rights mean that postcommunist states are particularly well prepared to do battle against counterregime propaganda on the Internet. Expectations were that the Internet would weaken authoritarian regimes, but instead, postcommunist states have generally adapted older techniques to new spaces of contestation. In China, for example, techniques of mass indoctrination from the Maoist era utilized against suspected class enemies are relatively easy to adapt to ethnic minorities suspected of harboring separatist sentiments.[74] In noncommunist Singapore, the use of propaganda, as we will see in the next section, is less intrusive and much less physically coercive, but the overall goals are not dissimilar to China's efforts in its periphery.

PROPAGANDA IN SINGAPORE

From the early Cold War period, Malaya and the Crown Colony of Singapore collaborated with a US-funded anticommunist propaganda initiative: the "Campaign of Truth" under Presidents Harry Truman and Dwight Eisenhower. As British colonial power in the region waned, the American project targeted the ethnic Chinese diaspora in Southeast Asia initially through low-budget films and documentaries,[75] but later through a wide array of media and events, as well as a library. The films aimed to convince members of the diaspora to shun the Chinese Communist Party and remain loyal to their adopted homelands, despite their ethnolinguistic heritage. After the start of self-government in 1959, the Singapore's PAP, under the leadership of Lee Kuan Yew, temporarily limited the circulation of US materials for a year and "sought to manage U.S. [information] operations to further the party's nation-building programs."[76]

Although the results are difficult to demonstrate empirically,[77] US propaganda efforts in Singapore did appear to bear fruit, at least in comparison to other areas in Southeast Asia targeted by the Truman and Eisenhower administrations. Alternatively, one could argue that Singaporeans, as a multiethnic society of immigrants who were seeking material prosperity and who resided in a regional trading hub shaped since 1819 by British laissez-faire economic policies, were perhaps more receptive to the liberal ideas the United States was promoting than were other countries in Southeast Asia at the time.[78] However, it is worth noting that US efforts were only one initiative in a complex and diverse informational ecosystem. Although communist propaganda and texts were officially censored by the colonial government, the Communist Party was very active in Singapore at the time, organizing workers and students. Moreover, the humiliating defeat of British troops by the Japanese in Singapore during World War II and the prolonged process of decolonization had undermined the prestige of liberal political and economic ideas in Asia. The United States sought primarily to shape ultimate values rather than engage in questioning facts or specific policies. Finally, the aim of US propaganda was oriented toward grand strategy rather than comprehensive planning. In other words, US information operations in a foreign territory such as Singapore would not raise concerns for Hayek. While Singapore (and Malaysia) to this day prohibit the screening of films that show the (now anemic) Malayan Communist Party in a positive light,[79] the focus of propaganda efforts has shifted to protecting social stability and regime legitimacy.

The state in contemporary Singapore, with its highly educated, cosmopolitan population, which enjoys one of the highest standards of living in the world, complements basic censorship and propaganda with a more sophisticated messaging and information management strategy[80]— particularly since the state seeks to be an attractive location for the regional headquarters of foreign firms and a hub for the creative arts. In essence, the state has had to move beyond its "survivalist and developmental state" framework.[81] Senior officials relate the challenge of managing flows of information most often to the need to maintain social stability. The task is portrayed as a battle to prevent the circulation of rumors or, more recently, to contain "fake news." Because Singapore is a multiethnic society, its leaders are particularly sensitive to information that could spark communal tension or radicalize individuals to commit acts of terrorism.[82] Thus, similar to the situation with the Chinese party/state in the XUAR, intercommunal harmony and antiradicalization are major goals of domestic propaganda efforts. And as it is with the Chinese state in its core areas and with the Vietnamese state, defending and enhancing regime legitimacy is also a major objective.

An example of Singapore's antiradicalization propaganda efforts came in the wake of the September 11, 2001, terrorist attacks on the United States and the discovery of a thirty-four-member Jemaah Islamiyah cell planning attacks in Singapore in October 2001. Three years later the Islamic Religious Council of Singapore (MUIS) organized the Singapore Muslim Identity project. In addition to affirming the role of Singaporean Muslims in society, the project aimed to separate Singaporean Muslims from extremist teachings by groups outside of Singapore. While the religious council claimed their efforts were an autonomous response by religious authorities within the local Muslim community, MUIS is ultimately a "state sponsored religious bureaucracy with statutory board status." Moreover, the message put forward by MUIS was completely congruent with the state, despite different means of dissemination.[83] MUIS was eventually restructured to monitor closely mosques and madrassahs, and a registry of *asatizah* (religious teachers) was established.[84]

Two decades later, the Singaporean government's discourse continues to focus on extremism, exclusionary practices, and radicalization (although public officials have noticeably dropped the simplistic juxtaposition of "moderate Muslims" with "Islamic extremists") and to urge constant vigilance against "extremist" interpretations and deeds.[85] In essence, the Singaporean state's discourse, not unlike that of many other states around the world, continues to problematize and securitize Muslim identity, particularly the Malay/Muslim minority within the city-state. An analysis of speeches by public officials reveals a particular scrutiny of Muslim cultural practices that promote exclusion from interaction with non-Muslims, as well as a paternalistic encouragement of a "modern" disposition toward "science, technology, maths, and computers,"[86] which implies that Muslims are inherently traditional and backward. While singling out the minority community for surveillance and securitization, the discourse has also begun to address "Islamophobia" as a broader societal problem that induces alienation in the minority community. The discursive shift appears more balanced, but the inclusion of Islamophobia reaffirms how crucial the role of the illiberal state is to holding together a fragile multiethnic and multireligious society and protecting it from existential threats.[87]

Singapore's propaganda efforts are becoming more sophisticated. In 2012, for example, the Ministry of Communication and Information created a state-operated fact-checking website called "Factually."[88] The website also exposes the names of individuals and organizations who post the information under discussion. From 2017 onward, in response to events in the United States and United Kingdom, elected officials in Singapore began securitizing the issue of "fake news" by positing it as an existential threat to individual reputations, the economy, communal harmony, societal stability, electoral integrity, and thus the sovereignty of the state itself. In 2018 the Ministry of Communication and the Ministry of Law circulated a green paper titled "Deliberate Online Falsehoods," which led to the formation of a Select Parliamentary Committee to address the issue.[89] Subsequently, in May 2019 the government passed the Protection from Online Falsehoods and Manipulation Act (POFMA) to order official corrections next to news or social media posts that harm any entity on the enumerated list of public interests. Internet sites that repeatedly publish misleading information are listed as "declared online locations." While the new law is the latest in a legal framework of anti-falsehood laws that trace back to the Sedition Act of 1948, the new laws also broadly expanded the scope and powers of the state on issues of speech and expression, where it already exercised extensive authority, and extended that oversight more thoroughly to the Internet, where its grip was weaker. Moreover, the laws sideline the judiciary and due process by permitting the government to order that "fake news" be taken down within hours of its being posted online.[90] "Fake news" was not defined clearly, and interpretation of the term was left to the discretion of the state.[91]

Of course, in countering "fake news," state agents are not merely correcting potentially damaging information; rather, the correction of misleading news is frequently mixed with an explanation and defense of the government's policies and state institutions while portraying the state as the authoritative source of veracity.[92] In other words, the modern and sophisticated political-capitalist state, rather than subverting facts to support the ends of public policy, uses cherry-picked facts to defend regime legitimacy and "expose" regime dissidents as generally uninformed, unreliable, or openly mendacious. The direct involvement of the state, as opposed to an autonomous and disinterested third party or the judiciary, in fact-checking and exposing dissidents reveals the state's deep insecurity about its own legitimacy.

Conclusion

Hayek's midcentury theory of propaganda under totalitarian regimes needs to be significantly modified to better understand how those regimes historically interfaced with knowledge production, particularly in academia. It is certainly an oversimplification to argue, as Hayek did, that totalitarian regimes "undermine one of the foundations of all morals: the sense of and the respect for truth."[93] While it is undoubtedly true that socialists and fascists often adopted absurd slogans (e.g., "We stand for the purity of Marxist-Leninist theory in surgery!")[94] and mouthed patent falsehoods, a focus on ideological buffoonery and blatant mendacity may obscure more than it reveals—particularly the sociological element in intra-academic rivalries that led to the absurd slogans. Hayek's theory oddly treads too lightly on the deep complicity of knowledge producers in the physical sciences, social sciences, and humanities under a totalitarian state—which is strange, given Hayek's contempt for academics, scientists, and engineers who willingly collaborated with totalitarian regimes, as well as "collectivist" intellectuals in liberal regimes.[95]

In the twenty-first century, political-capitalist regimes display increasingly sophisticated approaches to information management and dissemination with their core populations but rely upon crude approaches to co-opt or discipline minorities along their peripheries. To update Hayek's theory, the image of the masses as passive recipients of the state's "complete ethical code" will need to be discarded, since political-capitalist regimes do not possess a monopoly on the means of communication and the reliance on market allocation of resources negates the need for comprehensive planning and thus a comprehensive hierarchy of social values.[96] Far from seeking to erode notions of truth and morality, contemporary political-capitalist regimes increasingly seek to champion morally righteous behavior and to become distributors of empirically valid facts that ensure regime viability in their selective interventions. The growing sophistication of state propaganda, even if contested domestically, implies that liberals should anticipate nimble resistance to the seductive soft power of liberalism.

[CHAPTER TWELVE]

The Socialist Roots of Nazism

All antiliberal forces are combining against everything that is liberal.

Arthur Moeller van den Bruck (1923)

Arthur Moeller van den Bruck's *Germany's Third Empire* (1923; reprinted posthumously in 1930) was highly influential among the Young Conservatives and national socialists in the interwar period. The quoted passage is part of a bitter screed in which the author prays for and prophesies the end of liberalism in Germany. More broadly, Moeller van den Bruck attacks the age of reason for turning thinking man into calculating man and denying the primacy of nationalism.[1] The author desperately hoped that Germany, guided by non-Marxian socialism and Prussian values, would rise from its ashes a totalitarian state.[2]

Hayek's choice to quote this particular passage from Moeller van den Bruck is slightly peculiar. Moeller van den Bruck was not describing a historical reality so much as projecting a fantasy. At the time he was writing, Germany had defaulted on its reparations, and France and Belgium had occupied the Ruhr Valley. Illiberal forces had yet to "combine" against the liberal regime, and support for the Nazi Party (Nationalsozialistische Deutsche Arbeiterpartei, or NSDAP) actually dropped from two million votes in May 1924 to under one million in December 1924.[3] Hitler would not be appointed chancellor for another decade. Thus, the epigraph does not confirm Hayek's argument that socialists and national socialists converged to exorcise liberalism from Germany, although it does document that vehemently antiliberal sentiment existed on the far right.

Unfortunately, the quote by itself also does not shed much light on the chapter's theme, that is, "the socialist roots of Nazism." Moeller van den Bruck did not transition from socialism to national socialism—his rabid anti-Semitism toward Marx foreclosed that possibility. In fact, he argues at one point that socialism is an offshoot of the liberalism he despises: "Socialism[,] which grew up beneath and alongside liberalism, demands justice."[4] At another point he critiques Marx for not realizing that "national socialism might be a condition precedent of universal socialism; that men can only live if their nations live also."[5] In other words, and in contrast to Hayek, Moeller van den Bruck argues that national socialism is logically anteced-ent to universal socialism. A better quote for Hayek from Moeller van den Bruck for the purposes of this chapter might have been, "[German social-ists] can turn their backs on intellectual socialism which has deceived them and adopt an emotional socialism which opens wider vistas than Marxist calculations."[6] Moeller van den Bruck believed that Bolshevism was Rus-sian and that German socialism would be a "corporative conception of state and economics, which must perhaps have a revolutionary foundation, but will then seek conservative stability."[7] For Moeller van den Bruck, socialism did not evolve into national socialism; socialism reflected the national char-acteristics of the soil in which it took root. As the chapter illustrates, Hayek would obviously disagree with Moeller van den Bruck's thesis.

∴

How International Socialism Became National Socialism

In contrast to the arc of Moeller van den Bruck's thought, Hayek seeks to illustrate and explain the pattern whereby intellectuals (e.g., Werner Som-bart, Johann Plenge, Paul Lensch) converted from socialism to fascism in the early twentieth century. The historical oddity of this pattern was that national socialism prior to World War I was regarded with contempt by the great majority of Germans. Hayek's puzzle to solve in this chapter, there-fore, is how views held by a "reactionary minority" came to gain the sup-port of the great majority.[8]

Hayek is not content to accept conventional explanations that look to either (1) social history (the social impact of Germany's defeat in World War I and the Great Depression) or (2) reactionary ideology (the supposed "capitalist reaction to the advance of socialism").[9] The first thesis is dis-counted, since the emergence of national-socialist thought was actually coeval with World War I in Germany. For example, two classics of national-socialist thought were published during the war; Werner Sombart's *Händ-ler und Helden* (Merchants and Heroes) was published in 1915, and Johan Plenge's *1789 and 1914* was published in 1916. Moreover, Hayek believes the German defeat in World War I actually sustained the "war hysteria of 1914" and helped to advance national socialism.[10] The second thesis, that fascism emerged from a bourgeois reaction to socialism, is rejected because the Germans lacked a sufficiently powerful bourgeoisie to counter the advance of socialist ideas. Hayek implies that socialism was in the very air that the

German bourgeoisie breathed, from the French Revolution to the start of World War I; the German middle class would not have been able intellectually to construct a compelling counterhegemonic ideology ex nihilo.

Hayek argues instead that national socialism evolved from ideas developed and popularized by socialists over a century and a half. Existing socialist ideas would come to be fused with militant nationalism from 1914 onward. In other words, national socialism was not simply an irrational response to historical and political events in the interwar period; rather, it had a well-established intellectual pedigree that allowed it to emerge during the Great War itself.

Of course, Hayek is careful to reiterate his point from the beginning of the book that while German thinkers were critical in the development of both socialism and national socialism, these ideas were not exclusively German. Hayek revisits the work of R. D. Butler in tracing the intellectual roots of national socialism in part to an Englishman, Houston Stewart Chamberlain (1855–1927), and a Scotsman, Thomas Carlyle (1795–1881).[11] Although Hayek agrees with the lineages Butler traces, he is critical of the teleological element in Butler's argument. Hayek traces the origins of the link between socialism and national socialism back to three specific German intellectuals: Johann Gottlieb Fichte (1762–1814), Johann Karl Rodbertus (1805–1875), and Ferdinand Lassalle (1825–1864).

To solve the chapter's puzzle, Hayek essentially traces out a few key tasks that cleared the way for the emergence and consolidation of national socialism in Germany.

The first step in the expansion of national-socialist ideology was the denigration of the liberal tradition in Germany. Liberal ideas had flowered in Germany since the late eighteenth century. Thus, early twentieth-century conservative authors, such as Oswald Spengler (1880–1936), diminished and dismissed early liberal reformers, such as Karl August Fürst von Hardenberg (1750–1822) and Alexander von Humboldt (1769–1859), as "English" plants left behind on German soil by Napoleon.[12] Next, the "anticapitalist forces of the Right and of the Left" converged and "drove out from Germany everything that was liberal."[13] Revolutionary socialists and national socialists even united in their opposition to the residual "liberal elements" of socialism, that is, its support of internationalism and democracy.[14]

This part of Hayek's narrative is overstated. Liberalism did return to prominence after the Great War under the Weimar Republic (1918–33). The image that the German parliament was dysfunctional and confused throughout the Weimar Era has been challenged empirically. Coalition governments during the Weimar Era were short-lived, to be sure, but this is not attributable to either a lack of ideological coherence among the parties or an electoral law that permitted too many parties to be represented, despite conventional wisdom.[15] Moreover, the NSDAP struggled to survive during the Weimar Republic and only formed a government in 1933. After Hitler's failed coup attempt in 1923, the Nazis were officially banned until 1925, and Hitler was not allowed to speak in public until 1928. The share of seats in parliament for the NSDAP dropped from 6.8 percent in 1924 to 2.4 percent in 1928. The silencing of Hitler had a significant impact on the coherence of the national socialists even as they worked around official limitations. As late as March 1933, the last contested multiparty election before the Weimar Republic was dissolved, the NSDAP only held 44.51 percent of seats.[16] Even the German National People's Party (Deutschnationale Volkspartei, or DNVP), which would serve as the coalition partner that brought Hitler to power, was dominated by its "liberal wing" until 1928.[17] Of course, the Weimar Republic's liberal parties could not ultimately withstand the polarized ideological battles and economic crises. But Spengler's claim that liberal ideas were driven out by the "German Revolution" of 1914 is hyperbolic. A more accurate statement is simply that a deep and abiding hatred of liberalism served to provide a common ground between the socialists and national socialists in Germany. This shared terrain facilitated the movement of socialist intellectuals to the national-socialist camp for the first half of the twentieth century. However, the rise of national socialism was not linear, and the Nazi Party did benefit from the economic crises and political turbulence that racked the Weimar Republic.

The second step was the conversion of laborers and students to the ideology of national socialism. From the start of World War I, a litany of former socialist intellectuals who had converted to national socialism led workers and students into the national-socialist camp through their popular writings and public lectures.[18] The logic here is that as workers and students increased the ranks of national socialism, "nationalist-socialism" would eventually become a mobilizable asset ripe for political entrepreneurs.

Hayek does not provide empirical evidence to support this claim. While Hayek is likely correct in arguing that national socialism appealed to workers and students around the start of World War I, it is difficult to confirm his assertion empirically. The torchbearer of national socialism, the NSDAP, was not created until after World War I out of the German Workers' Party, or DAP, formed in 1919. There were some direct links between the intellectual forefathers of national socialism and the Nazi Party, for example, the meeting between Hitler and his longtime hero Houston Stewart Chamberlain in 1923.[19] There were also a wide range of prewar *völkisch* (ethno-/ racial-)nationalist groups that would inspire the NSDAP after the Great War. In other words, it is indisputable that the intellectual origins of national socialism predate even World War I, but it is difficult to confirm the extent of adherence to these ideas among workers and students.

Contemporary scholarship on the membership of the Nazi Party, based on a sample of the party's two master files (1925–45) seized by the Allies in 1945, demonstrates that the party did recruit broadly from a range of social classes, including workers, the "old middle class," and the "new middle class," during the Weimar Republic. The old middle class, made up of artisans, merchants, and small independent farmers, constituted over half (53 percent) of party joiners (i.e., new members) between 1925 and 1932.[20] The working class constituted the next largest group (40 percent) of all party joiners between 1925 and 1932.[21] The highest proportion of party joiners from the working class came from several import-oriented industrial branches, and there was "an overrepresentation of skilled workers and an underrepresentation of semiskilled and unskilled workers."[22] The new middle class, which consisted of white-collar private and civil service employees, had emerged at the dawn of the twentieth century in tandem with increase in industrialization and government. By 1933 this combined group constituted about 7 percent of the total population; 4 percent of the general population were civil servants, and 3 percent were private white-collar workers.[23] The NSDAP did well with public-sector employees, owing in part to their efforts to block the liberal (German Democratic Party [Deutsche Demokratische Partei, or DDP]) and socialist (Social Democratic Party [Sozialdemokratische Partei Deutschlands, or SPD]) parties' plan for "democratizing" the civil service and Chancellor Heinrich Brüning's austerity program of 1930–31.[24] While only 4 percent of the NS-DAP members were civil servants, it must be kept in mind that joining an extremist political party was declared illegal from 1929 to 1932. There were also significant economic, physical-safety, and social costs to joining the party before 1933. When the ban on civil servants' joining the NSDAP was lifted in 1933, civil servants came to constitute 10 percent of the NSDAP. The Nazis also performed well with white-collar workers in the private sector.[25] Most surprisingly, the Nazis disproportionately attracted women to the party despite their overtly antifeminist policies (e.g., calling for married women to be removed from the workforce): 96 percent of new white-collar female party members were unmarried, compared to only 46 percent of white-collar male party joiners who were unmarried.[26] Of course, as a share of the general population, only 6 percent of women were members of the NSDAP, compared to 11 percent of men, from 1925 to 1932.[27] Moreover, women did not tend to vote in large numbers for radical parties, that is, the Communist Party (Kommunistische Partei Deutschlands, or KPD) or the NSDAP, in the elections between 1924 and 1933.[28]

The third step in the growth of national socialism was the forging of a link between socialism and militant nationalism. With the start of the Great War in 1914, socialist intellectuals begin to depict the war as a battle between states representing clashing political and economic ideologies. Hayek uses Sombart as an exemplar of this disposition: "In his war book this old socialist welcomed the 'German War' as the inevitable conflict between the commercial civilization of England and the heroic culture of Germany. His contempt for the commercial view of the English people, who had lost all warlike instincts, is unlimited."[29] Sombart contrasts British values of individualism, commercialism, and bourgeois comfort with the Germanic values of the people's community (*Volksgemeinschaft*), the deification of the state, and martial virtue. Anticapitalism and illiberalism were therefore tied to one particular nation and state, and hence to a nationalist vision of socialism.

Sombart's crude juxtaposition was subsequently refined by Johann Plenge in *1789 and 1914: The Symbolic Years in the History of the Political Mind* (1916). Plenge contrasts the French Revolution's ideal of freedom with the German wartime ideal of organization. In effect, he excommunicates Marx from the socialist camp for prematurely attempting to fuse the two incompatible ideals through Marx's gestures toward a communist utopia. Organization is the essence of socialism for Plenge, and the ideal reaches its apogee in the German Empire. In other words, like Sombart, Plenge's socialism becomes tied to a particular nation and state. The war permits socialists to witness for the first time a comprehensively planned economy and a society working toward a unified purpose. For Plenge, the needs of the war economy under Kaiser Wilhelm II (1859–1941) gives birth to national socialism, which he views as an evolutionary culmination and a gift to humanity.[30] The conservative historian Oswald Spengler would extend these ideas to argue that there were essentially three regime types: the liberal parliamentarism of the English, the social democracy of the French, and the illiberal and antidemocratic authoritarian socialism of Prussian Germany. The Nazi constitutional theorist Carl Schmitt (1888–1985) would further restructure Spengler's notion into three dialectic stages: the absolute state of the seventeenth and eighteenth centuries, the neutral state of nineteenth-century liberalism, and the totalitarian state, in which state and society are equal.[31] The contempt for liberalism and democracy, along with the celebration of socialism, militarism, and authoritarianism, came to be paired with the belief that Germany's national socialism was the fortunate culmination of world-historical struggles.

Finally, Hayek demonstrates how national-socialist intellectuals naturalized their ideas as part of German culture by tracing the fetish for organization, administration, and planning, which culminates in policies such as the Nazi regime's Four-Year Plan, implemented by Hermann Göring (1893–1946), back to the late nineteenth century.[32] The emphasis on organization, administration, and planning was viewed as a kind of proto-socialism. In 1920, for example, Spengler argued that Chancellor Otto von Bismarck's (1815–1898) deliberate organization of economic activity progressively became more socialist.[33] In 1933 Moeller van den Bruck added that, unlike parliamentarism, which hands the conduct of public business to private persons, the "Prussian idea" was that everyone should be a state official. For him, the choice that the German people uniquely had to solve "*for* the world" came down to whether trade and private property would dominate the state or the state would command trade and socialize property. Thus, Prussia-led Germany, a rigidly militaristic, aristocratic, and authoritarian state, was depicted as an early socialist state, in contrast to English liberalism and commercialism. The defeat of "German" socialism by (English) liberalism in World War I is used by Moeller van den Bruck to argue for the creation of a purified and fundamentalist (i.e., "undefiled by Western liberal ideas") socialism in a future "Third Reich."[34]

Political Capitalism, Corporatism, and Nationalism

What does the recent increased emphasis on nationalism in political-capitalist states imply? Is it analogous to the transition from socialism to national socialism in the early twentieth century?

Nationalism as a socially constructed ideology may serve as a mechanism for states to shape values, channel collective action, and foster militarism. In formerly socialist states, nationalism is a more flexible and useful ideological framework than socialism, particularly since the end of the Cold War and the delegitimation of revolutionary socialism. When combined with political capitalism, nationalist ideology may intensify authoritarianism, but the end result is not national socialism.

SIMILARITIES

To be sure, there are striking similarities between the one-party states of (German) national socialism and (e.g., Chinese, Vietnamese, or Singaporean) political capitalism.

First, both national socialism and political capitalism share a derogation of human and civil rights. Wherever the individual is subordinated to the collective, it is not surprising that human rights and civil rights are undermined, particularly for those outside of the majority community.

Second, both national socialism and political capitalism forged or built upon existing corporatist institutions to manage group (e.g., labor or ethnic) relations—although both regime types have had a complex relationship to these entities. In the discipline of political science, fascism is generally classified as a subspecies of the genus "corporatism,"[35] which Phillipe C. Schmitter defined as

> ... a system of interest representation in which the constituent units are organized into a limited number of singular, compulsory, noncompetitive, hierarchically ordered and functionally differentiated categories, recognized or licensed (if not created) by the state and granted a deliberate representational monopoly within their respective categories in exchange for observing certain controls on their selection of leaders and articulation of demands and supports.[36]

In contrast to the pluralism that characterizes liberal democratic regimes, a state-corporatist regime views labor groups or syndicates in society as part of a(n organic) whole to be integrated for the smooth functioning of the body politic. A corporatist state, therefore, usually recognizes one (and only one) labor union or association as the representative of a particular sector. The state works with the recognized union or association to set and implement policy objectives; the relationship may be consensual but is more frequently dominated by state manipulation and coercion of the syndicate.[37] In return for their cooperation, syndicates are empowered by the state to discipline their members and prevent the emergence of alternative, independent unions or associations. The state's aim is to generate industrial peace, social harmony, and rapid economic growth. In contrast to liberalism, which views the autonomous organization of interest groups by free individuals as a mechanism for *limiting* state power, corporatism views the state's coordination of syndicates or associations as fundamental to *enhancing* the power of the state.[38]

German national socialism, as a particular variant of fascism, publicly proclaimed a desire to use the state to mediate between labor syndicates and the owners of capital to achieve national objectives—that is, until it formed a government. National socialism seemed to represent a novel combination of syndicalism and nationalism in the early twentieth century and thus a rejection of both liberalism and socialism.[39] Ideas of the political and economic corporatist state (*Ständestaat*) were championed by Othmar Spann,[40] an Austrian intellectual with close ties to the NSDAP, and Arthur Moeller van den Bruck in the early 1920s. The idea of corporatism was not new; rather it built on an existing corporatist tradition. Elements of social corporatism, such as the Zentralarbeitgemeinschaft (Central Work Community), a roundtable of apex unions and employers, or the Reichswirtschaftsrat (Reich Economic Council), were implemented during the early years of the Weimar Republic and in turn modeled corporatist arrangements for compulsory labor during the Great War.[41] During the hyperinflation period in 1923, the Parliament also restricted the freedom of collective bargaining and initiated compulsory state arbitration.[42] Under the Nazi regime, nominally corporatist boards were established (e.g., the Reich Food Corporation or Reichsnährstand, and the Reich Chamber of Culture, or Reichskulturkammer); but these generally failed to form self-governing bodies, as the Nazis refused to place any limits on the führer or to contemplate a body politic divided into "estates."[43] Labor unions were dissolved in 1933 and forced to join the German Labor Front (Deutsche Arbeitsfront), but that body did not assume control over wage bargaining. However, in 1934 the Ministry of Labor did create an arbitration body populated by "factory leaders" and "labor trustees," which had the power to set minimum wages.[44]

Political capitalism also contains elements of corporatism. Milanovic's articulation of the concept of political capitalism implies a situation in which ". . . the technocratic bureaucracy of the state, for the purpose of delivering high economic growth and gaining political legitimacy, became the agent of building an indigenous capitalism" in "backward and colonized societies."[45] Thus, it is not surprising that political capitalism, as exercised in China, for example, has been influenced by the state corporatism of the neighboring East Asian developmental states (Japan, South Korea, and Taiwan) as well as the corporatist structures built into the Soviet state that China emulated from the outset. As a revolutionary communist state, Maoist China's corporatist structures simply became a "transmission belt" for mobilizing industrial workers and peasant groups once the business sector was effectively annihilated.[46] After liberalization, China had to develop new associations, including business-sector associations, to loosen the state's control over the economy. The Party hoped to dominate economic activity through surrogate associations, rather than a transmission belt, and thereby encourage greater initiative and competition within each sector.[47] Zhang and Zeng argue that beyond creating capitalist associations or institutions, the state is also engaged in creating a capitalist class—but this line of argument does not contradict Milanovic's theory.[48]

In contemporary China, the political-capitalist state relies on technocrats and party apparatchiks to guide relations between labor organizations and owners of capital. Employees in SOEs and even several private and foreign-owned corporations, are required to be members of state-created, enterprise-level unions; alternative labor representation is legally prohibited. Business and trade associations are almost all formed and subsidized by the state; even the leadership is usually chosen by the state. These organizations serve to educate members about state policies and directives.[49] As the Chinese state has sought to support the decentralization of decision-making, local governments have gained greater "local corporatist" authority, at times even working against the wishes of the national government and peak-level industrial associations.[50] The state-corporatist system in China has thus moved quite a distance from the transmission belt approach under Mao Zedong. Nevertheless, the state still retains the authority to rein in any organization that becomes too autonomous from the state. As Jonathan Unger and Anita Chan note: This is a government that does not want the genie to escape from the bottle. It does not want a business constituency to embed itself in broad-based associations that the businesspeople can increasingly influence. The government wants to prevent the development of any association that can muster even a soft challenge to the government's unilateral control—notwithstanding the fact that businesspeople in China have shown no inclination to mount any challenges at all to the Party's domination.[51]

It is also worth mentioning that Vietnam developed state-corporatist institutions beginning in the mid-twentieth century to manage interest groups and permit limited participation in economic management.[52] These mass organizations, headed by members of the Communist Party, represent different social groups (e.g., workers, peasants/farmers, women, students/youth, and the chamber of commerce and industry) that interface with the state and have at least some influence on policy debates.[53] Of course, there are other informal linkages to state officials, and new social groups have emerged since liberalization.

Finally, Singapore also uses corporatism to manage labor relations as well as its multicultural society. The leadership of the omnibus National Trade Union Congress (NTUC), which by 1995 represented 98.5 percent of total union membership and 90 percent of unions on the island, are members of the ruling PAP. Leaders from the constituent unions of the NTUC are also expected to be supporters of the PAP. Moreover, since the late 1970s, the PAP has been replacing union leaders who had come up through the ranks with an appointed technocratic elite. Sandra Suarez argues that the "great majority of unionized workers in Singapore have no independent capacity for political action."[54] This is evident by the near absence of disruptive labor actions in the city-state.[55]

A specific form of corporatism known as "tripartism," in which state, labor, and employers coordinate policy, describes Singapore's approach. In 1960, in an early experiment, the government created the Industrial Arbitration Court with a proto-tripartite structure borrowed from Australia's tribunal model. Later, in 1972, the state created a full-blown tripartite institution, the National Wages Council (NWC), with equal representation from government, employers, and workers to recommend wage rates annually that were in line with the PAP's economic growth strategies. The corporatist-tripartite arrangement was further strengthened in 1980 with the fusion of the Singapore Employer's Federation and the National Employer's Council into the Singapore National Employers' Federation (SNEF) at the behest of the Ministry of Labour.[56] Notably, wage-increase recommendations require unanimous agreement by the NWC representatives, and deliberations are confidential.[57]

The use of corporatism in Singapore's societal management is evident from the exclusive role of the state, which "... legitimat[es] and enfranchis[es] group and individual participation in public affairs, while also being responsible for managing the harmonious interaction among these groups and individuals."[58] Norman Vasu goes so far as to argue that divisions between the communities of Singapore are essential to the preservation of the state's corporatism. Artificial divisions between the different cultural groups permit a transcendent and enlightened elite to segment and discipline the otherwise fractious public.[59] Social divisions are maintained through political (e.g., the Group Representation Constituency system), economic (e.g., race-based socioeconomic assistance), and social institutions (e.g., "mother tongue" language education and housing policy racial quotas).[60] The narrative of preserving "cultural harmony" (based on discrete and essentialized "racial" classifications) and protecting "unique" cultural traits thus legitimates authoritarian practices. Despite the best efforts of the state to preserve and perpetuate cultural differences, however, the system may be breaking down as a sense of national identity comes to prevail, particularly in response to the intense competition in the labor force with foreign permanent residents, naturalized citizens, and guest workers. Rather than accepting the emergence of a national identity, the state has sought to further entrench multiculturalism and to emphasize the potential threat of communal discord.[61] Thus, the ideology of nationalism, while instrumentally useful as a prophylactic against foreign intervention and to legitimate mandatory national service, is viewed skeptically by the corporatist state in Singapore.

DIFFERENCES

Despite the collectivist and corporatist commonalities between national socialism and political capitalism, there are also distinct differences.

First, national socialism, when it is not outright hostile toward capitalism and the bourgeoisie, is economically autarchic in its ambition; political capitalism is mercantilist within the context of a liberal international trade regime. Long before coming to power, the Nazis' Twenty-five Points (1920) was hostile to all capitalism except artisanal production. However, once in power the Nazi regime sought to collaborate with big business to rearm the country. Industrialists collaborated, despite these overtly autarchic policies, in exchange for the emasculation of labor unions.[62] Ultimately, the Nazis despised the bourgeoisie not for exploiting their workers, but for their "softness."[63] For national socialists, autarchy is a means of establishing and preserving state sovereignty and national unity. Political capitalism is not oriented toward developing autarchy, except perhaps in the defense industry. Even if a political-capitalist regime wanted to create an autarchic economy, in the current era of globalization a reliance on global and regional value chains to spur industrial development rules out this possibility.

Second, national socialism is geared toward comprehensive planning in the service of the military; political capitalism permits a wide scope for market allocation of resources. While a political-capitalist state may seek to develop a military capable of protecting trade routes and deterring foreign aggression, the economy is not geared toward comprehensive planning.

Third, nationalism and militarism are used instrumentally in a political-capitalist system; nationalism and militarism are fundamentally constitutive of national socialism.

The amplification of nationalism that reemerged with China's Patriotic Education Campaign of the 1990s was the party/state's response to the Tiananmen Square Massacre of 1989. The articulation of the "Chinese Dream" in 2012 and the launching of the Patriotic Education in the New Era campaign in 2019 are Xi Jinping's attempts to build on these earlier endeavors to exploit nationalism and reground the party, state, and ruler's legitimacy.[64] While a few scholars have characterized Xi Jinping's ambition as "national-socialism with Chinese characteristics," that is, a form of fascism, most China scholars would not accept this line of argument.[65] It is correct that Xi has restored the primacy of the party and reversed the growing autonomy of society to organize itself under his predecessor. Xi's cult of personality, signaled by the elevation of so-called Xi Jinping Thought to the status of state dogma, is reminiscent of totalitarian regimes. Relatedly, Xi has also undermined Deng Xiaoping's principle of collective leadership.

However, militarism—beyond a defense of core territorial interests—is not a component of Xi Jinping's strategy. While China has increased military spending in line with its growing prosperity, it would not be correct to interpret China under Xi Jinping as a militaristic society:

> Despite this new positioning, China is not yet a global power, and its "new assertiveness" under Xi Jinping has more to do with the way other powers perceive it than with an actual radical change in its foreign policy, as, for the most part, it shows a great deal of continuity with Chinese foreign policy of previous decades. Nevertheless, its economic transformation and its increasing integration with the global market will have repercussions on China's international presence. It seems that China is, so far, acting within the international legal order and is hesitant about becoming a "revolutionary state" as that will lead to isolation in the international system, as in the 1960s and 1970s.[66]

By contrast, nationalism and militarism are fundamental to national socialism. As Antonio Gramsci realized, although fascism had broad cross-class appeal, military "veterans, nationalists, and legionaries" were a significant bloc within fascism.[67] El-Ojeili adds, citing Michael Mann, that "fascism is inseparable from marching, uniforms, danger, guns, fighting, [and] distinctively 'encaging' young men in paramilitary organizations that proved vital for fascism's successes."[68] Fascism, whether German or Japanese, Italian or Portuguese, Romanian or Hungarian, is intimately tied to nationalism and militarism wherever it emerges autonomously.

George Mosse, building on the work of Gustave Le Bon, sees the reliance upon nationalism in fascism as a response to fin-de-siècle alienation:

> The conservatism of crowds was reborn in fascism itself as the instinct for national traditions and for the restoration of personal bonds, like the family, which seemed fragmented in modern society. This conservatism was closely connected with the longing for an end to alienation, for belonging to a definite group. But the group had to be a traditional one, and it had to represent the restoration of the traditional morality. Hitler, for example, believed mass movements necessary because they enabled man to step out of his workshop, where he feels small, and to be surrounded by "thousands and thousands of people with like convictions." Alienation was to be exorcized, but on the basis of accepting a view of man as both irrational and conservative. Similarly in Italy an historically centred nationalism was to provide the "national consensus."[69]

Again, nationalism and militarism were not merely instrumental to fascism; they were constitutive. As Ernst Nolte writes, "Fascism begins at the point where nationalism becomes radicalized and, therefore, changed."[70] Radical or ultranationalism was particularly promoted by veterans as a means of restoring the comradeship, equality of sacrifice, and leadership of their military experience.[71] At times, this form of nationalism was overlaid with religion (e.g., with existing religion in the case of the Belgian Rexist Party; or with the deification of the state itself as the foundation of a political religion) and racism (e.g., German Nazism toward Jews and East Europeans or Italian fascism toward Libyans and Ethiopians),[72] but the point was primarily to unify the *Volk* and usher in a national revival in order to midwife the birth of a "new man."

Fourth, national socialism (and fascism more generally) has historically come to power in cooperation with conservative or traditional elites. Robert Paxton argues that this historical context, which induces a struggle between the leader, conservatives, party functionaries, and state functionaries, is why fascist regimes appear so shapeless and febrile.[73] Political capitalism, which emerges in postcommunist or strong one-party states that have eradicated traditional or conservative elites, is closer to Stalinism in this regard, since there is no traditional or conservative elite to constrain the exercise of power from their inherited and autonomous bases.

Conclusion

The differences between national socialism and political capitalism outweigh the similarities, even as political-capitalist regimes instrumentally deploy nationalism to preserve regime legitimacy. In any case, unlike the links between socialism and national socialism, there is no evidence of ideological conversion from national socialism to political capitalism or vice versa. Thus it is wise, in the battle of ideas, to maintain the distinctions between antiliberal regime types.

CHAPTER THIRTEEN

The Totalitarians in Our Midst

When authority presents itself in the guise of organization, it develops charms fascinating enough to convert communities of free people into totalitarian States.

The Times (1937)

Although not named in Hayek's epigraph, the passage is from an editorial preface to William Henry Beveridge's third and final article (printed on the same page) in a series titled "The Home Front in War: III.—A General Staff," published in *The Times* (London) on February 24, 1937—two years before Britain's entry into World War II.

Beveridge, a Fabian socialist economist, was the director of the London School of Economics (LSE) from 1919 to 1937. (Hayek had joined the LSE in 1931.) Beveridge's report in 1942, "Social Insurance and Allied Services," would serve as the foundation of the British welfare state after World War II.

In the editorial introduction, the *Times* editor argues in favor of social planning and combining reconstruction and rearmament against the possibility of another war in Europe. A larger section of the original article needs to be quoted to provide proper context.

Once committed to the practice of extracting good from evil, and of making a virtue of necessity, we may well find that its application is not restricted to material concerns. The transition from an individualist to a coordinated economy is not the only task which confronts modern democratic statesmanship. The old antagonism between authority and liberty has assumed new and formidable shape. *When authority presents itself in the guise of organization it develops charms fascinating enough to convert communities of free peoples into totalitarian States.* The dilemma which presents itself is very real. Either the outward tokens of a free life must be sacrificed or freedom itself will be imperiled, for in the modern world improvisation in support of the best of political causes will fail against organized and mechanized tyranny. For democracy this dilemma is personified by the expert, without whom Government fumbles its grip on social needs, but whose word prevails, not because it persuades, but because it commands. Yet in truth difficulties arise only because the remnants of the *laissez-faire* tradition still hang about the conception of freedom. To be free, as nineteenth-century thought saw it, was to be released from the shackles of obsolete authority. To be free, as twentieth-century thought is beginning to see it, is to organize that the gains of freedom shall not be precarious but shall be wrought into the very texture of a people's life. The light of nearly twenty years' further experience shows vividly what is involved in making the world safe for democracy. It was not enough to organize victory. The need was so to organize the peace-making and peace itself that victory might be set beyond challenge. Because that need was not met organization must exert itself now to avert a danger of renewed war which greater foresight could never have allowed to emerge. But there is nothing anti-democratic in this process, and the steps taken to preserve freedom can also serve to extend it. That is the lesson as it is presented now, and, because he has already mastered it, Sir William Beveridge sees in an adequately protected home front not one huge national dug-out but a healthier and more evenly prosperous England. [Emphasis added][1]

To summarize, the editor is arguing that authority disguised as organization is dangerous and likely to spawn a totalitarian state even in a free society. However, liberal democracy and freedom will lose to totalitarianism if some "outward tokens of a free life" are not sacrificed. The editor believes Beveridge to be arguing that society cannot rely on a spontaneous order when confronting a totalitarian state. Freedom needs to be enfolded into the life of a people through organization. It was the failure of the Allied powers in World War I to "organize the peace-making" that explains the precipice on which Europe found itself by 1937.

It should be clear that *The Times* was not endorsing a position with which Hayek would wholeheartedly agree. For his epigraph, Hayek extracts only the snippet of the argument with which he agrees.

∴

This chapter is a fierce, frontal counterattack against realism in the disciplines of political science and international relations, German scientists and engineers who served the Nazi regime, and monopolistic owners of capital. For Hayek, the realists and scientists are an example of the "totalitarians in our midst." Here Hayek traces the spread of illiberal Germanic thinking into English political thought.

Hayek argues that the outrages committed by totalitarian regimes give liberal societies the false impression that such a system of government could not arise in their countries. A more accurate picture of the potential for sociopolitical transformation comes into focus when one examines contemporary liberal societies in contrast to totalitarian societies a generation or two before their regime change. The telling characteristics that Hayek emphasizes are (1) the increasing similarity between the left and right ends of the political spectrum, (2) the increasing veneration of the state, (3) the admiration of power, (4) the preference for "bigness" for its own sake, (5) the enthusiasm for the "organization" of everything, and (6) the inability to accept organic growth.[2]

Hayek is particularly distressed by Britons who neglect their own iconic English liberal thinkers and politicians in favor of German ones. Ironically, given his argument about changing British preferences, Hayek cites Keynes' "nightmare," that is, a caustic review by Keynes of a German economist who argued for the continuing mobilization of industry in peacetime in order to create an organically unified state along Platonist lines.

In portraying Nazism as a radical alien ideology, Hayek does continue to conflate liberalism with the totality of "Western civilization."[3] This only creates confusion, since he previously argued that socialism emerged as a reaction to the liberalism of the French Revolution and that socialist intellectual trends set the stage for national socialism. The argument is clearer if we discard the conflation of liberalism with Western civilization.

Amoral Realists

Hayek demonstrates the penetration of German ideas in the English intellectual world by selecting two books from the realist thinker E. H. Carr: *The Twenty Years' Crisis* and the *Conditions of Peace*.[4] The willingness of Carr, a self-described adherent of the German historical school of realism, to pit his argument against English liberalism and individualism, thinly disguised by the labels of "utopianism" or "idealism," is revealing. Hayek is scandalized by the realists' willingness to openly advocate expediency as a moral principle in international relations. Hayek exposes the fact that utopianism or idealism, as caricatured by the realists, is ultimately liberal and individualist, since "it ma[kes] the human conscience the final court of appeal."[5] Realists' unwillingness to respect even the most fundamental principle of civil and international law, that is, that pacts must be respected, generates an amoral, anarchic order that they posit as ontological. Hence, it is not surprising that Carr is unable to distinguish the national socialists' identification of their national interest with universal right from similar assertions by liberal politicians in the United States and the United Kingdom.

Hayek equates Carr's erasure of the distinction between society and state to the Nazi theoretician Carl Schmitt's definition of totalitarianism.[6] Similarly, Carr's defense of propaganda is linked to the fascist regimentation of opinion. Hayek accuses Carr of overtly Nazi sympathies and an abiding hostility to liberal democracy, national self-determination, and laissez-faire economics.[7] Hayek's accusations were not libelous; in 1937, after a visit to Nazi Germany, Carr had written that Germany under the Nazis "was almost a free country as compared with Russia."[8] Hayek also finds Carr repeating the arguments of Friedrich List against free trade, glorifying war as a means of creating social solidarity, and predicting the inevitable triumph of authoritarian collectivism. Carr had even openly admired Hitler's effort to create a large planned and integrated economic area under German hegemony.[9]

Ironically, Carr is usually more associated with the political Left than the political Right. Contemporary international relations scholars—relying on the work of Carr's biographer and research assistant Jonathan Haslam, and on writings by Carr praising the Soviet Union in the early 1930s—tend to identify Carr as having been influenced by the life and works of Marx, Fyodor Dostoevsky, and Mikhail Bakunin, each of whom were the subjects of biographies Carr wrote in the 1930s.[10] Although Carr certainly read Marx directly, Carr's "Marxism" was mainly absorbed through the writing of the proponent of centralized state planning Karl Mannheim—an archrival of Hayek at the LSE.[11] Carr used Mannheim's critical sociology of knowledge to critique and deconstruct the rhetorical utopianism of his opponents, only to then turn around and embrace a utopian faith in statism himself—a trick not fully appreciated by many scholars who have sought to rigidly classify Carr as an unambiguous and "hard-nosed" realist.[12]

Carr's interwar praise for fascism, contempt for the nationalism of smaller states, and desire to see German power restored is generally ignored or dismissed as mere opportunism by international relations scholars today, despite the fact that the central policy recommendation of Carr's *Twenty Years' Crisis* is appeasement.[13] Moreover, Carr's own troubling postwar admission that "no doubt I was very blind" in admiring Hitler's regime is conveniently forgotten.[14] The fact that Carr, by his own admission, only *began* to see Hitler as a potential danger around 1938, after the annexation of Austria, may indicate that the supposedly uncompromising realist was not such a shrewd and farsighted analyst of international politics after all. In any case, *The Twenty Years' Crisis*, which endorsed Prime Minister Chamberlain's appeasement of Hitler, was first published in September 1939—well after *Kristallnacht*, the November 1938 pogrom against German Jewish citizens and synagogues, and the violation of the 1938 Munich Agreement, which resulted in Hitler's occupation of Czechoslovakia in March 1939. In fact, Carr argued in the first edition that Chamberlain's appeasement, resulting in the negotiated dismemberment of Czechoslovakia, was preferable to militarized conflict. He only mildly chastised Hitler for his military provocations, believing that Nazi Germany's cynicism regarding the role of morality in international relations was justified by the harsh treatment it had suffered at Versailles in 1919. His real critique was not that the Allies sought to appease Hitler, but that they appeased Hitler while verbally protesting his military aggression. In other words, the Allies should have accepted Germany's territorially expansionist demands on neighboring states as legitimate and used this accommodation to reconcile with Germany.[15] Unsurprisingly, Carr carefully scrubbed these sections from the second edition, published in 1946.

Once World War II was well underway, Carr would flop back to supporting the Soviet Union. He wrote nearly four hundred editorial articles for *The Times*, where he was the assistant editor from 1941 to 1946, arguing a pro-Soviet stance in foreign policy and advocating for recognizing and even supporting a Soviet sphere of influence in Eastern Europe. Casting aside ideological rivalries, he advocated the "practical" goal of ensuring political and economic security through centralized state planning.[16] Carr was not the typically misguided intellectual when it came the USSR; having served in Britain's Foreign Office from 1916 to 1936, Carr was well aware of the fundamentally brutal nature of the Soviet regime. Nevertheless, he saw in the Soviet experiment potential lessons for Western societies.

What bridged Carr's seemingly contradictory admiration for both Hitler's Germany and Stalin's Soviet Union was a deep distaste for the "anarchy of capitalism" following the Great Depression and his belief that expanding the role and scope of the state was inevitable, admirable, and worthy of emulation by Western states, particularly Great Britain.[17] Carr's firm faith in this "inevitability" led him to endorse appeasement of both the Nazis in the 1930s and the Soviets in the 1940s.[18] As the epitome of an influential mid-century British public intellectual, Carr's woefully shortsighted admiration for internally and externally expansive states starkly exemplified the danger that flowed from British intellectual circles' denigration of liberalism. The fact that Carr is still taught today in the field of international relations as the paragon of a no-nonsense realist and a founding father of the critical-theory camp indicates that Hayek's critique failed to penetrate.[19]

Servile Scientists

Hayek reminds his readers that, in addition to intellectuals, there were many scientists and engineers who served the national-socialist regime: "It is well known that particularly the scientists and engineers, who had so loudly claimed to be the leaders on the march to a new and better world, submitted more readily than almost any other class to the new tyranny."[20] He blames the German education system, which abandoned the humanities in favor of "realities" over the century before World War II. Hayek argues that scientists easily fall for the vain, superstitious belief that science is competent in areas of moral philosophy. This superstition leads the scientist to stray into discussions of politics while masking their passions with a veneer of science. More broadly, Hayek sees scientists as displaying an impatience with laymen and contempt for aspects of social life that are not organized by "superior minds."

Hayek relies on the English embryologist and geneticist Conrad Hal Waddington's book *The Scientific Attitude* to demonstrate his line of argument. Hayek illustrates that Waddington was under the sway of a fatalistic outlook on history influenced by Marxism. He ridicules Waddington for the assertion that freedom of thought would be preserved in a totalitarian state.[21] While Hayek's brief illustrative case study is interesting, the discussion of Waddington by itself is hardly compelling to a critical reader.

Corporatist Collaborators

Two other (nonintellectual) entities advanced the movement toward totalitarianism: organized capital and organized labor. The commonality between the two forces was support for the monopolistic organization of industry, which evolves into corporatism. Organized capital and labor are led invariably by the capitalist organizers of monopoly, but they acquire the support of organized labor under the logic that a monopolist can afford to pay higher wages. Although monopolistic capitalists do not aim to build a totalitarian state, they are often shortsighted in believing that they will retain their autonomy in any regime. Hayek expresses his skepticism that private ownership of monopolistic industries would long be tolerated by a totalitarian state: "The decisions which the managers of such an organized industry would constantly have to make are not decisions which any society will long leave to private individuals. A state which allows such enormous aggregations of power to grow up cannot afford to let this power rest entirely in private control."[22] Hayek is correct that a totalitarian state will naturally seek to limit the accumulation of economic power outside the state. However, in a political-capitalist system, the state need not seek to capture and nationalize concentrations of private power. The absence of the rule of law, the use of anticorruption campaigns to neuter rising oligarchs, and the discretionary power of technocratic bureaucrats can all work to retain state autonomy without terminating a reliance on the market economy.

Hayek sought a small but muscular state capable of controlling monopolies, but he preferred to leave monopolies in private hands if the only alternative was the establishment of state monopolies: "Where the power which ought to check and control monopoly becomes interested in sheltering and defending its appointees, where for the government to remedy an abuse is to admit responsibility for it, and where criticism of the actions of monopoly means criticism of the government, there is little hope of monopoly becoming the servant of the community."[23]

Conclusion

Hayek's attack on the pragmatic public intellectual, the haughty scientist, the scheming captain of industry, and the colluding union boss seeks to illustrate that the seeds of illiberalism are widespread in the elite circles of an open society such as Great Britain. What unites these individuals is a desire to organize the spontaneous, chaotic, and seemingly muddled order around them for aesthetic pleasure, power, influence, and personal or collective material gain. Hayek is warning the reader that authority disguised as organization is dangerous to a liberal society, and that the proponents of organization are well placed to advocate for their grand strategies and designs. Of course, if a truly totalitarian state comes to power, that state would undoubtedly seek to destroy or subordinate these independent bases of power and influence. A political-capitalist regime can be more flexible with rival sources of power and influence, as it can rely on anticorruption campaigns and rule by law to neutralize selective threats, retain state autonomy, and still reap the benefits of a market economy. Authority now presents itself in a more complex guise.

CHAPTER FOURTEEN

Material Conditions and Ideal Ends

Is it just or reasonable, that most voices against the main end of government should enslave the less number that would be free? More just it is, doubtless, if it come to force, that a less number compel a greater to retain, which can be no wrong to them, their liberty, than that a greater number, for the pleasure of their baseness, compel a less most injuriously to be their fellow slaves. They who seek nothing but their own just liberty, have always the right to win it, whenever they have the power, be the voices never so numerous that oppose it.

John Milton (1660)

There are parallels between Hayek's *Road to Serfdom* and Milton's *Readie and Easie Way to Establish a Free Commonwealth* (1660). The two pamphlets argue, in the face of an impending sociopolitical transformation, in favor of "returning" to an almost utopian vision of republican government that will protect against the tyranny of the majority. Nevertheless, Milton's understanding that liberty flows from a government of the wise and godly is quite distinct from that demonstrated by Hayek, who emphasized the individual as best placed to make use of their own knowledge in matters of opinion and taste.[1]

Thus one sees over the course of three centuries a dramatic evolution in thinking about freedom.[2] The earlier strand insists on the role of a republic guided by a moral and educated elite against the tyranny of the brute majority. The latter strand insists on the autonomy of the free market as a logical extension of a free individual and resists arbitrary efforts to channel the market mechanism (and hence the individual) for the good of the many.[3] There is a shared distrust of the rude masses, but later theorists also reject the guiding hand of a group of philosopher-kings in favor of the invisible hand of impersonal market forces.

The multiple references to Milton in this chapter and throughout *The Road to Serfdom* are not superficial. Hayek felt compelled to defend Milton against "a host of American and English detractors." In particular, Hayek took umbrage at the American poet Ezra Pound, who became enamored with fascism while living in Italy from 1924 to 1945.[4] While Pound was often scathing in his assessment of Milton, it should be noted that Pound was primarily focused on Milton's Latinized poetic style, not his political stance.[5] Nonetheless, in Hayek's mind there was a clear connection between Pound's denigration of Milton as a poet and the denigration of liberalism. Later in the chapter, Hayek tellingly quotes a passage from a sonnet by William Wordsworth (1770–1850) written in 1802:

> It is not to be thought of that the Flood
> Of British freedom, which, to the open sea
> Of the world's praise, from dark antiquity
> Hath flowed, "with pomp of water, unwithstood,"
> [. . .] In our halls is hung
> Armoury of the invincible Knights of old:
> We must be free or die, who speak the tongue
> That Shakespeare spake; the faith and morals hold
> Which Milton held.—In every thing we are sprung
> Of Earth's first blood, have titles manifold.[6]

But Hayek could easily have quoted another of Wordsworth's sonnets dedicated to liberty, "London, 1802":

> Milton! thou should'st be living at this hour:
> England hath need of thee: She is a fen
> Of stagnant waters: altar, sword, and pen,
> Fireside, the heroic wealth of hall and bower,
> Have forfeited their ancient English dower
> Of inward happiness. We are selfish men;
> Oh! raise us up, return to us again;
> And give us manners, virtue, freedom, power.
> Thy soul was like a Star, and dwelt apart:
> Thou hadst a voice whose sound was like the sea:
> Pure as the naked heavens, majestic, free,
> So didst thou travel on life's common way,
> In cheerful godliness; and yet thy heart
> The lowliest duties on herself did lay.[7]

For Hayek as for Wordsworth, Milton's morals, poetry, and politics were intertwined; to disparage any aspect of Milton was seen as an affront to the totality of what the man symbolizes.

More speculatively, Hayek's defense of Milton might also be seen as a counterpoint to the final lines of William Blake's (1757–1827) preface to his epic visionary poem *Milton: A Poem in Two Books* (c. 1808). Blake's preface echoes scenes from Milton's *Paradise Lost*, although Blake believed that Milton wanted him (i.e., Blake) to expose the errors of Milton's doctrine of political, social, and sexual repression.[8] While Blake admired Milton's iconoclastic political radicalism and republicanism, he rejected Milton's theological puritanism.[9] Blake's poem, which had not circulated widely until it was set to music in 1916 by Sir Hubert Parry, would herald the spirit of the suffragist movement during World War I and, later, post–World War II Britain's lofty ambitions. In particular, before acquiring the broadly patriotic significance it holds today, the hymn came to be associated with the Christian Socialist prime minister Clement Attlee (1945–51) and the Labour Party:

> I will not cease from Mental Fight,
> Nor shall my Sword sleep in my hand:
> Till we have built Jerusalem,
> In England's green & pleasant Land.

These familiar words would also conclude the memorial service in 1946 to Hayek's friend and intellectual rival John Maynard Keynes.[10] In the postwar era, it is precisely this fevered spirit, held by an overwhelming majority of British citizens, to use the government to create a new Jerusalem that Hayek sought to moderate.

∴

Transcending Materialism?

Has humanity (or at least that small sliver of humanity that resides in the high-income economies and earns a high income) entered a postmaterialist age? Haven't the material considerations fostered by capitalism become subordinate to higher ideal ends? Hasn't capitalism failed to create either equality or freedom for the masses? These are the questions that frame the fourteenth chapter.

It is worth recalling that in Hayek's time, European fascists and socialists had answered all of these questions in the affirmative. For example, Mussolini wrote: "Fascism denies the materialist conception of happiness as a possibility, and abandons it to its inventors, the economists of the first half of the nineteenth century."[11] Mussolini would go on to argue that fascism's general attitude toward life was not confined to the "superficial" material world, which atomized the individual, but rather expanded into a spiritual attitude that championed "organic" social bonds.[12] Fascism promised to fulfill the Marxian prophecy of overcoming the alienation and fragmentation generated by capitalism.

Similarly, Hayek's foil at the start of the chapter, Peter F. Drucker, argues in *The End of Economic Man: A Study of Totalitarianism* (1939) that laissez-faire capitalism and Marxian communism had failed to capture the imagination of the twentieth century because they were predicated on the rationality of the economic order—a belief that was destroyed by World War I and the Great Depression—and had failed to deliver freedom and equality in the economic sphere.[13] The Great War destroyed any illusion of the international solidarity of the working class,[14] and the Great Depression destroyed the image of an internally rational economic logic. These ideas lived on, of course, but only as hollow shells once their spiritual promise was revealed to be empty. Drucker writes,

> If socialism cannot establish the classless society its aims must of necessity become limited to improving the social and economic lot of the workers. . . .
>
> But the appeal of socialism had not been based originally upon its promise to bring better bargaining conditions for unskilled workers. It owed its strength and its very existence as a creed to the promise to bring a new social order and to establish equality. Without this appeal the belief in socialism has no basis and disintegrates. Its continued existence becomes dependent upon the belief in the capitalist creed and the capitalist order of which it has become a part—though as integral opposition.[15]

And despite the material comfort that capitalism supplies, Drucker also deems it a failure, at least in terms of delivering substantive and even formal equality and freedom: "The failure to establish equality by economic freedom has destroyed the belief in capitalism as a social system in spite of material blessings, not only for the proletariat but among the very middle classes who have benefited most economically and socially."[16] Hayek rejects all of these notions of material transcendence; he notes instead the primacy of economic concerns in social reform efforts. In particular, concepts of liberty, equality, and security are increasingly expressed in economic rather than political, spiritual, or philosophical criteria.[17] Hayek asserts that a postmaterialist age is not on the horizon, despite the repeated false assertions that capitalism is the barrier to an era of plenty and equality.

Hayek's argument is aimed at the psychological unwillingness of individuals to accept arguments premised on scarcity or notions of trade-offs, that is, economic arguments. This resistance reflects in modern man a "revolt against the impersonal forces to which in the past he submitted, even though they have often frustrated his individual efforts."[18] Hayek's counterargument is clever: he does not seek to convince his reader that economic forces are in fact rational.

Rationality and Submission

Hayek introduces the notion that nonrational submission to market forces allowed a complex order to emerge. The market is not a rational order, it lies in between instinct and reason. Moreover, the market order is built on a moral and cultural foundation supplied in part by religion and superstition, which are irrational.[19] Despite the market's impersonal and nonrational character, submission to it enables the growth of civilization. Civilization creates the possibility of reason, although it is not grounded on reason.

Hayek is not reflexively antirational; he seeks to praise the general disposition that rejects submission without critical scrutiny: "This revolt is an instance of a much more general phenomenon, a new unwillingness to submit to any rule or necessity the rationale of which man does not understand; it makes itself felt in many fields of life, particularly in that of morals; and it is often a commendable attitude."[20] However, a skeptical outlook paired with a general resistance to economic logic opens the door to magical thinking. In part, this resistance to notions of scarcity is driven by pseudotheories of "potential plenty," to be unleashed after the defeat of capitalism. Popular critiques of capitalism are often internally incoherent and convoluted, because they mistake the effects of monopoly for that of competition. Hayek argues that the refusal to submit to forces whose logic cannot be made fully intelligible to the individual threatens the broader civilizational order: "It was men's submission to the impersonal forces of the market that in the past has made possible the growth of a civilization which without this could not have developed; it is by thus submitting that we are every day helping to build something that is greater than any one of us can fully comprehend."[21] The argument is consistent with Hayek's general theory of knowledge. The market is far too complex for an individual to digest intellectually. At best, an individual will detect proximate relations of cause and effect, but the broader structural framework will elude her. Hayek writes:

> A complex civilization like ours is necessarily based on the individual's adjusting himself to changes whose cause and nature he cannot under-

stand: why he should have more or less, why he should have to move to another occupation, why some things he wants should become more difficult to get than others, will always be connected with such a multitude of circumstances that no single mind will be able to grasp them; or, even worse, those affected will put all the blame on an obvious immediate and avoidable cause, while the more complex interrelationships which determine the change remain hidden to them.[22]

Hayek's critique of the obstinate rationalist man echoes the words of Adam Smith in *The Theory of Moral Sentiments*:

The man of system, on the contrary, is apt to be very wise in his own conceit; and is often so enamoured with the supposed beauty of this own ideal plan of government, that he cannot suffer the smallest deviation from any part of it. He goes on to establish it completely and in all its parts, without any regard either to the great interests, or to the strong prejudices which may oppose it. He seems to imagine that he can arrange the different members of a great society with as much ease as the hand arranges the different pieces upon a chess-board. He does not consider that the pieces upon the chess-board have no other principle of motion besides that which the hand impresses upon them; but that, in the great chess-board of human society, every single piece has a principle of motion of its own altogether different from that which the legislature might chuse to impress upon it. . . .

Some general, and even systematical, idea of the perfection of policy and law, may no doubt be necessary for directing the views of the statesman. But to insist upon establishing, and upon establishing all at once, and in spite of all opposition, every thing which that idea may seem to require, must often be the highest degree of arrogance.[23]

While the rationalist (or "constructivist," in Hayek's phrasing) refuses to submit to forces beyond intelligibility and critical scrutiny, he is not dissimilar to Smith's man of system, who views his fellow citizens as a pawns and society as mechanistically organized. These two individuals are two sides of the same coin because their view of society relies on mechanical thinking.

Hayek condemns this form of rationalism:

The refusal to yield to forces which we neither understand nor can recognize as the conscious decisions of an intelligent being is the product of an incomplete and therefore erroneous rationalism. It is incomplete because it fails to comprehend that the coordination of the multifarious individual efforts in a complex society must take account of facts no individual can completely survey. And it fails to see that, unless this complex society is to be destroyed, the only alternative to submission to the impersonal and seemingly irrational forces of the market is submission to an equally uncontrollable and therefore arbitrary power of other men.[24]

The stark dichotomy between submission to impersonal market forces and submission to personalized, arbitrary power seems too extreme. Of course, Hayek is not arguing that the market is sacrosanct or that men ought not make laws to regulate it. As noted earlier (see chapter 3), Hayek endorsed the use of uniform regulations of market actors. His main intent is to encourage his readers to recognize the limits of rationalism against the sublime aura of a complex civilizational order.

Individual Freedom and Single Purpose

Utopian schemes abound when societies delude themselves into believing they can transcend market forces, for example, by setting a unified purpose for a whole society. Hayek argues that individual freedom cannot exist in a society organized to fulfill a single purpose, with the exceptions of total war and temporary disaster. Existential threats that require an immediate concentration of resources permit freedom to survive in the long run, and thus it is logical to sacrifice short-term for long-term freedom; but a free society cannot function on a permanent war footing.

Writing in the midst of a world war, Hayek was naturally eager to restore individual freedoms and the market order in peacetime. However, he worried that unions would resist the reimposition of a competitive system, which would certainly result in unemployment and declines in wages as the intensity of wartime demand faded. In particular, he was concerned that the aim of full employment would capture the attention of a society already fully mobilized for war. Given that the painful reallocation of labor following wartime mobilization would necessarily entail either coercive reassignment or prolonged unemployment until workers accepted lower wages, it is clear why a society would seek to pursue full employment rather than return to a market order. A state could easily use an expansionary monetary policy to provide the illusion of full employment in the short run. In the long run, prolonged monetary expansion would undermine labor productivity, reduce real wages, and entrench inflationary expectations in wage negotiations. He describes the theft of wages through inflation as "concealed and underhanded."[25] His underlying message is clear: there are no short cuts to achieving full employment in a free society. Intervention in the market mechanism inhibits the ability of the market to self-adjust to changes in demand and productivity. In the long run, monetary manipulation sets the stage for a much more painful readjustment than if society has submitted to market forces at the outset.

Hayek assumed that Great Britain would be a poor country after the war, as it was indebted and impaired by the war effort. Reconstruction would require balancing consumption with needed reconstruction and industrial overhaul. He feared, however, that Britain would adopt redistributive policies to stave off the appeal of socialism among the workers. Hayek supports a basic minimum income for all but hopes to block claims for a higher level of economic security or efforts to prevent immigration: "Let a uniform minimum be secured to everybody by all means; but let us admit at the same time that with this assurance of a basic minimum all claims to a privileged security of particular classes must lapse, that all excuses disappear for allowing groups to exclude newcomers from sharing their relative prosperity in order to maintain a special standard of their own."[26] While Hayek certainly supported working to improve the general level of wealth, he was always skeptical of utopian schemes and shortcuts. Nevertheless, he presciently warns his reader, "The one thing modern democracy will not bear without cracking is the necessity of a substantial lowering of the standards of living in peacetime or even prolonged stationariness of its economic conditions."[27] The challenge of adjustment for Western Europe would be significantly eased with the announcement of the Marshall Plan (formally known as the European Recovery Plan) in 1948. However, in the twenty-first century, the stagnation of wages in the middle and lower classes over several decades has resulted in tensions in the major democracies.

Individual Morality and Ideal Ends

Hayek anticipates and rejects the counterargument that socialism or collectivism, while admittedly likely to threaten economic prospects, is still preferable as it promotes "much higher values." He notes that half a century of "collectivism" in Britain has hardly raised moral standards and more likely lowered those standards. While he detects a much greater indignity toward the inequities of capitalist society in his generation than in previous ones, he notes no changes in positive standards or moral principles. It is likely that Hayek would make the same observation if he were alive today.

Hayek reminds his reader that only in the context of free choice and individual responsibility can one confer moral value on decisions. Hayek cites Milton's "Areopagitica": "If every action which is good or evil in a man of ripe years were under pittance and prescription and compulsion, what were virtue but a name, what praise should then be due to well-doing, what gramercy to be sober, just, or continent?"[28] Hayek's critique of collectivism on this front is that it aims to relieve the individual from responsibility and is therefore antimoral. Where the individual cannot arrange their own life and take responsibility for the consequences of their own decisions, morality cannot exist. And where morality and individual responsibility are absent, there can only be a demand for obedience or compulsion to accept collective goals. Even if these collective goals are decided through democratic elections, Hayek contends that moral values are not at stake, since the individual is not asked to sacrifice lower values to sustain higher ones.

Hayek sees that individuals of his generation are being asked not to sacrifice their material comfort, but to regard the moral values of liberalism (i.e., liberty, independence, the rights-bearing individual, democracy, etc.) as anachronistic. Hayek claims that the sacrosanct rights of the individual are increasingly being supplanted by the rights of closed groups and nations. Although Hayek is quite vague in this section, he seems to be expressing indignation at the emergence of forced detention camps in liberal societies during World War II, or perhaps he is thinking of the policy of partition: ". . . and the grossest violations of the most elementary rights of the individual, such as are involved in the compulsory transfer of populations, are more and more often countenanced even by supposed liberals." Hayek also takes a swipe at realism in international relations, an argument he will pursue in the next chapter, and the priority given to exigency in foreign affairs: "When we are reminded, as more and more frequently happens, that one cannot make omelettes without breaking eggs, the eggs which are broken are almost all of the kind which a generation or two ago were regarded as the essential bases of civilized life. And what atrocities committed by powers with whose professed principles they sympathize have not been readily condoned by many of our so-called 'liberals'?"[29] As an immigrant, Hayek makes a special appeal to the English people not to forget their heritage as liberals:

> And if one who, whatever the law may say, must forever remain a foreigner, may be allowed to say so, it is one of the most disheartening spectacles of our time to see to what extent some of the most precious things which England, for example, has given to the world are now held in contempt in England herself. The English hardly know to what degree they

differ from most other people in that they all, irrespective of party, hold to a greater or less extent the ideas which in their most pronounced form are known as liberalism.[30]

Hayek's attempt to flatter his English hosts is understandable, but not convincing or compelling. He goes so far as to quote Milton, saying, "Let not England forget her precedence of teaching nations how to live."[31] Today the passages seem awkward and anachronistic at best.

The underlying point of Hayek's flattery, however, is that the British need to prepare for a battle of ideas with the Germans after the war is concluded. Hayek is urging the British not to regurgitate back to the Germans their own stale ideas: state socialism, *Realpolitik*, "scientific" planning, corporatism. Hayek is asking liberals to gird their loins and be true to their own traditions, for the Germans ". . . might be convinced that the way they have chosen was wrong—but nothing will ever convince them that the British or Americans will be better guides on the German path." Hayek states that what chastened Germans want now is protection from the "monster state" and an opportunity to build their own little worlds.[32] A similar disposition is advisable for liberals facing the challenge of political capitalism today.

Postmaterialism and Political Capitalism

Leaders of contemporary political-capitalist regimes are under no illusion that a postmaterialist age has emerged in their societies. In fact, in much of the world the quest for material wealth, economic growth, and personal security continues apace. Political-capitalist regimes and their societies increasingly see the market as a mechanism to generate plenty, not a barrier to generalized prosperity. Their worldview is still characterized by the recognition of persistent scarcity, the need to make trade-offs, and (at least selective) submission to impersonal market forces.

There is greater attention to the environmental consequences of rapid growth and improving the quality of life for ordinary citizens,[33] but sustaining relatively high levels of growth is still seen as a priority among most citizens and decision makers. In China, while women, youth, and better-educated individuals with postmaterialist values do show more concerns about the environmental impacts of high growth, people from more CO_2-dependent economic regions tend to be *less* concerned about global warming and climate change than those from less CO_2-dependent economic regions.[34] This may simply reflect economic self-interest. And overall, the intensity of concern about global warming and climate change in China is low, just above the level of "neither concerned nor unconcerned," and quite similar to that in the United States.[35]

While Hayek would not oppose uniform environmental regulations to protect individual well-being and a community's quality of life, the generally pragmatic posture of political-capitalist leaders confirms Hayek's skepticism about emerging postmaterialist values and the related hostility toward capitalism. Similarly, a study of ten prosperous countries found that Singapore scored below the mean, indicating that its citizens were slightly more materialistic than postmaterialistic. Notably, the United States scored the lowest, followed by Australia and Japan. The study concluded that regime type and level of welfare shape an individual's postmaterialistic values more than individual or national economic level.[36]

Postmaterialism and Liberal Meritocratic Regimes

Hayek would note with concern, however, the perennial discussion of postmaterialism in liberal meritocratic societies. Today's scholars of postmaterialism continue to assert an intergenerational shift in value priorities, but with new (and sometimes contradictory) twists. Douglas Booth, for example, argues that aspects of postmaterialism may be vital to the preservation of political liberalism. According to him, postmaterialist virtues are associated with freedom of expression, social and sexual tolerance, a humane society, and democracy. These virtues are in turn associated with a willingness to join voluntary associations, pursue creativity in the world of work, and engage in political action.[37] Edmund Cheng, Hiu-Fung Chung, and Anthony Cheng argue that individuals with postmaterialist values and high levels of life dissatisfaction are more likely to engage in radicalized political actions (e.g., strikes and boycotts), but increased life satisfaction weakens the relationship between postmaterialism and participation in conventional political actions (e.g., voting).[38] Dimitri Gugushvili finds that postmaterialists favor reduced economic growth, but at the national level, economic affluence results in greater support for reduced growth regardless of attitudes toward postmaterialism, suggesting that politicians can be bolder in advancing policies that reduce economic growth.[39]

Undoubtedly Hayek would not be impressed by these recent reformulations of an outmoded variant of midcentury modernization theory. As noted earlier, Hayek argues that the political ideals of the past (e.g., liberty, equality, and security) are increasingly understood and expressed in economic terms. Contemporary postmaterialist progressives continue to phrase their demands for social change or social justice primarily in economic terms (e.g., a living wage, emissions taxes, reparations, affirmative action, and socialized medicine). In essence, the main social and political problems in society are still understood to be fundamentally economic or material in scope and solution. Moreover, regardless of survey results showing support for "degrowth" (or *décroissance*) to protect the environment in the abstract, there is virtually no support in actual political practice for deliberately cutting economic growth even in a few select sectors of the economy in affluent countries. Indeed, as Hayek noted earlier, demanding a lowering or even a freeze in the standard of living in peacetime would break almost any democracy.[40]

Hayek would also reiterate that Drucker's *End of Economic Man*, a foundational postmaterialist text, was originally published in 1939 as fascist, liberal, and communist forces collided. Ronald Inglehart's "silent revolution" hypothesis and survey research on intergenerational change from "acquisitive" to "postbourgeois" values (broadened later to the notion of "materialist" and "postmaterialist") in advanced industrial societies was first published in the *American Political Science Review* in 1971—inspired by the May 1968 Paris student protests.[41] It would seem, then, that claims of generational transcendence of materialism achieve prominence with major shifts in economic policy, political events, and popular culture.

Notably, Inglehart published a major follow-up study on materialism and postmaterialism in 1981,[42] just as the neoliberal revolution would unleash pent-up market forces across the high-income countries and challenge the assumption of intracohort stability in value priorities.[43] In 2017 Inglehart and Pippa Norris explained that strong "period effects" owing to significant economic growth but an unequal distribution of wealth since the 1980s had overwhelmed postmaterialist "cohort effects" and resulted in growing support for authoritarian, xenophobic, populist parties among the less educated, older, and less secure in society.[44] The reactionary reversal seemed puzzling: Inglehart, while never completely ruling out the possibility of a backlash, had argued in 1981 that postmaterialism was a "deeply rooted" value, despite the period effects that increased support for materialism owing to inflation and economic turbulence from 1973 to 1978. He had also ruled out life-cycle effects, that is, changes in political attitudes as an individual or cohort ages. Moreover, he had argued that despite being a minority overall, postmaterialists outnumbered materialists in key areas (i.e., higher education, management, and civil service); older cohorts and the Western European political class were becoming increasingly postmaterialist; and postmaterialists were giving rise to a "New Class."[45] As late as 1997, Paul Abramson, Susan Ellis, and Inglehart concluded that "the weight of the evidence demonstrates that the long-term trend toward post-materialism in Western Europe is driven by generational replacement," thus making the triumph of postmaterialism seem inevitable.[46]

Inglehart and Norris awkwardly explained the unexpected reactionary trend by analogizing the xenophobic survival strategies of a fictional starving "tribe" protecting its territory from outsiders with today's high-income countries experiencing economic growth with an inequitable distribution of gains and increased undocumented immigration.[47] From a global perspective, the analogy is odd, since the authoritarian, xenophobic, and populist wave is emerging within the most prosperous and most physically secure regions on the planet and in human history, particularly with the decline in nuclear tensions brought about by the end of the Cold War and a dramatic drop in interstate warfare.

The wealthy regions of the planet are so prosperous that their failure to gravitate toward postmaterialism is surprising. Today, as opposed to two centuries ago, the citizenship premium/penalty is so great that where one is born has a greater influence on one's lifetime income than the social class into which one is born.[48] As Milanovic notes, "People living in the United States tend to have higher incomes, at any given percentile of the national income distribution, than people living in poor countries."[49] Therefore, even with rising inequality and stagnant real wages for the lower half of the income brackets, the poorer citizens of high-income countries tend to be dramatically better off than the citizens of low-income countries and even most of the citizens of middle-income countries in the world. Undoubtedly, Inglehart and Norris would emphasize that it is the subjective *perception* of relative deprivation and insecurity within a country that is the most salient factor supporting the backlash—but this maneuver complicates the argument, which grounds the formation of durable values in preadult experience (and even periodic shifts in attitude) in objective material prosperity and physical security as measured by aggregate economic data (e.g., GNP per capita in PPP) and military events.[50]

Instead of accepting that their theory had been falsified, the authors argued that an aging but materialist cohort overwhelmed the young and progressive postmaterialist cohort within the ruling strata of elites from the 1980s onward. The authors also targeted the political Left's abandonment of redistributive economic issues in favor of cultural (i.e., postmaterialist) struggles in the 1980s as paving the way for increased inequality and hence the xenophobic backlash decades later.[51] In other words, the argument shifted from viewing postmaterialism as the gradual but inevitable outcome of modernization to seeing postmaterialism as a dialectical element that planted the seeds of its own destruction.

Regardless of the value of the completely reworked narrative, Ingle-hart's parsimonious argument, even with its narrow focus on "advanced industrial societies," still cannot credibly explain why countries in East Asia (e.g., South Korea) have remained less postmaterialist than the world average after well over half a century of an economic boom and peace, which brought several of them near the top for economic performance year after year. Although the answer may lie in the differing nature of the provision of state welfare in each region,[52] this theory cannot explain the variance in levels of postmaterialism even within groups of states with similar welfare regimes in an era of global financial market integration that readily transmits economic shocks across interconnected countries.[53] Beyond the OECD countries, the argument cannot explain why a poor, food insecure-, and existentially threatened country in South Asia (i.e., India) might have been more liberal, tolerant, and democratic than much more prosperous countries in the mid-twentieth century, other than to deny that such a possibility could even have occurred, as it would violate the scarcity hypothesis and Maslow's hierarchy of needs, on which the entire model is built.[54] Finally, it cannot explain why a liberal and democratic country such as India is becoming dramatically less liberal, tolerant, and open-minded more than three decades after it became more economically and physically secure from existential threats.

Even if there is a lasting generational shift away from prioritizing "physical sustenance and safety" and toward more ethereal notions of "belonging, self-expression and the quality of life" in high-income countries that will outlast the current reactionary turn, these polarized values do not logically imply irreconcilable social tensions. In a commercial society, materialist as well as postmaterialist desires can easily be combined, commodified, differentiated, and transformed into scarce rival goods through cunning marketing and sales. For example, sustenance can be transformed into a mode of self-expression, belonging, and quality of life through the marketing of exclusive culinary experiences. Environmentalism, personal safety, and self-expression can all be commodified and rendered as consumable goods thus blurring the distinction between material and postmaterial values and limiting the political saliency of the distinction. At the very least, the notion that postmaterialism is "intrinsically anti-capitalist" is certainly overstated.[55]

Anticapitalist rhetoric notwithstanding, one mainly notes a shift from the accumulation of basic goods and experiences among the economically less prosperous to the accumulation of more refined goods along with more exclusive experiences (and goods that facilitate the accumulation of those experiences) among the more prosperous segments of the population. Rather than an emerging social divide in high-income countries in which the less prosperous (i.e., the "working class") value things and the more prosperous ("middle class") value experiences, one sees both segments pursuing similar goods and experiences at different "trim levels," so to speak, or across different brands of varying prestige.[56]

If the hypothesis of a lasting intergenerational divide between materialist and postmaterialist values is still valid, the exclusive epistemological reliance on the World Values Survey is problematic. Presenting behavioral data on average hours worked and worker productivity by age cohort, as well as real prices of durable consumer goods and housing, would be more compelling. One would expect to see a decline in hours worked, lower productivity, and declining real prices for durable consumer goods and real estate as the younger generation opts for less materialistic pursuits and less acquisitive lifestyles. Inglehart did argue at one point that the emergence of postmaterialism is associated with lower rates of economic growth, but this finding could also be attributed to other independent variables.[57]

Conclusion

Materialism has not been transcended by a younger generation of postmaterialists either in liberal meritocratic or political-capitalist societies. In liberal meritocratic societies, the postwar fever to use the state to build a New Jerusalem and a more equitable society seems to have subsided in most quarters. If anything, there is now a fever to use the state to protect against global economic competition and labor migration, that is, to entrench massive global inequalities in the distribution of material wealth. Even contemporary anticapitalists in liberal meritocratic societies frame their demands for social and environmental justice in material terms as often as not. Meanwhile, the citizens of political-capitalist societies, even those who deal daily with the consequences of rapid environmental degradation and unfettered industrialization, express little desire to transcend materialism.

For the liberal, this is not a cause for celebration. While Hayek is a staunch defender of individual liberty and the extended order of the market, he also advocates for basic economic security as well as environmental regulation and preservation. As the next chapter illustrates, Hayek had hoped for a gradual expansion of the free flow of capital, goods, and even labor through interstate federalism in order to build a more just world.

CHAPTER FIFTEEN

The Prospects of International Order

Of all checks on democracy, federation has been the most efficacious and the most congenial [; but, becoming associated with the Red Republic, with feudalism, with the Jesuits, and with slavery, it has fallen into disrepute, and is giving way to centralism.] The federal system limits and restrains the sovereign power by dividing it and by assigning to Government only certain defined rights. It is the only method of curbing not only the majority but the power of the whole people [and it affords the strongest basis for a second chamber, which has been found the essential security for freedom in every genuine democracy].

Lord Acton (1878)

Lord Acton actually used the term "federalism" rather than "federation" in his review of Thomas Erskine May's *Democracy in Europe*, from which Hayek takes this epigraph.[1] Federalism is the philosophy or doctrine that guides federal political systems. Federal political systems may be categorized as union states (e.g., the Republic of India), federations (e.g., the United States of America post-1789), confederations (e.g., Switzerland 1291–1848), and so on. The three models exist along a continuum, with union states conferring the greatest power on the federal government and confederations the least. A federation implies a set of territories with shared sovereign constitutional authority over their respective territories and joint legislative powers. In a federation, neither the federal government nor the regions may alter one another's power without a mutually participatory constitutional amendment process. In a federation, power is "non-centralized;" it cannot devolve from the center to the regions, as that would imply that the center takes primacy over them.[2]

The rest of the passage from which the epigraph is drawn may be recondite to a modern audience. A few details will perhaps help to clarify Lord Acton's position. First, the "Red Republic" is a reference to the 1848 Revolution in France, which ended the July Monarchy of Louis Philippe I, who had ruled France since 1830. The 1848 Revolution ushered in the short-lived French Second Republic, which collapsed a few years later when its president, Louis-Napoléon Bonaparte, declared himself Emperor

Napoleon III in 1852 and established the Second Empire. During this odd interregnum, the Second Republic came to be associated with the decentralization of power from Paris to the provinces. Supporters of the Second Empire, who sought to legitimate the new regime with references to the French Revolution of 1789, argued that decentralization represented a challenge to the Jacobin doctrine of popular sovereignty as well as national unity.[3] Thus, federalism or decentralization was curiously made to appear antidemocratic and conservative by its monarchical critics. Second, feudalism, as a system in which local lords acquired suzerainty under the sovereign power of a king or emperor, exposed local inhabitants to increased exploitation, oppression, and tyranny.[4] In the European historical context federalism was easily linked to feudal oppression. Third, the reference to Jesuits invokes the smear of ultramontanism, or the belief, in the wake of the Protestant Reformation, that the Society of Jesus supported papal intervention in French affairs, in contrast to loyalist French Catholics. It is for similar reasons that Jesuits were suppressed in most of Western Europe from 1759 until 1815. In this light, federalism appears to create divided loyalties, domestic strife, and external intervention. Fourth, undoubtedly, for most British intellectuals of the late nineteenth century, federalism would have been blamed for permitting the longevity of America's "peculiar institution," as Tocqueville termed it, of slavery and its eventual Civil War. To this extent, federalism could be seen by its critics as permitting barbarism to endure. It is worth noting that Lord Acton supported the Confederate States of America in the American Civil War, believing as he did in the notion that "states' rights" trumped the most fundamental human right—a convoluted error in upholding the core principles of liberalism.[5] It is probably for this reason that Hayek, a great admirer of Acton, passed over this part of the passage.

In spite of the negative associations that had accrued to federalism, Acton defends the constitutional practice as a mechanism to protect against tyranny. More interestingly, Acton views federalism as a protection against the "whole people," as it empowers a second chamber (e.g., the US Senate) to secure the rule of law in a changing democratic polity. Acton was generally as suspicious of parliamentary authority as he was of absolutist monarchy. As he argued in his second set of Cambridge lectures, the French Revolution and Declaration of the Rights of Man, despite their monumental significance, had two grave faults. First, the French sacrificed liberty to equality.[6] Second, the absolutism of the king became the absolutism of the assembly.[7] Acton reasoned that while it was awful to be oppressed by a minority, it was worse to be oppressed by a majority. The masses may resist oppression by a minority through collective action, "but from the absolute will of an entire people there is no appeal, no redemption, no refuge but treason."[8] Protection from majority oppression must be manifold if liberty is to endure.

In a bicameral legislature, the upper house, constituted to represent the constituent political units rather than the people, protects the "permanent reign of law against the arbitrary revolutions of opinion."[9] Thus, the upper house essentially preserves a secularized notion of the Hebrew concept of "higher law," which recognizes the dignity of the individual, freedom of conscience, and individual rights.[10]

Acton also believed that a society that includes distinct national polities (without oppressing them), residing in separate, cohesive settlements, results in "more perfect" liberty. A society that contains multiple nations effectively emulates the role of federalism or a strong independent church vis-à-vis civil authority. A central government that grants privilege, autonomy, and separate law to its minority populations so that they can preserve their self-identity and traditions is by definition a government that is limited and decentralized.[11] At a fundamental level, Acton's outlook displays a distrust of parliaments as guardians of liberty, in part because these institutions are predicated on the assumption of national unity. Much as the crown needed to be checked by the power of the parliament, parliament itself needs to be checked by provincial legislatures, local self-government, an independent church, and adherence to tradition.[12]

Borrowing from these insights, Hayek seeks a supranational federation as a mechanism for reducing economically induced international friction and thus preserving a liberal order and, ultimately, individual liberty.[13] Based in part on an essay he originally published in 1939, "The Economic Conditions of Interstate Federalism," he argues that economic planning is generally predicated on restrictions to the flow of bodies, goods, and capital across borders, which may disrupt careful centralized planning.[14]

In contrast, Hayek seeks to create a liberal order that will empower workers and entrepreneurs (particularly in the postcolonial world after World War II) and permit the frictionless flow of goods and capital.

∴

Federalism and Civil War

To comprehend Hayek's approach to the international order, one might begin with his understanding of the structural causes of war and peace. In this light, there is an interesting parallel between Hayek's reading of the eco-

nomic causes of European civil war (specifically World War II) and Lord
Acton's effort to trace the economic origins of the American Civil War.

Acton believed that Thomas Jefferson's Embargo Act of 1807, which "virtually put an end to American international trade" in order to punish the
British and French for violating American neutrality in international waters,
set several precedents that led to one of America's greatest calamities. Jefferson's embargo harmed the export-oriented New England states. Christopher Lazarski writes in his biography of Lord Acton: "Instead of hurting
Britain and France, it hurt domestic producers, in particular the shipping
industry. The northern states, mainly those in New England, vigorously
protested this policy, which painfully hit one region of the country for the
benefit of the whole."[15] Consequently, it was the New England states that
first raised the issue of nullification of federal laws and threatened secession
from the Union. Although the law was rescinded in 1809, these issues would
resurface with the Hartford Convention of 1814, in which the New England
Federalist Party again discussed secession in response to the Louisiana Purchase, the War of 1812, and laws restricting free trade. Later, South Carolina's nullification crisis in response to the federal tariffs of 1828 and 1832,
which South Carolinians felt were imposed at the behest of Northern industrialists, would rekindle regional tensions, except this time from a Southern
perspective.[16] Underlying these tensions was the fact that two distinct political economies were managed by a federal system that could be captured and
directed to legislate on behalf of sectional interests. Notes Lazarski:

> The North was increasingly dominated by the town, focused on industrial production and trade, and experiencing rapid population growth.
> The South remained rural and agricultural, without a large influx of immigrants. While young industries in the North needed protection from
> English competition and supported tariffs and duties, the conservative
> South, paradoxically, advocated free trade. Selling most of their cotton
> abroad, Southerners understood that tariffs in international trade would
> be suicidal for their agriculture.[17]

As Roland Hill states in his biography of Lord Acton, "By abuse of federal
authority, South and North had each alternately attempted policies of economic victimization against the other."[18] Ultimately, of course, it was the
secession of the Southern states in response to the election of President
Abraham Lincoln, who opposed the expansion of slavery into the western territories (i.e., the extension of the Southern economic model), that
started the Civil War. The use of the federal state's power to protect the
economy of a particular region at the expense of other regions destroyed

the ability of federalism both to check the power of majoritarian democracy and to maintain the equality of the states.[19]

Just as protracted economic friction within a federal system opens the prospect of secession and civil war, protracted economic friction between states opens the prospect for interstate coercion and war. Thus, like Acton in his economic reading of the American Civil War, Hayek traces the underlying cause of World War II to a retreat from the open trading system. As Hayek asserts at the outset of the chapter, "In no other field has the world yet paid so dearly for the abandonment of nineteenth-century liberalism as in the field where the retreat began: in international relations."[20] In this assessment, Hayek joined many other political economists of his generation. In fact, the Bretton Woods intergovernmental financial institutions (i.e., the International Monetary Fund, the World Bank, and the ill-fated International Trade Organization) designed by Keynes and Harry Dexter White were specifically structured to restore and preserve a modified (or socially "embedded") liberal order as the keystone in the arch between international peace and prosperity.[21] However, Hayek does not embrace a modified or embedded liberal order managed by intergovernmental institutions at the international scale. Although he often encourages a flexible and dynamic approach to a revived liberalism, Hayek—echoing Acton's reflexive support of the South, except on a global scale—would reject a modification of the market order for the sake of social stability and prosperity in one region at the expense of another.

POLANYI'S CRITIQUE

To appreciate Hayek's position, it is useful to juxtapose it with Karl Polanyi's popular (if woolly) critique of unfettered markets in *The Great Transformation* (1944).[22] Polanyi argued that a socially "disembedded" or self-regulating market order that emerged as part of a laissez-faire liberal project in the late nineteenth century generated a spontaneous, "natural," and dialectical social reaction against the unrestrained market on the part of the urban working strata of Europe (although in emergencies it also generated a defense of the market in those social strata connected to the land).[23] For Hayek, the willingness to provide wealthier countries with safeguards against disembedded market competition came at the direct but hidden expense of workers and entrepreneurs in middle- and low-income countries. Hayek illuminates the injustice of seemingly benign compromises within the liberal market order on the international scale when he writes,

> To the worker in a poor country the demand of his more fortunate colleague to be protected against his low-wage competition by minimum-

wage legislation, supposedly in his interest, is frequently no more than a means to deprive him of his only chance to better his conditions by overcoming natural disadvantages by working at wages lower than his fellows in other countries. And to him the fact that he has to give the product of ten hours of his labor for the product of five hours of the man elsewhere who is better equipped with machinery is as much 'exploitation' as that practiced by any capitalist.[24]

By extension, one might speculate that social stability and equality cannot be achieved in the core of wealthy countries by regulating the market without displacing that instability and inequality to the periphery of poorer countries.

Polanyi would agree with Hayek that social protection in Europe historically came at the expense of the colonized countries. Polanyi wrote in 1944:

But if the organized states of Europe could protect themselves against the backwash of international free trade, the politically unorganized colonial peoples could not. The revolt against imperialism was mainly an attempt on the part of exotic peoples to achieve the political status necessary to shelter themselves from the social dislocations caused by European trade policies. The protection that the white man could easily secure for himself, through the sovereign status of his communities was out of reach of the colored man as long as he lacked the prerequisite, political government.[25]

Where Polanyi and Hayek diverge is in imposing an alternative order. Polanyi is primarily nostalgic about an era prior to the forced introduction of self-regulating market relations on "exotic peoples." Although traditional economic institutions are destroyed by colonizers, Polanyi insists that it is actually the provision of peace by the colonial power that shatters traditional patriarchal authority and results in cultural degeneration. Polanyi compares the colonized peoples of the mid-twentieth century to the poor of England in the mid-nineteenth century, implying an inevitable fate as new institutions are gradually assimilated and the colonized peoples are transformed into "semidomesticated animals," akin to the pauperized masses in England at the dawn of its Industrial Revolution.[26]

In any case, although Polanyi had condemned nineteenth-century liberalism for failing to anticipate the need to dampen the pace of economic change to allow for social adjustment during the British Industrial Revolution, he understood all too well that resistance by the crown to the first and

second enclosure movements was politically reactionary, generally ineffective, and harmful to society's overall economic progress.[27] In other words,
while the movement to allay market forces buys time for social adjustment,
it is neither necessarily politically progressive nor economically rational as
a long-term policy.

Hayek argues for a postwar international order that champions individual workers and entrepreneurs regardless of location or race rather than
choosing between an international order that either creates social stability
in high-income countries at the expense of middle- and low-income countries and colonies or seeks to overturn the exploitative relations between
stronger and weaker nations along the murky lines of social justice. This
is not a poststatist utopian vision; states would still play a critical role in
facilitating markets in this framework. Similarly, Hayek does not rule out
the role of intergovernmental organizations or regional confederations of
states; such organizations can play a critical role in limiting the power of
the state to coerce individuals. Finally, Hayek's rejection of social justice
as an objective of states or intergovernmental organizations should not
be read as an embrace of racism or neocolonialism. Rather, Hayek views
adjudicating between rival social-justice claims as impractical and morally
fraught. Nevertheless, the clear subtext of Hayek's vision of international
order is a liberal defense of colonized peoples against realist efforts to re-
subjugate brown and black peoples through the delegation of power and
moral authority to a new intergovernmental organization.

The stakes were tremendous. Hayek feared that if the international order could not be managed, the cycle of economic collapse and war that he
had witnessed twice in his lifetime would recur. As Richard Ebeling writes,

> For liberals like Hayek, once World War II was over, unless something
> was done to calm the international scene, the cycle of nationalistic con-
> frontation and conflict would raise its dangerous head all over again.
> More wars, more economic barriers against international collabora-
> tion and material betterment, more antagonisms among and between
> peoples due to the atavistic ideas of race, linguistic or cultural identity
> imposed through government coercion and command; more national
> socialism through economic planning for national greatness.[28]

The International Scale

Hayek predicts that a centrally planned international system would lead
poorer countries to chafe against restraints imposed by supranational plan-

ning. He scathingly predicts that continued dominance by the wealthy countries via international organizations after the end of World War II would become highly problematic from a racial perspective: "Can there be much doubt that this would mean a more or less conscious endeavour to secure the dominance of the white man, and would rightly be so regarded by all other races?"[29] This position represented a shift from his earlier thinking in 1939, when he had written:

> Nor is it even possible to give here further consideration to such important problems as those of monetary policy or colonial policy which will, of course, continue to exist in a federation. On the last point it may, however, be added that the question which probably would be raised first, i.e., whether colonies ought to be administered by states or by the federation, would be of comparatively minor importance. With a real open-door policy for all members of the federation, the economic advantages derived from the possession of colonies, whether the colonies were administered federally or nationally, would be approximately the same to all members of the federation. But, in general, it would undoubtedly be preferable that their administration should be a federal and not a state matter.[30]

In other words, prior to the outbreak of World War II, Hayek could not conceive that the age of imperialism was about to end—in fact, the discussion of the "colonial problem" is mainly an afterthought in his first essay on interstate federalism. Hayek's prewar liberal approach was simply to negate the economic advantages of the imperial preference system by creating a "real open-door policy" for all colonies on the model of the Great Powers' dominance of China between 1842 and 1895 and between 1899 and 1937. In essence, the economic advantages of imperialism and spheres of influence would be rendered nominal through genuine free trade, but the territorial integrity and political stability of the colonies would be guaranteed by an interstate federation. Toward the end of the war, however, Hayek no longer sees the need to prop up a hollowed out imperial project.

By the same token, after the war the prospect that the "European races" would submit to the redistributive demands of a supranational entity strikes Hayek as entirely unrealistic. Hayek's assertions are predicated on a racialized worldview—that is, the reification of the concept of race as a meaningful social category—but not a racist one. The reference to European races (plural) alongside the use of "the white man" indicates that Hayek was not particularly wedded to the crude racial categories (white, black, brown, yellow, etc.) commonly used in the early twentieth century.

Hayek is certainly aware of the massive inequality between and within nation-states in the mid-twentieth century, but this does not lead him to concede the need for a centralized national or supranational plan. For Hayek, selecting a public rank ordering of priorities (e.g., economic equality) requires the subordination of those who prefer an alternative goal.[31] Moreover, rival claims to priority assistance in equalizing incomes must be adjudicated, which transfers even more power to the state: "There exists no basis which allows us to decide whether the claims of the poor Rumanian peasant are more or less urgent than those of the still poorer Albanian, or the needs of the Slovakian mountain shepherd greater than those of his Slovenian colleague. But if raising their standards of life is to be effected according to a unitary plan, somebody must deliberately balance the merits of all these claims and decide between them."[32] Hayek argues that to impose one's moral views or rank ordering of values by coercion results in an ethically impossible situation: a moral view imposed on others against their will renders that moral view immoral. In any case, given Hayek's preference for spontaneous order, there hardly seems to be a justification for seeking to predetermine or impose a particular rank ordering of values.

The only way in which a hierarchy of values can be imposed morally is if one believes in a mystical "general will" that is unproblematically conveyed through democratic voting processes. As Ebeling notes, echoing later critiques of the concept of "society" by Hayek, "But there is no 'general will,' or higher communal or collective good. There are only individuals with their own ideas, beliefs, values and visions of what is good, better or best. In spite of the near mystical aura around which the idea of democracy is enveloped . . . it is merely a political mechanism for, as the phrase goes, 'counting heads, rather than breaking them.'"[33]

Of course, Hayek's general argument on the international scale is essentially an extension of his argument on the national scale. Hayek believes that, owing to the fragmentation and dispersal of knowledge among individuals, aggressive schemes for interventionist planning on a transnational scale are even more impractical than those for interventionist planning on the national scale and are likely to increase coercion between states. He reasons that the information problems that arise from planning on a domestic scale would be even greater on the much larger, dispersed, and complex international scale. Hayek adds that many types of centralized national planning require the elimination of "extraneous influences" and the creation of numerous restrictions on the "movements of men and goods."[34] It is unclear why Hayek emphasizes only the type of national planning that seeks to eliminate (as opposed to regularize and regulate) extraneous influences. However, he is correct that centralized national planning—and, by extension, international planning—would necessarily impose at least some restrictions or hindrances on the free movement of labor, capital, and goods in order to facilitate plan implementation and promote social stability. It is the restrictions on the flow of goods, in particular, that would likely increase friction between nation-states and hence tempt stronger states to use coercion to achieve their objectives.

Later in *Law, Legislation, and Liberty*, Hayek would reluctantly concede the need for some restrictions on the free movement of individuals across national boundaries. In part, these restrictions on the idea of an open society would result either from the efforts of wealthier countries to secure for their citizens above-average standards of living or from differences in national and ethnic traditions, which, paradoxically, would not be mitigated so long as restrictions on migration continue: "We must face the fact that we here encounter a limit to the universal application of those liberal principles of policy which the existing facts of the present world make unavoidable."[35] Notably, however, Hayek does not seek to restrict migration on racial or ethnic grounds; he would not support contemporary racist immigration policies, as one of his critics falsely alleges.[36] Rather, Hayek argues that freedom of migration to liberal societies ought to be restricted to those who voluntarily agree to adhere to liberal principles:

> These limits do not constitute fatal flaws in the argument since they imply merely that, like tolerance in particular, liberal principles can be consistently applied only to those who themselves obey liberal principles, and cannot always be extended to those who do not. The same is true of some moral principles. Such necessary exceptions to the general rule do therefore provide no justification for similar exceptions within the sphere in which it is possible for government consistently to follow liberal principles.[37]

At the international level, Hayek is skeptical that planning of economic life can be accomplished without a reliance on force and compulsion as the degree of commonality declines.[38] In a footnote on British imperialism, Hayek states that British "colonial development" entailed ". . . the imposition of certain values and ideals on those whom they try to assist. It is, indeed, this experience which has made even the most internationally minded of colonial experts so very sceptical of the practicability or an "international" administration of colonies."[39] Hayek is not so naive as to believe that colonial development policies were actually aimed at "assisting" colonized subjects. He is not a subscriber to Rudyard Kipling's notion of the "white man's burden." Hayek adds, "To undertake the direction of economic life of people with widely divergent ideals and values is to assume responsibilities which commit one to the use of force. . . . This is true even if we assume the dominant power to be as idealistic and unselfish as we can possibly conceive. But how small is the likelihood that it will be unselfish, and how great the temptations!"[40] Even a regional order drawn from a common civilizational core (e.g., Western Europe) may lack the moral or normative basis for supranational planning. Hayek believes that enthusiasm for international cooperation dissipates as soon as one imagines one's preferred policy is a minority view in any cooperative organization. On the surface, the noncoercive evolution and expansion of the European Union from either the 1951 Treaty of Paris or the 1958 Treaty of Rome to the present would seem to challenge this argument, notwithstanding the tensions since the Eurozone crisis of 2009 and the defection of the United Kingdom in 2020. However, the European Union does not even remotely represent Hayek's understanding of supranational centralized economic planning. Hayek was clearly thinking of the Third Reich's *Grossraumwirtschaft* and the Soviet Union as examples of (coercive) supranational planned economies. The European Union's social model attempts to combine market-based wealth generation with generous redistributive policies.[41]

Nevertheless, even contemporary intergovernmental financial and development bureaucracies that seek to promote market economies (e.g., the Bretton Woods institutions) attempt to massage the imposition of a hierarchy of values on behalf of stronger and wealthier states by treating international economic policy-making as a technical task managed by objective experts. Hayek would easily see through the effort to neutralize the political and moral aspects of economic policy-making, since economic policies necessarily impact the distribution of scarce resources.[42] And while existing intergovernmental financial institutions are generally not devoted to centralized planning and allocation of resources (except for cartels, e.g., OPEC [Organization of the Petroleum Exporting Countries]), Hayek sees the danger if such bodies were to come into existence. He argues that transferring economic control over any essential commodity or service from the state to an intergovernmental body dedicated to centralized economic planning would represent one of the most significant transfers of power to any authority. Control over economic resources determines the fate of industries, nation-states, and ultimately individual lives.

Outsiders cannot effectively question or control a power that enshrouds itself in technical expertise. Even governments, which jointly establish these bodies, would have difficulty holding them accountable without the cooperation of most member states. Thus, Hayek encourages resistance to a concentration of power in autonomous international planning bodies, even if the administrators are "the most faithful guardians of the trust placed in their care."[43]

REALISM UNMASKED

For Hayek, the most that can be achieved successfully in international relations is to establish the "rules of the game" and uphold the rule of law: "If anything is evident, it should be that, while nations might abide by formal rules on which they have agreed, they will never submit to the direction which economic planning involves—that while they may agree on the rules of the game, they will never agree on the order of preference in which the rank of their own needs and the rate at which they are allowed to advance is fixed by majority vote."[44] It is noteworthy that Hayek is arguing not as a "hard-boiled realist" but as a liberal. In fact, in his day, his argument was pitched *against* realists, who supported giving economic power to intergovernmental organizations to regulate the affairs of colonized peoples:

> What is evidently at the back of the minds of the not altogether unpracticable "realists" who advocate these schemes is that, while the great powers will be unwilling to submit to any superior authority, they will be able to use those "international" authorities to impose their will on the smaller nations within the area in which they exercise hegemony. There is so much "realism" in this that by thus camouflaging the planning authorities as "international" it might be easier to achieve the condition under which international planning is alone practicable, namely, that it is in effect done by one single predominant power. This disguise would, however, not alter the fact that for all the smaller states it would mean a much more comprehensive subjection to an external power, to which no real resistance would any longer be possible, than would be involved in the renunciation of a clearly defined part of political sovereignty.[45]

In essence, internationalism is a mask for the exertion of hegemonic dominance. Here Hayek's logic temporarily transfers to smaller nation-states and peoples the status of individuals in liberalism. Much as liberalism aims to recognize the competence of individuals in their own sphere and minimize coercion, Hayekian liberalism argues that individual states should not be subordinated to the will of more powerful nation-states on an international scale: "It is significant that the most passionate advocates of a centrally directed economic New Order for Europe should display, like their Fabian and German prototypes, the most complete disregard of the individuality and of the rights of small nations."[46] Hayek's ire was once again reserved for the British diplomat and scholar E. H. Carr (1892–1982), one of the founders of classical realism and a convert to socialism. At the time Hayek wrote *The Road to Serfdom*, Carr would have been celebrated as the author of *The Twenty Years' Crisis* and an advocate for a spheres-of-influence approach to managing world order. As noted earlier, Carr notoriously argued for a German sphere of influence in Eastern Europe and supported a policy of appeasement toward Hitler, support that he would later withdraw. During World War II Carr, an assistant editor at *The Times*, advocated "a form of common market involving some sort of supranational planning," with centralized control in a social-democratic framework.[47] Carr was calling not for a world government, but for an intermediate organizational configuration between the national and the global dominated by three or four multinational, regional civilizations (e.g., the United States, United Kingdom, the Soviet Union, and China).[48]

It should be noted that an intergovernmental authority is by no means ruled out in Hayek's vision, but Hayek insists that such an authority should be strictly circumscribed by the rule of law and a division of powers. A Hayekian intergovernmental body would mainly seek to enforce peace and facilitate market exchange on an international scale. As Hayek had previously argued in "The Economic Conditions of Interstate Federalism," lowering impediments to the movement of people, goods, and capital would be immensely beneficial from a material standpoint and help to reduce frictions that might lead to war.[49] Hayek believes that the proper model for an intergovernmental body is the ultraliberal laissez-faire (or "night-watchman") state.[50] In other words, an intergovernmental body should not seek to implement on an international scale the type of planned projects and social-justice initiatives that increasingly typified modern states after the dawn of the twentieth century.

The ideal model is one of a confederation of independent states from similar geographic regions (e.g., a European confederation).[51] The main aim of Hayek's approach is to devolve power to the (regional) international scale and the local scale in order to weaken the nation-state. In this desire for devolution, Hayek sees himself as firmly within the liberal tradition. It is only with the emergence of *Realpolitik* in the twentieth century that the liberal dream came to be seen as "unpracticable and utopian."[52]

The National Scale

From an economic perspective, and unlike Keynes at Bretton Woods, Hayek does not embrace the nation-state as the "natural" site for accumulation of "excess" capital:

Those who are so ready to ride roughshod over the rights of small states are, of course, right in one thing: we cannot hope for order or lasting peace after this war if states, large or small, regain unfettered sovereignty in the economic sphere. But this does not mean that a new superstate must be given powers which we have not learned to use intelligently even on a national scale, that an international authority ought to be given power to direct individual nations how to use their resources.[53]

Hayek believes that nationalism is ultimately an artificial means for creating "economic solidarity" and restricting the access of outsiders to resources through protectionism and redistributive policies.[54] Liberalism foregrounds the individual rather than the nation-state. Given the preference for the individual, citizenship in a nation-state is essentially conceptualized either as a rent that accrues to beneficiaries without merit or as a barrier to trade and free movement, depending on the country in question. Thus, Hayek argues, "It is neither necessary nor desirable that national boundaries should mark sharp differences in standards of living, that membership of a national group should entitle one to a share in a cake altogether different from that in which members of other groups share."[55] International trade in a liberal framework should be between individuals rather than states organized as trading bodies. The role of the liberal state is to preserve order and facilitate market exchange between individuals, not to engage in exchange directly on behalf of individuals.

In any case, Hayekian liberalism does not recognize the concept of "national resources" upon which national planning is often predicated. Resources are no more the exclusive property of nation-states than individual human beings are the property of their government. Hayek argues that states managing trade in natural resources do not generate either order or peace in the international trading system. In fact, since states are sovereign actors and coercive entities by definition, the division of natural resources among states only incentivizes and encourages the use of violent means to achieve economic objectives.

Of course, the artificial solidarity of nationalism is not the only ideology through which barriers to free trade in goods and the free movement of labor and capital can be legitimated. The European Union, for example, has maintained robust agricultural subsidies and protections, despite the development of a form of pooled sovereignty beyond the nation-state.[56] Adam Smith had long predicted that producer groups and merchants would naturally collude to raise prices or secure subsidies.[57] Similarly, redistributive policies could reemerge at the supranational level if one concedes that national solidarity is not the only rationale for the pursuit of social justice.[58]

Redistributive policies may simply be the preference of a large majority if they are risk averse or normatively intolerant of large inequalities in the distribution of wealth. Hayek's preference for an ultraminimalist international order bound by the rule of law would limit prospects for protectionism, subsidies, and redistributive policies.

From a political perspective, Hayek contends, democracy is best fostered and preserved at the local level. Accountable government becomes meaningless when power is centralized in remote spaces and in complex bureaucratic structures.

> We shall not rebuild civilization on the large scale. It is no accident that on the whole there was more beauty and decency to be found in the life of the small peoples, and that among the large ones there was more happiness and content in proportion as they had avoided the deadly blight of centralization. Least of all shall we preserve democracy or foster its growth if all the power and most of the important decisions rest with an organization far too big for the common man to survey or comprehend. Nowhere has democracy ever worked well without a great measure of local self-government, providing a school of political training for the people at large as much as for their future leaders.[59]

In part, the need for a small scale is part of the knowledge problem that Hayek has already laid out. Hayek contends that the needs of others cannot be well understood beyond the scope of interaction with one's neighbors. A reliance on theories or ideologies is deceptive in giving the illusion of knowledge, whereas knowledge warehoused in remote bureaucratic structures hampers the "creative impulses of the private person."

Hayek favors a world order in which small states, and by extension, small communities and individuals can thrive. In fact, a central purpose of an international authority would be to limit the powers of the state over the individual in order to safeguard peace.[60] Of course, he realizes that preserving peace paradoxically requires a powerful authority that is prevented from abusing the power it is able to wield. On the one hand, Hayek's approach is feasible only if there is a strong normative agreement on fundamental liberal principles—that is, if we agree that limiting power may also prevent the use of power for desirable purposes. On the other hand, liberalism only requires adherence to a minimalist doctrine and is therefore more practical than creating comprehensive institutions with universal mandates. Given the failures of the League of Nations, it was not unreasonable for Hayek to suggest a more minimalist route for the successor organizations that would be built at the conclusion of the war.

Political Capitalism and Federalism

Political-capitalist regimes have used mechanisms to exploit the benefits of economic liberalism and decentralization domestically without conceding political rights to individual citizens (including secure private property rights).[61] Thus, in contrast to Lord Acton's dictum in the chapter's epigraph, (extremely asymmetric) federalism, rather than limiting or restraining sovereign power by dividing it, can be made to enhance sovereign power by further undermining the rule of law and promoting performance legitimacy through policy experimentation. Internationally, rather than develop a form of supranational federation with a liberal framework to reduce regional economic friction, political-capitalist regimes may use development assistance to enhance peace, security, and regime viability. If economic friction does emerge, political-capitalist regimes can easily exploit federal structures and sectional interests in liberal capitalist regimes to weaken their resolve.

Domestically, Special Economic Zones (SEZs) in political-capitalist regimes arguably represent an extremely asymmetric, top-down type of federal political system; they are a kind of a maximal variant of the union state model of federalism, in which the center grants a geographic region autonomy or, more accurately in this case, exemption from national laws, policies, taxes, tariff barriers, and regulatory standards. SEZs stretch the core concept of federalism—that it is a hierarchy of governments with delineated scope of authority for each government[62]—to its breaking point, and some scholars would argue that SEZs are a distinct phenomenon altogether.[63] Others have labeled the broader political system (which includes the relationship between the central party/state and local governments) as "federalism, Chinese Style," or federalism with Chinese characteristics.[64] Of course, SEZs are not unique to China or political-capitalist regimes; there are currently over four thousand SEZs in almost half of the countries in the world.[65] Regardless of the classificatory label, however, SEZs are useful for strengthening political-capitalist regimes in particular.

The main advantage of SEZs is that they permit an authoritarian capitalist regime to create exceptional liberal spaces without undertaking broader political (or economic) reforms outside of the designated zone. Moreover, SEZs hold the rule of law in abeyance, as they essentially represent discretionary policy.[66] While federal regions are often granted autonomy because of long-standing historical, linguistic, and cultural differences, SEZs are often created as top-down economic policy experiments to attract foreign direct investment. Despite the lack of institutionalized durability in SEZs, a political-capitalist regime's need for performance legitimacy provides market actors with a credible commitment signal. Nevertheless, as discretionary policy instruments, SEZs are easier to unwind than historically and culturally differentiated autonomous regions.

Internationally, China's Belt and Road Initiative (BRI), launched in 2013, may be viewed as a core mechanism to promote peace and security by reducing economic friction. And while China is a member of many multilateral organizations, its diplomatic practice shows a preference for bilateralism.[67] Officially, the BRI program was designed for infrastructural development with China's neighbors, but the program is quite flexible, and with its maritime component it can accommodate countries from any region. For example, China's efforts to broker peace in Yemen's civil war by linking postwar reconstruction with participation in the BRI is ". . . evidence of the ways in which this new global platform is being integrated into the existing architecture of international peace and security."[68] Moreover, cooperation through the program can range from experimental pilot projects to comprehensive joint planning. The initiative consists of a series of bilateral arrangements that are often presented as an "alternative Chinese model of development." Barry Naughton argues that

> despite the general developmental overtones, the basic philosophy behind the BRI is one of exercising greater international influence by providing benefits to a broad range of developing economies and tying them more closely to China.
>
> . . . one of the most fundamental objectives of the BRI is to improve the infrastructure linking China to its neighbors. Transport infrastructure—highways and railroads, including high-speed railroads—will reduce transaction costs and pull nations closer together economically. . . . This infrastructure diplomacy is thus the functional equivalent of a trade pact: It draws countries closer together, and implicitly creates higher economic barriers to countries outside the "club."[69]

Finally, political-capitalist regimes have found that trade wars against federations are advantageous. Federations, which are often characterized by geographic units with sectoral differentiation (e.g., predominantly agricultural states or counties, manufacturing states or counties), are easily manipulated in a trade war with targeted tariffs. Sung Eun Kim and Yotam Margalit, as well as Thiemo Fetzer and Carlo Schwarz, find, for example, that in a 2018 trade dispute between the United States and China, Chinese retaliatory tariffs against the Trump administration "systematically targeted US goods that had production concentrated in Republican-supporting counties, particularly when located in closely contested Congressional districts."[70] Moreover, the surgical strategy worked: in the next election, voters in those districts punished the incumbent party at the polls.

Conclusion

Although federalism has the potential to restrain sovereign power; enhance individual freedom; facilitate the flow of capital, goods, and labor; and promote domestic and international cooperation, it needs liberalism as a guiding ideology. Without a liberal ideology, a democratic federal system or interstate federation is easily taken over and used to promote sectoral, regional, and majoritarian interests at the expense of its constituent units and minorities. Additionally, an illiberal federalism can work to entrench global asymmetries by promoting protectionism and externalizing the costs of adjustment to shifting market signals onto weaker states. A federal structure at the national or regional level can easily buckle under the strain of trade-related friction between its composite parts or with other political entities.

The challenge of political capitalism makes the revival of liberalism even more pressing, since political-capitalist regimes can use extremely asymmetric federalism to enhance sovereign power and thus enhance performance legitimacy, development assistance to bind foreign states in relations of dependence, and targeted tariffs to weaken democratic trade partners with federal political structures. Economic liberalism may reduce the temptation to initiate bilateral trade wars in the first place while also enhancing resilience by fostering more competitive industries.

Conclusion

In a succinct final note, Hayek concludes that the main point of his book was to hammer out the principles by which we ought to live together rather than to sketch a detailed plan. The main principles, for Hayek, are the freedom of the individual and the creation of conditions for progress, rather than the planning of progress itself.[1] He returns to his basic assertion that world order in the quarter century prior to World War II was not a continuation of the liberal order of the nineteenth century. Of course, his aim is not to drag society back to the nineteenth century, but to recover the principles of liberalism from that era and refashion them for the next generation.

Hayek tells his young readers that they are right to doubt the economic ideas of their elders. But they are incorrect to believe that those ideas are merely an extension of the liberal ideas of the nineteenth century. In the revivalist spirit with which he began, he ends with a call to try again to make a world safe for free people: "If in the first attempt to create a world of free men we have failed, we must try again."[2]

Rising to the Challenge

The challenge of political capitalism in the twenty-first century is distinctly different from that presented by socialism in the twentieth century. First, political capitalism is ultimately a form of capitalism (albeit one that is usually fused with an autonomous, authoritarian state and a technocratic bureaucracy). Although China is the most salient example, political capitalism is also arguably practiced in countries as dissimilar as Singapore and Rwanda, Botswana and Algeria, or Malaysia and Ethiopia.[3] In this light, a Cold War–style strategy of ideological and military containment to limit the spread of political capitalism makes little sense, given the ideological diversity of states that seem to adhere to the model and their general lack of coordinated hostility toward liberal meritocratic capitalism. Second, and in sharp contrast to most socialist regimes, political-capitalist regimes are characterized by strong economic performance. This performance, in turn, strengthens regime legitimacy, resources, and durability. Third, the nature of the contemporary global economy restricts the willingness and even ability of transnational corporations to unwind regional and global value chains rapidly. In other words, the economic and technological isolation of political-capitalist regimes is unlikely. Political-capitalist regimes are worthy adversaries of liberal meritocratic capitalism.

Most important, the political-capitalist mode of governance becomes more attractive as liberal capitalism comes to be associated with political incompetence and instability, mediocre economic performance, highly concentrated ownership of capital, and a lack of intergenerational social mobility.[4] Thus, a credible solution to the challenge of political capitalism would entail fixing the problems with liberal meritocratic capitalism to make it more attractive to other countries. Luckily, the main problems of liberal meritocratic capitalism can be fixed without abandoning core liberal principles.

Hayekian liberalism is not intrinsically averse to planning for market competition, the regulation of industry, a minimum income, or even a (Thatcherite) people's capitalism; liberalism is not libertarianism or a type of economic fundamentalism. Moreover, Hayekian liberalism supports international economic unions, fundamental human rights, anti-imperialist struggles, the free flow of labor, and a moral framework for international relations; liberalism is not nationalist, imperialist, or realist. Liberalism is not conservative, even though it fights to conserve individual liberty and the free market, ideals that may align with the interests of conservatives in a liberal capitalist regime. Liberalism is progressive, principled, reasonable, and universal. To conclude with Hayek's parting words:

The guiding principle that a policy of freedom for the individual is the only truly progressive policy remains as true today as it was in nineteenth century.[5]

Acknowledgments

This book grew out of discussions about Friedrich Hayek with my "States and Markets" class and my "Economic Freedom" and "The Fate of Liberty" seminars at Hobart and William Smith Colleges. The passion with which my students engaged Hayek's political thought and the recent literature on comparative political economy helped me to see the need to write this book. The arguments presented here are particularly inspired by the writings of Peter Boettke and Branko Milanovic, to whom I am deeply indebted for their lucid prose, penetrating insights, and kind encouragement. Jeremy Shearmur and an anonymous reviewer provided excellent, detailed guidance and critical commentary. Joseph Mink was kind enough to read an early draft of the prospectus and offer his wise advice. Kevin Dunn generously invited me to present a chapter to his seminar. I would like to thank my editor at the University of Chicago Press, Chad Zimmerman, for his faith in the project. I am grateful to the Institute for Humane Studies for their generous support (IHS016563) for manuscript preparation. Charles King lent his keen eyes and gentle humor for final proofing and indexing.

Stacey Philbrick Yadav provided both inspiration and critical reflection on my interpretation of Hayek. She has patiently endured my obsession with Hayek for many, many years. Needless to say, any remaining faults in the text are my own.

This book is dedicated to my daughters, Kieran and Lila: may they always enjoy the fruits of liberty.

Vikash Yadav
Pittsford, New York

Notes

PREFACE

1. For a discussion of the formalization of Hayek's economic theories, see Bruce Caldwell, *Hayek's Challenge: An Intellectual Biography of F. A. Hayek* (Chicago: University of Chicago Press, 2008).

2. For a discussion of the political project associated with Hayek and neoliberalism, see Philip Mirowski and Dieter Plehwe, eds., *The Road from Mont Pèlerin: The Making of the Neoliberal Thought Collective*, 1st Harvard University Press paperback ed. (Cambridge, MA: Harvard University Press, 2015); Daniel Stedman Jones, *Masters of the Universe: Hayek, Friedman, and the Birth of Neoliberal Politics* (Princeton, NJ: Princeton University Press, 2014).

3. For leftist critiques of Hayek, see Quinn Slobodian, *Globalists: The End of Empire and the Birth of Neoliberalism* (Cambridge, MA: Harvard University Press, 2018); Corey Robin, *The Reactionary Mind: Conservatism from Edmund Burke to Sarah Palin* (Oxford and New York: Oxford University Press, 2013); David Harvey, *A Brief History of Neoliberalism* (Oxford and New York: Oxford University Press, 2011).

4. There is a small but important circle of philosophers, including Norman Barry, John Gray, Chandran Kukathas, Jeremy Shearmur, Roland Kley, Brian Lee Crowley, and Raymond Plant, who have critically engaged Hayek's work. I will discuss relevant aspects of their arguments in the course of this book.

5. Milton Friedman and Adam Meyerson, "Letters: Who Is a Conservative?," *Policy Review* (Fall 1994): 90.

6. Robin, *The Reactionary Mind*. For a discussion of leftist engagement with Hayek, see Simon Griffiths, "'Comrade Hayek' or the Revival of Liberalism? Andrew Gamble's Engagement with the Work of Friedrich Hayek," *Journal of Political Ideologies* 12, no. 2 (2007): 189–210, https://doi.org/10.1080/13569310701285032.

7. Daron Acemoglu and James A. Robinson, *The Narrow Corridor: States, Societies, and the Fate of Liberty* (New York: Penguin Press, 2019).

8. Peter J. Boettke and Scott M. King, "Hayek and the Hayekians on the Political Order of a Free People," in *Hayek's Tensions: Reexamining the Political Economy and Philosophy of F. A. Hayek*, ed. Stefanie Haeffele, Solomon Stein, and Virgil Storr (Arlington, VA: Mercatus Center, George Mason University, 2020), 9–10.

9. Friedrich A. Hayek, *The Road to Serfdom: Text and Documents; The Definitive*

Edition, ed. Bruce Caldwell, vol. 2 of *The Collected Works of F. A. Hayek* (Chicago: University of Chicago Press, 2007), 37.

10. Peter J. Boettke, "On Reading Hayek: Choice, Consequences and *The Road to Serfdom*," *European Journal of Political Economy* 21, no. 4 (December 2005): 1042, https://doi.org/10.1016/j.ejpoleco.2004.08.005.

11. Hayek, *The Road to Serfdom*, 9–11.

12. Ibid., 38. Hayek states that he first sketched out the argument for *The Road to Serfdom* in a 1938 article titled "Freedom and the Economic System" published in *Contemporary Review* and later expanded it in 1939 in the Public Policy Pamphlets series published by the University of Chicago Press.

13. Peter J. Boettke, *F. A. Hayek: Economics, Political Economy and Social Philosophy* (London: Palgrave Macmillan, 2018); Caldwell, *Hayek's Challenge*; Alan O. Ebenstein, *Friedrich Hayek: A Biography* (Chicago: University of Chicago Press, 2003).

14. Friedrich A. Hayek, *The Constitution of Liberty: The Definitive Edition*, ed. Ronald Hamowy, vol. 17 of *The Collected Works of F. A. Hayek* (Chicago: University of Chicago Press, 2011), 47.

15. An older Hayek would reluctantly support restrictions on immigration on the basis of acculturation difficulties and resentment by local populations. Hayek cited the example of Polish and Czech immigration to Vienna prior to World War II and the establishment of separate Komensky schools with instruction in the Czech language, which resulted in violent anti-Semitic riots. Although in principle Hayek supported the "free movement of men," he feared that a dramatic change in immigration policy would rekindle strong nationalist sentiments that he felt were otherwise waning. See Friedrich A. Hayek, "The Politics of Race and Immigration," *The Times*, February 11, 1978; Friedrich A. Hayek, "Origins of Racialism," *The Times*, March 1, 1978; Friedrich A. Hayek, "Integrating Immigrants," *The Times*, March 9, 1978.

INTRODUCTION

1. Branko Milanovic, *Capitalism, Alone: The Future of the System That Rules the World* (Cambridge, MA: Belknap Press, 2019).

2. Amitav Acharya, *The End of American World Order*, 1st ed. (Cambridge, UK and Medford, MA: Polity Press, 2014); Alexander Cooley and Daniel H. Nexon, *Exit from Hegemony: The Unraveling of the American Global Order* (Oxford and New York: Oxford University Press, 2020).

3. Keith Tribe, "Liberalism and Neoliberalism in Britain, 1930–1980," in *The Road from Mont Pèlerin: The Making of the Neoliberal Thought Collective*, ed. Philip Mirowski and Dieter Plehwe, 1st Harvard University Press paperback ed. (Cambridge, MA: Harvard University Press, 2015), 68.

4. Hayek, *The Road to Serfdom*, 74.

5. William Poole, "Hayek on *The Road to Serfdom*," *Journal of Private Enterprise* 32, no. 1 (Spring 2017): 19–22.

6. Other candidates for this label include Malaysia, Laos, Algeria, Tanzania, Angola, Botswana, Ethiopia, and Rwanda.

7. Milanovic, *Capitalism, Alone*, 95. Although Randall Holcombe also uses the term

"political capitalism" in his recent work, my use of the term is confined to Milanovic's definition. Holcombe's conceptualization of political capitalism, which builds on Max Weber's typology, Gabriel Kolko's reading of the US Progressive Era, and public choice theory, is quite distinct from Milanovic's original typology of political capitalism and liberal meritocratic capitalism. In Holcombe's use of the term, economic and political elites cooperate for mutual benefit. The elite shape state regulation, spending, and taxation to maintain their own status. Holcombe's cites the German and Italian fascist/corporatist economies and the United States as examples. By contrast, Milanovic's concept, on which I frame the case studies of China, Vietnam, and Singapore, the postcommunist or one-party state maintains autonomy from the economic elite. The Leninist-capitalist party/state is not dependent on the economic elite except to the extent that they are useful as a class in helping to generate performance legitimacy for the regime. However, as the Chinese party/state has demonstrated episodically after earthquakes and floods, and more systematically since the COVID-19 pandemic, the party/state is more than willing to assert authority ruthlessly over the concerns of economic elites if the party/state perceives an opportunity to demonstrate competence at crisis containment and management. In fact, the party/state deliberately seeks to keep economic elites off balance and to remind them of their subordinate status to the party/state through anticorruption campaigns. See Randall G. Holcombe, "Political Capitalism," *Cato Journal* 35, no. 1 (2015): 41–66; Randall G. Holcombe, *Political Capitalism: How Economic and Political Power Is Made and Maintained* (Cambridge and New York: Cambridge University Press, 2018). Paul Aligica and Vlad Tarko articulate the concept of "state capitalism," which is similar to Milanovic's concept but should be kept distinct. Their concept of "state capitalism" in *Capitalist Alternatives* builds upon Ian Bremmer's article "The State Comes of Age," *Foreign Affairs* (May 2009): 40–55; and Edward Luttwak's concept of "geo-economics," in "From Geopolitics to Geoeconomics: Logic of Conflict, Grammar of Commerce," *National Interest* 20 (Summer 1990): 17–23. However, state capitalism encompasses a fairly diverse range of countries, including China and Vietnam, but also petroleum-exporting countries (such as Norway, Qatar, and Russia), as well as countries with large state-owned enterprises (e.g., India, Morocco, and Kazakhstan). Aligica and Tarko argue that state capitalism is marked by economic systems in which "the state functions as the leading economic actor and uses markets primarily for political gain." Unfortunately, as I will argue, this portrait as applied to China is rather dated. The Chinese economy is increasingly characterized by market competition domestically and a diminishing role for state-owned enterprises as a share of the total market. Overall, Aligica and Tarko's deductive taxonomy is vague once the process of coding and interpretation begins, despite their extensive and sophisticated elaboration of the possible permutations. The concept of state capitalism does not provide the reader with significant analytical tools (beyond the introduction of market prices) that could be used to distinguish it from "real" or "actually existing" Soviet socialism or even classical French mercantilism. This is problematic since, despite certain authoritarian continuities, there are dramatic political and economic differences before and after liberalization in China and Vietnam (e.g., dramatic increases in productivity and efficiency, income inequality, and corruption—the last one due to access to offshore havens; the emergence of hypernationalism; intensified individual surveillance; sophisticated information management; and growing corporatist arrangements). See: Paul Dragos Aligica and Vlad Tarko, *Capitalist Alternatives: Models, Taxonomies, Scenarios* (London: Routledge, 2015), 6, 18–19, 26, 30, 34.

8. Milanovic, *Capitalism, Alone*, 67.

9. Ibid., 92–93.

10. Ibid., 94; Barry Naughton, "Is China Socialist?," *Journal of Economic Perspectives* 31, no. 1 (2017): 11.

11. Milanovic, *Capitalism, Alone*, 87.

12. Panthea Pourmalek, review of Branko Milanovic, *Capitalism, Alone: The Future of the System That Rules the World*, *Journal of East Asian Studies* 20, no. 1 (March 2020): 128, https://doi.org/10.1017/jea.2019.45.

13. Ibid., 129.

14. Robert Kuttner, "Can We Fix Capitalism?," *New York Review of Books* 67, no. 14 (2020): 71–72.

15. Juan Carlos Perez, "Amazon Records First Profitable Year in Its History," *Computerworld*, January 28, 2004, accessed October 1, 2022, https://www.computerworld.com/article/2575106/amazon-records-first-profitable-year-in-its-history.html.

16. Drew Hendricks, "5 Successful Companies That Didn't Make a Dollar for 5 Years," Inc.com, July 7, 2014, accessed October 1, 2022, https://www.inc.com/drew-hendricks/5-successful-companies-that-didn-8217-t-make-a-dollar-for-5-years.html.

17. Jonathan Crider, "Just How Much Does Tesla Get in Subsidies Anyways?," CleanTechnica, August 3, 2020, accessed October 1, 2022, https://cleantechnica.com/2020/08/03/tesla-subsidies-how-much/.

18. Kuttner, "Can We Fix Capitalism?," 72.

19. Peter Bengsten, "China's Forced Labor Problem," *Diplomat*, March 21, 2018, accessed October 1, 2022, https://thediplomat.com/2018/03/chinas-forced-labor-problem/.

20. Kuttner, "Can We Fix Capitalism?," 72.

21. Anthony Go Yeh, Fiona F. Yang, and Jiejing Wang, "Economic Transition and Urban Transformation of China," *Urban Studies* 52, no. 15 (2015): 2827.

22. Ibid., 2828.

23. Naughton, "Is China Socialist?," 12.

24. Ibid.

25. Ibid., 13.

26. Milanovic, *Capitalism, Alone*, 73; Daron Acemoglu and James A. Robinson, *Why Nations Fail: The Origins of Power, Prosperity, and Poverty*, 1st ed. (New York: Crown, 2012), 436–39.

27. Daron Acemoglu and James A. Robinson, *The Narrow Corridor: States, Societies, and the Fate of Liberty* (New York: Penguin Press, 2019), 72.

28. This is not to deny that elites frequently store their excess wealth outside the country and prefer to educate their children in the West. These behaviors do not indicate that the political or economic system is unsustainable.

29. Acemoglu and Robinson, *Why Nations Fail*, 91–92.

30. Milanovic, *Capitalism, Alone*, 87–91; Naughton, "Is China Socialist?," 7.

31. Naughton, "Is China Socialist?," 7.

32. Ibid., 7.

33. Acemoglu and Robinson, *Why Nations Fail*, 441.

34. Edward Steinfeld, "Teams of Rivals: China, the United States, and the Race to Develop Technologies for a Sustainable Energy Future," in *China's Global Engagement: Cooperation, Competition, and Influence in the 21st Century*, ed. Jacques de Lisle and Avery Goldstein (Washington, DC: Brookings Institution Press, 2017), 98.

35. Ibid., 98.

36. Acemoglu and Robinson, *Why Nations Fail*, 442.

37. World Bank, "GNI per Capita, Atlas Method (Current US$) | Data," Database, World Bank, 2020, accessed October 1, 2022, https://data.worldbank.org/indicator/NY.GNP.PCAP.CD.

38. World Bank, "GDP Growth (Annual %)—Upper Middle Income, China," Database, accessed October 1, 2022, https://data.worldbank.org/indicator/NY.GDP.MKTP.KD.ZG?locations=XT-CN.

39. Acemoglu and Robinson, *The Narrow Corridor*, 234.

40. Hayek, *The Constitution of Liberty*, 52, 55, 81.

41. John Gray, "Hayek on Liberty, Rights, and Justice," *Ethics* 92, no. 1 (1981): 77, https://doi.org/10.1086/292299.

42. Ibid., 74–75.

43. Roland Kley, *Hayek's Social and Political Thought* (Oxford: Clarendon Press, 1994), 5–6, https://doi.org/10.1093/acprof:oso/9780198279167.001.0001.

44. Gray, "Hayek on Liberty, Rights, and Justice," 78.

45. Ibid., 84.

46. Milanovic, *Capitalism, Alone*, 12.

47. Ibid., 13.

48. Ibid., 217.

49. Richard E. Baldwin, *The Great Convergence: Information Technology and the New Globalization* (Cambridge, MA: Belknap Press, 2016).

50. Ibid., 7.

51. Ibid., 12.

52. Milanovic, *Capitalism, Alone*, 81.

53. Martin Wolf, *The Shifts and the Shocks: What We've Learned—and Have Still to Learn—from the Financial Crisis* (New York: Penguin Press, 2015).

54. Cooley and Nexon, *Exit from Hegemony*, 3.

55. Ibid., 7.

56. Amitav Acharya, *The End of American World Order*, 2nd ed. (Cambridge, UK and Medford, MA: Polity Press, 2018), 46–76.

57. Ibid., 46.

58. Ibid., 51.

59. William J. Clinton, "Speech to the Democratic National Committee," Denver, CO, August 27, 2008, accessed October 1, 2022, https://youtu.be/fl7Jc8tNxck.

60. Tribe, "Liberalism and Neoliberalism in Britain," 70.

61. Ibid., 73.

62. Gilles Deleuze and Félix Guattari, *A Thousand Plateaus: Capitalism and Schizophrenia* (Minneapolis: University of Minnesota Press, 1987); Gyanendra Pandey, "Encounters and Calamities," in *Selected Subaltern Studies*, ed. Ranajit Guha and Gayatri Chakravorty Spivak (Oxford and New York: Oxford University Press, 1988).

63. Tribe, "Liberalism and Neoliberalism in Britain," 74.

64. Ibid., 71–72.

65. After all, how does one explain Indira Gandhi's electoral defeat and ouster after the Emergency period in India?

66. Milanovic, *Capitalism, Alone*, 70–71.

67. Ibid., 71.

68. See also Gareth Dale, "Justificatory Fables of Ordoliberalism: Laissez-Faire and the 'Third Way,'" *Critical Sociology* 45, nos. 7–8 (2019): 1050–51, https://doi.org/10.1177/0896920519832638.

69. Hayek, *The Road to Serfdom*, 73–74.

70. Ibid., 74–75.

71. Amartya Sen, *Development as Freedom* (New York: Anchor Books, 2000); Gurcharan Das, *India Grows at Night: A Liberal Case for a Strong State* (New Delhi: Penguin Books, 2012); Chiaki Nishiyama, "Arguments for the Principles of Liberty and the Philosophy of Science," *Il Politico* 32, no. 2 (1967): 336–47.

72. Michel Foucault, *Discipline and Punish: The Birth of the Prison* (New York: Vintage Books, 1995).

73. Chris Matthew Sciabarra, *Marx, Hayek, and Utopia* (Albany: State University of New York Press, 1995), 16.

74. Imre Lakatos and Alan Musgrave, eds., *Criticism and the Growth of Knowledge*, vol. 4, *Proceedings of the International Colloquium in the Philosophy of Science, London 1965* (Cambridge and New York: Cambridge University Press, 2004).

75. Robert Skidelsky, *John Maynard Keynes: The Return of the Master* (New York: PublicAffairs, 2010); see also Mirowski and Plehwe, *The Road from Mont Pèlerin*, 58–59.

76. Hayek, *The Road to Serfdom*, 48.

77. Andrew Farrant, "Hayek, Orwell, and *The Road to Serfdom*," in *Hayek: A Collaborative Biography*, ed. Robert Leeson (London: Palgrave Macmillan, 2015), 152–82, https://doi.org/10.1057/9781137479259_3.

78. Ibid., 160.

79. Hayek, *The Road to Serfdom*, 58.

80. Poole, "Hayek on *The Road to Serfdom*," 19–22.

81. Hayek, *The Road to Serfdom*, 59.

82. Sciabarra, *Marx, Hayek, and Utopia*, 12.

83. Boettke and King, "Hayek and the Hayekians," 13.

84. Alexis de Tocqueville, *Democracy in America*, ed. Philips Bradley, trans. Henry

Reeve and Francis Bowen, vol. 2 (New York: Alfred A. Knopf, 1945), 319; quoted in Hayek, *The Road to Serfdom*, 49.

85. Bruce Caldwell and Leonidas Montes, "Friedrich Hayek and His Visits to Chile," *Review of Austrian Economics* 28, no. 3 (September 2015): 261–309, https://doi.org/10 .1007/s11138-014-0290-8.

86. Andrew Farrant, Edward McPhail, and Sebastian Berger, "Preventing the 'Abuses' of Democracy: Hayek, the 'Military Usurper' and Transitional Dictatorship in Chile?," *American Journal of Economics and Sociology* 71, no. 3 (2012): 518–20, https:// doi.org/10.1111/j.1536-7150.2012.00824.x.

87. Ibid., 521–22.

CHAPTER ONE

1. Hayek, *The Road to Serfdom*, 65.

2. Arthur Schlesinger Jr., "The 'Hundred Days' of F.D.R.," *New York Times*, April 10, 1983, sec. Books, accessed October 1, 2022, https://archive.nytimes.com/www.nytimes .com/books/00/11/26/specials/schlesinger-hundred.html.

3. Roger Daniels, *Franklin D. Roosevelt: Road to the New Deal, 1882–1939* (Urbana: University of Illinois Press, 2018), 135, https://doi.org/10.5406/j.ctt174d23g.

4. Ibid., 137.

5. Schlesinger, "The 'Hundred Days' of F.D.R."

6. John Milton, *Paradise Lost*, book 2, lines 432–33. Hayek would later criticize Roosevelt's "Four Freedoms" (particularly "freedom from want" and "freedom from fear") speech and the embodiment of these ideals in the United Nation's Universal Declaration of Human Rights (1948). Friedrich A. Hayek, *Law, Legislation and Liberty: A New Statement of the Liberal Principles of Justice and Political Economy* (London and New York: Routledge, 2012), 263–64.

7. Skidelsky, *Keynes*, 70.

8. Kim Phillips-Fein, "Business Conservatives and the Mont Pèlerin Society," in *The Road from Mont Pèlerin*, ed. Philip Mirowski and Dieter Plehwe (Cambridge, MA: Harvard University Press, 2015), 280–81.

9. Ibid., 285.

10. Ibid., 283–89. Despite Phillips-Fein's assertion of anti-Semitism, it is worth noting that Crane happily promoted Ludwig von Mises, who was known to be Jewish.

11. Hayek, *The Road to Serfdom*, 205.

12. Jacques Derrida, *Specters of Marx: The State of the Debt, the Work of Mourning and the New International* (New York: Routledge, 2006).

13. Hayek, *The Road to Serfdom*, 65.

14. Ibid., 65.

15. Adam Smith, *An Inquiry into the Nature and Causes of the Wealth of Nations*, ed. R. H. Campbell and Andrew S. Skinner, vol. 1 of *The Glasgow Edition of the Works and Correspondence of Adam Smith* (Indianapolis: Liberty Classics, 1981), 456 (book 4, chap. 2, para. 9).

16. Hayek, *The Road to Serfdom*, 65.

17. Ibid., 66.

18. Ibid., 61.

19. Ibid. Hayek attribute the origins of national socialism to Thomas Carlyle (a Scotsman) and Houston Stewart Chamberlain (an Englishman).

20. Ibid., 66.

21. Ibid., 66–67 n. 2.

22. Ibid., 67.

23. Sean Irving, "Hayek's Neo-Roman Liberalism," *European Journal of Political Theory* 19, no. 4 (July 17, 2017): 560, https://doi.org/10.1177/1474885117718370; Friedrich A. Hayek, "The Counter-Revolution of Science (Part I)," *Economica* 8, no. 29 (1941): 11, https://doi.org/10.2307/2549519.

24. Hayek, *The Road to Serfdom*, 68.

25. Sen, *Development as Freedom*, 232–33.

26. Ibid., 233.

27. Ibid., 234.

28. Ibid., 235–36.

29. Ibid., 238–40.

30. Das, *India Grows at Night*, 11.

31. Ibid., 52.

32. Myeong-seok Kim, "Choice, Freedom, and Responsibility in Ancient Chinese Confucianism," *Philosophy East and West* 63, no. 1 (2013): 17–19; Rina Marie Camus, "I Am Not a Sage but an Archer: Confucius on Agency and Freedom," *Philosophy East & West* 68, no. 4 (2018): 1042–53, https://doi.org/10.1353/pew.2018.0096.

33. Sen, *Development as Freedom*, 234–35.

34. Kim, "Choice, Freedom, and Responsibility," 21.

35. Ibid., 21–28.

36. Roy Tseng, "The Idea of Freedom in Comparative Perspective: Critical Comparisons between the Discourses of Liberalism and Neo-Confucianism," *Philosophy East and West* 66, no. 2 (2016): 552.

37. Ibid., 542.

38. Caldwell, *Hayek's Challenge*, 141.

39. Max Weber, *The Protestant Ethic and the Spirit of Capitalism* (London and New York: Routledge, 2001).

40. Ibid.

41. Chandran Kukathas, "Does Hayek Speak to Asia?," *Independent Review* 4, no. 3 (2000): 419–29.

42. Hayek, *The Road to Serfdom*, 68.

43. Ibid., 69.

44. Ibid., 68–69.

45. Geoffrey Ashton, "Role Ethics or Ethics of Role-Play? A Comparative Critical

Analysis of the Ethics of Confucianism and the Bhagavad Gītā," *Dao : A Journal of Comparative Philosophy* 13, no. 1 (2014): 13, https://doi.org/10.1007/s11712-013-9354-x.

46. Abram Steen, "'Over This Jordan': Dying and the Nonconformist Community in Bunyan's *Pilgrim's Progress*," *Modern Philology* 110, no. 1 (2012): 50, https://doi.org/10.1086/667706.

47. Joseph Cropsey, "The General Foundation of Smith's System," in *Polity and Economy* (Dordrecht: Springer Netherlands, 1957), 1–55, https://doi.org/10.1007/978-94-011-9383-2_1.

48. Hilary Wainwright, "It's Never Too Late to Move Beyond the Choices of the Cold War," *Guardian (London)*, February 20, 2006; Sciabarra, *Marx, Hayek, and Utopia*, 2.

49. Mancur Olson, *The Logic of Collective Action: Public Goods and the Theory of Groups*, Harvard Economic Studies 124 (Cambridge, MA: Harvard University Press, 2003); Robert Michels, *Political Parties: A Sociological Study of the Oligarchical Tendencies of Modern Democracy*, introd. Seymour Martin Lipset, trans. Eden and Cedar Paul (New York: Free Press, 2016).

50. Hayek, *The Road to Serfdom*, 69.

51. Ibid., 69–70; Acemoglu and Robinson, *Why Nations Fail*, 182–83.

52. Hayek, *The Road to Serfdom*, 70.

53. Ibid., 66.

54. Sciabarra, *Marx, Hayek, and Utopia*.

55. Hayek, *Law, Legislation and Liberty*, 501.

56. Hayek, *The Road to Serfdom*, 66.

57. Hayek had intended in 1947 to name his group the "Acton-Tocqueville Society." The group ultimately took the name of the location of the first meeting, a resort at Mont Pèlerin in Switzerland, in the canton of Vaud. Stefan Kolev, Nils Goldschmidt, and Jan-Otmar Hesse, "Debating Liberalism: Walter Eucken, F. A. Hayek and the Early History of the Mont Pèlerin Society," *Review of Austrian Economics* 33, no. 4 (2020 2019): 4, https://doi.org/10.1007/s11138-019-0435-x.

58. Mirowski and Plehwe, *The Road from Mont Pèlerin*. Jeremy Shearmur takes issues with Philip Mirowski's use of the term "thought collective," arguing that there were four distinct camps within the MPS: Mises and the radical non-interventionists; the German conservative liberals, such as Rüstow and Röpke; Hayek; and the American professional economists, such as Friedman and Stigler. There were also important tensions between Popper and Hayek. See Jeremy Shearmur, "No 'Thought Collective': Some Historical Remarks on the Mont Pèlerin Society," paper presented at the History of Economic Thought Society of Australia, Sydney, July 13, 2015; Jeremy Shearmur, *Hayek and After: Hayekian Liberalism as a Research Programme* (London and New York: Routledge, 2003), 4–5, 63–64, 81, https://doi.org/10.4324/9780203438343.

59. Jones, *Masters of the Universe*, 80.

60. Hayek, *Law, Legislation and Liberty*, 62.

61. Jones, *Masters of the Universe*, 48–49, 62–63; Karl Popper, *The Open Society and Its Enemies* (Princeton, NJ: Princeton University Press, 2020), 603–4, n. 4.

62. Hayek, *Law, Legislation and Liberty*, 62.

63. Hayek, *The Road to Serfdom*, 69.

64. Ibid., 69.

65. For a more sophisticated explanation and multi-causal framework, see Weber, *The Protestant Ethic and the Spirit of Capitalism*.

66. Smith, *An Inquiry into . . . the Wealth of Nations*, 1:381–427.

67. Ibid. 1:448.

68. Hayek, *The Road to Serfdom*, 70.

69. Ibid., 70–71.

70. Ibid., 71.

71. Ibid., 74.

72. Ibid., 75.

73. Ibid., 59.

74. In "Why I Am Not a Conservative," Hayek argues for a triangular political map, with conservatives, socialists, and liberals at each vertex. See Hayek, *The Constitution of Liberty*, 520. A contemporary variant of this left-equals-right outlook is known as "horseshoe theory" and is popularly credited to the French philosopher Jean-Pierre Faye.

75. Hayek, *The Road to Serfdom*, 245.

76. Ibid., 79.

77. Slavoj Žižek, "The Two Totalitarianisms," *London Review of Books*, March 17, 2005, accessed October 10, 2022, https://www.lrb.co.uk/the-paper/v27/n06/slavoj -zizek/the-two-totalitarianisms.

78. Hayek, *The Road to Serfdom*, 71.

79. Karl Polanyi, *The Great Transformation* (Boston, MA: Beacon Press, 1944).

80. Tribe, "Liberalism and Neoliberalism in Britain," 76; Jones, *Masters of the Universe*, 183.

81. Boettke, *F. A. Hayek*, 40; Jones, *Masters of the Universe*, 201–5.

82. Hayek, *The Constitution of Liberty*, 522.

83. Hayek, *The Road to Serfdom*, 72.

THE GARDEN ANALOGY

1. Ibid., 71.

2. Ibid., 72.

CHAPTER TWO

1. Friedrich Hölderlin, *Hyperion, or, The Hermit in Greece*, trans. Howard Gaskill (Cambridge: Open Book Publishers, 2019), 27–28.

2. Ibid., 152.

3. John W. Hoffmeyer, "Poetics of History, Logics of Collapse: On Heidegger's Hölderlin," *German Quarterly* 93, no. 3 (2020): 374–89.

4. In the foreword to the novel, Hölderlin writes, "Those who merely sniff my flower mistake its nature, and so do those who pluck it merely for instruction." Hölderlin, *Hyperion*, 5.

5. Hayek, *The Road to Serfdom*, 54.

6. Boettke, *F. A. Hayek*, 25.

7. Hayek, *The Road to Serfdom*, 104–5.

8. Ibid., 82.

9. Boettke, "On Reading Hayek," 1048.

10. Boettke, *F. A. Hayek*, 26.

11. Hayek, *The Road to Serfdom*, 77; Alexis de Tocqueville, "Tocqueville on Socialism," trans. Ronald Hamowy, "Tocqueville's Critique of Socialism (1848)," accessed May 19, 2021, https://oll.libertyfund.org/page/tocqueville-s-critique-of-socialism-1848.

12. Hayek, *The Road to Serfdom*, 76.

13. Ibid.

14. Ibid.

15. Ibid., 77.

16. Ibid.

17. Ibid., 78.

18. Hayek neglects to note that a liberal order, which sustains competition and prevents collusion, is also likely to result in a redistribution of wealth through the operation of the market.

19. Hayek, *The Road to Serfdom*, 78.

20. Ibid., 79.

21. Alan Johnson, "The New Communism: Resurrecting the Utopian Delusion," *World Affairs* 175, no. 1 (2012): 62–70.

22. Nathan Sperber, "The Many Lives of State Capitalism: From Classical Marxism to Free-Market Advocacy," *History of the Human Sciences* 32, no. 3 (2019): 100–124. As Sperber notes, Lenin's use of the term "state capitalism" in reference to the USSR was positive, since Lenin saw state capitalism as a precursor to genuine socialism.

23. Johnson, "The New Communism," 68–69.

24. Hayek, *The Road to Serfdom*, 80–82.

25. Ibid., 245.

26. Ibid., 246.

27. Ibid., 246–47.

28. Ibid., 247–48.

29. Ibid., 148.

30. Ibid.

31. Norman P. Barry, "The Road to Freedom: Hayek's Social and Economic Philosophy," in *Hayek, Co-Ordination and Evolution: His Legacy in Philosophy, Politics,*

Economics, and the History of Ideas, ed. Jack Birner and Rudy van Zijp, 1st ed. (London and New York: Routledge, 1994), 147, https://doi.org/10.4324/9780203004241.

32. Hayek, *The Road to Serfdom*, 148.

33. Ibid., 152; Juan Ramón Rallo, "Hayek Did Not Embrace a Universal Basic Income," *Independent Review* 24, no. 3 (2020): 350–51.

34. Hayek, *The Constitution of Liberty*, 427.

35. Rallo, "Hayek Did Not Embrace a Universal Basic Income," 352.

36. Hayek, *The Road to Serfdom*, 78.

37. Milanovic, *Capitalism, Alone*, 201–2.

38. Ibid., 48; Margaret Thatcher, "'The New Renaissance'—Speech to Zurich Economic Society," Margaret Thatcher Foundation, March 14, 1977, accessed October 10, 2022, https://www.margaretthatcher.org/document/103336.

39. Milanovic, *Capitalism, Alone*, 47–48.

40. Ibid., 46.

41. Ibid., 42–44.

42. Ibid., 46.

43. Thiem H. Bui, "Deconstructing the 'Socialist' Rule of Law in Vietnam: The Changing Discourse on Human Rights in Vietnam's Constitutional Reform Process," *Contemporary Southeast Asia* 36, no. 1 (2014): 89, https://doi.org/10.1355/cs36-1d.

44. Hayek was critical of the Universal Declaration of Human Rights. See Hayek, *Law, Legislation and Liberty*, 263–64.

45. Pitman B. Potter, "China and the International Human Rights Legal Regime," in *China's Global Engagement: Cooperation, Competition, and Influence in the 21st Century*, ed. Jacques deLisle and Avery Goldstein (Washington, DC: Brookings Institution Press, 2017), 297–99.

46. Richard McGregor, *The Party: The Secret World of China's Communist Rulers* (New York: Harper Perennial, 2012), 197–98.

47. Björn Alexander Düben, "Xi Jinping and the End of Chinese Exceptionalism," *Problems of Post-Communism* 67, no. 2 (2020): 117, https://doi.org/10.1080/10758216 .2018.1535274.

48. Ibid., 118.

49. Ibid., 118–19.

50. Ibid., 120.

51. Giao Cong Vu and Kien Tran, "Constitutional Debate and Development on Human Rights in Vietnam," *Asian Journal of Comparative Law* 11, no. 2 (2016): 241–42, https://doi.org/10.1017/asjcl.2016.27.

52. Rachel Ellett and Diep Phan, "The Emperor's Law Stops at the Village Gate: Questioning the Primacy of Formal Institutions in Vietnam's Land Law Reform," *Journal of Southeast Asian Economies* 37, no. 3 (2020): 237–39, https://doi.org/10.1355/ ae37-3a.

53. Vu and Tran, "Constitutional Debate and Development on Human Rights in Vietnam," 244–46.

NOTES TO PAGES 48–54 › 223

54. Tom Ginsburg, "Does Law Matter for Economic Development? Evidence From East Asia," *Law & Society Review* 34, no. 3 (2000): 833, https://doi.org/10.2307/3115145.

55. Vu and Tran, "Constitutional Debate and Development on Human Rights in Vietnam," 252–53.

56. Li-Ching Ho, "'Freedom Can Only Exist in an Ordered State': Harmony and Civic Education in Singapore," *Journal of Curriculum Studies* 49, no. 4 (2017): 491, https://doi.org/10.1080/00220272.2016.1155648.

57. Lynette J. Chua, "Pragmatic Resistance, Law, and Social Movements in Authoritarian States: The Case of Gay Collective Action in Singapore," *Law & Society Review* 46, no. 4 (2012): 718, 722, https://doi.org/10.1111/j.1540–5893.2012.00515.x.

58. Kenneth Paul Tan, "Choosing What to Remember in Neoliberal Singapore: The Singapore Story, State Censorship and State-Sponsored Nostalgia," *Asian Studies Review* 40, no. 2 (2016): 232, https://doi.org/10.1080/10357823.2016.1158779.

59. Ibid., 238.

60. Marco Verweij and Riccardo Pelizzo, "Singapore: Does Authoritarianism Pay?," *Journal of Democracy* 20, no. 2 (2009): 22, https://doi.org/10.1353/jod.0.0076.

61. Ibid., 20–23.

62. Düben, "Xi Jinping and the End of Chinese Exceptionalism," 120; Verweij and Pelizzo, "Singapore: Does Authoritarianism Pay?," 22–23.

CHAPTER THREE

1. Hayek, *The Road to Serfdom*, 83. A *dreyfusard* was a supporter of Alfred Dreyfus, a captain of Jewish heritage, who was falsely convicted of treason by the French military in a scandalous miscarriage of justice that lasted from 1894 to 1906. The *dreyfusards* were pro-republic and anticlerical, while their opponents supported the military and the Catholic Church.

2. Ludovic Frobert, "Elie Halévy and Philosophical Radicalism," *Modern Intellectual History* 12, no. 1 (April 2015): 129, 132, https://doi.org/10.1017/S1479244314000377.

3. Ibid., 131.

4. Ibid., 137–39.

5. Friedrich Hayek, "Dr. Bernard Mandeville," in *The Collected Works of Friedrich Hayek* (Chicago: University of Chicago Press, 1991), 3:91.

6. H. S. Jones, "The Era of Tyrannies: Elie Halévy and Friedrich von Hayek on Socialism," *European Journal of Political Theory* 1, no. 1 (July 1, 2002): 54, 59–60, https://doi.org/10.1177/1474885102001001005.

7. Ibid., 55.

8. Ibid., 62–63.

9. Hayek, *The Road to Serfdom*, 83.

10. Max Weber, *From Max Weber: Essays in Sociology*, ed. Hans Gerth and Charles Wright Mills (Oxford and New York: Oxford University Press, 1959).

11. Hayek, *The Road to Serfdom*, 85.

12. Theodore A. Burczak, *Socialism after Hayek* (Ann Arbor: University of Michigan Press, 2006), 2, https://doi.org/10.3998/mpub.93585.

13. Whether a post-Hayekian or "libertarian Marxism," which achieves social justice without centralized state planning, is possible is debatable, particularly if it is also to abjure the coercion of individuals. See ibid.

14. Walter L. Adamson, "Gramsci's Interpretation of Fascism," *Journal of the History of Ideas* 41, no. 4 (1980): 621, https://doi.org/10.2307/2709277.

15. Traute Rafalski, "Social Planning and Corporatism: Modernization Tendencies in Italian Fascism," trans. Michel Vale, *International Journal of Political Economy* 18, no. 1 (1988): 13.

16. Peter Temin, "Soviet and Nazi Economic Planning in the 1930s," *Economic History Review* 44, no. 4 (1991): 573, https://doi.org/10.2307/2597802.

17. Rural citizens were prohibited from alienating their private property. Prices of agricultural products were controlled by marketing boards using fixed prices.

18. Temin, "Soviet and Nazi Economic Planning in the 1930s," 582.

19. Ibid., 576–77.

20. Ibid., 580.

21. Jon Simons, "Benjamin's Communist Idea: Aestheticized Politics, Technology, and the Rehearsal of Revolution," *European Journal of Political Theory* 15, no. 1 (January 1, 2016): 45, https://doi.org/10.1177/1474885114543569.

22. Ibid., 55 n. 97.

23. Hayek, *The Road to Serfdom*, 86.

24. Ibid., 86.

25. Ibid., 84.

26. Ibid., 86–87.

27. Ibid., 87.

28. Ibid., 87.

29. Ibid., 88.

30. Milanovic, *Capitalism, Alone*, 87–89.

31. Daniel C. K. Chow, "Rising Nationalism: China's Regulation of Investment Trade," in *China's Global Engagement: Cooperation, Competition, and Influence in the 21st Century*, ed. Jacques deLisle and Avery Goldstein (Washington, DC: Brookings Institution Press, 2017), 71–72.

32. Ibid., 72.

33. "Global 500," *Fortune*, August 2020, accessed October 1, 2022, https://fortune.com/global500/2020/.

34. Ben Hillman, "Law, Order and Social Control in Xi's China," *Issues and Studies—Institute of International Relations* 57, no. 2 (2021): 2, 8, https://doi.org/10.1142/S1013251121500065.

35. Ibid., 12–14.

36. Konstantin M. Wacker, "Restructuring the SOE Sector in Vietnam," *Journal of Southeast Asian Economies* 34, no. 2 (2017): 285, https://doi.org/10.1355/ae34–2c.

37. Vu Quoc Ngu, "Total Factor Productivity Growth of Industrial State-Owned Enterprises in Vietnam, 1976–98," *ASEAN Economic Bulletin* 20, no. 2 (2003): 160–62.

38. Hai Hong Nguyen, "Resilience of the Communist Party of Vietnam's Authoritarian Regime since Đổi Mới," *Journal of Current Southeast Asian Affairs* 35, no. 2 (2016): 43, https://doi.org/10.1177/186810341603500202.

39. Chua Beng Huat, "State-Owned Enterprises, State Capitalism and Social Distribution in Singapore," *Pacific Review* 29, no. 4 (2016): 500–501, https://doi.org/10.1080/09512748.2015.1022587.

40. Shamsul M. Haque and Jose A. Puppim de Oliveira, "Building Administrative Capacity under Developmental States in Chile and Singapore: A Comparative Perspective," *International Review of Administrative Sciences* 87, no. 2 (2021): 227, https://doi.org/10.1177/0020852320943656.

41. Ibid., 227.

42. Mark R. Thompson, review of Chua Beng Huat, *Liberalism Disavowed: Communitarianism and State Capitalism in Singapore* (Singapore: NUS Press, 2017), *Journal of Southeast Asian Studies (Singapore)* 51, no. 4 (2020): 645.

43. Ian Vásquez and Fred McMahon, *The Human Freedom Index 2020: A Global Measurement of Personal, Civil, and Economic Freedom* (Washington, DC: CATO Institute and Fraser Institute, 2020), 7.

44. Ibid., 22–24.

45. "Plan v. Market," *Economist*, November 5, 2016.

46. Ibid.

47. Stephan Haggard, *Developmental States* (Cambridge and New York: Cambridge University Press, 2018), 71–72.

48. Mei-Lin Goh, Douglas Sikorski, and Wing-Keong Wong, "Government Policy for Outward Investment by Domestic Firms: The Case of Singapore's Regionalisation Strategy," *Singapore Management Review* 23, no. 2 (2001): 30.

49. Ibid., 40–41.

50. Ibid, 41–42.

51. Haggard, *Developmental States*, 91–92.

52. Ibid, 92.

53. Ibid, 93.

54. Chalmers A. Johnson, *MITI and the Japanese Miracle: The Growth of Industrial Policy, 1925—1975* (Stanford, CA: Stanford University Press, 2007).

55. For a discussion of corporatism, see chap. 12.

56. Hayek, *The Road to Serfdom*, 89; Atul Kohli, *State-Directed Development: Political Power and Industrialization in the Global Periphery* (Cambridge and New York: Cambridge University Press, 2004).

57. Hayek, *The Road to Serfdom*, 89.

CHAPTER FOUR

1. Hayek, *The Road to Serfdom*, 91.

2. Roger Griffin, "Mussolini Predicted a Fascist Century: How Wrong Was He?," *Fascism* 8, no. 1 (July 1, 2019): 2, https://doi.org/10.1163/22116257–00801001.

3. Carl T. Schmidt, *The Corporate State in Action: Italy under Fascism* (Oxford and New York: Oxford University Press, 1939), 41–43, 56; Didier Musiedlak, "Mussolini, Charisma and Decision-Making.," *Portuguese Journal of Social Science* 8, no. 1 (April 2009): 32.

4. David Rifkind, "'Everything In the State, Nothing Against the State, Nothing Outside the State': Corporativist Urbanism and Rationalist Architecture in Fascist Italy," *Planning Perspectives* 27, no. 1 (January 2012): 53.

5. Schmidt, *The Corporate State in Action*, 80–81.

6. Ibid., 82.

7. Ibid., 76.

8. Rifkind, "'Everything In the State, Nothing Against the State, Nothing Outside the State'," 53.

9. Claire Giordano and Ferdinando Giugliano, "A Tale of Two Fascisms: Labour Productivity Growth and Competition Policy in Italy, 1911–1951," *Explorations in Economic History* 55 (2015): 25–38, https://doi.org/10.1016/j.eeh.2013.12.003.

10. Franklin Hugh Adler, "Why Mussolini Turned on the Jews," *Patterns of Prejudice* 39, no. 3 (September 2005): 296, https://doi.org/10.1080/00313220500198235.

11. Amanda Minervini, "Mussolini Speaks: History Reviewed," *Massachusetts Review* 60, no. 1 (2019): 194, https://doi.org/10.1353/mar.2019.0031.

12. Ibid., 194–98; Giorgio Bertellini, "Duce/Divo: Masculinity, Racial Identity, and Politics among Italian Americans in 1920s New York City," *Journal of Urban History* 31, no. 5 (July 2005): 693, https://doi.org/10.1177/0096144205275981.

13. Bertellini, "Duce/Divo."

14. Lawrence Squeri, "Who Benefited from Italian Fascism: A Look at Parma's Landowners," *Agricultural History* 64, no. 1 (1990): 20.

15. Baldwin, *The Great Convergence*.

16. Ibid.

17. Hayek, *The Road to Serfdom*, 92.

18. Ibid., 92–93.

19. Ibid., 93.

20. Ibid., 95.

21. Ibid.

22. "Can Big Data Help to Resurrect the Planned Economy?," *Global Times*, June 14, 2017, https://www.globaltimes.cn/content/1051715.shtml; Jesús Fernández-Villaverde, "Artificial Intelligence Can't Solve the Knowledge Problem," *Public Discourse* (blog), July 29, 2021, accessed October 1, 2022, https://www.thepublicdiscourse.com/2021/07/76963/.

23. Paul Cockshott, "How Feasible Are Jack Ma's Proposals for Computerized Planning?," *World Review of Political Economy* 10, no. 3 (Fall 2019): 302–3.

24. Allenna Leonard, "The Viable System Model and Its Application to Complex Organizations," *Systemic Practice and Action Research* 22, no. 4 (2009): 230–31, https://doi.org/10.1007/s11213–009–9126-z.

25. George Eaton, "Project Cybersyn: The Afterlife of Chile's Socialist Internet," *New Statesman* 147, no. 5433 (2018): 16.

26. Farrant, McPhail, and Berger, "Preventing the 'Abuses' of Democracy," 524.

27. Cockshott, "How Feasible Are Jack Ma's Proposals?," 307–8.

28. Ibid. 305.

29. Ibid., 308–14.

30. Fernández-Villaverde, "Artificial Intelligence Can't Solve the Knowledge Problem."

31. Ibid.

32. "Can Big Data Help to Resurrect the Planned Economy?"

33. Yoko Kubota, "Jack Ma Urges Beijing to Ease Up—Market, Not Regulator, Should Determine How Technology Evolves, Tycoon Tells AI Session," *Wall Street Journal*, September 18, 2018, Eastern ed. , 2108088534.

34. Eswar Prasad, "Jack Ma Paid for Taunting China [op-ed]," *New York Times*, April 30, 2021, sec. A23.

35. George Calhoun, "What Really Happened to Jack Ma?," *Forbes*, June 24, 2021, accessed July 30, 2021, https://www.forbes.com/sites/georgecalhoun/2021/06/24/what-really-happened-to-jack-ma/?sh=13fdd1b17c7e.

36. Hayek, *The Road to Serfdom*, 96.

37. Ibid.

38. Ibid., 97.

39. Ibid., 98.

40. Mark Pennington, "Hayek on Complexity, Uncertainty and Pandemic Response," *Review of Austrian Economics* 34, no. 2 (2021): 207, https://doi.org/10.1007/s11138–020–00522–9.

41. Assuming that the purpose of a highway system is to facilitate civilian use and commerce rather than military defense and rapid troop deployment.

42. Hayek, *The Road to Serfdom*, 98.

43. Michel Foucault, *The History of Sexuality: An Introduction*, vol. 1 (New York: Vintage Books, 1990), 95–96.

44. Pennington, "Hayek on Complexity, Uncertainty and Pandemic Response," 205.

CHAPTER FIVE

1. Friedrich A. Hayek, *The Road to Serfdom: Text and Documents; The Definitive Edition*, ed. Bruce Caldwell, vol. 2 of *The Collected Works of F. A. Hayek* (Chicago: University of Chicago Press, 2007), 100; from Smith, *An Inquiry into . . . the Wealth of Nations*, 1:456.

2. H. Goodacre, "Limited Liability and the Wealth of 'Uncivilised Nations': Adam Smith and the Limits to the European Enlightenment," *Cambridge Journal of Economics* 34, no. 5 (September 1, 2010): 860, https://doi.org/10.1093/cje/beq007.

3. John Kenneth Galbraith, *Economics in Perspective: A Critical History* (Princeton, NJ: Princeton University Press, 2017), 77, https://doi.org/10.2307/j.ctt1vwmhch; Smith, *An Inquiry into . . . the Wealth of Nations*, 1:463, 467.

4. Hayek, *The Road to Serfdom*, 100–101. By "thin" I mean vague and indeterminate. Hayek himself states that the social goal or common purpose is "usually vaguely described" as the common good or general welfare. He adds, "It does not need much reflection to see that these terms have no sufficiently definite meaning to determine a particular course of action." Thin concepts may be useful in fabricating consensus, but they often mask thicker concepts that are peculiar to certain societies or factions. On notions of "thin" and "thick" moral concepts, see Kwame Anthony Appiah, *Cosmopolitanism: Ethics in a World of Strangers* (New York: Norton, 2007), 46–47.

5. Hayek, *The Road to Serfdom*, 101.

6. Ibid., 101.

7. Foucault, *Discipline and Punish*; Foucault, *The History of Sexuality*. Hayek might respond, as he did in his critique of John Kenneth Galbraith, that Foucault's argument is a non sequitur. Hayek argued that all of our desires beyond the bare necessities are obviously shaped by the civilization in which we live. To diminish the value of these desires as artificial because they are not innate or absolutely necessary for survival is to misunderstand the role of humans as social creatures. Of course, Foucault's argument is not confined to the incitement of desire for goods and services but includes the internalization and embodiment of a disciplinary apparatus. See Friedrich A. Hayek, *Studies in Philosophy, Politics and Economics* (London: Routledge & Kegan Paul, 1967), 313–17.

8. Hayek, *The Road to Serfdom*, 106.

9. Ibid., 102.

10. Ibid., 103.

11. Even within liberal societies there are increasing fractures in values along the lines of race and ethnicity, religiosity, gender/sexual identity, and even the belief in science. The result has been recrudescent tribalism and contending fundamentalisms. See Stephen Holmes, *The Anatomy of Antiliberalism* (Cambridge, MA: Harvard University Press, 1993).

12. Hayek, *The Road to Serfdom*, 105.

13. Ibid., 108.

14. Ibid., 110.

15. Ibid., 124.

16. Ibid., 124.

17. Weber, *From Max Weber*; Hayek, *The Road to Serfdom*, 129.

18. Hayek, *The Road to Serfdom*, 128.

19. Ibid., 133.

CHAPTER SIX

1. Karl Mannheim, *Man and Society in an Age of Reconstruction*, trans. Edward Shils (London: Routledge & Kegan Paul, 1940), 180. Hayek did not include the full sentence in his epigraph.

2. Although the sociology department and the Institute for Social Research were housed in the same building, Manneheim had "virtually no contact" with the Institute, according to his assistant, Norbert Elias. See Rolf Wiggershaus, *The Frankfurt School: Its History, Theories and Political Significance*, trans. Michael Robertson (Cambridge and Cambridge, MA: Polity Press and MIT Press, 1994), 111.

3. Mannheim, *Man and Society in an Age of Reconstruction*, 379–81.

4. Jefferson Pooley, "Edward Shils' Turn against Karl Mannheim: The Central European Connection," *American Sociologist* 38, no. 4 (2007): 365, 371, https://doi.org/10.2307/27700518.

5. Ibid., 374.

6. Hayek, *The Road to Serfdom*, 73–74.

7. Richard M. Ebeling, "The Geneva Connection, a Liberal World Order, and the Austrian Economists," *Review of Austrian Economics*, May 2019, 8, n. 3, https://doi.org/10.1007/s11138–019–00450–3.

8. Mannheim, *Man and Society in an Age of Reconstruction*, 181.

9. In *The Constitution of Liberty*, Hayek will come to embrace common law as favorable to the evolution of the rule of law. Hayek, *The Constitution of Liberty*, 297–98. For a detailed critique of Hayek's "exaggerated" reverence for the rule-of-law concept, at least from the Anglo-American tradition (as opposed to Hayek's preference for the Kantian *Rechtsstaat* tradition), see Joseph Raz, "The Rule of Law and Its Virtue," in *The Authority of Law: Essays on Law and Morality* (Oxford and New York: Oxford University Press, 1979), https://doi.org/10.1093/acprof:oso/9780198253457.003.0011; Herman Finer, *The Road to Reaction* (Boston, MA: Little, Brown, 1945), 45–59.

10. Hayek, *The Road to Serfdom*, 246–47.

11. Tim Rogan, *The Moral Economists: R. H. Tawney, Karl Polanyi, E. P. Thompson, and the Critique of Capitalism* (Princeton, NJ: Princeton University Press, 2017), 117.

12. Mannheim, *Man and Society in an Age of Reconstruction*, 176; Hayek, *The Road to Serfdom*, 73.

13. Rogan, *The Moral Economists*, 118–19.

14. Ibid., 123–24.

15. Kolev, Goldschmidt, and Hesse, "Debating Liberalism," 9.

16. Rogan, *The Moral Economists*, 124–25.

17. Kolev, Goldschmidt, and Hesse, "Debating Liberalism," 13–14.

18. As opposed to, for example, the British concept, which implies the supremacy of Parliament, or the American concept, in which the seat of sovereignty rests with the "constitutional disposition of powers" and thus ultimately in the people who can amend the Constitution. See Finer, *The Road to Reaction*, 45–67.

19. Hayek, *The Road to Serfdom*, 112.

20. Ibid., 112–13.

21. Ibid., 112.

22. Ibid.114.

23. Daniel Nientiedt, "Hayek's Treatment of Legal Positivism," *European Journal of Law and Economics* 51, no. 3 (2021): 568, https://doi.org/10.1007/s10657-021 -09684-8.

24. Hayek, *The Road to Serfdom*, 119 n. 7.

25. Nientiedt, "Hayek's Treatment of Legal Positivism," 568.

26. Hayek, *The Road to Serfdom*, 113.

27. Dorottya Sallai and Gerhard Schnyder, "What Is 'Authoritarian' About Authoritarian Capitalism? The Dual Erosion of the Private–Public Divide in State-Dominated Business Systems," *Business & Society* 60, no. 6 (2021): 1317, https://doi.org/10.1177/0007650319898475.

28. Hayek, *The Road to Serfdom*, 119.

29. Nientiedt, "Hayek's Treatment of Legal Positivism," 564. Kelsen also wrote a letter of introduction for Karl Popper to meet with Hayek in 1935, even though Kelsen and Hayek did not see eye to eye. Ebenstein, *Friedrich Hayek*, 156.

30. Hayek, *The Road to Serfdom*, 113.

31. Ibid.

32. Ibid., 115.

33. Ibid., 117. Shearmur might add that Hayekians ought to note that liberalism generates wealth spontaneously and minimizes coercion, and that these benefits are more valuable than economic equality. See Shearmur, *Hayek and After*, 139.

34. Hayek, *The Road to Serfdom*, 117 n. 5.

35. Ibid., 118.

36. Milanovic also distinguishes between classical capitalism (e.g., laissez-faire pre–World War I UK), social-democratic capitalism (e.g., post–World War II Europe and the United States), and liberal meritocratic capitalism (i.e., the contemporary United States). Milanovic, *Capitalism, Alone*, 12–21.

37. Wendy Ng, "Changing Global Dynamics and International Competition Law: Considering China's Potential Impact," *European Journal of International Law* 30, no. 4 (2019): 1426, https://doi.org/10.1093/ejil/chz066.

38. Bui, "Deconstructing the 'Socialist' Rule of Law in Vietnam," 89.

39. Ibid., 78.

40. Ibid., 79–80.

41. Ibid., 80–81.

42. Sek Keong Chan, "The Courts and the 'Rule of Law' in Singapore: A Lecture Delivered at the Rule of Law Symposium," *Singapore Journal of Legal Studies* (December 2012): 215–16.

43. Ibid., 219–21.

44. Ibid., 223.

45. Li-ann Thio, "Between Apology and Apogee, Autochthony: The 'Rule of Law' Beyond the Rules of Law in Singapore," *Singapore Journal of Legal Studies* (December 2012): 269–70.

46. Luyao Che, "The Chinese Conception of the Rule of Law and Its Embodiment under the 'Belt and Road' Initiative (BRI)," *Journal of World Trade* 55, no. 1 (2021): 175.

47. Ibid., 174.

48. Ibid. 182.

49. Fitch Solutions, "Vietnam Trade and Investment Risk Report—Q1 2021" (London: Fitch Solutions, 2021), 4.

50. Ibid., 17–18.

51. Habibul Haque Khondker, "Globalization and State Autonomy in Singapore," *Asian Journal of Social Science* 36, no. 1 (2008): 49, https://doi.org/10.1163/156853108X267585.

52. Ali M. Nizamuddin, "Multinational Corporations and Economic Development: The Lessons of Singapore," *International Social Science Review* 82, nos. 3–4 (2007): 156.

53. Fitch Solutions, "Vietnam Trade and Investment Risk Report—Q1 2021," 19.

54. Michael Intal Magcamit, "Trading in Paranoia: Exploring Singapore's Security-Trade Linkages in the Twenty-First Century," *Asian Journal of Political Science* 23, no. 2 (2015): 185, https://doi.org/10.1080/02185377.2014.999248.

55. Choon Yin Sam, "Economic Nationalism in Singapore and Thailand: The Case of the Shin Corporation—Temasek Holdings Business Deal," *South East Asia Research* 16, no. 3 (2008): 450, https://doi.org/10.5367/000000008787133427.

56. Ng, "Changing Global Dynamics and International Competition Law," 1423.

57. Eleanor M. Fox, "Should China's Competition Model Be Exported? A Reply to Wendy Ng," *European Journal of International Law* 30, no. 4 (2019): 1434, https://doi.org/10.1093/ejil/chaa010.

58. Ng, "Changing Global Dynamics and International Competition Law," 1426.

59. Fox, "Should China's Competition Model Be Exported?," 1435.

60. Youngjoon Lee, "The Rule of Law, Anti-Corruption and Land Expropriation: Evidence from China," *China (National University of Singapore. East Asian Institute)* 18, no. 4 (2020): 96–98.

61. Susan H. Whiting, "Authoritarian 'Rule of Law' and Regime Legitimacy," *Comparative Political Studies* 50, no. 14 (2017): 1908, 1913, https://doi.org/10.1177/0010414016688008.

62. Ginsburg, "Does Law Matter for Economic Development?," 846; John Gillespie, "Exploring the Limits of the Judicialization of Urban Land Disputes in Vietnam," *Law & Society Review* 45, no. 2 (2011): 268, https://doi.org/10.1111/j.1540-5893.2011.00434.x.

63. Marco Zappa, "The Rise of Governance and the Japanese Intermediation in Transitional Vietnam: The Impact of Japanese Knowledge-Based Aid to Vietnam in the Doi Moi Years," *Studia Politica* 20, no. 1 (2020): 18–19.

64. Khondker, "Globalization and State Autonomy in Singapore," 49.

65. Choon-Piew Pow, "Consuming Private Security: Consumer Citizenship and Defensive Urbanism in Singapore," in "Crime and Control in Asia," ed. Maggy Lee

and Karen Joe Laidler, special issue, *Theoretical Criminology* 17, no. 2 (2013): 185–86, https://doi.org/10.1177/1362480612472782.

66. Ibid., 186.

67. Hayek would not concur that a one-party state could be autonomous from society since it is by definition a reflection of a partisan or popular bias. However, it is clear that the political-capitalist state can act against the interests of even very influential firms and "celebrity entrepreneurs" in the economy (e.g., Jack Ma's Alibaba Group in China, discussed earlier).

68. Peter B. Evans, *Embedded Autonomy: States and Industrial Transformation* (Princeton, NJ: Princeton University Press, 1995).

69. McGregor, *The Party*, 32.

70. John B. Knight, "China as a Developmental State," *World Economy* 37, no. 10 (2014): 1341, https://doi.org/10.1111/twec.12215.

71. Li Yang, Filip Novokmet, and Branko Milanovic, "From Workers to Capitalists in Less than Two Generations: A Study of Chinese Urban Top Group Transformation between 1988 and 2013," *British Journal of Sociology* 72, no. 3 (June 2021): 482, https://doi.org/10.1111/1468-4446.12850.

72. Martin Painter, "The Politics of State Sector Reforms in Vietnam: Contested Agendas and Uncertain Trajectories," *Journal of Development Studies* 41, no. 2 (2005): 266–67, https://doi.org/10.1080/0022038042000309241.

73. Ibid., 267–68.

74. Tu Phuong Nguyen, "Rethinking State-Society Relations in Vietnam: The Case of Business Associations in Ho Chi Minh City," *Asian Studies Review* 38, no. 1 (2014): 87–106, https://doi.org/10.1080/10357823.2013.872598.

75. Robert Gregory, "Combating Corruption in Vietnam: A Commentary," *Asian Education and Development Studies* 5, no. 2 (2016): 230, https://doi.org/10.1108/AEDS-01-2016-0010.

76. Khondker, "Globalization and State Autonomy in Singapore," 48; Martin Gainsborough, "The (Neglected) Statist Bias and the Developmental State: The Case of Singapore and Vietnam," *Third World Quarterly* 30, no. 7 (2009): 1324, https://doi.org/10.1080/01436590903134957.

77. Khondker, "Globalization and State Autonomy in Singapore," 50–53.

78. Only 12.68 percent of China's land was arable in 2018. World Bank, "Arable Land (% of Land Area)—China | Data," accessed August 12, 2021, https://data.worldbank.org/.

79. Ng, "Changing Global Dynamics and International Competition Law," 1428.

80. Chan, "The Courts and the 'Rule of Law' in Singapore," 212.

CHAPTER SEVEN

1. Hilaire Belloc, *The Servile State*, 1st American ed. (New York: Henry Holt, 1946).

2. Edward McPhail, "Does the Road to Serfdom Lead to the Servile State?," *European Journal of Political Economy* 21, no. 4 (2005): 1001, https://doi.org/10.1016/j.ejpoleco.2004.10.005.

3. Ibid., 1003.

4. Hayek, *The Road to Serfdom*, 67 n. 4.

5. McPhail, "Does the Road to Serfdom Lead to the Servile State?," 1006.

6. Ibid., 1007.

7. Hayek, *The Road to Serfdom*, 126.

8. Charles E. Lindblom, "Market and Democracy—Obliquely," *PS: Political Science & Politics* 28, no. 4 (1995): 685, https://doi.org/10.2307/420518.

9. Hayek, *The Road to Serfdom*, 127 n. 4.

10. Ibid., 127.

11. Farrant, "Hayek, Orwell, and *The Road to Serfdom*."

12. Hayek, *The Road to Serfdom*, 129. One might object that Hayek is interested in physical rather than social mobility. However, it is clear from the context that Hayek is concerned about the freedom of individuals to choose their own occupation, which would include the aspiration for social mobility even if that aspiration generates an inefficient use of labor resources or waste owing to failure in a new occupation or enterprise. Notably, on the previous page, Hayek had written, "Nothing makes conditions more unbearable than the knowledge that no effort of ours can change them; and even if we should never have the strength of mind to make the necessary sacrifice, the knowledge that we could escape if we only strove hard enough makes many otherwise intolerable positions bearable."

13. Raymond Plant, "Neo-Liberalism and the Theory of the State: From *Wohlfahrtsstaat* to *Rechtsstaat*," *Political Quarterly* 75, no. s1 (2004): 25–26, https://doi.org/10.1111/j.1467-923X.2004.620_1.x.

14. Milanovic, *Capitalism, Alone*, 27, 46.

15. Hayek, *Law, Legislation and Liberty*, 289–90.

16. For theoretical and public-policy examples, see Andreas Bergh, "Yes, There Are Hayekian Welfare States (at Least in Theory)," *Econ Journal Watch* 12, no. 1 (2015): 22; Andreas Bergh, "Hayekian Welfare States: Explaining the Coexistence of Economic Freedom and Big Government," *Journal of Institutional Economics* 16, no. 1 (2020): 1–12, https://doi.org/10.1017/S1744137419000432.

17. Hayek, *The Road to Serfdom*, 130.

18. Ibid., 131.

19. Ibid., 131–32.

20. Michael Löwy, "From Marx to Ecosocialism," *Capitalism, Nature, Socialism* 13, no. 1 (2002): 122–25, https://doi.org/10.1080/104557502101245413.

21. Andreas Malm, "Marx on Steam: From the Optimism of Progress to the Pessimism of Power," *Rethinking Marxism* 30, no. 2 (2018): 173, https://doi.org/10.1080/08935696.2017.1417085.

22. Andreas Malm and Dominic Mealy, "'To Halt Climate Change, We Need an Ecological Leninism': An Interview with Andreas Malm," *Jacobin*, June 15, 2020, https://jacobinmag.com/2020/06/andreas-malm-coronavirus-covid-climate-change.

23. Damian F. White, "Ecological Democracy, Just Transitions and a Political Ecol-

ogy of Design," *Environmental Values* 28, no. 1 (2019): 31–53, https://doi.org/10.3197/096327119X15445433913569.

24. Pennington, "Hayek on Complexity, Uncertainty and Pandemic Response," 204.

25. A more complete specification of property rights would confine many environmental disputes to the realm of tort law. Graham Dawson, "Austrian Economics and Climate Change," *Review of Austrian Economics* 26, no. 2 (2013): 184, https://doi.org/10.1007/s11138-012-0174-8.

26. Hayek, *The Constitution of Liberty*, 492; Dawson, "Austrian Economics and Climate Change," 191.

27. Hayek, *The Road to Serfdom*, 87; Andries Nentjes, "Austrian View on Environmental Protection," in *Modern Applications of Austrian Thought*, ed. Jürgen G. Backhaus (London: Routledge, 2005), 358.

28. Hayek, *The Constitution of Liberty*, 494.

29. Pennington, "Hayek on Complexity, Uncertainty and Pandemic Response," 207.

30. Dawson, "Austrian Economics and Climate Change," 191–92.

31. Ibid., 192.

32. Hayek, *The Constitution of Liberty*, 497.

33. Nentjes, "Austrian View on Environmental Protection," 359.

34. Dawson, "Austrian Economics and Climate Change," 183–84.

35. I thank Jeremy Shearmur for this insight.

36. Nentjes, "Austrian View on Environmental Protection," 360.

CHAPTER EIGHT

1. Hayek, *The Road to Serfdom*, 134.

2. Harold Acton, "Lord Acton," *Chicago Review* 15, no. 1 (1961): 40, https://doi.org/10.2307/25293642.

3. Ibid., 33.

4. Christopher Lazarski, *Power Tends to Corrupt: Lord Acton's Study of Liberty* (DeKalb: Northern Illinois University Press, 2012), 38.

5. Ibid., 197.

6. Ibid., 188.

7. Ibid., 191.

8. Ibid., 230.

9. Ibid., 231.

10. Ibid., 240.

11. Ibid., 250–51.

12. Hayek, *The Road to Serfdom*, 134.

13. Ibid., 135.

14. Ibid.

15. Ibid., 135 n. 2.

16. Ibid., 136.

17. Ibid., 137.

18. Brian Lee Crowley, *The Self, the Individual, and the Community: Liberalism in the Political Thought of F. A. Hayek and Sidney and Beatrice Webb* (Oxford and New York: Oxford University Press, 1987), 27.

19. Eugene Goodheart, "Individualism versus Equality," *Salmagundi*, nos. 172–73 (2011): 148; Alvin B. Tillery, "Tocqueville as Critical Race Theorist: Whiteness as Property, Interest Convergence, and the Limits of Jacksonian Democracy," *Political Research Quarterly* 62, no. 4 (2009): 639–52. Hayek effectively concedes this point later in his career when he states that the law between master and servant, landlord and tenant, creditor and debtor, organized business and its customers, has been shaped by the ruling groups and may be incompatible with justice and the ideal of the rule of law. Hayek advocates using legislation to quickly replace such laws and bring them in line with rule-of-law principles. Gottfried Dietze, "The Necessity of State Law," in *Liberty and the Rule of Law* (College Station: Texas A&M University Press, 1979), 78.

20. Tillery, "Tocqueville as Critical Race Theorist," 644.

21. Ibid., 645.

22. Hector J. Massey, "Lord Acton's Theory of Nationality," *Review of Politics* 31, no. 4 (1969): 500.

23. Ibid., 502.

24. Ibid., 503.

25. Ibid., 504.

26. Hayek, *The Road to Serfdom*, 137.

27. Smith, *An Inquiry into . . . the Wealth of Nations*, 1:418–19.

28. Hayek, *The Road to Serfdom*, 139.

29. Sen, *Development as Freedom*, 130–31.

30. Ibid. 93.

31. Ibid., 95.

CHAPTER NINE

1. Hayek attributes the passage from which the epigraph comes to "Nikolai Lenin," a pseudonym for Vladimir Illych Ulyanov (1870–1924).

2. V. I. Lenin, *State and Revolution*, ed. Todd Chretien (Chicago: Haymarket Books, 2014), 121–42.

3. Ibid., 140.

4. Paul Le Blanc, *Leon Trotsky* (London: Reaktion Books, 2015), 107.

5. Ibid., 107.

6. Deborah Duff Milenkovitch, "Trotsky's *The Revolution Betrayed*: A Contemporary Look," *Comparative Economic Studies (Pre-1990)* 29, no. 3 (Fall 1987): 41.

7. Ibid., 41.

8. Le Blanc, *Leon Trotsky*, 108.

9. Ibid., 108–9.

10. Milenkovitch, "Trotsky's *The Revolution Betrayed*," 43; Leon Trotsky, *The Revolution Betrayed*, trans. Max Eastman (Mineola, NY: Dover, 2004), 57.

11. Milenkovitch, "Trotsky's *The Revolution Betrayed*," 43; Trotsky, *The Revolution Betrayed*, 207.

12. Milenkovitch, "Trotsky's *The Revolution Betrayed*," 44; Alec Nove, "Trotsky, Markets, And East European Reforms," *Comparative Economic Studies (Pre-1990)* 29, no. 3 (Fall 1987): 31.

13. Hayek, *The Road to Serfdom*, 148.

14. Ibid., 148.

15. Ibid.

16. Ibid..

17. Ibid., 148–49.

18. Goodheart, "Individualism versus Equality," 142.

19. Ibid., 144.

20. Hayek, *The Road to Serfdom*, 152.

21. Ibid., 149.

22. Ibid.

23. John Gerard Ruggie, "International Regimes, Transactions, and Change: Embedded Liberalism in the Postwar Economic Order," *International Organization* 36, no. 2 (1982): 379–415.

24. Hayek, *The Road to Serfdom*, 153.

25. Ibid., 152.

26. Ibid.

27. Ibid., 154.

28. Milanovic, *Capitalism, Alone*, 84, fig. 3.1.

CHAPTER TEN

1. John Emerich Edward Dalberg-Acton, "Acton-Creighton Correspondence | Online Library of Liberty," April 5, 1887, accessed October 1, 2022, https://oll.libertyfund .org/title/acton-acton-creighton-correspondence.

2. Lazarski, *Power Tends to Corrupt*, 46.

3. John Emerich Edward Dalberg-Acton, *The History of Freedom and Other Essays* (London: Macmillan, 1907), 77–78.

4. Ibid., 78.

5. Ibid.

6. Hayek, *The Road to Serfdom*, 165.

7. Ibid., 165.

8. Power is conceptualized by Hayek as an intangible, fungible, and expandable force with material and psychic effects. Although power is not static, it cannot be extinguished.

9. Hayek, *The Road to Serfdom*, 160.

10. Ibid., 158.

11. Ibid.

12. Ibid., 158–59.

13. Ibid., 159.

14. Ibid., 160.

15. Weber, *From Max Weber*, 110.

16. Hayek, *The Road to Serfdom*, 161.

17. Ibid., 161–62.

18. Ibid., 162.

19. Ibid., 162 n. 4.

20. Ibid., 163–64.

21. Ibid., 166.

22. Friedrich A. Hayek, *New Studies in Philosophy, Politics, Economics, and the History of Ideas* (London: Routledge and Kegan Paul, 1978), 59.

23. Hayek, *The Road to Serfdom*, 167–68.

24. Ibid.

25. Ibid., 169.

26. Ibid., 168.

27. Barbara Demick, "A Tale of China's Two Great Cities: The Beijing-Shanghai Rivalry Is a Powerful Undercurrent in Politics and Culture," *Los Angeles Times*, October 4, 2010.

28. Weigang Gong, Meng Zhu, Burak Gürel, and Tian Xie, "The Lineage Theory of the Regional Variation of Individualism/Collectivism in China," *Frontiers in Psychology* 11 (January 20, 2021): 596762–596762, https://doi.org/10.3389/fpsyg.2020.596762.

29. Liza G. Steele and Scott M. Lynch, "The Pursuit of Happiness in China: Individualism, Collectivism, and Subjective Well-Being during China's Economic and Social Transformation," *Social Indicators Research* 114, no. 2 (2013): 442–43, https://doi.org/10.1007/s11205-012-0154-1.

30. Ibid., 450.

31. Zhang Long, John A. Parnell, and Eric B. Dent, "Individualism, Collectivism and Management in China: Does Atlas Shrug in China?," *Journal of Asia-Pacific Business* 20, no. 3 (2019): 181–82, https://doi.org/10.1080/10599231.2019.1647076.

32. Qiu Cheng and Kinglun Ngok, "Welfare Attitudes towards Anti-Poverty Policies in China: Economical Individualism, Social Collectivism and Institutional Differences," *Social Indicators Research* 150, no. 2 (2020): 679–94, https://doi.org/10.1007/s11205-020-02313-y.

33. Thang Dinh Truong, Philip Hallinger, and Kabini Sanga, "Confucian Values and School Leadership in Vietnam: Exploring the Influence of Culture on Principal Decision Making," *Educational Management Administration & Leadership* 45, no. 1 (2017): 79, https://doi.org/10.1177/1741143215607877.

34. Thi Minh Thi Tran, "Complex Transformation of Divorce in Vietnam under the Forces of Modernization and Individualism," *International Journal of Asian Studies* 18, no. 2 (2021): 226, https://doi.org/10.1017/S1479591421000024.

35. Charlene Tan, "'Our Shared Values' in Singapore: A Confucian Perspective," *Educational Theory* 62, no. 4 (2012): 449–63, https://doi.org/10.1111/j.1741-5446.2012 .00456.x.

36. Chua Beng Huat, *Liberalism Disavowed: Communitarianism and State Capitalism in Singapore* (Ithaca, NY: Cornell University Press, 2017), 22, https://doi.org/10 .7591/j.ctt1zkjz35.3.

CHAPTER ELEVEN

1. Edward Hallett Carr, *The Twenty Years' Crisis, 1919–1939: An Introduction to the Study of International Relations* (London: Macmillan, 1946), 132–33. As Bruce Caldwell notes, in his epigraph Hayek misquotes Carr slightly: Carr used the phrase "nationalisation of opinion" rather than "nationalization of thought."

2. Edward Hallett Carr, *Propaganda in International Politics*, Oxford Pamphlets on World Affairs 16 (London and New York: Oxford University Press, 1939), 4.

3. Carr, *The Twenty Years' Crisis, 1919–1939*, 134–35.

4. Ibid., 135.

5. Ibid., 142.

6. Hayek revisits Carr in chaps. 13 and 15 of *The Road to Serfdom*.

7. Hayek, *The Road to Serfdom*, 172–73.

8. Ibid., 173 n. 3. See, e.g., Oswald Spengler, *The Decline of the West*, trans. Charles Francis Atkinson (London: George Allen & Unwin, 1934), 2:350, 354, 356, 367, 371, 435.

9. Hayek, *The Road to Serfdom*, 174.

10. See also Thomas Hobbes, *Leviathan* (Harmondsworth: Penguin Books, 1988), 100–110 (part 1, chap. 4).

11. Hayek, *The Road to Serfdom*, 177.

12. Volker R. Remmert, "What's Nazi about Nazi Science? Recent Trends in the History of Science in Nazi Germany," *Perspectives on Science* 12, no. 4 (2004): 456, https:// doi.org/10.1162/1063614042776003.

13. Till Düppe and Sarah Joly-Simard, "Stalin's Pluralism: How Anti-Dogmatism Serves Tyranny," in *Research in the History of Economic Thought and Methodology: Including a Symposium on Economists and Authoritarian Regimes in the 20th Century*, vol. 38B (Bingley, UK: Emerald, 2020), 38–39, https://doi.org/10.1108/ S0743-41542020000038B003.

14. Bukharin was executed in 1938; Trotsky was assassinated in 1940.

15. Elena A. Zaitseva and Ernst Homburg, "Catalytic Chemistry under Stalin: Science and Scientists in Times of Repression," *Ambix* 52, no. 1 (2005): 48, https:// doi.org/10.1179/000269805X52904.

16. Düppe and Joly-Simard, "Stalin's Pluralism," 43.

17. Notably, as Düppe and Joly-Simard argue, Stalin would make a similar non-

dogmatic intervention in a debate on Slavic linguistics, setting off another flurry of academic activity.

18. Düppe and Joly-Simard, "Stalin's Pluralism," 43.

19. See, e.g., the scandal of Lysenkoism at the Institute of Genetics in the Soviet Academy of Sciences.

20. Zaitseva and Homburg, "Catalytic Chemistry under Stalin," 46.

21. Denis J. B. Shaw, "Mastering Nature through Science: Soviet Geographers and the Great Stalin Plan for the Transformation of Nature, 1948–53," *Slavonic and East European Review (1928)* 93, no. 1 (2015): 128, https://doi.org/10.5699/slaveasteurorev2.93.1.0120.

22. Zaitseva and Homburg, "Catalytic Chemistry under Stalin," 55.

23. Golfo Alexopoulos, "Medical Research in Stalin's Gulag," *Bulletin of the History of Medicine* 90, no. 3 (2016): 363–93, https://doi.org/10.1353/bhm.2016.0070.

24. Mark B. Adams, review of Ethan Pollock, *Stalin and the Soviet Science Wars* (Princeton, NJ: Princeton University Press, 2006), *Journal of Modern History* 81, no. 1 (2009): 246–47, https://doi.org/10.1086/598750.

25. Remmert, "What's Nazi about Nazi Science?," 458–59, 465.

26. Ibid., 457–58.

27. Robert L. Berger, "Nazi Science—The Dachau Hypothermia Experiments," *New England Journal of Medicine* 322, no. 20 (1990): 1435–40, https://doi.org/10.1056/NEJM199005173222006.

28. Remmert, "What's Nazi about Nazi Science?," 462–63.

29. Ibid., 469–70; Robert Proctor, "Nazi Science and Nazi Medical Ethics: Some Myths and Misconceptions," *Perspectives in Biology and Medicine* 43, no. 3 (2000): 335–46, https://doi.org/10.1353/pbm.2000.0024.

30. Proctor, "Nazi Science and Nazi Medical Ethics," 340.

31. Ibid., 341.

32. Remmert, "What's Nazi about Nazi Science?," 471.

33. Proctor, "Nazi Science and Nazi Medical Ethics."

34. Ibid., 337.

35. Ibid., 342–43.

36. Ibid., 344.

37. Ibid., 343.

38. David Shambaugh, "China's Propaganda System: Institutions, Processes and Efficacy," *China Journal (Canberra, A.C.T.)* 57, no. 57 (2007): 26, https://doi.org/10.1086/tcj.57.20066240.

39. Rogier Creemers, "Cyber China: Upgrading Propaganda, Public Opinion Work and Social Management for the Twenty-First Century," *Journal of Contemporary China* 26, no. 103 (2017): 98, https://doi.org/10.1080/10670564.2016.1206281. Although difficult to translate directly, *suzhi* may be understood as a kind of personal quality. The concept rationalizes the need for a paternalistic state to cultivate citizens with the proper personal qualities.

40. Ibid., 97.

41. Ibid.

42. Ibid., 88.

43. Fan Liang, Yuchen Chen, and Fangwei Zhao, "The Platformization of Propaganda: How Xuexi Qiangguo Expands Persuasion and Assesses Citizens in China," *International Journal of Communication* 15, no. Journal Article (2021): 1858, 1863–64.

44. Shambaugh, "China's Propaganda System," 26–27.

45. Liang, Chen, and Zhao, "The Platformization of Propaganda."

46. Ibid., 1859.

47. Ibid., 1864–67.

48. Ibid., 1869.

49. Siqin Kang and Jiangnan Zhu, "Do People Trust the Government More? Unpacking the Distinct Impacts of Anticorruption Policies on Political Trust," *Political Research Quarterly* 74, no. 2 (2021): 439, https://doi.org/10.1177/1065912920912016; Haifeng Huang, "A War of (Mis)Information: The Political Effects of Rumors and Rumor Rebuttals in an Authoritarian Country," *British Journal of Political Science* 47, no. 2 (2017): 283–311, https://doi.org/10.1017/S0007123415000253.

50. Tom Cliff, "Refugees, Conscripts, and Constructors: Developmental Narratives and Subaltern Han in Xinjiang, China," *Modern China* 47, no. 5 (2020 2021): 540–68, https://doi.org/10.1177/0097700420904020.

51. Ondřej Klimeš, "Advancing 'Ethnic Unity' and 'De-Extremization': Ideational Governance in Xinjiang under 'New Circumstances' (2012–2017)," *Chinese Journal of Political Science* 23, no. 3 (2018): 413, https://doi.org/10.1007/s11366-018-9537-8.

52. Ibid., 419–22.

53. Ibid., 426.

54. Ibid., 427.

55. Ibid., 430–31.

56. James Leibold, "Surveillance in China's Xinjiang Region: Ethnic Sorting, Coercion, and Inducement," *Journal of Contemporary China* 29, no. 121 (2020): 46–60, https://doi.org/10.1080/10670564.2019.1621529.

57. Suppression of religious minorities began in 1957 with the Communist Party's anti-rightist policy. Attacks on ethnic and religious minorities and their places of worship reached a fever pitch during the Cultural Revolution (1966–76). See Elizabeth Van Wie Davis, "Uyghur Muslim Ethnic Separatism in Xinjiang, China," *Asian Affairs: An American Review* 35, no. 1 (2008): 17, https://doi.org/10.3200/AAFS.35.1.15–30.

58. Cliff, "Refugees, Conscripts, and Constructors," 543.

59. James Waller and Mariana Salazar Albornoz, "Crime and No Punishment? China's Abuses against the Uyghurs," *Georgetown Journal of International Affairs* 22, no. 1 (2021): 100, https://doi.org/10.1353/gia.2021.0000; Suzanne E. Scoggins, "Propaganda and the Police: The Softer Side of State Control in China," *Europe-Asia Studies* 73, no. 1 (2021): 204, https://doi.org/10.1080/09668136.2020.1850644.

60. David Tobin, "A 'Struggle of Life or Death': Han and Uyghur Insecurities on China's North-West Frontier," *China Quarterly* 242 (June 2020), https://doi.org/10.1017/S030574101900078X.

61. Davis, "Uyghur Muslim Ethnic Separatism in Xinjiang, China," 17; Salih Hudayar, "When Human Rights, National Identity, Ethnicity, and Religious Persecution Collide," *Sur: International Journal on Human Rights* 16, no. 29 (2019): 180.

62. Waller and Albornoz state that there are four hundred such camps. See Waller and Albornoz, "Crime and No Punishment?," 100. Szadziewski states that satellite images have identified between twenty-eight and sixty-six camps. Henryk Szadziewski, "The Push for a Uyghur Human Rights Policy Act in the United States: Recent Developments in Uyghur Activism," *Asian Ethnicity* 21, no. 2 (2020): 211, https://doi.org/10.1080/14631369.2019.1605497.

63. Tobin, "A 'Struggle of Life or Death'," 302.

64. Ibid., 303.

65. Leibold, "Surveillance in China's Xinjiang Region," 59.

66. Ibid., 59–60.

67. Giang Nguyen-Thu, "From Wartime Loudspeakers to Digital Networks: Communist Persuasion and Pandemic Politics in Vietnam," *Media International Australia Incorporating Culture & Policy* 177, no. 1 (2020): 145, https://doi.org/10.1177/1329878X20953226.

68. Vu Lam, "Information and Communications Technologies, Online Activism, and Implications for Vietnam's Public Diplomacy," *Journal of Current Southeast Asian Affairs* 41, no. 1 (2021): 15, https://doi.org/10.1177/18681034211002850.

69. Mai Duong, "Blogging Three Ways in Vietnam's Political Blogosphere," *Contemporary Southeast Asia* 39, no. 2 (2017): 381, https://doi.org/10.1355/cs39-2e.

70. Ibid., 385.

71. Lam, "Information and Communications Technologies, Online Activism, and Implications for Vietnam's Public Diplomacy," 5–6.

72. Ibid., 13–15.

73. Ibid., 15.

74. Of course, the Maoist regime also persecuted the non-Han communities of Xinjiang, particularly during the Cultural Revolution.

75. Wai-Siam Hee, "Anti-Communist Films Sponsored by the US Government in Singapore and Malaya: On the New York Sound Masters Inc.," *Inter-Asia Cultural Studies* 19, no. 2 (2018): 310–27, https://doi.org/10.1080/14649373.2018.1463078.

76. S. R. Joey Long, "Winning Hearts and Minds: U.S. Psychological Warfare Operations in Singapore, 1955–1961," *Diplomatic History* 32, no. 5 (2008): 901, 925, https://doi.org/10.1111/j.1467-7709.2008.00734.x.

77. For survey data on the effectiveness of US efforts, see ibid., 926–27.

78. Ibid., 903.

79. Hee, "Anti-Communist Films Sponsored by the US Government in Singapore and Malaya," 313.

80. Tan, "Choosing What to Remember in Neoliberal Singapore."

81. Ibid., 235.

82. Lasse Schuldt, "Official Truths in a War on Fake News: Governmental Fact-Checking in Malaysia, Singapore, and Thailand," *Journal of Current Southeast Asian Affairs* 40, no. 2 (2021): 356, https://doi.org/10.1177/18681034211008908.

83. Muneerah Ab Razak, "'World-Class Muslims': Examining the Discursive Construction of a Singapore Muslim Identity," *Muslim World* 109, no. 3 (2019): 417–18, https://doi.org/10.1111/muwo.12300.

84. Ibid., 420.

85. Ibid., 426–27.

86. Ibid., 425.

87. Ibid., 426.

88. Accessed October 10, 2022, https://www.gov.sg/factually.

89. Ric Neo, "The Securitisation of Fake News in Singapore," *International Politics* 57, no. 4 (2019): 728, https://doi.org/10.1057/s41311-019-00198-4.

90. Ibid., 733.

91. Ibid., 733–34.

92. Schuldt, "Official Truths in a War on Fake News," 344, 356–63.

93. Hayek, *The Road to Serfdom*, 172.

94. Ibid., 177.

95. Ibid., 178–79.

96. Ibid., 172.

CHAPTER TWELVE

1. Arthur Moeller van den Bruck, *Germany's Third Empire*, trans. E. O. Lorimer (London: George Allen & Unwin, 1934), 112–13.

2. Ibid., 11, 37–45.

3. Ibid., 10–11.

4. Ibid., 37.

5. Ibid., 44.

6. Ibid., 57.

7. Ibid., 74.

8. Hayek, *The Road to Serfdom*, 182.

9. Ibid.

10. Ibid., 183.

11. Ibid., 181; Rohan D'Olier Butler, *The Roots of National Socialism, 1783–1933* (London: Faber & Faber, 1941), 158, 167–74, 193, 223–24, 282.

12. Hayek, *The Road to Serfdom*, 190.

13. Ibid., 182.

14. Ibid.

15. Sibylle H. Lehmann, "Chaotic Shop-Talk or Efficient Parliament? The Reichstag, the Parties, and the Problem of Governmental Instability in the Weimar Republic," *Public Choice* 144, nos. 1–2 (2010): 102, https://doi.org/10.1007/s11127–009–9505–0.

16. Ibid., 85, 87, 98.

17. C. Stogbauer, "The Radicalisation of the German Electorate: Swinging to the Right and the Left in the Twilight of the Weimar Republic," *European Review of Economic History* 5, no. 2 (2001): 258, https://doi.org/10.1017/S1361491601000107.

18. Hayek, *The Road to Serfdom*, 183.

19. Samuel Koehne, "Were the National Socialists a *Völkisch* Party? Paganism, Christianity, and the Nazi Christmas," *Central European History* 47, no. 4 (2014): 764, https://doi.org/10.1017/S0008938914001897.

20. William Brustein, "The Nazi Party and the German New Middle Class, 1925–1933," *American Behavioral Scientist* 41, no. 9 (1998): 1240, https://doi.org/10.1177/0002764298041009005.

21. In the Brustein-Falter sample of Nazi Party membership, there were 42,004 observations from the pre-1933 period. The sample contains nearly three thousand cases for each of the early years to 1933, and roughly eight thousand cases for each of the years from 1930 to 1932. Brustein, "The Nazi Party and the German New Middle Class," 1251, 1258–59 n. 2.

22. Ibid., 1240.

23. Ibid., 1253.

24. Ibid., 1247.

25. Ibid., 1254–57.

26. Ibid., 1249–50.

27. Ibid., 1250.

28. Marc Debus and Martin Ejnar Hansen, "Representation of Women in the Parliament of the Weimar Republic: Evidence from Roll Call Votes," *Politics & Gender* 10, no. 3 (2014): 345–46, https://doi.org/10.1017/S1743923X1400021X.

29. Hayek, *The Road to Serfdom*, 183.

30. Ibid., 184–85.

31. Ibid., 190 n. 32.

32. Ibid., 186–87. Hayek incorrectly (or perhaps impishly) used the phrase "Five-Year Plan," but Hermann Göring's task in 1936 entailed implementing the Second Four-Year Plan (*Vierjahrsplan*) in preparation for an expected war with the Soviet Union. The First Four-Year Plan, begun in 1933, was terminated before its completion.

33. Ibid., 190–91.

34. Ibid., 191.

35. A corporatist state need not embrace the strong monopolistic party system characteristic of fascist Italy and Nazi Germany. Corporatism has been used to describe a wide variety of political entities, including Switzerland, Sweden, the Netherlands, Norway, Denmark, Austria, Spain, Portugal, Brazil, Chile, Peru, Greece, Mexico, and Yugo-

slavia. Schmitter actually is skeptical whether Nazi Germany was a corporatist state after 1936. See Philippe C. Schmitter, "Still the Century of Corporatism?," *Review of Politics* 36, no. 1 (1974): 99, 104 n. 53, 113 n. 113, 123, https://doi.org/10.1017/S0034670500022178.

36. Ibid., 93–94.

37. Jonathan Unger and Anita Chan, "State Corporatism and Business Associations in China: A Comparison with Earlier Emerging Economies of East Asia," ed. C. Lattemann and W. Zhang, *International Journal of Emerging Markets* 10, no. 2 (2015): 179, https://doi.org/10.1108/IJOEM-09-2014-0130.

38. Of course, as with all neat social-science categories, reality is messy. A few liberal democratic societies from Europe and East Asia to Australia have developed "societal corporatist" arrangements in industrial sectors of their economy, but the unions are still beholden to their members rather than the state. Ibid., 179–80.

39. Robert O. Paxton, "The Five Stages of Fascism," *Journal of Modern History* 70, no. 1 (1998): 11, https://doi.org/10.1086/235001.

40. On the young Hayek's relations with Spann, see Caldwell, *Hayek's Challenge*, 138–40; Ebenstein, *Friedrich Hayek*, 38.

41. Klaus Neumann, "Inter-War Germany and the Corporatist Wave, 1918–1939," in *Corporatism and Fascism: The Corporatist Wave in Europe*, ed. Antonio Costa Pinto (London and New York: Routledge, 2017), 128–30.

42. Ibid., 131.

43. Ibid., 135.

44. Ibid., 137.

45. Qian Forrest Zhang and Hongping Zeng, "Politically Directed Accumulation in Rural China: The Making of the Agrarian Capitalist Class and the New Agrarian Question of Capital," *Journal of Agrarian Change* 21, no. 4 (2021): 698, https://doi.org/10.1111/joac.12435.

46. Unger and Chan, "State Corporatism and Business Associations in China," 183.

47. Ibid., 183.

48. Zhang and Zeng, "Politically Directed Accumulation in Rural China," 698.

49. Unger and Chan, "State Corporatism and Business Associations in China," 184.

50. Ibid., 186.

51. Ibid., 190.

52. Yeonsik Jeong, "The Rise of State Corporatism in Vietnam," *Contemporary Southeast Asia* 19, no. 2 (1997): 152–71, https://doi.org/10.1355/CS19-2C.

53. Benedict J. Tria Kerkvliet, "An Approach for Analysing State-Society Relations in Vietnam," in "Negotiating the State in Vietnam," special issue, *Sojourn* 16, no. 2 (2018): 238–78, https://doi.org/10.1355/sj33-Sg; Martin Gainsborough, "The Myth of a Centralised Socialist State in Vietnam: What Kind of a Myth?," *Journal of Current Southeast Asian Affairs* 36, no. 3 (2017): 7, https://doi.org/10.1177/186810341703600305.

54. Sandra Suarez, "Political and Economic Motivations for Labor Control: A Comparison of Ireland, Puerto Rico, and Singapore," *Studies in Comparative International Development* 36, no. 2 (2001): 75, https://doi.org/10.1007/BF02686209.

55. There have been only a handful of strikes and very few man-days lost in Singapore in the last half century. Peter Sheldon, Bernard Gan, and David Morgan, "Making Singapore's Tripartism Work (Faster): The Formation of the Singapore National Employers' Federation in 1980," *Business History* 57, no. 3 (2015): 442, fig. 1, https://doi .org/10.1080/00076791.2014.983484.

56. Ibid., 438–39, 444.

57. Thomas J. Bellows, "Economic Challenges and Political Innovation: The Case of Singapore," *Asian Affairs: An American Review* 32, no. 4 (2006): 235–36, https://doi.org/10.3200/AAFS.32.4.231–255; Sheldon, Gan, and Morgan, "Making Singapore's Tripartism Work (Faster)," 447–48.

58. Norman Vasu, "Governance through Difference in Singapore: Corporatism's Composition, Characteristics, and Complications," *Asian Survey* 52, no. 4 (2012): 736.

59. Ibid., 736.

60. Ibid., 743.

61. Ibid., 750–53.

62. Paxton, "The Five Stages of Fascism," 5–6 n. 17.

63. Ibid., 7.

64. Walter C. Clemens Jr., "Grand Illusions and Delusions," *Asian Perspective* 45, no. 3 (2021): 673.

65. Ibid., 673; Jean-Philippe Beja, "Xi Jinping's China: On the Road to Neo-Totalitarianism," *Social Research* 86, no. 1 (2019): 203–30.

66. Maria Adele Carrai, "Chinese Political Nostalgia and Xi Jinping's Dream of Great Rejuvenation," *International Journal of Asian Studies* 18, no. 1 (2020): 9, https:// doi.org/10.1017/S1479591420000406.

67. Adamson, "Gramsci's Interpretation of Fascism," 617–18.

68. Chamsy el-Ojeili, "Reflecting on Post-Fascism: Utopia and Fear," *Critical Sociology* 45, nos. 7–8 (2019): 1154, https://doi.org/10.1177/0896920518768867.

69. George L. Mosse, "Introduction: The Genesis of Fascism," *Journal of Contemporary History* 1, no. 1 (1966): 16, https://doi.org/10.1177/002200946600100103.

70. Ernst Nolte, "What Fascism Is Not: Thoughts on the Deflation of a Concept: Comment," *American Historical Review* 84, no. 2 (1979): 389–94.

71. Mosse, "Introduction: The Genesis of Fascism," 17; George L. Mosse, "Two World Wars and the Myth of the War Experience," *Journal of Contemporary History* 21, no. 4 (1986): 491–513, https://doi.org/10.1177/002200948602100401; George L. Mosse, "National Cemeteries and National Revival: The Cult of the Fallen Soldiers in Germany," *Journal of Contemporary History* 14, no. 1 (1979): 1–20, https://doi.org/10 .1177/002200947901400101.

72. Emilio Gentile, "Fascism as Political Religion," *Journal of Contemporary History* 25, nos. 2–3 (1990): 229–51, https://doi.org/10.1177/002200949002500204.

73. Paxton, "The Five Stages of Fascism," 18.

CHAPTER THIRTEEN

1. "The Home Front," *The Times*, February 24, 1937.

2. Hayek, *The Road to Serfdom*, 193–94.

3. Ibid., 196.

4. Hayek quotes Carr in the epigraph to chap. 11. Hayek will conclude the attack on realism and Carr in chap. 15.

5. Hayek, *The Road to Serfdom*, 197.

6. Ibid., 198 n. 16.

7. Ibid., 198.

8. Robert William Davies, "Carr's Changing Views of the Soviet Union," in *E. H. Carr: A Critical Appraisal*, ed. Michael Cox (New York: Palgrave, 2000), 102.

9. Hayek, *The Road to Serfdom*, 199.

10. Milan Babik, "Realism as Critical Theory: The International Thought of E. H. Carr," *International Studies Review* 15, no. 4 (2013): 502, https://doi.org/10.1111/misr .12075.

11. Mannheim's work was discussed in chap. 6. See Babik, "Realism as Critical Theory," 503; Charles Jones, "Carr, Mannheim, and a Post-Positivist Science of International Relations," *Political Studies* 45, no. 2 (1997): 232–46, https://doi.org/10.1111/ 1467–9248.00078.

12. Peter Wilson, "Radicalism for a Conservative Purpose: The Peculiar Realism of E. H. Carr," *Millennium* 30, no. 1 (2001): 132, https://doi.org/10.1177/ 03058298010300010901. For an example of an attempt to unambiguously code Carr as a realist, see John J. Mearsheimer, "E. H. Carr vs. Idealism: The Battle Rages On," *International Relations* 19, no. 2 (June 2005): 139–52, https://doi.org/10.1177/ 0047117805052810. On Carr's preference for utopianism, see Davies, "Carr's Changing Views of the Soviet Union," 92–93, 105.

13. Wilson, "Radicalism for a Conservative Purpose," 132.

14. Davies, "Carr's Changing Views of the Soviet Union," 102.

15. Edward Hallett Carr, *The Twenty Years' Crisis, 1919–1939* (London: Palgrave Macmillan, 2016), xliii, xlvi, lxxxix–xcviii.

16. Wilson, "Radicalism for a Conservative Purpose," 134.

17. Davies, "Carr's Changing Views of the Soviet Union," 96; Wilson, "Radicalism for a Conservative Purpose," 129.

18. Davies, "Carr's Changing Views of the Soviet Union," 91.

19. Babik, "Realism as Critical Theory."

20. Hayek, *The Road to Serfdom*, 200–201.

21. Ibid., 203–4.

22. Ibid., 205.

23. Ibid., 206.

CHAPTER FOURTEEN

1. William Levine, "'A Permanent, Nationalized, Learned Order': The Humanistic Displacement of Milton's Politics in Coleridge's Later Cultural Criticism," *Wordsworth Circle* 25, no. 3 (1994): 157.

2. Hayek would insist that his outlook derives from liberalism, but there are "neo-Roman" (i.e., republican) elements in his later definition of freedom, particularly in *The Constitution of Liberty* (1960). See Irving, "Hayek's Neo-Roman Liberalism."

3. Ibid., 554.

4. Hayek, *The Road to Serfdom*, 220 n. 8.

5. Todd H. Sammons, "A Periplum of Pound's Pronouncements on John Milton," *Paideuma* 19, nos. 1–2 (1990): 147–61.

6. William Wordsworth, *Poetical Works* (London: Ward, Lock, 1881), 188.

7. Ibid.

8. Paul Miner, "Blake: Milton inside 'Milton,'" *Studies in Romanticism* 51, no. 2 (2012): 234–35.

9. Cato Marks, "Writings of the Left Hand: William Blake Forges a New Political Aesthetic," *Huntington Library Quarterly* 74, no. 1 (2011): 43–70, https://doi.org/10.1525/hlq.2011.74.1.43.

10. Robert Skidelsky, *John Maynard Keynes*, 1st American ed. (New York: Viking, 1986), 478.

11. Paul Morrison, *The Poetics of Fascism: Ezra Pound, T. S. Eliot, Paul de Man* (Oxford and New York: Oxford University Press, 1996), 7.

12. Ibid., 8.

13. Ibid., 7.

14. Peter F. Drucker, *The End of Economic Man: A Study of the New Totalitarianism* (New York: John Day, 1939), 35.

15. Ibid., 30–32.

16. Ibid., 40.

17. Hayek, *The Road to Serfdom*, 210.

18. Ibid., 211.

19. Ibid., 212.

20. Ibid., 211.

21. Ibid., 212.

22. Ibid., 211–12.

23. Adam Smith, *The Theory of Moral Sentiments*, ed. D. D. Raphael and A. L. Macfie, vol. 1 of *The Glasgow Edition of the Works and Correspondence of Adam Smith* (Indianapolis: Liberty Classics, 1982), 233–34.

24. Hayek, *The Road to Serfdom*, 212.

25. Ibid., 214.

26. Ibid., 215.

27. Ibid., 216.

28. Ibid.

29. Ibid., 218–19.

30. Ibid., 219.

31. Ibid., 220 n. 8.

32. Ibid., 221.

33. Kian Cheng Lee, "Re-Envisioning Citizen Diplomacy: A Case Study of a Multi-faceted, Transnational, People's Republic of China 'Ethnopreneur,'" *Journal of Current Chinese Affairs* 48, no. 2 (2019): 131–32, https://doi.org/10.1177/1868102620907240.

34. Xinsheng Liu, Feng Hao, Kent Portney, and Yinxi Liu, "Examining Public Concern about Global Warming and Climate Change in China," *China Quarterly* 242 (June 2020): 461, https://doi.org/10.1017/S0305741019000845.

35. Ibid., 469.

36. Seongkyung Cho and In-Jin Yoon, "The International Comparison of Post-Materialism: The Effects of Welfare Characteristics and Individual Security," *Development and Society* 44, no. 3 (2015): 507, 525, https://doi.org/10.21588/dns.2015.44.3.006.

37. Douglas E. Booth, "Post-Materialism's Social Class Divide: Experiences and Life Satisfaction," *Journal of Human Values* 27, no. 2 (2021): 141–42, https://doi.org/10.1177/0971685820946180.

38. Edmund W. Cheng, Hiu-Fung Chung, and Anthony Cheng, "Life Satisfaction and the Conventionality of Political Participation: The Moderation Effect of Post-Materialist Value Orientation," *International Political Science Review* (May 20, 2021): 19251212110065, https://doi.org/10.1177/01925121211006567.

39. Dimitri Gugushvili, "Public Attitudes toward Economic Growth versus Environmental Sustainability Dilemma: Evidence from Europe," *International Journal of Comparative Sociology* 62, no. 3 (2021): 224–40, https://doi.org/10.1177/00207152211034224.

40. Hayek, *The Road to Serfdom*, 216.

41. Ronald Inglehart, "Values, Objective Needs, and Subjective Satisfaction among Western Publics," *Comparative Political Studies* 9, no. 4 (1977): 429–58, https://doi.org/10.1177/001041407700900403; Ronald Inglehart, "Changing Values in Japan and the West," *Comparative Political Studies* 14, no. 4 (1982): 447, https://doi.org/10.1177/0010414082014004002.

42. Ronald Inglehart, "The Silent Revolution in Europe: Intergenerational Change in Post-Industrial Societies," *American Political Science Review* 65, no. 4 (1971): 991–1017, https://doi.org/10.2307/1953494; Ronald Inglehart, "Post-Materialism in an Environment of Insecurity," *American Political Science Review* 75, no. 4 (1981): 880–900, https://doi.org/10.2307/1962290.

43. Kyriaki I. Kafka and Pantelis C. Kostis, "Post-Materialism and Economic Growth: Cultural Backlash, 1981–2019," *Journal of Comparative Economics* 49, no. 4 (2021): 901–17, https://doi.org/10.1016/j.jce.2021.04.001.

44. Ronald Inglehart and Pippa Norris, "Trump and the Populist Authoritarian

Parties: The Silent Revolution in Reverse," *Perspectives on Politics* 15, no. 2 (2017): 444, https://doi.org/10.1017/S1537592717000111.

45. Inglehart, "Post-Materialism in an Environment of Insecurity," 880, 883, 886–87, 892.

46. Paul R. Abramson, Susan Ellis, and Ronald Inglehart, "Research in Context: Measuring Value Change," *Political Behavior* 19, no. 1 (1997): 41, https://doi.org/10.1023/A:1024845706077.

47. Inglehart and Norris, "Trump and the Populist Authoritarian Parties," 443–44.

48. Branko Milanovic, *Global Inequality: A New Approach for the Age of Globalization* (Cambridge, MA: Belknap Press, 2018), 128–31.

49. Ibid., 133.

50. Ronald F. Inglehart, "After Postmaterialism: An Essay on China, Russia and the United States; A Comment," *Canadian Journal of Sociology* 41, no. 2 (2016): 213, 220.

51. Inglehart and Norris, "Trump and the Populist Authoritarian Parties," 444.

52. Cho and Yoon, "The International Comparison of Post-Materialism," 496.

53. Ibid., 527.

54. Notably, India extended the franchise to all adults with independence in 1947, long before the United States gave substantive voting rights to its African American population and before several European countries extended suffrage to female citizens. Inglehart and Norris simply claim without offering evidence from any low-income countries that "postmaterialists are less conformist, more open to new ideas, less authoritarian, and more tolerant of outgroups. But these values depend on high levels of economic and physical security. They did not emerge in low-income countries, and were most prevalent among the younger and more secure strata of high-income countries." Inglehart and Norris, "Trump and the Populist Authoritarian Parties," 444.

55. Booth, "Post-Materialism's Social Class Divide," 142.

56. Recent postmaterialism scholars argue that the less prosperous ("working class") join voluntary groups, participate in political activities, and pursue creativity and independence at work at lower rates than the more prosperous ("middle class"), but this narrow definition of "postmaterialist experiences" is more likely a function of time and practical constraints owing to the nature of work for those with lower skill premiums. It is unclear why the scholars did not simply measure hours devoted to recreational activity as a component of postmaterialist experiences.

57. Kafka and Kostis, "Post-Materialism and Economic Growth," 902.

CHAPTER FIFTEEN

1. Dalberg-Acton, *The History of Freedom and Other Essays*, 98. The sections enclosed in square brackets are from the original text by Lord Acton but are not included in Hayek's epigraph.

2. Brendan O'Leary, "Federalism and Federation," in *The Princeton Encyclopedia of Self-Determination* (Princeton, NJ: Princeton University Press, 2021), accessed October 1, 2022, https://pesd.princeton.edu/node/431.

3. Sudhir Hazareesingh, *From Subject to Citizen: The Second Empire and the Emer-*

gence of Modern French Democracy (Princeton, NJ: Princeton University Press, 2014), 80, 120.

4. Bernard Moses, "Antecedents of Swiss Federalism," *Overland Monthly and Out West Magazine* 40., no. 65 (1888): 474.

5. From Acton's perspective in the early 1860s, the antebellum United States, like ancient Athens, exercised "mature liberty" and thus could be excused for practicing slavery and limiting the franchise. In other words, slavery and inequality were less evil than unlimited authority or barbarism. Although Acton certainly recognized that the US Constitution was a "monstrous fraud" from the perspective of liberalism, he was more interested in the effects that the doctrine of states' rights and federalism produced by checking the power of the central government, i.e., "a community more powerful, more prosperous, more intelligent, and more free than any other which the world has seen." To the extent that (legal) slavery freed the property owner from manual labor while protecting the slave from arbitrary "immorality," Acton saw the practice as contributing to "the growth of civilization." He was confident that slavery would be abolished through the natural evolution of society. By 1866 Acton had modified his complacent view and declared that slavery, as it was practiced in America, was unquestionably immoral; however, he still sided with the South, as revealed by his correspondence with General Robert E. Lee. Lazarski, *Power Tends to Corrupt*, 56, 142, 161–62, 239; Gertrude Himmelfarb, *Lord Acton: A Study in Conscience and Politics* (Chicago: University of Chicago Press, 1952), 79–80, 82.

6. See chap. 8.

7. G. P. Gooch, "Lord Acton: Apostle of Liberty," *Foreign Affairs*, July 1947, 635.

8. Dalberg-Acton, *The History of Freedom and Other Essays*, 11; Gooch, "Lord Acton: Apostle of Liberty," 637.

9. Dalberg-Acton, *The History of Freedom and Other Essays*, 13; Gooch, "Lord Acton: Apostle of Liberty," 637.

10. Lazarski, *Power Tends to Corrupt*, 238.

11. Ibid., 234–35.

12. Ibid., 235.

13. Victor J. Vanberg, "Constitutionalism, Federalism, and Limited Government: Hayekian Arguments in Political Scientists' Perspective," in *Revisiting Hayek's Political Economy*, ed. Peter J. Boettke and Virgil Henry Storr, vol. 21 of *Advances in Austrian Economics* (Bingley, UK: Emerald Group, 2017), 125, 130.

14. Friedrich A. Hayek, *Individualism and Economic Order* (Chicago: University of Chicago Press, 1980); Friedrich A. Hayek, "The Economic Conditions of Interstate Federalism," *New Commonwealth Quarterly* 5, no. 2 (September 1939): 131–49.

15. Lazarski, *Power Tends to Corrupt*, 152.

16. Ibid., 152–53, 165.

17. Ibid., 153.

18. Roland Hill, *Lord Acton* (New Haven, CT: Yale University Press, 2000), 115.

19. Dalberg-Acton, *The History of Freedom and Other Essays*, 20–21.

20. Hayek, *The Road to Serfdom*, 223.

21. Ruggie, "International Regimes, Transactions, and Change."

22. Philip Mirowski, "Polanyi vs Hayek?," *Globalizations* 15, no. 7 (2018): 899, https://doi.org/10.1080/14747731.2018.1498174.

23. Polanyi, *The Great Transformation*, 190–91.

24. Hayek, *The Road to Serfdom*, 227.

25. Polanyi, *The Great Transformation*, 182–83.

26. Ibid., 290–91, 293.

27. Ibid., 33, 35–37.

28. Ebeling, "The Geneva Connection, a Liberal World Order, and the Austrian Economists," 549.

29. Hayek, *The Road to Serfdom*, 226 n. 5.

30. Hayek, *Individualism and Economic Order*, 269.

31. Hayek, *The Road to Serfdom*, 228.

32. Ibid..

33. Ebeling, "The Geneva Connection, a Liberal World Order, and the Austrian Economists," 550.

34. Hayek, *The Road to Serfdom*, 223.

35. Hayek, *Law, Legislation and Liberty*, 396.

36. Arun Kundnani, "The Racial Constitution of Neoliberalism," *Race & Class* 63, no. 1 (2021): 61, https://doi.org/10.1177/0306396821992706.

37. Hayek, *Law, Legislation and Liberty*, 396.

38. Hayek, *The Road to Serfdom*, 224.

39. Ibid., 226 n. 4.

40. Ibid., 226.

41. Alberto Mingardi, "The European Union According to Hayek," *Wall Street Journal*, March 23, 2012, sec. Opinion, accessed October 10, 2022, https://www.wsj.com/articles/SB10001424052702304636404577299471982641512.

42. Hayek, *The Road to Serfdom*, 229.

43. Ibid.

44. Ibid., 230.

45. Ibid., 230–31.

46. Ibid., 231.

47. Jonathan Haslam, "'We Need a Faith': The Historian E. H. Carr," *History Today*, August 1, 1983, 37.

48. Or Rosenboim, *The Emergence of Globalism* (Princeton, NJ: Princeton University Press, 2017), 54–55, https://doi.org/10.2307/j.ctt1qlxrts.

49. Hayek, "The Economic Conditions of Interstate Federalism."

50. Hayek, *The Road to Serfdom*, 232.

51. Hayek uses the term "federation" but, given the minimal powers he permits, "confederation" is a more accurate term.

52. Hayek, *The Road to Serfdom*, 234.

53. Ibid., 231.

54. Ibid., 223.

55. Ibid., 223–24.

56. Glyn Morgan, "Hayek, Habermas, and European Integration," *Critical Review* 15, nos. 1–2 (2003): 4–5, https://doi.org/10.1080/08913810308443572.

57. Smith, *An Inquiry into . . . the Wealth of Nations*, 1:145.

58. Morgan, "Hayek, Habermas, and European Integration," 6–7.

59. Hayek, *The Road to Serfdom*, 234.

60. Ibid., 235.

61. Gabriella Montinola, Yingyi Qian, and Barry R. Weingast, "Federalism, Chinese Style: The Political Basis for Economic Success in China," *World Politics* 48, no. 1 (1995): 50, https://doi.org/10.1353/wp.1995.0003.

62. Ibid., 55.

63. Lotta Moberg and Vlad Tarko, "Special Economic Zones and Liberalization Avalanches," *Journal of Entrepreneurship and Public Policy* 10, no. 1 (2021): 122, https://doi.org/10.1108/JEPP-01-2021-0008.

64. Montinola, Qian, and Weingast, "Federalism, Chinese Style," 52–53.

65. Moberg and Tarko, "Special Economic Zones and Liberalization Avalanches," 120.

66. Ibid., 122.

67. Srikanth Kondapalli, "Regional Multilateralism with Chinese Characteristics," in *China and the World*, ed. David Shambaugh (Oxford University Press, 2020), 313, https://doi.org/10.1093/oso/9780190062316.003.0015.

68. Katherine Morton, "China's Global Governance Interactions," in *China and the World*, ed. David Shambaugh (Oxford and New York: Oxford University Press, 2020), 169, https://doi.org/10.1093/oso/9780190062316.003.0008.

69. Barry Naughton, "China's Global Economic Interactions," in *China and the World*, ed. David Shambaugh (Oxford and New York: Oxford University Press, 2020), 125–26, https://doi.org/10.1093/oso/9780190062316.003.0006.

70. Sung Eun Kim and Yotam Margalit, "Tariffs as Electoral Weapons: The Political Geography of the US–China Trade War," *International Organization* 75, no. 1 (2021): 1–38, https://doi.org/10.1017/S0020818320000612; Thiemo Fetzer and Carlo Schwarz, "Tariffs and Politics: Evidence from Trump's Trade Wars," *Economic Journal* 131, no. 636 (2021): 1717–41, https://doi.org/10.1093/ej/ueaa122.

CONCLUSION

1. Hayek, *The Road to Serfdom*, 237.

2. Ibid., 238.

3. Milanovic, *Capitalism, Alone*, 96–97.

4. Ibid., 12–21.

5. Hayek, *The Road to Serfdom*, 238.

Bibliography

Ab Razak, Muneerah. "'World-Class Muslims': Examining the Discursive Construction of a Singapore Muslim Identity." *Muslim World* 109, no. 3 (2019): 417–30. https://doi.org/10.1111/muwo.12300.

Abramson, Paul R., Susan Ellis, and Ronald Inglehart. "Research in Context: Measuring Value Change." *Political Behavior* 19, no. 1 (1997): 41–59. https://doi.org/10.1023/A:1024845706077.

Acemoglu, Daron, and James A. Robinson. *The Narrow Corridor: States, Societies, and the Fate of Liberty.* New York: Penguin Press, 2019.

———. *Why Nations Fail: The Origins of Power, Prosperity, and Poverty.* 1st ed. New York: Crown, 2012.

Acharya, Amitav. *The End of American World Order.* 1st ed. Cambridge, UK and Medford, MA: Polity Press, 2014.

———. *The End of American World Order.* 2nd ed. Cambridge, UK and Medford, MA: Polity Press, 2018.

Acton, Harold. "Lord Acton." *Chicago Review* 15, no. 1 (1961): 31–44. https://doi.org/10.2307/25293642.

Adams, Mark B. Review of Ethan Pollock, *Stalin and the Soviet Science Wars. Journal of Modern History* 81, no. 1 (2009): 246–48. https://doi.org/10.1086/598750.

Adamson, Walter L. "Gramsci's Interpretation of Fascism." *Journal of the History of Ideas* 41, no. 4 (1980): 615–33. https://doi.org/10.2307/2709277.

Adler, Franklin Hugh. "Why Mussolini Turned on the Jews." *Patterns of Prejudice* 39, no. 3 (2005): 285–300. https://doi.org/10.1080/00313220500198235.

Alexopoulos, Golfo. "Medical Research in Stalin's Gulag." *Bulletin of the History of Medicine* 90, no. 3 (2016): 363–93. https://doi.org/10.1353/bhm.2016.0070.

Aligica, Paul Dragos, and Vlad Tarko. *Capitalist Alternatives: Models, Taxonomies, Scenarios.* London: Routledge, 2016.

Appiah, Kwame Anthony. *Cosmopolitanism: Ethics in a World of Strangers.* New York: Norton, 2007.

Ashton, Geoffrey. "Role Ethics or Ethics of Role-Play? A Comparative Critical Analysis of the Ethics of Confucianism and the Bhagavad Gītā." *Dao: A Journal of Comparative Philosophy* 13, no. 1 (2014): 1–21. https://doi.org/10.1007/s11712-013-9354-x.

Babik, Milan. "Realism as Critical Theory: The International Thought of E. H. Carr." *International Studies Review* 15, no. 4 (2013): 491–514. https://doi.org/10.1111/misr.12075.

Baldwin, Richard E. *The Great Convergence: Information Technology and the New Globalization*. Cambridge, MA: Belknap Press, 2016.

Barry, Norman P. "The Road to Freedom: Hayek's Social and Economic Philosophy." In *Hayek, Co-Ordination and Evolution: His Legacy in Philosophy, Politics, Economics, and the History of Ideas*, edited by Jack Birner and Rudy van Zijp. 1st ed. London and New York: Routledge, 1994. https://doi.org/10.4324/9780203004241.

Beja, Jean-Philippe. "Xi Jinping's China: On the Road to Neo-Totalitarianism." *Social Research* 86, no. 1 (2019): 203–30.

Belloc, Hilaire. *The Servile State*. 1st American ed. New York: Henry Holt, 1946.

Bellows, Thomas J. "Economic Challenges and Political Innovation: The Case of Singapore." *Asian Affairs: An American Review* 32, no. 4 (2006): 231–55. https://doi.org/10.3200/AAFS.32.4.231-255.

Bengsten, Peter. "China's Forced Labor Problem." *Diplomat*, March 21, 2018. Accessed October 1, 2022. https://thediplomat.com/2018/03/chinas-forced-labor-problem/.

Berger, Robert L. "Nazi Science—The Dachau Hypothermia Experiments." *New England Journal of Medicine* 322, no. 20 (1990): 1435–40. https://doi.org/10.1056/NEJM199005173222006.

Bergh, Andreas. "Hayekian Welfare States: Explaining the Coexistence of Economic Freedom and Big Government." *Journal of Institutional Economics* 16, no. 1 (2020): 1–12. https://doi.org/10.1017/S1744137419000432.

———. "Yes, There Are Hayekian Welfare States (at Least in Theory)." *Econ Journal Watch* 12, no. 1 (2015): 22.

Bertellini, Giorgio. "Duce/Divo: Masculinity, Racial Identity, and Politics among Italian Americans in 1920s New York City." *Journal of Urban History* 31, no. 5 (July 2005): 685–726. https://doi.org/10.1177/0096144205275981.

Boettke, Peter J. *F. A. Hayek: Economics, Political Economy and Social Philosophy*. London: Palgrave Macmillan, 2018.

———. "On Reading Hayek: Choice, Consequences and The Road to Serfdom." *European Journal of Political Economy* 21, no. 4 (December 2005): 1042–53. https://doi.org/10.1016/j.ejpoleco.2004.08.005.

Boettke, Peter J., and Scott M. King. "Hayek and the Hayekians on the Political Order of a Free People." In *Hayek's Tensions: Reexamining the Political Economy and Philosophy of F. A. Hayek*, edited by Stefanie Haeffele, Solomon M. Stein, and Virgil Henry Storr. Arlington, VA: Mercatus Center at George Mason University, 2020.

Booth, Douglas E. "Post-Materialism's Social Class Divide: Experiences and Life Satisfaction." *Journal of Human Values* 27, no. 2 (2021): 141–60. https://doi.org/10.1177/0971685820946180.

Brustein, William. "The Nazi Party and the German New Middle Class, 1925–1933." *American Behavioral Scientist* 41, no. 9 (1998): 1237–61. https://doi.org/10.1177/0002764298041009005.

Bui, Thiem H. "Deconstructing the 'Socialist' Rule of Law in Vietnam: The Changing Discourse on Human Rights in Vietnam's Constitutional Reform Process." *Contemporary Southeast Asia* 36, no. 1 (2014): 77–100. https://doi.org/10.1355/cs36-1d.

Burczak, Theodore A. *Socialism after Hayek*. Ann Arbor: University of Michigan Press, 2006. https://doi.org/10.3998/mpub.93585.

Butler, Rohan D'Olier. *The Roots of National Socialism, 1783–1933*. London: Faber & Faber, 1941.

Caldwell, Bruce. *Hayek's Challenge: An Intellectual Biography of F. A. Hayek.* Chicago: University of Chicago Press, 2008.

Caldwell, Bruce, and Leonidas Montes. "Friedrich Hayek and His Visits to Chile." *Review of Austrian Economics* 28, no. 3 (September 2015): 261–309. https://doi.org/10.1007/s11138-014-0290-8.

Calhoun, George. "What Really Happened to Jack Ma?" *Forbes*, June 24, 2021. Accessed July 30, 2021. https://www.forbes.com/sites/georgecalhoun/2021/06/24/what-really-happened-to-jack-ma/.

Camus, Rina Marie. "I Am Not a Sage but an Archer: Confucius on Agency and Freedom." *Philosophy East & West* 68, no. 4 (2018): 1042–61. https://doi.org/10.1353/pew.2018.0096.

"Can Big Data Help to Resurrect the Planned Economy?" *Global Times*, June 14, 2017. Accessed October 1, 2022. https://www.globaltimes.cn/content/1051715.shtml.

Carr, Edward Hallett. *Propaganda in International Politics.* Oxford Pamphlets on World Affairs 16. London: Oxford University Press, 1939.

———. *The Twenty Years' Crisis, 1919–1939.* London: Palgrave Macmillan, 2016.

———. *The Twenty Years' Crisis, 1919–1939: An Introduction to the Study of International Relations.* London: Macmillan, 1946.

Carrai, Maria Adele. "Chinese Political Nostalgia and Xi Jinping's Dream of Great Rejuvenation." *International Journal of Asian Studies* 18, no. 1 (2020): 1–19. https://doi.org/10.1017/S1479591420000406.

Chan, Sek Keong. "The Courts and the 'Rule of Law' in Singapore: A Lecture Delivered at the Rule of Law Symposium." *Singapore Journal of Legal Studies* (December 2012): 209–31.

Che, Luyao. "The Chinese Conception of the Rule of Law and Its Embodiment under the 'Belt and Road' Initiative (BRI)." *Journal of World Trade* 55, no. 1 (2021): 171–96.

Cheng, Edmund W., Hiu-Fung Chung, and Anthony Cheng. "Life Satisfaction and the Conventionality of Political Participation: The Moderation Effect of Post-Materialist Value Orientation." *International Political Science Review* (2021): 19251212110065. https://doi.org/10.1177/01925121211006567.

Cheng, Qiu, and Kinglun Ngok. "Welfare Attitudes towards Anti-Poverty Policies in China: Economical Individualism, Social Collectivism and Institutional Differences." *Social Indicators Research* 150, no. 2 (2020): 679–94. https://doi.org/10.1007/s11205-020-02313-y.

Cho, Seongkyung, and In-Jin Yoon. "The International Comparison of Post-Materialism: The Effects of Welfare Characteristics and Individual Security." *Development and Society* 44, no. 3 (2015): 495–533. https://doi.org/10.21588/dns.2015.44.3.006.

Chow, Daniel C. K. "Rising Nationalism: China's Regulation of Investment Trade." In *China's Global Engagement: Cooperation, Competition, and Influence in the 21st Century,* edited by Jacques deLisle and Avery Goldstein. Washington, DC: Brookings Institution Press, 2017.

Chua Beng Huat. *Liberalism Disavowed: Communitarianism and State Capitalism in Singapore.* Ithaca, NY: Cornell University Press, 2017. https://doi.org/10.7591/j.cttlzkjz35.3.

———. "State-Owned Enterprises, State Capitalism and Social Distribution in Singapore." *Pacific Review* 29, no. 4 (2016): 499–521. https://doi.org/10.1080/09512748.2015.1022587.

Chua, Lynette J. "Pragmatic Resistance, Law, and Social Movements in Authoritarian States: The Case of Gay Collective Action in Singapore." *Law & Society Review* 46, no. 4 (2012): 713–48. https://doi.org/10.1111/j.1540-5893.2012.00515.x.

Clemens, Walter C., Jr. "Grand Illusions and Delusions." *Asian Perspective* 45, no. 3 (2021): 671–82.

Cliff, Tom. "Refugees, Conscripts, and Constructors: Developmental Narratives and Subaltern Han in Xinjiang, China." *Modern China* 47, no. 5 (2021): 540–68. https://doi.org/10.1177/0097700420904020.

Clinton, William J. "Speech to the Democratic National Committee." Denver, CO, August 27, 2008. Accessed October 1, 2022. https://youtu.be/fl7Jc8tNxck.

Cockshott, Paul. "How Feasible Are Jack Ma's Proposals for Computerized Planning?" *World Review of Political Economy* 10, no. 3 (2019): 302–15.

Cooley, Alexander, and Daniel H. Nexon. *Exit from Hegemony: The Unraveling of the American Global Order*. Oxford and New York: Oxford University Press, 2020.

Creemers, Rogier. "Cyber China: Upgrading Propaganda, Public Opinion Work and Social Management for the Twenty-First Century." *Journal of Contemporary China* 26, no. 103 (2017): 85–100. https://doi.org/10.1080/10670564.2016.1206281.

Crider, Jonathan. "Just How Much Does Tesla Get in Subsidies Anyways?" *CleanTechnica*, August 3, 2020. Accessed October 1, 2022. https://cleantechnica.com/2020/08/03/tesla-subsidies-how-much/.

Cropsey, Joseph. "The General Foundation of Smith's System." In *Polity and Economy*, 1–55. Dordrecht: Springer Netherlands, 1957. https://doi.org/10.1007/978-94-011-9383-2_1.

Crowley, Brian Lee. *The Self, the Individual, and the Community: Liberalism in the Political Thought of F. A. Hayek and Sidney and Beatrice Webb*. Oxford: Clarendon Press, 1987.

Dalberg-Acton, John Emerich Edward. "Acton-Creighton Correspondence | Online Library of Liberty," April 5, 1887. Accessed October 1, 2022. https://oll.libertyfund.org/title/acton-acton-creighton-correspondence.

———. *The History of Freedom and Other Essays*. London: Macmillan, 1907.

Dale, Gareth. "Justificatory Fables of Ordoliberalism: Laissez-Faire and the 'Third Way.'" *Critical Sociology* 45, no. 7–8 (2019): 1047–60. https://doi.org/10.1177/0896920519832638.

Daniels, Roger. *Franklin D. Roosevelt: Road to the New Deal, 1882–1939*. Urbana: University of Illinois Press, 2018. https://doi.org/10.5406/j.ctt174d23g.

Das, Gurcharan. *India Grows at Night: A Liberal Case for a Strong State*. New Delhi: Penguin Books, 2012.

Davies, Robert William. "Carr's Changing Views of the Soviet Union." In *E. H. Carr: A Critical Appraisal*, edited by Michael Cox. New York: Palgrave, 2000.

Davis, Elizabeth Van Wie. "Uyghur Muslim Ethnic Separatism in Xinjiang, China." *Asian Affairs: An American Review* 35, no. 1 (2008): 15–29. https://doi.org/10.3200/AAFS.35.1.15–30.

Dawson, Graham. "Austrian Economics and Climate Change." *Review of Austrian Economics* 26, no. 2 (2013): 183–206. https://doi.org/10.1007/s11138-012-0174-8.

de Tocqueville, Alexis. *Democracy in America*. Edited by Philips Bradley. Translated by Henry Reeve and Francis Bowen. Vol. 2. New York: Alfred A. Knopf, 1945.

———. "Tocqueville on Socialism." Translated by Ronald Hamowy. In *Tocqueville's*

Critique of Socialism (1848). Accessed May 19, 2021. https://oll.libertyfund.org/page/tocqueville-s-critique-of-socialism-1848.

Debus, Marc, and Martin Ejnar Hansen. "Representation of Women in the Parliament of the Weimar Republic: Evidence from Roll Call Votes." *Politics & Gender* 10, no. 3 (2014): 341–64. https://doi.org/10.1017/S1743923X1400021X.

Deleuze, Gilles, and Félix Guattari. *A Thousand Plateaus: Capitalism and Schizophrenia.* Minneapolis: University of Minnesota Press, 1987.

Demick, Barbara. "A Tale of China's Two Great Cities: The Beijing-Shanghai Rivalry Is a Powerful Undercurrent in Politics and Culture." *Los Angeles Times*, October 4, 2010.

Derrida, Jacques. *Specters of Marx: The State of the Debt, the Work of Mourning and the New International.* New York: Routledge, 2006.

Dietze, Gottfried. "The Necessity of State Law." In *Liberty and the Rule of Law.* College Station: Texas A&M University Press, 1979.

Drucker, Peter F. *The End of Economic Man: A Study of the New Totalitarianism.* New York: John Day, 1939.

Düben, Björn Alexander. "Xi Jinping and the End of Chinese Exceptionalism." *Problems of Post-Communism* 67, no. 2 (2020): 111–28. https://doi.org/10.1080/10758216.2018.1535274.

Duong, Mai. "Blogging Three Ways in Vietnam's Political Blogosphere." *Contemporary Southeast Asia* 39, no. 2 (2017): 373–92. https://doi.org/10.1355/cs39-2e.

Düppe, Till, and Sarah Joly-Simard. "Stalin's Pluralism: How Anti-Dogmatism Serves Tyranny." In *Research in the History of Economic Thought and Methodology: Including a Symposium on Economists and Authoritarian Regimes in the 20th Century*, 38B:37–54. Bingley, UK: Emerald Publishing Limited, 2020. https://doi.org/10.1108/S0743-41542020000038B003.

Eaton, George. "Project Cybersyn: The Afterlife of Chile's Socialist Internet." *New Statesman* 147, no. 5433 (2018): 16–17.

Ebeling, Richard M. "The Geneva Connection, A Liberal World Order, and the Austrian Economists." *Review of Austrian Economics* 33 (2020): 535–54. https://doi.org/10.1007/s11138-019-00450-3.

Ebenstein, Alan O. *Friedrich Hayek: A Biography.* Chicago: University of Chicago Press, 2003.

Ellett, Rachel, and Diep Phan. "The Emperor's Law Stops at the Village Gate: Questioning the Primacy of Formal Institutions in Vietnam's Land Law Reform." *Journal of Southeast Asian Economies* 37, no. 3 (2020): 233–50. https://doi.org/10.1355/ae37-3a.

el-Ojeili, Chamsy. "Reflecting on Post-Fascism: Utopia and Fear." *Critical Sociology* 45, nos. 7–8 (2019): 1149–66. https://doi.org/10.1177/0896920518768867.

Evans, Peter B. *Embedded Autonomy: States and Industrial Transformation.* Princeton, NJ: Princeton University Press, 1995.

Farrant, Andrew. "Hayek, Orwell, and The Road to Serfdom." In *Hayek: A Collaborative Biography*, edited by Robert Leeson, 152–82. London: Palgrave Macmillan, 2015. https://doi.org/10.1057/9781137479259_3.

Farrant, Andrew, Edward McPhail, and Sebastian Berger. "Preventing the 'Abuses' of Democracy: Hayek, the 'Military Usurper' and Transitional Dictatorship in Chile?" *American Journal of Economics and Sociology* 71, no. 3 (2012): 513–38. https://doi.org/10.1111/j.1536-7150.2012.00824.x.

Fernández-Villaverde, Jesus. "Artificial Intelligence Can't Solve the Knowledge Problem." *Public Discourse* (blog), July 29, 2021. Accessed October 1, 2022. https://www.thepublicdiscourse.com/2021/07/76963/.

Fetzer, Thiemo, and Carlo Schwarz. "Tariffs and Politics: Evidence from Trump's Trade Wars." *Economic Journal* 131, no. 636 (2021): 1717–41. https://doi.org/10.1093/ej/ueaa122.

Finer, Herman. *The Road to Reaction.* Boston: Little, Brown, 1945.

Fitch Solutions. "Vietnam Trade and Investment Risk Report—Q1 2021." London: Fitch Solutions, 2021.

Foucault, Michel. *Discipline and Punish: The Birth of the Prison.* New York: Vintage Books, 1995.

———. *The History of Sexuality: An Introduction.* Vol. 1. New York: Vintage Books, 1990.

Fox, Eleanor M. "Should China's Competition Model Be Exported?: A Reply to Wendy Ng." *European Journal of International Law* 30, no. 4 (2019): 1431–40. https://doi.org/10.1093/ejil/chaa010.

Friedman, Milton, and Adam Meyerson. "Letters: Who Is a Conservative?" *Policy Review: Washington* (Fall 1994): 90.

Frobert, Ludovic. "Elie Halévy and Philosophical Radicalism." *Modern Intellectual History* 12, no. 1 (April 2015): 127–50. https://doi.org/10.1017/S1479244314000377.

Gainsborough, Martin. "The Myth of a Centralised Socialist State in Vietnam: What Kind of a Myth?" *Journal of Current Southeast Asian Affairs* 36, no. 3 (2017): 119–43. https://doi.org/10.1177/186810341703600305.

———. "The (Neglected) Statist Bias and the Developmental State: The Case of Singapore and Vietnam." *Third World Quarterly* 30, no. 7 (2009): 1317–28. https://doi.org/10.1080/01436590903134957.

Galbraith, John Kenneth. *Economics in Perspective: A Critical History.* Princeton, NJ: Princeton University Press, 2017. https://doi.org/10.2307/j.cttlvwmhch.

Gentile, Emilio. "Fascism as Political Religion." *Journal of Contemporary History* 25, nos. 2–3 (1990): 229–51. https://doi.org/10.1177/002200949002500204.

Gillespie, John. "Exploring the Limits of the Judicialization of Urban Land Disputes in Vietnam." *Law & Society Review* 45, no. 2 (2011): 241–76. https://doi.org/10.1111/j.1540-5893.2011.00434.x.

Ginsburg, Tom. "Does Law Matter for Economic Development? Evidence From East Asia." *Law & Society Review* 34, no. 3 (2000): 829–56. https://doi.org/10.2307/3115145.

Giordano, Claire, and Ferdinando Giugliano. "A Tale of Two Fascisms: Labour Productivity Growth and Competition Policy in Italy, 1911–1951." *Explorations in Economic History* 55 (2015): 25–38. https://doi.org/10.1016/j.eeh.2013.12.003.

"Global 500." *Fortune*, August 2020. Accessed October 1, 2022. https://fortune.com/global500/2020/.

Goh, Mei-Lin, Douglas Sikorski, and Wing-Keong Wong. "Government Policy for Outward Investment by Domestic Firms: The Case of Singapore's Regionalisation Strategy." *Singapore Management Review* 23, no. 2 (2001): 23.

Gong, Weigang, Meng Zhu, Burak Gürel, and Tian Xie. "The Lineage Theory of the Regional Variation of Individualism/Collectivism in China." *Frontiers in Psychology* 11 (2020): 596762. https://doi.org/10.3389/fpsyg.2020.596762.

Gooch, G. P. "Lord Acton: Apostle of Liberty." *Foreign Affairs*, July 1947.

Goodacre, H. "Limited Liability and the Wealth of 'Uncivilised Nations': Adam Smith and the Limits to the European Enlightenment." *Cambridge Journal of Economics* 34, no. 5 (2010): 857–67. https://doi.org/10.1093/cje/beq007.

Goodheart, Eugene. "Individualism versus Equality." *Salmagundi* 172–73 (2011): 142–57.

Gray, John. "Hayek on Liberty, Rights, and Justice." *Ethics* 92, no. 1 (1981): 73–84. https://doi.org/10.1086/292299.

Gregory, Robert. "Combating Corruption in Vietnam: A Commentary." *Asian Education and Development Studies* 5, no. 2 (2016): 227–43. https://doi.org/10.1108/AEDS -01–2016–0010.

Griffin, Roger. "Mussolini Predicted a Fascist Century: How Wrong Was He?" *Fascism* 8, no. 1 (July 1, 2019): 1–8. https://doi.org/10.1163/22116257–00801001.

Griffiths, Simon. "'Comrade Hayek' or the Revival of Liberalism? Andrew Gamble's Engagement with the Work of Friedrich Hayek." *Journal of Political Ideologies* 12, no. 2 (2007): 189–210. https://doi.org/10.1080/13569310701285032.

Gugushvili, Dimitri. "Public Attitudes toward Economic Growth Versus Environmental Sustainability Dilemma: Evidence from Europe." *International Journal of Comparative Sociology* 62, no. 3 (2021): 224–40. https://doi.org/10.1177/ 00207152211034224.

Haggard, Stephan. *Developmental States.* Cambridge and New York: Cambridge University Press, 2018.

Haque, Shamsul M., and Jose A Puppim de Oliveira. "Building Administrative Capacity under Developmental States in Chile and Singapore: A Comparative Perspective." *International Review of Administrative Sciences* 87, no. 2 (2021): 220–37. https://doi.org/10.1177/0020852320943656.

Harvey, David. *A Brief History of Neoliberalism.* Oxford and New York: Oxford University Press, 2011.

Haslam, Jonathan. "'We Need a Faith': The Historian E. H. Carr." *History Today.*, August 1, 1983.

Hayek, Friedrich A. *Individualism and Economic Order.* Chicago: University of Chicago Press, 1980.

———. "Integrating Immigrants." *The Times*, March 9, 1978.

———. *Law, Legislation and Liberty: A New Statement of the Liberal Principles of Justice and Political Economy.* London: Routledge, 2012.

———. *New Studies in Philosophy, Politics, Economics, and the History of Ideas.* London: Routledge & Kegan Paul, 1978.

———. "Origins of Racialism." *The Times*, March 1, 1978.

———. *Studies in Philosophy, Politics and Economics.* London: Routledge & Kegan Paul, 1967.

———. *The Constitution of Liberty: The Definitive Edition.* Edited by Ronald Hamowy. Vol. 17 of *The Collected Works of F. A. Hayek.* Chicago: University of Chicago Press, 2011.

———. "The Counter-Revolution of Science (Part I)." *Economica* 8, no. 29 (1941): 9– 36. https://doi.org/10.2307/2549519.

———. "The Economic Conditions of Interstate Federalism." *New Commonwealth Quarterly* 5, no. 2 (September 1939): 131–49.

———. "The Politics of Race and Immigration." *The Times*, February 11, 1978.

———. *The Road to Serfdom: Text and Documents; The Definitive Edition.* Edited by

Bruce Caldwell. Vol. 2 of *The Collected Works of F. A. Hayek*. Chicago: University of Chicago Press, 2007.

Hazareesingh, Sudhir. *From Subject to Citizen: The Second Empire and the Emergence of Modern French Democracy*. Princeton, NJ: Princeton University Press, 2014.

Hee, Wai-Siam. "Anti-Communist Films Sponsored by the US Government in Singapore and Malaya: On the New York Sound Masters Inc." *Inter-Asia Cultural Studies* 19, no. 2 (2018): 310–27. https://doi.org/10.1080/14649373.2018.1463078.

Hendricks, Drew. "5 Successful Companies That Didn't Make a Dollar for 5 Years." Inc.com, July 7, 2014. Accessed October 1, 2020. https://www.inc.com/drew-hendricks/5-successful-companies-that-didn-8217-t-make-a-dollar-for-5-years.html.

Hill, Roland. *Lord Acton*. New Haven, CT: Yale University Press, 2000.

Hillman, Ben. "Law, Order and Social Control in Xi's China." *Issues and Studies: Institute of International Relations* 57, no. 2 (2021): 2150006–21. https://doi.org/10.1142/S1013251121500065.

Himmelfarb, Gertrude. *Lord Acton: A Study in Conscience and Politics*. Chicago: University of Chicago Press, 1952.

Ho, Li-Ching. "'Freedom Can Only Exist in an Ordered State': Harmony and Civic Education in Singapore." *Journal of Curriculum Studies* 49, no. 4 (2017): 476–96. https://doi.org/10.1080/00220272.2016.1155648.

Hobbes, Thomas. *Leviathan*. Harmondsworth: Penguin Books, 1988.

Hoffmeyer, John W. "Poetics of History, Logics of Collapse: On Heidegger's Hölderlin." *German Quarterly* 93, no. 3 (2020): 374–89.

Holcombe, Randall G. "Political Capitalism." *Cato Journal* 35, no. 1 (2015): 41–66.

———. *Political Capitalism: How Economic and Political Power Is Made and Maintained*. Cambridge and New York: Cambridge University Press, 2018.

Hölderlin, Friedrich. *Hyperion, or, The Hermit in Greece*. Translated by Howard Gaskill. Cambridge: Open Book, 2019.

Holmes, Stephen. *The Anatomy of Antiliberalism*. Cambridge, MA: Harvard University Press, 1993.

"The Home Front." *The Times*. February 24, 1937.

Huang, Haifeng. "A War of (Mis)Information: The Political Effects of Rumors and Rumor Rebuttals in an Authoritarian Country." *British Journal of Political Science* 47, no. 2 (2017): 283–311. https://doi.org/10.1017/S0007123415000253.

Hudayar, Salih. "When Human Rights, National Identity, Ethnicity, and Religious Persecution Collide." *Sur: International Journal on Human Rights* 16, no. 29 (2019): 187–90.

Inglehart, Ronald. "Changing Values in Japan and the West." *Comparative Political Studies* 14, no. 4 (1982): 445–79. https://doi.org/10.1177/0010414082014004002.

———. "Post-Materialism in an Environment of Insecurity." *American Political Science Review* 75, no. 4 (1981): 880–900. https://doi.org/10.2307/1962290.

———. "The Silent Revolution in Europe: Intergenerational Change in Post-Industrial Societies." *American Political Science Review* 65, no. 4 (1971): 991–1017. https://doi.org/10.2307/1953494.

———. "Values, Objective Needs, and Subjective Satisfaction among Western Publics." *Comparative Political Studies* 9, no. 4 (1977): 429–58. https://doi.org/10.1177/001041407700900403.

Inglehart, Ronald F. "After Postmaterialism: An Essay on China, Russia and the United States: A Comment." *Canadian Journal of Sociology* 41, no. 2 (2016): 213.

Inglehart, Ronald, and Pippa Norris. "Trump and the Populist Authoritarian Parties: The Silent Revolution in Reverse." *Perspectives on Politics* 15, no. 2 (2017): 443–54. https://doi.org/10.1017/S1537592717000111.

Irving, Sean. "Hayek's Neo-Roman Liberalism." *European Journal of Political Theory* 19, no. 4 (July 17, 2017): 553–70. https://doi.org/10.1177/1474885117718370.

Jeong, Yeonsik. "The Rise of State Corporatism in Vietnam." *Contemporary Southeast Asia* 19, no. 2 (1997): 152–71. https://doi.org/10.1355/CS19-2C.

Joey Long, S. R. "Winning Hearts and Minds: U.S. Psychological Warfare Operations in Singapore, 1955–1961." *Diplomatic History* 32, no. 5 (2008): 899–930. https://doi.org/10.1111/j.1467-7709.2008.00734.x.

Johnson, Alan. "The New Communism: Resurrecting the Utopian Delusion." *World Affairs* 175, no. 1 (2012): 62–70.

Johnson, Chalmers A. *MITI and the Japanese Miracle: The Growth of Industrial Policy, 1925–1975*. Stanford, CA: Stanford University Press, 2007.

Jones, Charles. "Carr, Mannheim, and a Post-Positivist Science of International Relations." *Political Studies* 45, no. 2 (1997): 232–46. https://doi.org/10.1111/1467-9248.00078.

Jones, Daniel Stedman. *Masters of the Universe: Hayek, Friedman, and the Birth of Neoliberal Politics*. Princeton, NJ: Princeton University Press, 2014.

Jones, H. S. "The Era of Tyrannies: Elie Halévy and Friedrich von Hayek on Socialism." *European Journal of Political Theory* 1, no. 1 (July 1, 2002): 53–69. https://doi.org/10.1177/1474885102001001005.

Kafka, Kyriaki I., and Pantelis C. Kostis. "Post-Materialism and Economic Growth: Cultural Backlash, 1981–2019." *Journal of Comparative Economics* 49, no. 4 (2021): 901–17. https://doi.org/10.1016/j.jce.2021.04.001.

Kang, Siqin, and Jiangnan Zhu. "Do People Trust the Government More? Unpacking the Distinct Impacts of Anticorruption Policies on Political Trust." *Political Research Quarterly* 74, no. 2 (2021): 434–49. https://doi.org/10.1177/1065912920912016.

Kerkvliet, Benedict J. Tria. "An Approach for Analysing State-Society Relations in Vietnam." *Sojourn: Journal of Social Issues in Southeast Asia* 16, no. 2 (2001): 238–78. https://doi.org/10.1355/sj33-Sg.

Khondker, Habibul Haque. "Globalization and State Autonomy in Singapore." *Asian Journal of Social Science* 36, no. 1 (2008): 35–56. https://doi.org/10.1163/156853108X267585.

Kim, Myeong-seok. "Choice, Freedom, and Responsibility in Ancient Chinese Confucianism." *Philosophy East and West* 63, no. 1 (2013): 17–38.

Kim, Sung Eun, and Yotam Margalit. "Tariffs as Electoral Weapons: The Political Geography of the US–China Trade War." *International Organization* 75, no. 1 (2021): 1–38. https://doi.org/10.1017/S0020818320000612.

Kley, Roland. *Hayek's Social and Political Thought*. Oxford: Clarendon Press, 1994. https://doi.org/10.1093/acprof:oso/9780198279167.001.0001.

Klimeš, Ondřej. "Advancing 'Ethnic Unity' and 'De-Extremization': Ideational Governance in Xinjiang under 'New Circumstances' (2012–2017)." *Chinese Journal of Political Science* 23, no. 3 (2018): 413–36. https://doi.org/10.1007/s11366-018-9537-8.

Knight, John B. "China as a Developmental State." *World Economy* 37, no. 10 (2014): 1335–47. https://doi.org/10.1111/twec.12215.

Koehne, Samuel. "Were the National Socialists a *Völkisch* Party? Paganism, Christianity, and the Nazi Christmas." *Central European History* 47, no. 4 (2014): 760–90. https://doi.org/10.1017/S0008938914001897.

Kohli, Atul. *State-Directed Development: Political Power and Industrialization in the Global Periphery*. Cambridge and New York: Cambridge University Press, 2004.

Kolev, Stefan, Nils Goldschmidt, and Jan-Otmar Hesse. "Debating Liberalism: Walter Eucken, F. A. Hayek and the Early History of the Mont Pèlerin Society." *Review of Austrian Economics* 33, no. 4 (2020): 1–31. https://doi.org/10.1007/s11138 -019-0435-x.

Kondapalli, Srikanth. "Regional Multilateralism with Chinese Characteristics." In *China and the World*, edited by David Shambaugh, 313–40. Oxford and New York: Oxford University Press, 2020. https://doi.org/10.1093/oso/9780190062316.003 .0015.

Kubota, Yoko. "Jack Ma Urges Beijing to Ease Up—Market, Not Regulator, Should Determine How Technology Evolves, Tycoon Tells AI Session." *Wall Street Journal*. September 18, 2018, Eastern ed. 2108088534.

Kukathas, Chandran. "Does Hayek Speak to Asia?" *Independent Review* 4, no. 3 (2000): 419–29.

Kundnani, Arun. "The Racial Constitution of Neoliberalism." *Race & Class* 63, no. 1 (2021): 51–69. https://doi.org/10.1177/0306396821992706.

Kuttner, Robert. "Can We Fix Capitalism?" *New York Review of Books* 67, no. 14 (2020): 71.

Lakatos, Imre, and Alan Musgrave, eds. *Criticism and the Growth of Knowledge*. Vol. 4 of Proceedings of the International Colloquium in the Philosophy of Science, London 1965. Cambridge: Cambridge University Press, 2004.

Lam, Vu. "Information and Communications Technologies, Online Activism, and Implications for Vietnam's Public Diplomacy." *Journal of Current Southeast Asian Affairs* 41, no. 1 (2021): 3–33. https://doi.org/10.1177/18681034211002850.

Lazarski, Christopher. *Power Tends to Corrupt: Lord Acton's Study of Liberty*. DeKalb: Northern Illinois University Press, 2012.

Le Blanc, Paul. *Leon Trotsky*. London: Reaktion Books, 2015.

Lee, Kian Cheng. "Re-Envisioning Citizen Diplomacy: A Case Study of a Multifaceted, Transnational, People's Republic of China 'Ethnopreneur.'" *Journal of Current Chinese Affairs* 48, no. 2 (2019): 127–47. https://doi.org/10.1177/1868102620907240.

Lee, Youngjoon. "The Rule of Law, Anti-Corruption and Land Expropriation: Evidence from China." *China: An International Journal* 18, no. 4 (2020): 85–101.

Lehmann, Sibylle H. "Chaotic Shop-Talk or Efficient Parliament? The *Reichstag*, the Parties, and the Problem of Governmental Instability in the Weimar Republic." *Public Choice* 144, no. 1/2 (2010): 83–104. https://doi.org/10.1007/s11127-009 -9505-0.

Leibold, James. "Surveillance in China's Xinjiang Region: Ethnic Sorting, Coercion, and Inducement." *Journal of Contemporary China* 29, no. 121 (2020): 46–60. https://doi.org/10.1080/10670564.2019.1621529.

Lenin, V. I. *The State and Revolution*. Edited by Todd Chretien. Chicago: Haymarket, 2014.

Leonard, Allenna. "The Viable System Model and Its Application to Complex Organizations." *Systemic Practice and Action Research* 22, no. 4 (2009): 223–33. https://doi.org/10.1007/s11213-009-9126-z.

Levine, William. "'A Permanent, Nationalized, Learned Order': The Humanistic Displacement of Milton's Politics in Coleridge's Later Cultural Criticism." *Wordsworth Circle* 25, no. 3 (1994): 154–59.

Liang, Fan, Yuchen Chen, and Fangwei Zhao. "The Platformization of Propaganda: How Xuexi Qiangguo Expands Persuasion and Assesses Citizens in China." *International Journal of Communication* 15 (2021): 1855–74.

Lindblom, Charles E. "Market and Democracy—Obliquely." *PS: Political Science & Politics* 28, no. 4 (1995): 684–88. https://doi.org/10.2307/420518.

Liu, Xinsheng, Feng Hao, Kent Portney, and Yinxi Liu. "Examining Public Concern about Global Warming and Climate Change in China." *China Quarterly* 242 (2020): 460–86. https://doi.org/10.1017/S0305741019000845.

Long, Zhang, John A. Parnell, and Eric B. Dent. "Individualism, Collectivism and Management in China: Does Atlas Shrug in China?" *Journal of Asia-Pacific Business* 20, no. 3 (2019): 166–88. https://doi.org/10.1080/10599231.2019.1647076.

Löwy, Michael. "From Marx to Ecosocialism." *Capitalism, Nature, Socialism* 13, no. 1 (2002): 121–33. https://doi.org/10.1080/104557502101245413.

Magcamit, Michael Intal. "Trading in Paranoia: Exploring Singapore's Security-Trade Linkages in the Twenty-First Century." *Asian Journal of Political Science* 23, no. 2 (2015): 184–206. https://doi.org/10.1080/02185377.2014.999248.

Malm, Andreas. "Marx on Steam: From the Optimism of Progress to the Pessimism of Power." *Rethinking Marxism* 30, no. 2 (2018): 166–85. https://doi.org/10.1080/08935696.2017.1417085.

Malm, Andreas, and Dominic Mealy. "'To Halt Climate Change, We Need an Ecological Leninism': An Interview with Andreas Malm." *Jacobin*, June 15, 2020. Accessed October 1, 2022. https://jacobinmag.com/2020/06/andreas-malm-coronavirus-covid-climate-change.

Mannheim, Karl. *Man and Society in an Age of Reconstruction.* Translated by Edward Shils. London: Routledge & Kegan Paul, 1940.

Marks, Cato. "Writings of the Left Hand: William Blake Forges a New Political Aesthetic." *Huntington Library Quarterly* 74, no. 1 (2011): 43–70. https://doi.org/10.1525/hlq.2011.74.1.43.

Massey, Hector J. "Lord Acton's Theory of Nationality." *Review of Politics* 31, no. 4 (1969): 495–508.

McGregor, Richard. *The Party: The Secret World of China's Communist Rulers.* New York: Harper Perennial, 2012.

McPhail, Edward. "Does the Road to Serfdom Lead to the Servile State?" *European Journal of Political Economy* 21, no. 4 (2005): 1000–1011. https://doi.org/10.1016/j.ejpoleco.2004.10.005.

Mearsheimer, John J. "E. H. Carr vs. Idealism: The Battle Rages On." *International Relations* 19, no. 2 (June 2005): 139–52. https://doi.org/10.1177/0047117805052810.

Michels, Robert. *Political Parties: A Sociological Study of the Oligarchical Tendencies of Modern Democracy.* With an introduction by Seymour Martin Lipset. Translated by Eden and Cedar Paul. London and New York: Routledge, 2016.

Milanovic, Branko. *Capitalism, Alone: The Future of the System That Rules the World.* Cambridge, MA: Belknap Press, 2019.

———. *Global Inequality: A New Approach for the Age of Globalization.* Cambridge, MA: Belknap Press, 2016.

Milenkovitch, Deborah Duff. "Trotsky's The Revolution Betrayed: A Contemporary Look." *Comparative Economic Studies* 29, no. 3 (Fall 1987): 40.

Miner, Paul. "Blake: Milton Inside 'Milton.'" *Studies in Romanticism* 51, no. 2 (2012): 233–76.

Minervini, Amanda. "Mussolini Speaks: History Reviewed." *Massachusetts Review* 60, no. 1 (2019): 194–204. https://doi.org/10.1353/mar.2019.0031.

Mingardi, Alberto. "The European Union According to Hayek." *Wall Street Journal.* March 23, 2012, Opinion section.

Mirowski, Philip. "Polanyi vs Hayek?" *Globalizations* 15, no. 7 (2018): 894–910. https://doi.org/10.1080/14747731.2018.1498174.

Mirowski, Philip, and Dieter Plehwe, eds. *The Road from Mont Pèlerin: The Making of the Neoliberal Thought Collective.* Cambridge, MA: Harvard University Press, 2015.

Moberg, Lotta, and Vlad Tarko. "Special Economic Zones and Liberalization Avalanches." *Journal of Entrepreneurship and Public Policy* 10, no. 1 (2021): 120–39. https://doi.org/10.1108/JEPP-01-2021-0008.

Moeller van den Bruck, Arthur. *Germany's Third Empire.* Translated by E. O. Lorimer. London: George Allen & Unwin, 1934.

Montinola, Gabriella, Yingyi Qian, and Barry R. Weingast. "Federalism, Chinese Style: The Political Basis for Economic Success in China." *World Politics* 48, no. 1 (1995): 50–81. https://doi.org/10.1353/wp.1995.0003.

Morgan, Glyn. "Hayek, Habermas, and European Integration." *Critical Review: A Journal of Politics and Society* 15, no. 1–2 (2003): 1–22. https://doi.org/10.1080/08913810308443572.

Morrison, Paul. *The Poetics of Fascism: Ezra Pound, T. S. Eliot, Paul de Man.* Oxford and New York: Oxford University Press, 1996.

Morton, Katherine. "China's Global Governance Interactions." In *China and the World,* edited by David Shambaugh, 156–80. Oxford and New York: Oxford University Press, 2020. https://doi.org/10.1093/oso/9780190062316.003.0008.

Moses, Bernard. "Antecedents of Swiss Federalism." *Overland Monthly and Out West Magazine* 11, no.65. (1888): 474–88.

Mosse, George L. "Introduction: The Genesis of Fascism." *Journal of Contemporary History* 1, no. 1 (1966): 14–26. https://doi.org/10.1177/002200946600100103.

———. "National Cemeteries and National Revival: The Cult of the Fallen Soldiers in Germany." *Journal of Contemporary History* 14, no. 1 (1979): 1–20. https://doi.org/10.1177/002200947901400101.

———. "Two World Wars and the Myth of the War Experience." *Journal of Contemporary History* 21, no. 4 (1986): 491–513. https://doi.org/10.1177/002200948602100401.

Musiedlak, Didier. "Mussolini, Charisma and Decision-Making." *Portuguese Journal of Social Science* 8, no. 1 (April 2009): 31–41.

Naughton, Barry. "China's Global Economic Interactions." In *China and the World,* edited by David Shambaugh, 113–36. Oxford and New York: Oxford University Press, 2020. https://doi.org/10.1093/oso/9780190062316.003.0006.

———. "Is China Socialist?" *Journal of Economic Perspectives* 31, no. 1 (2017): 3–24.

Nentjes, Andries. "Austrian View on Environmental Protection." In *Modern Applications of Austrian Thought,* edited by Jürgen G. Backhaus. London: Routledge, 2005.

Neo, Ric. "The Securitisation of Fake News in Singapore." *International Politics* 57, no. 4 (2019): 724–40. https://doi.org/10.1057/s41311-019-00198-4.

Neumann, Klaus. "Inter-War Germany and the Corporatist Wave, 1918–1939." In *Corporatism and Fascism: The Corporatist Wave in Europe*, edited by Antonio Costa Pinto. London: Routledge, Taylor & Francis, 2017.

Ng, Wendy. "Changing Global Dynamics and International Competition Law: Considering China's Potential Impact." *European Journal of International Law* 30, no. 4 (2019): 1409–30. https://doi.org/10.1093/ejil/chz066.

Ngu, Vu Quoc. "Total Factor Productivity Growth of Industrial State-Owned Enterprises in Vietnam, 1976–98." *ASEAN Economic Bulletin* 20, no. 2 (2003): 158–73.

Nguyen, Hai Hong. "Resilience of the Communist Party of Vietnam's Authoritarian Regime since Đổi Mới." *Journal of Current Southeast Asian Affairs* 35, no. 2 (2016): 31–55. https://doi.org/10.1177/186810341603500202.

Nguyen, Tu Phuong. "Rethinking State-Society Relations in Vietnam: The Case of Business Associations in Ho Chi Minh City." *Asian Studies Review* 38, no. 1 (2014): 87–106. https://doi.org/10.1080/10357823.2013.872598.

Nguyen-Thu, Giang. "From Wartime Loudspeakers to Digital Networks: Communist Persuasion and Pandemic Politics in Vietnam." *Media International Australia Incorporating Culture & Policy* 177, no. 1 (2020): 144–48. https://doi.org/10.1177/1329878X20953226.

Nientiedt, Daniel. "Hayek's Treatment of Legal Positivism." *European Journal of Law and Economics* 51, no. 3 (2021): 563–76. https://doi.org/10.1007/s10657-021-09684-8.

Nishiyama, Chiaki. "Arguments for the Principles of Liberty and the Philosophy of Science." *Il Politico* 32, no. 2 (1967): 336–47.

Nizamuddin, Ali M. "Multinational Corporations and Economic Development: The Lessons of Singapore." *International Social Science Review* 82, nos. 3–4 (2007): 149–62.

Nolte, Ernst. "What Fascism Is Not: Thoughts on the Deflation of a Concept: Comment." *The American Historical Review* 84, no. 2 (1979): 389–94.

Nove, Alec. "Trotsky, Markets, And East European Reforms." *Comparative Economic Studies* 29, no. 3 (1987): 30.

O'Leary, Brendan. "Federalism and Federation." In *The Princeton Encyclopedia of Self-Determination*. Princeton, NJ: Princeton University Press, 2021. Accessed October 1, 2022. https://pesd.princeton.edu/node/431.

Olson, Mancur. *The Logic of Collective Action: Public Goods and the Theory of Groups.* Harvard Economic Studies 124. Cambridge, MA: Harvard University Press, 2003.

Painter, Martin. "The Politics of State Sector Reforms in Vietnam: Contested Agendas and Uncertain Trajectories." *Journal of Development Studies* 41, no. 2 (2005): 261–83. https://doi.org/10.1080/0022038042000309241.

Pandey, Gyanendra. "Encounters and Calamities." In *Selected Subaltern Studies*, edited by Ranajit Guha and Gayatri Chakravorty Spivak. Oxford and New York: Oxford University Press, 1988.

Paxton, Robert O. "The Five Stages of Fascism." *Journal of Modern History* 70, no. 1 (1998): 1–23. https://doi.org/10.1086/235001.

Pennington, Mark. "Hayek on Complexity, Uncertainty and Pandemic Response." *Review of Austrian Economics* 34, no. 2 (2021): 203–20. https://doi.org/10.1007/s11138-020-00522-9.

Perez, Juan Carlos. "Amazon Records First Profitable Year in Its History." Computerworld, January 28, 2004. Accessed October 1, 2022. https://www.computerworld.com/article/2575106/amazon-records-first-profitable-year-in-its-history.html.

Phillips-Fein, Kim. "Business Conservatives and the Mont Pèlerin Society." In *The Road from Mont Pèlerin*, edited by Philip Mirowski and Dieter Plehwe. Cambridge, MA: Harvard University Press, 2015.

Plant, Raymond. "Neo-Liberalism and the Theory of the State: From *Wohlfahrtsstaat* to *Rechtsstaat*." *Political Quarterly* 75, no. s1 (2004): 24–37. https://doi.org/10.1111/j.1467-923X.2004.620_1.x.

"Plan v Market." *Economist*, November 5, 2016.

Polanyi, Karl. *The Great Transformation*. Boston, MA: Beacon Press, 1944.

Poole, William. "Hayek on The Road to Serfdom." *Journal of Private Enterprise* 32, no. 1 (2017): 11–28.

Pooley, Jefferson. "Edward Shils' Turn against Karl Mannheim: The Central European Connection." *American Sociologist* 38, no. 4 (2007): 364–82. https://doi.org/10.2307/27700518.

Popper, Karl. *The Open Society and Its Enemies*. Princeton, NJ: Princeton University Press, 2020.

Potter, Pitman B. "China and the International Human Rights Legal Regime." In *China's Global Engagement: Cooperation, Competition, and Influence in the 21st Century*, edited by Jacques deLisle and Avery Goldstein. Washington, DC: Brookings Institution Press, 2017.

Pourmalek, Panthea. Review of Branko Milanovic, *Capitalism, Alone: The Future of the System That Rules the World*. *Journal of East Asian Studies* 20, no. 1 (2020): 128–29. https://doi.org/10.1017/jea.2019.45.

Pow, Choon-Piew. "Consuming Private Security: Consumer Citizenship and Defensive Urbanism in Singapore." Edited by Maggy Lee and Karen Joe Laidler. *Theoretical Criminology* 17, no. 2 (2013): 179–96. https://doi.org/10.1177/1362480612472782.

Prasad, Eswar. "Jack Ma Paid for Taunting China: [Op-Ed]." *New York Times*, April 30, 2021, sec. A23.

Proctor, Robert. "Nazi Science and Nazi Medical Ethics: Some Myths and Misconceptions." *Perspectives in Biology and Medicine* 43, no. 3 (2000): 335–46. https://doi.org/10.1353/pbm.2000.0024.

Rafalski, Traute. "Social Planning and Corporatism: Modernization Tendencies in Italian Fascism." Translated by Michel Vale. *International Journal of Political Economy* 18, no. 1 (1988): 10–64.

Rallo, Juan Ramón. "Hayek Did Not Embrace a Universal Basic Income." *Independent Review* 24, no. 3 (2020): 347–59.

Raz, Joseph. "The Rule of Law and Its Virtue." In *The Authority of Law*. Oxford and New York: Oxford University Press, 1979. https://doi.org/10.1093/acprof:oso/9780198253457.003.0011.

Remmert, Volker R. "What's Nazi about Nazi Science? Recent Trends in the History of Science in Nazi Germany." *Perspectives on Science* 12, no. 4 (2004): 454–75. https://doi.org/10.1162/1063614042776003.

Rifkind, David. "'Everything In the State, Nothing Against the State, Nothing Outside the State': Corporativist Urbanism and Rationalist Architecture in Fascist Italy." *Planning Perspectives* 27, no. 1 (2012): 51–80.

Robin, Corey. *The Reactionary Mind: Conservatism from Edmund Burke to Sarah Palin.* Oxford and New York: Oxford University Press, 2013.

Rogan, Tim. *The Moral Economists: R. H. Tawney, Karl Polanyi, E. P. Thompson, and the Critique of Capitalism.* Princeton, NJ: Princeton University Press, 2017.

Rosenboim, Or. *The Emergence of Globalism: Visions of World Order in Britain and the United States, 1939–1950.* Princeton, NJ: Princeton University Press, 2017. https:// doi.org/10.2307/j.cttlq1xrts.

Ruggie, John Gerard. "International Regimes, Transactions, and Change: Embedded Liberalism in the Postwar Economic Order." *International Organization* 36, no. 2 (1982): 379–415.

Sallai, Dorottya, and Gerhard Schnyder. "What Is 'Authoritarian' about Authoritarian Capitalism? The Dual Erosion of the Private–Public Divide in State-Dominated Business Systems." *Business & Society* 60, no. 6 (2021): 1312–48. https://doi.org/10 .1177/0007650319898475.

Sam, Choon Yin. "Economic Nationalism in Singapore and Thailand: The Case of the Shin Corporation–Temasek Holdings Business Deal." *South East Asia Research* 16, no. 3 (2008): 433–59. https://doi.org/10.5367/000000008787133427.

Sammons, Todd H. "A Periplum of Pound's Pronouncements on John Milton." *Paideuma* 19, nos. 1–2 (1990): 147–61.

Schlesinger, Arthur, Jr. "The 'Hundred Days' of F.D.R." *New York Times*, April 10, 1983, Books section. Accessed October 1, 2022. https://archive.nytimes.com/www .nytimes.com/books/00/11/26/specials/schlesinger-hundred.html.

Schmidt, Carl T. *The Corporate State in Action: Italy under Fascism.* Oxford and New York: Oxford University Press, 1939.

Schmitter, Philippe C. "Still the Century of Corporatism?" *Review of Politics* 36, no. 1 (1974): 85–131. https://doi.org/10.1017/S0034670500022178.

Schuldt, Lasse. "Official Truths in a War on Fake News: Governmental Fact-Checking in Malaysia, Singapore, and Thailand." *Journal of Current Southeast Asian Affairs* 40, no. 2 (2021): 340–71. https://doi.org/10.1177/18681034211008908.

Sciabarra, Chris Matthew. *Marx, Hayek, and Utopia.* Albany: State University of New York Press, 1995.

Scoggins, Suzanne E. "Propaganda and the Police: The Softer Side of State Control in China." *Europe-Asia Studies* 73, no. 1 (2021): 200–220. https://doi.org/10.1080/ 09668136.2020.1850644.

Sen, Amartya. *Development as Freedom.* New York: Anchor Books, 2000.

Shambaugh, David. "China's Propaganda System: Institutions, Processes and Efficacy." *China Journal* 57 (2007): 25–58. https://doi.org/10.1086/tcj.57.20066240.

Shaw, Denis J. B. "Mastering Nature through Science: Soviet Geographers and the Great Stalin Plan for the Transformation of Nature, 1948–53." *Slavonic and East European Review* 93, no. 1 (2015): 120–46. https://doi.org/10.5699/slaveasteuro-rev2.93.1.0120.

Shearmur, Jeremy. *Hayek and After: Hayekian Liberalism as a Research Programme.* London and New York: Routledge, 2003. https://doi.org/10.4324/9780203438343.

———. "No 'Thought Collective': Some Historical Remarks on the Mont Pelerin Society." Presentation at History of Economic Thought Society of Australia, 2015. Accessed October 1, 2022. https://d3nr8uzk0yq0qe.cloudfront.net/media/upload/ documents/2015/June/Shearmur_HETSA_2015_Paper.pdf.

Sheldon, Peter, Bernard Gan, and David Morgan. "Making Singapore's Tripartism

Work (Faster): The Formation of the Singapore National Employers' Federation in 1980." *Business History* 57, no. 3 (2015): 438–60. https://doi.org/10.1080/00076791.2014.983484.

Simons, Jon. "Benjamin's Communist Idea: Aestheticized Politics, Technology, and the Rehearsal of Revolution." *European Journal of Political Theory* 15, no. 1 (January 1, 2016): 43–60. https://doi.org/10.1177/1474885114543569.

Skidelsky, Robert. *John Maynard Keynes*. 3 vols. 1st American ed. New York: Viking, 1986–2000.

———. *Keynes: The Return of the Master*. Rev. and updated. New York: PublicAffairs, 2010.

Slobodian, Quinn. *Globalists: The End of Empire and the Birth of Neoliberalism*. Cambridge, MA: Harvard University Press, 2018.

Smith, Adam. *An Inquiry into the Nature and Causes of the Wealth of Nations*. Edited by R. H. Campbell and Andrew S. Skinner. Vol. 1. The Glasgow Edition of the Works and Correspondence of Adam Smith. Indianapolis, IN: Liberty Classics, 1981.

———. *The Theory of Moral Sentiments*. Edited by D. D. Raphael and A. L. Macfie. The Glasgow Edition of the Works and Correspondence of Adam Smith. Indianapolis, IN: Liberty Classics, 1982.

Spengler, Oswald. *The Decline of the West*. Translated by Charles Francis Atkinson. London: George Allen & Unwin., 1934.

Sperber, Nathan. "The Many Lives of State Capitalism: From Classical Marxism to Free-Market Advocacy." *History of the Human Sciences* 32, no. 3 (2019): 100–124. https://doi.org/10.1177/0952695118815553.

Squeri, Lawrence. "Who Benefited from Italian Fascism: A Look at Parma's Landowners." *Agricultural History* 64, no. 1 (1990): 18–38. Accessed October 1, 2022. http://www.jstor.org/stable/3643180.

Steele, Liza G., and Scott M. Lynch. "The Pursuit of Happiness in China: Individualism, Collectivism, and Subjective Well-Being during China's Economic and Social Transformation." *Social Indicators Research* 114, no. 2 (2013): 441–51. https://doi.org/10.1007/s11205–012–0154–1.

Steen, Abram. "'Over This Jordan': Dying and the Nonconformist Community in Bunyan's *Pilgrim's Progress*." *Modern Philology* 110, no. 1 (2012): 49–73. https://doi.org/10.1086/667706.

Steinfeld, Edward. "Teams of Rivals: China, the United States, and the Race to Develop Technologies for a Sustainable Energy Future." In *China's Global Engagement: Cooperation, Competition, and Influence in the 21st Century*, edited by Jacques deLisle and Avery Goldstein. Washington, DC: Brookings Institution Press, 2017.

Stogbauer, C. "The Radicalisation of the German Electorate: Swinging to the Right and the Left in the Twilight of the Weimar Republic." *European Review of Economic History* 5, no. 2 (2001): 251–80. https://doi.org/10.1017/S1361491601000107.

Suarez, Sandra. "Political and Economic Motivations for Labor Control: A Comparison of Ireland, Puerto Rico, and Singapore." *Studies in Comparative International Development* 36, no. 2 (2001): 54–81. https://doi.org/10.1007/BF02686209.

Szadziewski, Henryk. "The Push for a Uyghur Human Rights Policy Act in the United States: Recent Developments in Uyghur Activism." *Asian Ethnicity* 21, no. 2 (2020): 211–22. https://doi.org/10.1080/14631369.2019.1605497.

Tan, Charlene. "'Our Shared Values' in Singapore: A Confucian Perspective." *Educational Theory* 62, no. 4 (2012): 449–63. https://doi.org/10.1111/j.1741–5446.2012.00456.x.

Tan, Kenneth Paul. "Choosing What to Remember in Neoliberal Singapore: The Singapore Story, State Censorship and State-Sponsored Nostalgia." *Asian Studies Review* 40, no. 2 (2016): 231–49. https://doi.org/10.1080/10357823.2016.1158779.

Temin, Peter. "Soviet and Nazi Economic Planning in the 1930s." *Economic History Review* 44, no. 4 (1991): 573–93. https://doi.org/10.2307/2597802.

Thatcher, Margaret. "'The New Renaissance'—Speech to Zurich Economic Society." Margaret Thatcher Foundation, March 14, 1977. Accessed October 1, 2022. https://www.margaretthatcher.org/document/103336.

Thio, Li-ann. "Between Apology and Apogee, Autochthony: The 'Rule of Law' beyond the Rules of Law in Singapore." *Singapore Journal of Legal Studies* (December 2012): 269–97. Accessed October 1, 2022. http://www.jstor.org/stable/24872213.

Thompson, Mark R. "Liberalism Disavowed: Communitarianism and State Capitalism in Singapore." *Journal of Southeast Asian Studies* 51, no. 4 (2020): 645.

Tillery, Alvin B. "Tocqueville as Critical Race Theorist: Whiteness as Property, Interest Convergence, and the Limits of Jacksonian Democracy." *Political Research Quarterly* 62, no. 4 (2009): 639–52.

Tobin, David. "A 'Struggle of Life or Death': Han and Uyghur Insecurities on China's North-West Frontier." *China Quarterly* 242 (June 2020): 301–23. https://doi.org/10.1017/S030574101900078X.

Tran, Thi Minh Thi. "Complex Transformation of Divorce in Vietnam Under the Forces of Modernization and Individualism." *International Journal of Asian Studies* 18, no. 2 (2021): 225–45. https://doi.org/10.1017/S1479591421000024.

Tribe, Keith. "Liberalism and Neoliberalism in Britain, 1930–1980." In *The Road from Mont Pèlerin: The Making of the Neoliberal Thought Collective*, edited by Philip Mirowski and Dieter Plehwe. Cambridge, MA: Harvard University Press, 2015.

Trotsky, Leon. *The Revolution Betrayed.* Translated by Max Eastman. Mineola, NY: Dover Publications, 2004.

Truong, Thang Dinh, Philip Hallinger, and Kabini Sanga. "Confucian Values and School Leadership in Vietnam: Exploring the Influence of Culture on Principal Decision Making." *Educational Management, Administration & Leadership* 45, no. 1 (2017): 77–100. https://doi.org/10.1177/1741143215607877.

Tseng, Roy. "The Idea of Freedom in Comparative Perspective: Critical Comparisons between the Discourses of Liberalism and Neo-Confucianism." *Philosophy East and West* 66, no. 2 (2016): 539–58.

Unger, Jonathan, and Anita Chan. "State Corporatism and Business Associations in China: A Comparison with Earlier Emerging Economies of East Asia." Edited by C. Lattemann and W. Zhang. *International Journal of Emerging Markets* 10, no. 2 (2015): 178–93. https://doi.org/10.1108/IJOEM-09-2014-0130.

Vanberg, Viktor J. "Constitutionalism, Federalism, and Limited Government: Hayekian Arguments in Political Scientists' Perspective." In *Revisiting Hayek's Political Economy*, edited by Peter J. Boettke and Virgil Henry Storr, vol. 21. Bingley: Emerald, 2017.

Vásquez, Ian, and Fred McMahon. *The Human Freedom Index 2020: A Global Measurement of Personal, Civil, and Economic Freedom.* Washington, DC: CATO Institute and Fraser Institute, 2020.

Vasu, Norman. "Governance through Difference in Singapore: Corporatism's Composition, Characteristics, and Complications." *Asian Survey* 52, no. 4 (2012): 734.

Verweij, Marco, and Riccardo Pelizzo. "Singapore: Does Authoritarianism Pay?" *Journal of Democracy* 20, no. 2 (2009): 18–32. https://doi.org/10.1353/jod.0.0076.

Vu, Giao Cong, and Kien Tran. "Constitutional Debate and Development on Human Rights in Vietnam." *Asian Journal of Comparative Law* 11, no. 2 (2016): 235–62. https://doi.org/10.1017/asjcl.2016.27.

Wacker, Konstantin M. "Restructuring the SOE Sector in Vietnam." *Journal of Southeast Asian Economies* 34, no. 2 (2017): 283–301. https://doi.org/10.1355/ae34–2c.

Wainwright, Hilary. "It's Never Too Late to Move Beyond the Choices of the Cold War." *Guardian (London)*, February 20, 2006.

Waller, James, and Mariana Salazar Albornoz. "Crime and No Punishment? China's Abuses against the Uyghurs." *Georgetown Journal of International Affairs* 22, no. 1 (2021): 100–111. https://doi.org/10.1353/gia.2021.0000.

Weber, Max. *From Max Weber: Essays in Sociology.* Edited by Hans Gerth and Charles Wright Mills. Oxford and New York: Oxford University Press, 1959.

———. *The Protestant Ethic and the Spirit of Capitalism.* London and New York: Routledge, 2001.

White, Damian F. "Ecological Democracy, Just Transitions and a Political Ecology of Design." *Environmental Values* 28, no. 1 (2019): 31–53. https://doi.org/10.3197/096327119X15445433913569.

Whiting, Susan H. "Authoritarian 'Rule of Law' and Regime Legitimacy." *Comparative Political Studies* 50, no. 14 (2017): 1907–40. https://doi.org/10.1177/0010414016688008.

Wiggershaus, Rolf. *The Frankfurt School: Its History, Theories and Political Significance.* Translated by Michael Robertson. Cambridge: Polity Press; Cambridge, MA: MIT Press, 1994.

Wilson, Peter. "Radicalism for a Conservative Purpose: The Peculiar Realism of E. H. Carr." *Millennium* 30, no. 1 (2001): 123–36. https://doi.org/10.1177/03058298010300010901.

Wolf, Martin. *The Shifts and the Shocks: What We've Learned—and Have Still to Learn—From the Financial Crisis.* New York: Penguin Press, 2015.

Wordsworth, William. *Poetical Works.* London: Ward, Lock, 1881.

World Bank. "Arable Land (% of Land Area)—China | Data." Accessed August 12, 2021. https://data.worldbank.org/.

———. "GDP Growth (Annual %)—Upper Middle Income, China." Database. Accessed December 14, 2020. https://data.worldbank.org/indicator/NY.GDP.MKTP.KD.ZG?locations=XT-CN.

———. "GNI per Capita, Atlas Method (Current US$) | Data." Database. World Bank, 2020. Accessed December 14, 2020. https://data.worldbank.org/indicator/NY.GNP.PCAP.CD.

Yang, Li, Filip Novokmet, and Branko Milanovic. "From Workers to Capitalists in Less than Two Generations: A Study of Chinese Urban Top Group Transformation between 1988 and 2013." *British Journal of Sociology* 72, no. 3 (June 2021): 478–513. https://doi.org/10.1111/1468–4446.12850.

Yeh, Anthony Go, Fiona F. Yang, and Jiejing Wang. "Economic Transition and Urban Transformation of China." *Urban Studies* 52, no. 15 (2015): 2822–48.

Zaitseva, Elena A., and Ernst Homburg. "Catalytic Chemistry under Stalin: Science and Scientists in Times of Repression." *Ambix* 52, no. 1 (2005): 45–65. https://doi.org/10.1179/000269805X52904.

Zappa, Marco. "The Rise of Governance and the Japanese Intermediation in Transitional Vietnam: The Impact of Japanese Knowledge-Based Aid to Vietnam in the Doi Moi Years." *Studia Politica* 20, no. 1 (2020): 9–146.

Zhang, Qian Forrest, and Hongping Zeng. "Politically Directed Accumulation in Rural China: The Making of the Agrarian Capitalist Class and the New Agrarian Question of Capital." *Journal of Agrarian Change* 21, no. 4 (2021): 677–701. https://doi.org/10.1111/joac.12435.

Žižek, Slavoj. "The Two Totalitarianisms." *London Review of Books*, March 17, 2005. Accessed October 1, 2022. https://www.lrb.co.uk/the-paper/v27/n06/slavoj-zizek/the-two-totalitarianisms.

Index

trade, 30, 47–48, 90, 92, 97, 135, 159, 162,
164, 191–92, 194, 198, 202, 205–6;
debt-financed, 11; exports, 3, 10, 62–
64, 66, 77, 92, 96, 192, 213; illiberalism
in, x; imports, 66, 157; international,
xiv; linkages, 11; and slavery, 31. *See
also* free trade
trade-offs, xi, xiv, 62, 97, 120, 147, 178, 183;
and utopian thought, 102–3
trade wars, 77, 192, 205–6; introduced,
xiv
training, political, 43, 117, 203
Treaty of Paris (1951), 199
Treaty of Rome (1958), 199
Treaty of Versailles (1919), 171
Tribe, Keith, 12–13
Trotsky, Leon, 110, 117–20, 122–23, 138,
238n14
Truman, Harry, 148–49
Trump, Donald, administration, 205
trust, societal, 64
truthiness, 148
Tseng, Roy, 26
Tsinghua University, 47–48, 61
Turkic peoples, in China, 145–47
Turner Broadcasting System, 4
Twenty Years' Crisis, The (Carr), 169–71,
201
Twitter, 65
"tyranny of the majority," 35, 86, 174, 191,
206; as potential pitfall of democracy,
79–81

uncertainty, 36, 45, 72–73, 75; benefits of,
x; and unknowability, 86
unemployment, 66, 115, 120–22, 180;
insurance, 45; under laissez-faire, 84
Unger, Jonathan, 162
Union of Soviet Socialist Republics
(USSR), 23, 33, 42, 52, 55, 69, 117–20,
123, 129, 137–39, 142, 161, 170–71, 199,
201, 221n22, 243n32
unions, 4, 64, 109, 112, 122, 160–62, 164,
172–73, 189, 204, 208, 244n38; competition and, 180; vis-à-vis government,
xiii; under Mussolini, 66
United Kingdom (UK), 151, 170, 199, 201;

since Great Depression, 20; leaving
liberalism, 29; as standard-bearer for
liberalism, 11. *See also* Britain; England; Great Britain
United Nations (UN), 48; Human Rights
Council, 90
United States (US), 9–12, 17, 20–21, 32, 71,
73, 121, 130, 140, 146, 149, 150–51, 170,
184, 186, 189, 201, 205, 213n7, 230n36,
249n54, 250n5; hegemony of, 11;
leaving liberalism, 29; limited welfare
of, 115; and operating losses, 4; and
planning, 5
universalism, 47, 90; and particularism,
129–31
University of Pennsylvania, 70
University of Vienna, 88
unselfishness, 199
Urumqi, ethnic violence in, 146
utilitarianism, 51, 52
utopianism, 29–30, 34, 36, 118–19, 158,
169–70, 174, 181, 195, 201, 246n12;
introduced, xiv; key concepts, 38–40,
43; and trade-offs, 102–3
Uyghurs, in China, 4, 145–47, 240n57,
241n62; Chinese government's atrocities against, 146

value chains, ix, 10, 164, 208
values, 1, 9, 18, 23–27, 41, 75–80, 82,
85, 98–99, 102, 107, 128–29, 133–34,
136–37, 141–42, 145, 149, 152–53, 158–
59, 181–88, 197–99, 228n11, 249n54;
hierarchy of, 197, 199; humane, 123;
introduced, xii; of market-based society, 43; ordering, 99
Vasu, Norman, 163
venture capital, 31
Victorian culture, 112
Vietnam, 35, 42, 48–50, 59, 61, 90–91, 93,
95, 133, 147–48, 150, 159, 162, 213n7;
political capitalism within, ix, 2
violence, 108, 114, 117–18, 122, 131, 146,
202, 212n15; fascist, 33, 66; necessary,
43; state, 80
Voigt, F. A., 33
Volk (concept), 137, 142, 166